CRUMBLING
EMPIRE

CRUMBLING
EMPIRE

The German Defeat in the East, 1944

SAMUEL W. MITCHAM, JR.

PRAEGER

Westport, Connecticut
London

Library of Congress Cataloging-in-Publication Data

Mitcham, Samuel W.
    Crumbling empire : the German defeat in the East, 1944 / by Samuel W. Mitcham, Jr.
        p. cm.
    Includes bibliographical references and index.
    ISBN 0–275–96856–1 (alk. paper)
    1. World War, 1939–1945—Eastern Front.   2. World War, 1939–1945—Germany.   I.
Title.
    D764.M527   2001
    940.54'21—dc21   00–049171

British Library Cataloguing in Publication Data is available.

Library of Congress Catalog Card Number: 00–049171
ISBN: 0–275–96856–1

First published in 2001

Praeger Publishers, 88 Post Road West, Westport, CT 06881
An imprint of Greenwood Publishing Group, Inc.
www.praeger.com

Printed in the United States of America

The paper used in this book complies with the
Permanent Paper Standard issued by the National
Information Standards Organization (Z39.48–1984).

10 9 8 7 6 5 4 3 2 1

Contents

Contents

Illustrations

TABLES

Photo essay follows page 162.

Introduction

This is the story of the end of an empire.

Anyone who has read Hitler's book, *Mein Kampf*, all the way through deserves a medal, for it is some of the most turgid reading in history. Such a person, however, would draw one inescapable conclusion: that establishing the German empire in the East was the primary reason Hitler went to war in 1939 and was a primary reason for the existence of the Third Reich in the first place. Hitler established this empire between 1936 and 1941. At first it was peaceful, as he annexed regions and countries via a combination of pressure and diplomacy (at least as the Nazis understood the term). In some places, such as the Balkans and Hungary, he was content with merely establishing German hegemony rather than direct rule. In 1939, however, diplomacy failed him, and he resorted to war; Poland became the first violent annexation of the Nazi era. In 1940 he turned his back on the East, because he was forced to deal with the French and British. This interruption in the eastern orientation of his policy was only a relatively brief pause, however; and the following year he turned his attention back to the East with a vengeance. He conquered Yugoslavia, invaded the Soviet Union, and overran much of European Russia, as well as the Ukraine, Belorussia (White Russia), Latvia, Estonia, Lithuania, and the Crimea. He also involved Hungary, Slovakia, Rumania, and (to a lesser degree) Bulgaria—his East European satellites—in the war as well. All told, he annexed an area twenty times the size of pre-1933 Germany. But he could not hold it.

This book is the story of the defeat of the German Army in the East. Germany was always a land power first and foremost and the defeat of the German Army and the defeat of the Third Reich are synonymous.

Although technically not part of the German Army, the Waffen-SS fought under army command. It will be considered separately here only to a limited degree.

Historical eras are sometimes clearly defined by events; more often, however, they are not. The German defeat in the East is a case in point. One could argue that the first seeds of this defeat were planted in the early 1920s, when Hitler began his rise to power, and that this book should begin at that point. Others might argue that it should begin in late 1942, when Hitler's eastern empire reached its maximum physical extent. Certainly one could make a case for either approach. This book, however, focuses on the period from June 1944 to February 1945, when the German Army and Waffen-SS in the East actually suffered their decisive defeats.

The German defeat at Stalingrad was, in my opinion, the turning point of the war and a serious defeat, but it can be considered decisive only in retrospect. Even after Stalingrad the German Army was still strong, and it came back immediately. Within two months, Field Marshal Erich von Manstein had launched a brilliant offensive, smashed several Soviet armies, and recaptured Kharkov, the fourth-largest city of the Soviet empire. Less than three months later, Hitler began a huge offensive at Kursk, which became the greatest tank battle of all time. The point is that, in the spring of 1943, German defeat was not a foregone conclusion. At this point, it was still conceivable that the Third Reich could impose a stalemate on its enemies and arrange a negotiated peace. The fact that Stalin was willing to negotiate confirms this argument. A reasonable person could not make this same statement in mid-February 1945. By the time Budapest fell, Germany had, in fact, been clearly and decisively defeated. Stalingrad is generally considered to be the largest military disaster ever suffered by the German armies in the East, but this is not true. It ranked only third. The Reich lost "only" 230,000 men when Field Marshal Paulus's 6th Army was destroyed in the Stalingrad campaign. It lost more than three hundred thousand men in the Battle of White Russia in June and July 1944, when Army Group Center was crushed. It lost approximately 270,000 more in the Rumanian campaign of August and September 1944, when General Friessner's Army Group South Ukraine was annihilated. Even then, it made a valiant attempt to stage a comeback in Hungary, but it failed. There was not much left for the defense of the Reich after the fall of Budapest. Ten weeks later, it was all over: Berlin had fallen, Hitler was dead, and the remnants of the High Command were concerned only with the details of surrender.

The Holocaust was arguably the most horrendous event of the twentieth century, and it morally defined the Third Reich as the most evil empire of that century, if not of all time (although Stalin's Soviet empire runs a close second); however, military historians and Holocaust historians are two different things. The purpose of this book is to study the crushing military defeats the German Wehrmacht suffered on the Eastern Front in the second half of 1944. The Holocaust will, therefore, be dealt with only to a limited degree, because it had only a limited impact on German military operations in the East in the last half of 1944. I do not want any reader, however, to mistakenly conclude that minimal coverage of the Holocaust suggests that I consider it to be of minimal importance. Quite the opposite, in fact, is true—the Holocaust was the realization of Hitler's "vision" for his government and largely defines what the Third Reich became. It is therefore largely beyond the scope of this book, but not entirely. There is an area of overlap between the history of the Holocaust and that of the Wehrmacht. This is obvious, because had the Third Reich not been defeated militarily, the Holocaust would never have ended. Also, the question of the degree of the German Army's involvement in the Holocaust (and therefore its guilt) is a significant issue, but not for this book. Large elements of the Wehrmacht in the East were deeply involved in the Holocaust in 1941. The German Army was much less involved in 1944. It was too busy being destroyed.

The SS, incidentally, was never part of the Wehrmacht (armed forces). Although units of the Waffen-SS (armed SS) were under the operational control of the military, they were not part of it. Even the SS combat formations were Nazi Party organizations.

On the other hand, the Ukrainian Nationalist movement will be considered in greater detail than the Holocaust. Let me state why, simply. There is no way the Jews were going to fight for Nazi Germany in the early 1940s. This is not true of the Ukrainians. Had Hitler handled the Ukrainians and certain other non-Russian minorities properly, he would have acquired significant allies. It is even conceivable that he would have won the war in the East. This makes the Ukrainian Nationalist movement a significant military factor on the Eastern Front in 1944. The conduct of the Ukrainian 14th SS Volunteer Grenadier Division is, in fact, an important indication of "what might have been" had Hitler handled the Soviet ethic minorities intelligently. He could, after all, have used them to win the war and turned on them later. But then, had Hitler handled the ethic minorities properly and intelligently, he would not have been Hitler.

I would like to thank Professor Melinda Mathews and Dianne Tilbury of the Interlibrary Loan Department of the University of Louisiana at Monroe for their assistance in acquiring source materials for this book. Thanks also go to the staffs of the U.S. National Archives, the U.S. Army War College, the U.S. Air Force's Air University, and the Bundesarchiv in Kolbenz for their assistance. I would also like to thank my long-suffering wife, Donna, for her patience and active assistance in the preparation of this manuscript. Thanks also go to Dr. Heather Staines for her help and patience. (I think I missed more deadlines on this book than for all of my previous books combined.)

The Cannae of Army Group Center

On September 1, 1939, the German Wehrmacht (armed forces) invaded Poland, igniting World War II. Contrary to popular myth, Adolf Hitler's war aim was never to conquer the world. He admired the British Empire and felt it served a very useful purpose for mankind, keeping the "subhuman" populations of Africa, India, and other places in check as it did. He certainly did not wish to destroy it; as early as 1924, when he lay out his program with astonishing candor in *Mein Kampf*, he stated that he wanted no war of revenge against England and France for what had happened in World War I. What Germany needed, he pounded out in a thousand speeches, was *Lebensraum*—living space. This, he pointed out, could only be obtained in the East—primarily at the expense of the Soviet Union.

Poland was the first eastern country to be forcibly annexed by the Greater German Reich. Adolf Hitler was stunned when London and Paris declared war on him on September 3, 1939. After Poland was conquered, he made peace overtures to the West. They were rejected. To the Nazi dictator's surprise, he found that he had lost credibility with the West—he had told one too many lies.

Hitler knew it would be impossible for him to successfully invade Russia with an undefeated England and France at his back. Reasonably confident that his 1939 alliance of convenience with Soviet dictator, Joseph Stalin, would hold for a year, he invaded France on May 10, 1940. Six weeks later, to the astonishment of the world, he dictated terms of peace to the French government.

Following the capitulation of France, Hitler again made a series of peace overtures to unconquered England, but they were not accepted. Sir Winston Churchill, prime minister since May 10, saw Adolf Hitler as the anti-Christ and a threat to Western civilization.[1] England fought on and survived the terror bombings and the U-boat blockade.

Although the British were not defeated, they were certainly beaten down. Hitler, who was by now accustomed to gambling on a grand scale, correctly guessed that England would not recover for some time—perhaps years. He decided he could conquer Russia in 1941, before the British could intervene. On June 22, 1941, he launched Operation Barbarossa: the invasion of the Soviet Union.

It was a fatal mistake and one of the turning points of the war.

In the forward European sectors alone, the Soviet Union outnumbered the Wehrmacht almost two to one in men, five to one in armored fighting vehicles (AFVs), and five to one in aircraft, although the German Army and Luftwaffe far outclassed it in initiative and leadership. The Russians, on the other hand, have often amazed the world with their incredible ability to endure hardships and suffering. Even after it suffered casualties numbering in the millions, the Red Army turned Hitler's legions back in front of the gates of Moscow. Then came Stalin's winter offensive of 1941–1942. Although it fell far short of the Communist dictator's goals, it nevertheless inflicted upon the German Army (*Heer*) its first defeat, and it was a serious one. German losses exceeded 30 percent and they were naturally higher in the combat arms. Losses of 50 percent in infantry and panzer grenadier (motorized infantry) units were not unusual. Because they lost so many of their best men, the German ground forces also lost much of their eliteness and *élan*. After the winter of 1941–1942, the Wehrmacht was never the same.

Dissatisfied with his generals, Adolf Hitler—who had been interfering in operational matters since 1938—sacked Field Marshal Walter von Brauchitsch, the commander in chief of the High Command of the Army (Oberkommando des Heer, or OKH) and replaced him himself. Hitler was now *Fuehrer* (leader) and chancellor of the Reich (empire), supreme commander of the Wehrmacht and commander in chief of the army. He issued his orders to the eastern armies through the chief of the General Staff of the army, whom he replaced more and more frequently.[2]

In 1941, Germany had launched offensives on three sectors of the Eastern Front—north, center, and south. In 1942, it had only enough strength to attack on one. Army Group South (subsequently divided into Army Groups A and B) pushed toward the Volga and the Caucasus but was finally defeated. The 6th Army was surrounded and destroyed at Stalingrad—by far the greatest military disaster in the history of the Third Reich to date. That winter, the Red Army surged forward again, only to be checked by the brilliant tactics of Field Marshal Erich von Manstein. A lull descended on the Eastern Front, but behind the lines there was feverish activity, as both sides prepared for the next battle.

In 1943, Germany could launch a major offensive in only part of one sector. Hitler chose to attack at Kursk, to pinch off a major Soviet salient. The offensive was slow in developing, and Stalin, who had prior knowledge of it, accepted the challenge. On July 5, Hitler struck. It was the greatest tank battle in history, and Germany was defeated. Now, although the Nazi dictator refused to accept the fact, all roads led backward for Nazi Germany.

As his military defeats compounded, Hitler's hatred and distrust of his generals increased. The Waffen-SS (armed SS)—a party formation which was under the tactical control of the Wehrmacht but not part of it—gained more and more power and influence in the conduct of the war. Hitler listened to his generals less and less and, insofar as was possible, surrounded himself only with the most compliant yes-men. His own creation, the High Command of the Wehrmacht (Oberkommando der Wehrmacht or OKW) gained more and more power and authority over military operations, at the expense of OKH, the traditional Prussian and Bavarian General Staff officers and army elite. OKW was clearly pro-Nazi and was headed by Field Marshal Wilhelm Keitel, a notorious yes-man who was privately referred to as "Lackey" by the other senior army generals. Even Hitler declared that Keitel had "the brains of a cinema usher" but, because of his doglike loyalty, kept him in power until the very end. The chief of the operations staff at OKW, Colonel General Alfred Jodl, was more talented than Keitel but was also clearly under the Fuehrer's spell. Less important positions at OKW and at Fuehrer Headquarters were filled by men with the same mindset. Hitler therefore was able to act with less and less restraint. He even sacked Field Marshal von Manstein, Germany's greatest strategic brain; Heinz Guderian, the Father of the *Blitzkrieg*; and Erwin Rommel, the famous "Desert Fox," among others. (Rommel and Guderian were recalled in 1943, Manstein was never reemployed.)

Hitler had been right about one thing: it did take Britain years to recover from her defeats of 1940, but in 1944 she was ready to reenter the battle on the European mainland. The United States, whose strength Hitler had grossly underestimated, was ready as well. On June 6, 1944, the Allies launched their D-day invasion. Rommel was able to check it but not destroy it. The Third Reich's chances of surviving the war were now not quite hopeless, but they were dangerously close to it.

In the East, meanwhile, all of eastern Europe and huge tracts of former Soviet territory were still part of the Nazi empire. As the summer of 1944 began everyone knew that Stalin and the Red Army were about to try to reconquer these regions. To defend his empire, Hitler turned to "politically correct," pro-Nazi generals and field marshals, such as Georg Lindemann, Ferdinand Schoerner, and Walter Model. The first senior Nazi general whom Stalin's armies would test that summer, however, was the least capable of them all: Ernst Busch.

Stalingrad is generally considered to be the largest military disaster suffered by Hitler's armies, but it was not. Field Marshal Paulus's 6th Army lost only 230,000 men at Stalingrad; Ernst Busch's Army Group Center

lost more than 300,000 men in the Vitebsk-Minsk battles, which Paul Carell called "The Cannae of Army Group Center."[3] It is not an uplifting story.

ERNST BUSCH: PORTRAIT OF A NAZI GENERAL

Ernst Busch was born on July 6, 1885, at Essen-Steele, in the Ruhr industrial district of western Germany. He decided early in life to become a
career army officer, worked hard at his chosen profession, and graduated
from the Gross-Lichterfelde Cadet Academy (Imperial Germany's West
Point) in 1904. He then joined the Westphalian 13th Infantry Regiment at
Muenster as an officer-cadet. He was commissioned as a second lieutenant
in the 57th Infantry Regiment in 1908, and in 1913 he was promoted to
first lieutenant and assigned to the War Academy at Kassel for further
training.[4] (See Appendix I for a table of comparative ranks.)

Busch spent almost all of the World War I period as an infantry commander on the Western Front. He was appointed company commander
upon the outbreak of hostilities and was promoted to captain in 1915.
Shortly afterward he was given command of a battalion in the 56th Infantry
Regiment. He fought in the battles of Reims and Namur, in the Artois
sector and in Flanders, at La Basse, Arras, and Verdun, and Champagne
area in 1918. He was awarded the *Pour le Mérite* ("Blue Max") for his
exceptional courage.

In 1919–1920, under the terms of the Treaty of Versailles, which ended
World War I, the German armed forces (which were called the Reichswehr
from 1919 to 1935) were reduced to 115,000 men. Of these, 100,000 were
allotted to the army (Reichsheer). The rest were assigned to the navy
(Reichsmarine). Germany was allowed no air force (Luftwaffe) under the
terms of the treaty.

Ernst Busch was selected for retention in the hundred-thousand-man
army. He held various staff and command assignments during the Weimar
Republic era (1919–1933). As a major, he was assigned to the staff of the
inspector of transport troops in the Reichswehr in 1925, and in 1930, while
serving as a battalion commander in the 9th Infantry Regiment, he was
promoted to lieutenant colonel. Two years later he was promoted to colonel and given command of the 9th Infantry Regiment at Potsdam.[5]

Ernst Busch was an "out-and-out" Nazi who followed Hitler with blind
obedience. He was a brutal man who said that he enjoyed sitting on the
People's Court tribunal, a body that frequently invoked the death penalty.
"This following story may give an idea of the man Busch," Lieutenant
Fabian von Schlabendorff, a member of his staff in 1944 and a lawyer in
civilian life, was to recall:

He told us one day that he had been a lay member of the National Socialists
People's Tribunal; and knowing nothing of law, had made up his mind from the

start to pass the death sentence upon everybody who was brought before the court. He had persevered in this practice, even when the learned judges were of other opinion. In the course of the conversation we came to discuss an astonishing order from Hitler that all parachutists, British and American alike, whether in uniform or civilian clothes, were to be shot at once. Busch did not hesitate to express his approval of this order. Disregarding his military rank, I emphatically opposed him. Busch, quite unperturbed, admitted that the order was a violation of international law, and added that, in fact, precautions had been taken to pass it on only by word of mouth, and to destroy immediately all written evidence that it had ever been sent to the Army Group.[6]

Busch's peacetime career was unexceptional until after Hitler assumed power in 1933, after which it was characterized by rapid promotion. He was a lieutenant colonel and number 176 on the German Army seniority list of 1932.[7] Nevertheless he was promoted to colonel soon after Hitler's rise, and in 1935 he was a major general, commanding the 23rd Infantry Division at Potsdam. He was promoted to lieutenant general in 1937 and was a rabid supporter of Hitler during the Blomberg-Fritsch crisis in early 1938, when the Fuehrer ousted both the minister of war and the commander in chief of the army, despite the objections of many of the generals. Busch's reward was quick in coming. On February 2, 1938, at the relatively early age of fifty-three, he received an accelerated promotion to general of infantry and later that month replaced anti-Nazi General Ewald von Kleist as commander of Wehrkreis (Military District) VIII (Silesia and later the Sudetenland).[8] In the fall of 1938 he blindly supported Hitler's plans to invade Czechoslovakia, despite the risks involved and the objections of dozens of more senior and experienced commanders. In the invasion of Poland, Busch's VIII Corps was on the left flank of Army Group South. It took Krakow, advanced along the Vistula, and ended the campaign near Lvov.[9]

Busch replaced Georg von Kuechler as commander of the 16th (formerly 3d) Army for the invasion of France. He did not understand tank tactics and did not believe the panzer thrust proposed by General Heinz Guderian would get beyond the Meuse, much less reach the English Channel; his most significant assignment in the campaign was to cover Guderian's left flank in the initial advance. In the second (mopping-up) phase of the campaign, he directed thirteen divisions (all infantry) and followed the panzers south into the French interior.[10] After the French surrender he was promoted to colonel general on July 19, 1940.

Busch's 16th Army remained in France until the spring of 1941, when it was sent to Poland, and was on the southern flank of Army Group North during Operation Barbarossa. Its primary missions were to cover the right flank of the 18th Army as it drove on Leningrad and to maintain contact with Army Group Center on its right (southern) flank. On June 27, 1941,

16th Army controlled seven divisions—again, all infantry.[11] Later that year it received reinforcements. Busch's forces penetrated the Soviet frontier defenses and advanced to Staraya Russa, which the three divisions of his X Corps took in the second week of August after bitter street fighting. In mid-August, X Corps was counterattacked by the Soviet 34th Army (eight infantry divisions, a cavalry corps, and an armored corps). General Erich von Manstein's LVI Panzer Corps had to be diverted from the advance on Leningrad to clear up matters. The brilliant Manstein described conditions around Staraya Russa as "shitty." He nevertheless managed to reverse the situation and surround the Soviet 34th Army, which was destroyed on August 23.[12]

Busch faced the Russian winter offensive of 1941–1942 with the XXXVIII, XXXIX Panzer, X, and II Corps: nine infantry divisions, one motorized division, and one SS motorized division on the line, with the 18th Motorized Division in reserve.[13] On January 9, in temperatures of minus sixty degrees Fahrenheit, he was struck by the Soviet 52nd, 11th, 34th, 3rd Shock, and 4th Shock Armies. Busch signaled his commanders that he had no reserves; they would have to hold where they were, as the Fuehrer had ordered a few days before. General of Infantry Count Walter von Brockdorff-Ahlefeldt's II Corps was surrounded near Demyansk on February 8, with more than 100,000 men. To the south, on January 28, Lieutenant General Theodor Scherer was encircled at Kholm with the headquarters of his 281st Security Division and some 5,500 men from various units. Meanwhile, in a heroic resistance, Lieutenant General Baron Theodor von Wrede's isolated 290th Infantry Division held up a large part of the Soviet 34th Army south of Lake Ilmen for weeks but was nearly wiped out in the process. Busch managed to save the vital city and supply base of Staraya Russa only by committing his last reserves (the 18th Motorized Division under Colonel Werner von Erdmannsdorff), and even then there was hand-to-hand fighting in the streets, right up to the doorstep of 16th Army's main supply depot. Contact with the left flank of Army Group Center was completely lost during this struggle. Colonel General von Kuechler, the recently appointed C-in-C of Army Group North, was so dissatisfied with Busch's leadership that he requested authorization from OKH (i.e., Hitler) to relieve him of his command. Permission was not forthcoming, however. Fortunately for the Germans, the main Soviet strike forces turned south, into the rear of Army Group Center, and headed for Vitebsk and Smolensk.[14] They were halted short of their objectives by General Walter Model's 9th Army.

As the Soviets exhausted themselves by attacking on a broad front and attempting to destroy all three German army groups, rather than contenting themselves with less ambitious objectives, Hitler and Kuechler reinforced the sagging 16th Army. That summer Busch was able to rescue Group Scherer at Kholm and reestablish ground contact with II Corps near Demyansk. That Corps, however, did not regain its freedom of maneuver until March 1943, when the Demyansk salient was evacuated.

From the spring of 1942 until 1944, the Soviet armies in the northern sector concentrated mainly against 18th Army, which was besieging Leningrad. Busch faced only secondary Soviet attacks and suffered no more serious defeats. He did not score any major victories either. Nevertheless, on February 1, 1943, he was promoted to field marshal, despite his rather mediocre record. He owed his advancement strictly to his pro-Nazi background and Hitler's favoritism, rather than to any distinguished performance on his part.

On October 28, 1943, Field Marshal Guenther von Kluge was seriously injured in an automobile accident. The next day Hitler named Ernst Busch to succeed him as commander in chief, Army Group Center. He had been promoted well beyond his capabilities. The results would be disastrous, as we shall see. Hitler valued Busch as a confirmed Nazi and as a yes-man; Busch, on the other hand, knew he had not really proven himself as a military commander, so he tended to rely on Hitler's judgment, even in tactical affairs. A Fuehrer order, to Busch, was something to be obeyed without question or thought of evasion. With this attitude, Busch was a thoroughly incompetent army group commander, a fact he would prove beyond a shadow of a doubt before 1944 was out.

THE CANNAE OF ARMY GROUP CENTER

From north to south, Army Group Center consisted of Colonel General Georg-Hans Reinhardt's 3rd Panzer Army (five infantry and four Luftwaffe field divisions); Colonel General Gotthard Heinrici's 4th Army (eighteen infantry and four Luftwaffe field divisions, plus the 18th Panzer and 25th Panzer Grenadier Divisions); General of Infantry Hans Jordan's 9th Army (fourteen infantry divisions and the battered 20th Panzer Grenadier Division); and Colonel General Walter Weiss's 2nd Army (eleven infantry and four panzer divisions, plus a security division). Busch also had six Hungarian infantry divisions, three German and one Slovak security divisions, and two field training divisions, for an army-group total of seventy-six divisions. This figure is very misleading, however. The Hungarian and Luftwaffe field units were next to useless, and the security and training divisions were not equipped for frontline combat. Security divisions, for example, normally consisted of two security regiments, small reconnaissance, engineer and signal components, and no artillery at all. Of the remaining fifty-five divisions, none were at full strength, and twenty-two were classified as remnants or *kampfgruppen* (battle groups)—divisions reduced to regimental strength by heavy casualties, albeit not without combat value.[15] By the following summer, Busch had combined and consolidated several of these units and would have thirty-eight infantry divisions on June 15, 1944. The average infantry division still would have only two thousand men in six frontline infantry battalions by that date.[16] (See Appendix II for an outline of German unit types and their approximate strengths.)

The Soviets attacked Army Group Center several times in the winter of 1943–1944. In the 4th Army's zone, the Soviets made four attempts to take Orsha (from October to the end of December 1943) but were defeated each time in heavy fighting, and the 3rd Panzer Army managed to hold Vitebsk—barely—against attacks by three Soviet armies. In these battles, Lieutenant General Rudolf Peschel's 6th Luftwaffe Field Division particularly distinguished itself, knocking out forty-seven Soviet tanks northeast of Vitebsk on January 5, 1944, alone. By January 8, however, it had only 436 men left. Busch's role in these victories was largely passive. In late 1943, for example, when General of Panzer Troops Georg-Hans Reinhardt, the panzer army commander, requested permission to withdraw his northernmost division, the 87th Infantry, Busch referred the matter to Hitler, who turned the request down. As a result, the division was encircled near Lobok on December 16. It escaped only when Reinhardt ordered it to break out against the Fuehrer's orders and only then in heavy fighting. It lost more than 1,500 of its five thousand men and all of its artillery, heavy equipment, and vehicles in the process. Lieutenant Colonel Helmut Geissler, the spearhead commander, was among those killed.[17]

Hitler also ordered 2nd Army, on Busch's southern flank, to stand firm, despite the fact that Model's Army Group North Ukraine was retreating to the Dnieper, exposing Busch's right (southern) flank. Rather than question the Fuehrer's judgment, Busch held the line by extending his frontage and committing the bulk of his panzer divisions to the south. As a result of this "stand fast" order, a sixty-mile gap developed between 2nd Army and Model's northern flank.[18]

The fighting in the winter of 1943–1944 was heavy, but Army Group Center managed to hold Vitebsk and Orsha, which guarded the fifty-mile land bridge between the Dvina and the Dnieper—the historic key to the Russian heartland. This represented a significant propaganda victory for the Germans, but elsewhere they were in serious trouble: the Siege of Leningrad was broken in mid-January, Army Group North was hurled back and lost contact with the northern wing of Army Group Center; 17th Army was smashed in the Crimea; and in the spring of 1944, the Ukraine was lost to Germany. When the spring thaw brought a lull on the Eastern Front, Germany's strategic situation was at a low ebb. Map 1.1 shows the situation in the East in the spring of 1944.

In May 1944, Germany had 2,242,649 men on the Eastern Front—the lowest total since the invasion began. They were opposed by 6,077,000 Soviet troops—the highest total ever. Stalin now had five hundred infantry divisions, forty artillery divisions, and three hundred armored or mechanized brigades, with more than nine thousand tanks, 10,500 guns, 2,300

Map 1.1
The Eastern Front, Spring 1944

multiple-tube rocket launchers, 4,200 antitank guns, and sixteen thousand fighters and bombers. The Third Reich had completely lost the initiative in all sectors. Army Group Center was in a particularly bad position. True, it was the strongest army group, with 792,196 men (as opposed to 540,965 in Army Group North, 400,542 in Army Group North Ukraine, and

508,946 in Army Group South Ukraine), but it was occupying a salient with both flanks exposed, and it barred the direct route to Berlin. At the closest point, Army Group Center was still only 290 miles from Moscow; at their closest point, the Russians were 550 miles from Berlin.[19] Clearly, if Stalin was going to destroy Nazi Germany, Army Group Center would have to be destroyed first.

By mid-May 1944, Army Group Center had a strength of forty-two infantry divisions (five of them Hungarian), four panzer divisions, three panzer grenadier divisions, three independent brigades, five security divisions, and a training division. On June 22, they were disposed as shown in Table 1.1. The frontline divisions were well dug in and in good positions. All had a forward trench line and two to four backup trench lines. Most of them were covered by minefields, and the approaches to the German main line of defense were heavily mined. The regiments had plenty of heavy and light machine guns and adequate ammunition. Each division was supported, on the average, by three to four artillery pieces and two assault guns or anti-tank guns per mile of front, although there was not enough artillery ammunition. There was not enough air support or infantry strength. Luftwaffe Colonel General Ritter Robert von Greim's 6th Air Fleet had only 839 aircraft, only forty of which were fighters, and he did not have enough fuel to keep them all flying.[20]

Three years of fighting on the Eastern Front had taken a terrible toll of the German infantry. Not all the German records from this period are extant but the figures for 4th and 9th Armies are. On June 20, XXVII Corps of 4th Army had three divisions. The 78th Assault Division had an effective strength of 5,712 men, ninety-nine guns, thirty-one assault guns and eighteen self-propelled 88 mm guns. The 25th Panzer Grenadier Division had 2,686 men, fifty-nine guns, forty-five assault guns and ten self-propelled 88 mm guns. The 260th Infantry had 2,554 men, fifty-nine guns, and no assault guns or 88s. The corps had twenty-seven assault guns and forty-five self-propelled 88 mm guns in its GHQ (general headquarters) units. According to the tables of organization, each German division should have had ten to twelve thousand men. Only one of XXVII Corps's divisions, thereafter, had more than half of its authorized strength. Adolf Hitler's preoccupation with creating new divisions rather than maintaining the ones he had further contributed to the declining numbers in the veteran divisions.

The divisions of the XXXIX Panzer Corps were in worse shape than those of XXVII Corps. The 12th Infantry Division had 3,604 men, forty-seven guns, and ten assault guns; the 31st Infantry had 2,448 men, forty-two guns, and ten assault guns; the 110th Infantry had 2,590 men, forty-two guns, and six assault guns; and the 337th Infantry Division had 3,775 men, eighty-one guns, and ten assault guns. None had any 88s. The corps commander, however, controlled fifty-eight tanks or assault guns and

Table 1.1
Order of Battle, Army Group Center, June 22, 1944

ARMY GROUP CENTER: Field Marshal Ernst Busch
  Chief of Staff: Lieutenant General Hans Krebs

3rd Panzer Army: Colonel General Georg-Hans Reinhardt
  Chief of Staff: Major General Otto Heidkaemper

IX Corps: General of Artillery Rolf Wuthmann
  Chief of Staff: Colonel Georg Praefke

  252nd Infantry Division: Lieutenant General Walter Melzer
  Corps Detachment D: Major General Bernhard Pamberg[1]

LIII Corps: General of Infantry Friedrich Gollwitzer
  Chief of Staff: Colonel Hans Schmidt

  206th Infantry Division: Lieutenant General Alfons Hitter
  246th Infantry Division: Major General Claus Mueller-Buelow
  4th Luftwaffe Field Division: Luftwaffe Lieutenant General Robert Pistorius
  6th Luftwaffe Field Division: Lieutenant General Rudolf Peschel

VI Corps: General of Artillery Georg Pfeiffer
  Chief of Staff: Colonel Willy Mantey

  197th Infantry Division: Colonel Theodor Preu[1]
  256th Infantry Division: Lieutenant General August Wuestenhagen
  299th Infantry Division: Lieutenant General Count Ralph von Oriola

4th Army: General of Infantry Kurt von Tippelskirch[2]
  Chief of Staff: Colonel Erich Dethleffsen

XXVII Corps: General of Infantry Paul Voelckers
  Chief of Staff: Colonel Joachim Staats

  25th Panzer Grenadier Division: Major General Paul Schuermann
  78th Assault Division: Lieutenant General Hans Traut
  260th Infantry Division: Major General Guenther Klammt

XXXIX Panzer Corps: General of Artillery Robert Martinek
  Chief of Staff: Lieutenant Colonel Martinek

  12th Infantry Division: Lieutenant General Rudolf Bamber
  31st Infantry Division: Lieutenant General Wilhelm Ochsner
  110th Infantry Division: Lieutenant General Eberhard von Kurowski
  337th Infantry Division: Lieutenant General Otto Schuenemann

XII Corps: Lieutenant General Vincenz Mueller
  Chief of Staff: Colonel Willy Deyhle

  18th Panzer Grenadier Division: Lieutenant General Karl Zutavern
  57th Infantry Division: Major General Adolf Trowitz
  267th Infantry Division: Lieutenant General Otto Drescher

Table 1.1 (*continued*)

9th Army: General of Infantry Hans Jordan
    Chief of Staff: Colonel Kurt Gundelach

XXXV Corps: Lieutenant General Baron Kurt-Juergen von Luetzow
    Chief of Staff:

    6th Infantry Division: Lieutenant General Walter Heyne
    45th Infantry Division: Major General Joachim Engel
    134th Infantry Division: Lieutenant General Ernst Philipp
    296th Infantry Division: Lieutenant General Arthur Kullner
    383rd Infantry Division: Lieutenant General Edmund Hoffmeister

XXXXI Panzer Corps: General of Artillery Hellmuth Weidling
    Chief of Staff: Colonel Klaus Berger

    35th Infantry Division: Lieutenant General Johann-Georg Richert
    36th Infantry Division: Major General Alexander Conrady
    129th Infantry Division: Major General Heribert von Larisch

LV Corps: General of Infantry Friedrich Herrlein
    Chief of Staff: Colonel Johannes Hoelz

    102nd Infantry Division: Major General Werner von Bercken
    292nd Infantry Division: Lieutenant General Richard John

2nd Army: Colonel General Walter Weiss
    Chief of Staff: Major General Henning von Tresckow

I Cavalry Corps: Lieutenant General Gustav Harteneck
    Chief of Staff: Lieutenant Colonel Kniess

    1st Hungarian Cavalry Division
    4th Cavalry Brigade: Colonel Lothar von Bischoffshausen

XXIII Corps: General of Engineers Otto Tiemann
    Chief of Staff: Colonel Heinz Langmann

    7th Infantry Division: Lieutenant General Fritz-Georg von Rappard
    203rd Security Division: Lieutenant General Rudolf Pilz
    17th Special Purposes Brigade Staff

VIII Corps[3]: General of Infantry Gustav Hoehne
    Chief of Staff: Colonel Eberhard von Schoenfeldt

    5th Jaeger Division: Lieutenant General Hellmuth Thumm
    211th Infantry Division: Lieutenant General Johann Heinrich Eckhardt
    12th Hungarian Reserve Division

XX Corps[3]: General of Artillery Baron Rudolf von Roman
    Chief of Staff: Colonel Wagner

    Corps Detachment E[4]: Lieutenant General Maximilian Felzmann
    3rd Cavalry Brigade: Colonel Baron Hans von Wolff

Table 1.1 (*continued*)

Army Reserves:
> 5th Hungarian Reserve Division
> 23rd Hungarian Reserve Division
> White Ruthenia Mil. Dist.: Gen. Count Edwin von Rothkirch und Trach
> 221st Security Division: Lieutenant General Herbert Lendle
> 391st Security Division: Lieutenant General Baron Albrecht Digeon von Monteton

Army Group Reserves:
> Panzer Grenadier Division "Feldherrnhalle": Major General Friedrich-Carl von Steinkeller
> 14th Infantry Division: Lieutenant General Hermann Floerke
> 20th Panzer Division: Lieutenant General Mortimer von Kessel
> 201st Security Division: Lieutenant General Alfred Jacobi
> 286th Security Division: Lieutenant General Hans Oschmann
> 390th Field Training Division: Lieutenant General Hans Bergen
> 707th Infantry Division: Major General Gustav Gihr

Notes:
[1] Acting commander.
[2] Acting commander, replacing Colonel General Gotthard Heinrici, who was ill.
[3] Not engaged in Operation Bagration.
[4] Including Division Groups 137 and 251.

Source: Kurt Mehner, ed., *Geheimen Tagesberichte*, vol. 10, p. 502.

forty-three self-propelled 88s, which he could commit at crisis points in the battle as the need arose.

The XII Corps included the 18th Panzer Grenadier Division (2,787 men, fifty-two guns, no assault guns), the 57th Infantry Division (2,136 men, thirty-eight guns, and six assault guns), and the 267th Infantry Division (2,498 men, forty-six guns, and nine assault guns). It no doubt had some assault guns and 88s in reserve, but this data is missing.

The 501st Heavy Panzer Battalion was in 9th Army reserve on June 20. It was equipped with twenty-nine PzKw VI Tiger tanks, which were superior to most Russian armor. The 14th Infantry Division was also in army reserve; although its figures are also missing, except for the fact that it had eight assault guns. It addition, Panzer Grenadier Division Feldherrnhalle (FHH), which was part of OKH (Hitler's) reserve, was positioned behind 4th Army. It had thirty-seven tanks and assault guns. Its tanks were PzKw IVs, which typically weighed 19.7 tons. They were considerably lighter than the Soviet main battle tank, the T-34s, which typically weighed 34.7 tons, or the KV-1, which might weigh fifty-two tons or more. (The weight of tanks varied according to model. See Appendix III for a brief description of German and Russian tank characteristics.)

In all, 4th Army had an effective strength of 30,830 men, 362 medium artillery pieces, 205 heavy guns, 246 assault guns, 40 tanks, and 116 self-propelled 88 mm flak guns, used primarily in an antitank role.[21] These figures, of course, exclude the units not reporting or whose records are missing, as well as any march (replacement) battalions that may have arrived from Germany.[22] All in all, 4th Army had about the same strength a strong corps would have had in 1939.

Ninth Army was somewhat stronger than 4th Army, having an infantry strength of 43,555, with seven thousand more in corps and army reserve. It also had seventy-six assault guns and 551 pieces of artillery. The 3rd Panzer Army, on Army Group Center's northern flank, was probably weaker than either 4th or 9th Armies. There were only three assault gun battalions and one heavy tank destroyer battalion (equipped with *Hornisse*, or Hornet, self-propelled antitank guns) in the entire army. This gave it a strength of sixty to eighty assault guns and tank destroyers.

In all, the average frontline division in Army Group Center had to defend fifteen to twenty miles of frontage, in an era when the average division could expect to hold only a six-mile front against a determined attack. (Map 1.2 shows the dispositions of Army Group Center on June 21, 1944.)

To make matters worse, replacements were inadequate. Since autumn 1943, almost 33 percent of the replacements sent to Army Group Center were *Volksdeutsche* (ethnic Germans) from the occupied territories.[23] They were, in general, not nearly as pro-Hitler as the men of the purely German divisions, and had little interest in risking their lives for the Third Reich. By the fifth year of the war, these replacements were considered unreliable. They were an indication that Nazi Germany was losing its real secret weapon: the high quality of its individual soldier.

In early May 1944, the Eastern Intelligence Branch of OKH predicted that the Soviet summer offensive would come south of the Pripyat Marshes, through Rumania, Hungary, and Slovakia, and into the Balkans, if it could get that far. Intelligence estimates stated that the sector north of the Pripyat would remain quiet even though Busch was concerned about signs of a troop buildup in the Kovel-Tarnopol area. Lieutenant General Adolf Heusinger, the Ia (chief of operations—see Appendix IV) of OKH, believed that the main attack would come against Model's Army Group North Ukraine, though he thought a secondary offensive against 2nd Army (the right flank of Army Group Center) was a likely possibility. Colonel General Kurt Zeitzler, the chief of the General Staff of OKH, agreed that the buildup at Kovel-Tarnopol could not be taken lightly and on May 10 proposed creating a reserve army on Busch's right flank to deal with a possible attack. (Since late 1941, as noted, Adolf Hitler had been commander in chief of OKH, and thus Zeitzler, as his chief executive officer, had far more com-

Map 1.2
Army Group Center, June 21, 1944

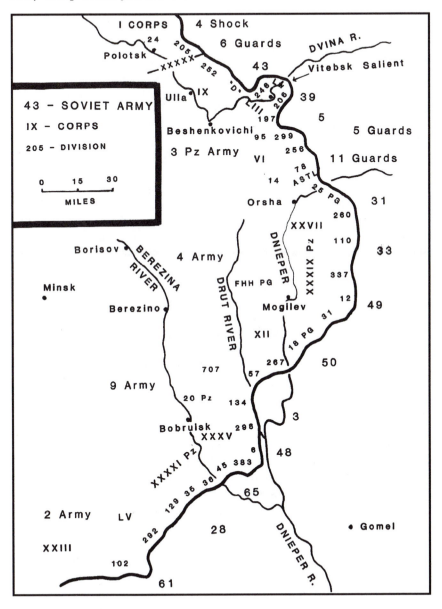

mand prerogatives than the typical chief of staff. He was, in fact, the military head of the High Command of the Army.) On Zeitzler's orders, OKH began reinforcing General of Infantry Friedrich Hossbach's LVI Panzer Corps (the nucleus of the reserve army) on Busch's right with tanks, artillery, and assault gun units.[24]

After Zeitzler suggested using the proposed reserve army for a surprise offensive, Walter Model, the C-in-C of Army Group North Ukraine, saw an opportunity to take LVI Panzer Corps away from his less alert colleague, Busch. On May 15 he asked the Fuehrer to give him LVI Panzer so he could try "an offensive solution." This idea, of course, appealed to the offensive-minded dictator, and over the next few days Model bombarded Hitler with intelligence reports (from his own intelligence office), suggesting the offensive north of the Carpathians would fall on Army Group North Ukraine and miss Army Group Center altogether. Hitler was soon convinced and on May 29 transferred LVI Panzer Corps to Model. Army Group Center gave up only 6 percent of its front but lost 15 percent of its divisions, 82 percent of its panzers, 23 percent of its assault guns, half of its tank destroyers, and approximately 25 percent of its heavy artillery.[25] General Weiss warned Busch that Model was trying to abscond with LVI Panzer, but the field marshal ignored him. When Hitler endorsed Model's plan, Busch surrendered the corps without a single protest.[26]

Meanwhile, Stalin and Stavka (the Soviet supreme headquarters) decided to concentrate their summer offensive against Army Group Center. It was codenamed Operation Bagration, after General Peter Nanovich Bagration, a prince killed during Napoleon's invasion of 1812. Stalin concentrated four fronts (each the size of an army group) opposite Army Group Center. North to south, they were the 1st Baltic Front (General Ivan Bagramian), supported by the 3rd Air Army; the 3rd Belorussian Front (General I. D. Chernyakovsky, a tank expert), supported by 1st Air Army; the 2nd Belorussian Front (General Matvei Vasilievich Zakharov), supported by 4th Air Army; and the 1st Belorussian Front (General Konstantin Rokossovskii), supported by 16th Air Army. The 1st Baltic and 3rd Belorussian Fronts were coordinated by Marshal Alexander Mikhailovich Vasilevskii, while Marshal Georgi Zhukov coordinated the 2nd and 1st Belorussian Fronts. Stalin increased their troop strengths by 60 percent, their tank and self-propelled gun strength by 300 percent, their artillery by 85 percent, and their already abundant air strength by 62 percent. By June 21, the 700,000 men of Army Group Center were facing 2,500,000 Russians, who were supported by more than 6,000 tanks and assault guns, over forty-five thousand guns and mortars, and seven thousand aircraft.[27] They outnumbered the German 6th Air Fleet 6.5 to one in airplanes and by an incredible fifty-eight to one in fighters.[28]

The Soviet deployment showed real tactical sophistication and showed how far the Red Army had come since 1941. Security and march discipline were very tight, and logistical arrangements were brilliant. By mid-June, Operation Bagration involved 38 percent of all rifle divisions in the Soviet Army, 40 percent of all of its tank and mechanized units, and 47 percent of all its aircraft. (The Red Air Force was part of the Soviet Army, not a separate branch of the service.) Although it was not possible to completely hide a buildup of this magnitude, no one on the German side realized how massive a superiority they had achieved by June 22, 1944, when the attack began.

General Hans Jordan, the acting commander of 9th Army, was alarmed over the buildup, but Busch hardly reacted at all. He was more concerned about his right flank and the chances of getting LVI Panzer Corps back after Model completed his offensive. Even his own chief of staff, Lieutenant General Hans Krebs, told Zeitzler that the Russians were building up and planning to launch a double envelopment against 9th Army, but he failed to convince the OKH chief that Army Group Center was facing more than a secondary offensive.[29] (See Appendix IV for an outline of the various German staff positions.) Busch seemed to agree. He turned down General Reinhardt's request to pull back the left flank of 3rd Panzer Army in order to shorten his front and gain more divisions. Using one of Hitler's favorite arguments, he told Reinhardt that such a move would free more Russian than German troops. "Under Busch," Ziemke wrote, "Headquarters, Army Group Center had become a mindless instrument for transmitting the Fuehrer's will."[30]

In April, Hitler designated Vitebsk, Orsha, Mogilev, and Bobruisk (Bobruysk) "fortified places," to be defended to the last man. All were to have a frontline division assigned to them except Vitebsk, which was to be defended by a corps of at least three divisions. Busch again accepted the Fuehrer's order without question. Back at the front, Jordan, the commander of the 9th Army, appealed to Busch to question the "fortified places" concept and to retreat to the Dnieper or the Beresina, forty-five miles farther west, a move that would reduce the army group's frontage by 150 miles.[31] He was backed up by the other army commanders, and their arguments must have been convincing, for on May 20 Busch visited Fuehrer Headquarters and requested permission to withdraw to the Dnieper or the Beresina, although he never questioned the "fortified places" policy. Hitler coolly rejected Busch's appeal, cynically remarking that he had not supposed Busch to be one of those generals who was always looking back over his shoulder. The remark was well calculated to influence Busch's attitude and subsequent behavior. Never again, he resolved, would he appear "disloyal": he would accept the Fuehrer's utterances without question and force his generals to do the same, even if the orders went against his own better judgment.[32] One member of his staff wrote that Busch was "a man inadequate to the military task entrusted to him, and who did not possess even the independence of mind of a man of average common sense."[33]

Although Hitler agreed that the major Russian offensive would come in eastern Galicia (east of Lvov), he was concerned about the low strength of 4th Army east of Mogilev. In mid-May, he expressed the wish that he could send it another division, but with the demands of the Italian Front and the Allied invasion looming in the West, he simply did not have one to spare.[34]

Stalin deliberately waited until after the Allies landed in Normandy to launch his offensive. On the night of June 19–20, 240,000 partisans arose in the Belorussian forests and cut almost all of Army Group Center's communications and rail lines. They accomplished little else of importance, and their performance—like that of their counterparts in France—varied from mediocre to rather pathetic, even against poorly armed, non-German, collaborationist police units. On June 22—the third anniversary of Hitler's invasion of the Soviet Union—the Red Army struck. The initial aerial and artillery bombardment was devastating. Over and above the organic artillery units of the Soviet divisions, corps and armies, Stavka had brought up ten artillery divisions, twenty-one independent artillery brigades, thirty-four independent artillery regiments, three mortar brigades, eighteen mortar regiments, three rocket-launcher divisions (equipped with the multibarreled, truck-mounted "Stalin organs"), a rocket-launcher brigade, and eleven rocket-launcher regiments. Then came the ground assault. The Soviets struck along a three-hundred-mile front with fourteen armies—118 rifle divisions in all. On the front line, they faced only thirty-four understrength German divisions. Although they struck all along the front, they focused on six break-in sectors, where they concentrated seventy-seven divisions. In these sectors, the Red committed a rifle division along every mile and a half to two miles of front—an average of 1,210 infantrymen per mile. The Germans met them with 131 men per mile. At the front, the Soviets had an infantry superiority of between nine and ten to one in infantry, thirty-five to one in artillery, and fifty-eight to one in fighter aircraft. Their superiority in armor was almost as great.

On the northern flank, General of Artillery Rolf Wuthmann's IX Corps of the 3rd Panzer Army was hit by twenty-nine infantry and eight tank divisions. The VI Corps, south of Vitebsk, was attacked by eighteen infantry and nine tank divisions. The Soviets' objective was clear: they wanted to encircle General of Infantry Friedrich Gollwitzer's LIII Corps at Vitebsk which was being pinned down by the Soviet 43rd and 39th Armies.[35] Meanwhile, in the army group's center, 4th Army was also under heavy attack. General of Infantry Paul Voelckers's XXVII Corps was facing twenty-five infantry and eleven tank divisions, and the XXXIX Panzer

Map 1.3
The Destruction of Army Group Center

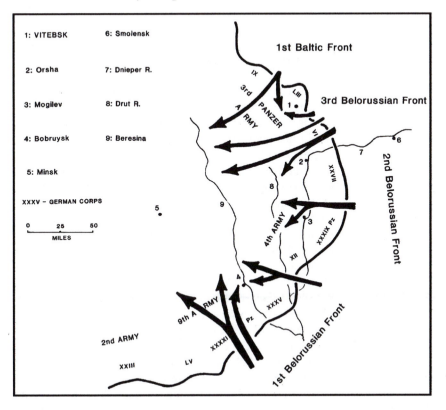

Corps met sixteen infantry and two armored divisions.[36] The next day, the offensive was extended to the zone of 9th Army, where the XXXXI Panzer Corps was smashed by twenty-three infantry and seven tank divisions, and XXXV Corps tried to hold against twenty-seven infantry and six tank divisions.[37] By now, Stalin had committed almost two hundred divisions, with six thousand tanks and assault guns, supported by seven thousand aircraft.[38] He was opposed by only thirty-four divisions with a few depleted tank regiments and forty aircraft (and these figures include Weiss's 2nd Army, which was not in Stalin's zone of attack). Busch's four mobile divisions—the 20th Panzer and 18th, 25th, and 60th Panzer Grenadier Divisions—had only about four hundred tanks and armored fighting vehicles combined. When the divisional assault gun battalions are factored in, German armored strength increases somewhat, but even by the most conservative estimates Army Group Center was outnumbered in armor by a ratio of 5:5 to one.[39] Map 1.3 shows the development of the offensive.

Busch was at the Berghof, where Hitler had his command post, when word of the offensive began, so he rushed back to his headquarters at Minsk without keeping his appointment with Hitler. Yet there was little he could do. By June 23, Corps Detachment D was smashed, the 252nd Infantry Division had lost Obol, 3rd Panzer Army had committed its last reserves, and the Red Army was closing in on Vitebsk from the north (see Map 1.4). Busch reported that he could not close 3rd Panzer Army's front without more divisions and asked for reinforcements from Army Group North Ukraine. He did not want to take troops away from 2nd Army, he said, because he still expected a Soviet attack toward Brest. OKH, meanwhile, took the 24th Infantry Division (along with the attached 909th Assault Gun Brigade) from Army Group North, assigned them to 3rd Panzer Army, and ordered Reinhardt to counterattack, rescue the 252nd Infantry, and restore the situation on Army Group Center's left flank. Wuthmann's IX Corps, however, was having a difficult time even holding its positions. By nightfall on June 23, Russian tanks were within five miles of the Headquarters 3rd Panzer Army.[40]

South of Vitebsk, Pfeiffer's VI Corps was also in serious trouble. The 197th, 299th, and 256th Infantry Divisions were subjected to massive attacks and were broken through in several places. General Pfeiffer managed to contain the penetrations only by using his last reserves. General of Infantry Kurt Tippelskirch, the acting commander of the 4th Army, gave him Major General Herbert Michaelis's 95th Infantry Division (then in 4th Army reserve), which he used to stabilize an eight-mile section of the front along the Pskov-Kiev road. It was not enough. The Reds broke through 197th Infantry Division and pushed it northwestwards, into the Vitebsk salient. By nightfall, the corridor to LIII Corps in Vitebsk was less than fourteen miles wide.

Early in the afternoon, Busch signaled OKH that 3rd Panzer Army could not restore the situation with its own resources. He recommended that LIII Corps be allowed to retreat and that Vitebsk be abandoned. He also called for reinforcements. Heusinger agreed and recommended that Army Group Center be granted the freedom of initiative to retreat to the Dnieper, but Hitler refused to permit any withdrawal. Meanwhile, on June 23, the front of the 4th Army began to crumble. All along the line the Russians were attacking with a newfound tactical skill, and even the veteran German divisions were no longer able to separate their infantry from the tanks. Soviet air-ground, ground-artillery, and close-air support was excellent; for the first time in the war, the Russian tactical performance neared German standards. After three years of fighting, the Soviet commanders had finally learned how to attack with tactical sophistication.

Map 1.4
The Vitebsk Salient

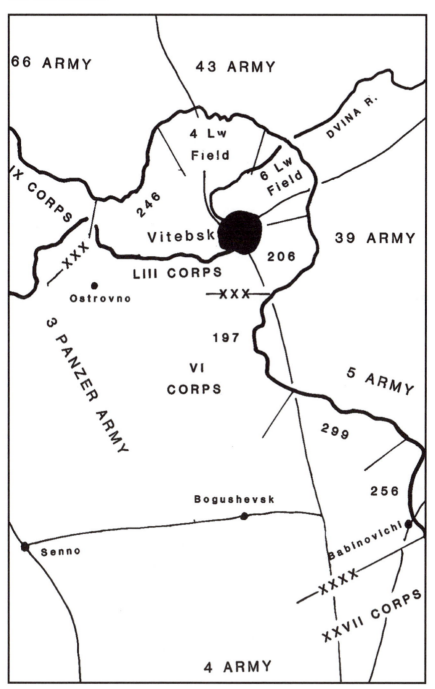

66 ARMY

43 ARMY

IX CORPS

4 Lw
Field

6 Lw
Field

DVINA R.

246

Vitebsk

206

39 ARMY

LIII CORPS

Ostrovno

XXX

3 PANZER ARMY

197

VI
CORPS

5 ARMY

299

256

Bogushevsk

Senno

Babinovichi

XXXX

XXVII CORPS

4 ARMY

Colonel General Gotthard Heinrici, the distinguished veteran commander of the 4th Army, had been away on sick leave since June 5. General von Tippelskirch, the acting commander, estimated that at the main focal points of the attack, one German battalion was fighting one Soviet division.[41] He signaled Krebs that XXXIX Panzer Corps was being attacked by ten Soviet divisions, while XXVII Corps was being attacked by a dozen more. He proposed that the army be allowed to retreat behind the Dnieper, but Busch refused to consider it. "Any voluntary abandonment of parts of the main line still intact is out of the question," he said.[42]

Tippelskirch had no choice but to try to halt the Russians at the front. He committed his main reserve. Lieutenant General Friedrich-Karl von Steinkeller's newly arrived 60th Panzer Grenadier Division "Feldherrn-halle" to the sector of the XXXIX Panzer Corps, with orders to stop up the hole east of Mogilev. General of Artillery Robert Martinek, the panzer corps commander, who did not have a single panzer unit, was astonished by this order. He asked Steinkeller just which hole he proposed to plug. "We've got nothing but holes here," he said. "Your place is back on the Berezina, so that we should have an interception line there for when we can't hold out on the Dnieper any longer. And that will be pretty soon!"[43]

But Hitler and Busch insisted that the front line be held. General Traut's 78th Assault Division—one of the best in the German Army—was overwhelmed, and XXVII Corps began to buckle. By June 24, it had knocked out 116 Soviet tanks since the offensive began, and the XXXIX Panzer destroyed thirty that day alone, but at a very heavy cost. The XXVII Corps was crushed. Busch sent it the only unit immediately available, the 2nd Security Regiment—a bicycle unit—and ordered it to hold the Russians on the Pskov-Kiev road southwest of Orekhovsk. This the XXVII Corps could not do.[44] By nightfall, 120 Soviet tanks had broken through. Things were no better in the zone of the XXXIX Panzer, where General Martinek signaled that the 337th Infantry Division now consisted of nothing but remnants. Only the divisions of Lieutenant General Vincenz Mueller's XII Corps managed to hold their positions, and only with difficulty.

In the zone of the 9th Army, the Russians fired a ninety-minute artillery barrage and then launched two major attacks. One was northeast of Bobruisk against XXXV Corps, the other to the south against XXXXI Panzer Corps. The former targeted the extreme right flank of Lieutenant General Trowitz's 57th Infantry Division (of the XII Corps), which was situated at the junction of the 4th and 9th Armies. It collapsed, and the Russians pushed beyond the German front. Army Group Center reacted quickly and placed all forces in the sector under the command of the 9th Army. It also released Major General Gustav Gihr's 707th Infantry Division to 9th Army, with orders to clean up the breakthrough. Busch also released 20th Panzer

Division to 9th Army, but only one unit at a time, to help it regain contact with 4th Army and restore its front.

At first, it looked as if the situation might, in fact, be quickly restored. The XXXV Corps knocked out eighty enemy tanks during the day, the 707th Infantry's counterattack achieved a measure of success, and to the south, XXXXI Panzer repulsed several Russian attacks; however, the Soviets managed to break through northwest of Cherven, at the junctions of the of the 36th and 35th Infantry Divisions. By nightfall, they had created a gap three miles wide at its spearhead and twelve miles wide at its base, and were already eight miles behind the original German front. The XXXXI Panzer Corps signaled 9th Army that it was under attack by fifteen infantry divisions and three tank units. General Jordan responded by transfering two infantry battalions and five batteries from LV Corps on his right flank, which was not under heavy attack. At 10 P.M. that night, Jordan ordered the 20th Panzer Division to turn about and head south, to deal with the threat to XXXXI Corps. It would, however, take a considerable amount of time to reconcentrate the division and move it from one flank of 9th Army to the other.

Busch met with Zeitzler at army group HQ in Minsk on June 24. By now the Soviets were attacking along more than 430 miles of frontage with more than two hundred divisions, all at or near full strength. Army Group Center faced them in the zones under attack with only twenty-eight divisions, almost all of which were very much understrength. Even now, however, the field marshal did not appeal for permission to conduct a general withdrawal, but, weakening from his previous resolution, he did ask permission to abandon Vitebsk and pull 3rd Panzer Army back to the southwest. Zeitzler, the chief of the General Staff, put this proposal to Hitler that afternoon but was turned down. All the Fuehrer would do was order the 212th and 290th Infantry (from Army Group North) and 5th Panzer Divisions (from Army Group North Ukraine) to Army Group Center. It would take days for them to arrive. Busch telephoned Hitler personally that evening, but the Fuehrer would not be persuaded: LIII Corps was to stay in the city.[45]

Meanwhile, inside the Vitebsk "fortified area," the situation was deteriorating rapidly. In the salient, it was the same old story: too few men to defend too much space. At Vitebsk, General Gollwitzer had only four depleted divisions—the 206th and 246th Infantry and the 4th and 6th Luftwaffe Field—to hold fifty-five miles of frontage. The total infantry strength of all four was 8,123, giving him an average strength of 150 men per mile of combat zone—about one man every twelve yards. His reserves consisted of one Luftwaffe special-services battalion, a battalion of heavy artillery, and two antitank companies—hardly enough to check two full Soviet armies. By the end of the first day of the offensive, Vitebsk was two-thirds surrounded.

"What can I do? What can I do?" Busch muttered to his chief of staff, Lieutenant General Krebs. It never occurred to him to take matters into his own hands. It was probably too late now in any event; the "fortified place" was already surrounded, and the Russians were rapidly pushing the rest of 3rd Panzer Army—IX and VI Corps—away from Vitebsk.[46] Sixth Corps on the right flank was in particularly poor condition. It had been attacked for four days by the Soviet 5th Tank Army (supported by more than five hundred heavy guns) and had almost been overwhelmed. All of its divisions were crushed, and Major General Count Ralph von Oriola's 299th Infantry Division was overrun on the morning of June 25. The corps, with the 95th, 14th, 256th, and 299th Infantry Divisions, was pushed into the zone of the 4th Army, which took control of it around noon. The veteran corps commander, General of Artillery Georg Pfeiffer, was fatally wounded in a Soviet air attack outside Mogilev about 8 P.M. on June 28 while trying to rally the pitiful remnants of his command. Certainly there was nothing he could have done on June 23, 24, or 25 to save Vitebsk.[47]

During the course of the battle, Hitler ordered that the Luftwaffe parachute a staff officer into Vitebsk to make sure that Gollwitzer understood that he was expected to hold until the end. Busch, naturally, passed the order down. The idea for this suicide mission was not dropped until General Reinhardt signaled Busch: "Tell the Fuehrer that if he stands by his order, there is only one officer in 3rd Panzer Army that can carry it out, and that is the commander. I am ready to execute the order!" Busch passed this dispatch on to OKH. An hour later, Hitler rescinded his order.[48]

On the evening of June 24, Hitler finally decided to allow General Gollwitzer to break out of Vitebsk with three of his four divisions, leaving only Lieutenant General Alfons Hitter's 206th Infantry Division behind. Gollwitzer disobeyed the spirit of Hitler's orders and carried most of the 206th with him when he cut his way out on June 25; however, LIII Corps only got a dozen miles before being surrounded again the next day. Lieutenant Generals Robert Pistorius and Rudolf Peschel, the commanders of the 4th and 6th Luftwaffe Field Divisions, were both killed as the Russians compressed the pocket. Gollwitzer finally gave up on the morning of June 27. He had 270 men with him when he surrendered, two-thirds of them wounded. General Hitter capitulated the same day. Twenty-seven thousand men were lost, most of them captured during the breakout.[49]

On the southern edge of the cauldron, the 1st Belorussian Front threw its full weight into the attack on June 24. On June 25, General Jordan requested permission to withdraw his 9th Army from the huge pocket forming between the Dnieper and the Beresina, but Busch retorted that the army's mission was to hold every foot of ground and not to give up anything voluntarily. "Having made a responsible report, one must accept the orders of his superiors even when he is convinced of the opposite," General Jordan wrote in 9th Army's war diary. "What is worse is to know that the completely inadequate direction from the army group is not a product of purposeful leadership trying to do its utmost but merely an attempt to carry out orders long overtaken by events."[50]

Jordan delayed several hours before committing his only sizable reserve, the 20th Panzer Division, to the battle on his southern flank, probably because he did not want to sacrifice it needlessly. Then it was delayed several more hours by the poor roads, which were now clogged with panic-stricken fugitives and refugees. When it did attack, it knocked out sixty Soviet tanks in one day (June 25), but it had only seventy-one operational tanks to begin with, and about half of these were PzKw IVs, which were marginal weapons on the Eastern Front in 1944. They were opposed by three hundred Russian tanks. The 20th Panzer Division lost about half of its tanks in this battle.[51] It could not prevent the Russians from breaking through General Edmund Hoffmeister's XXXXI Panzer Corps with strong armored forces and heading for Bobruisk. On Hoffmeister's left flank, meanwhile, the XXXV Corps was torn to bits on June 25. By nightfall, the XXXXI Panzer and XXXV Corps had knocked out 120 enemy tanks, but the 134th and 296th Infantry Divisions were smashed, the 35th Infantry Division was in remnants, and the rapidly moving Russians were bypassing the 707th and 134th Infantry Divisions southwest of Buda.

It is perhaps ironic that the German Army, which in 1940 stunned the world with its blitzkrieg method of mobile warfare, was the least mobile major army in Europe in 1944. This truth is not due to the fact that the German Army had retrogressed; the others had caught up with and then surpassed the Wehrmacht in every area of mobility. Anglo-Saxon (and primarily American) methods of mass production had irrevocably tilted the balance of power against it. The German panzer and panzer grenadier branches constituted only about 10.8 percent of the German Army in 1944. The vast majority of the German divisions were made up of horse-drawn units. In the typical infantry division, the only fully motorized unit was the ambulance company. The Red Army, on the other hand, had been so liberally supplied with American Lend-Lease equipment (especially 2.5-ton trucks) that it was one of the most mobile armies in the world by 1944. (The word *Studebaker* would be synonymous with *truck* in the USSR for many years to come.) Once the Soviets got behind a German infantry division—as was happening now—the German foot soldiers had little chance of catching up. They could only hope to escape, and even this depended on their comrades' stabilizing the front, so that they themselves would not have too far to travel.

On June 26, Busch flew to Obersalzburg and met with Hitler to try to get him to change his inflexible defense policies, but without success. The field marshal was accompanied by General Jordan, who had been ordered to Fuehrer Headquarters to explain his hesitant and confused instructions regarding the employment of the 20th Panzer Division. The meeting satisfied no one. Busch, possibly acting on Hitler's orders, sacked Jordan for irresolute leadership on June 27 and replaced him with General of Artillery Helmuth Weidling, the former commander of XXXXI Panzer Corps.[52] Weidling acted until his permanent replacement, General of Panzer Troops Nikolaus von Vormann, could arrive.[53] But it was again too late: the Russians virtually destroyed XXXXI Panzer Corps in three days of heavy fighting, bypassed Bobruisk, and fanned out behind 9th Army.[54] It is true that Jordan had initially committed the 20th Panzer too far north and too early, and then hesitated to commit it at the proper place; later, however, even if he had committed it a day sooner and had used it in the best theoretically possible manner, it would not have made the slightest difference.

Of the hundred thousand men in 9th Army, only thirty thousand escaped. Hoffmeister was among those captured, and the thirty-four thousand men of Lieutenant General Baron Kurt-Jurgen von Luetzow's XXXV Corps were surrounded in Bobruisk, where they came under heavy attack from the second wave of Soviet assault divisions. When Luetzow finally surrendered on June 29, only sixteen thousand of his men were left alive.[55] Four more German divisions had been destroyed. Meanwhile, Lieutenant Generals Ernst Phillipp and Karl Zutavern, the commanders of the 134th Infantry and the 18th Panzer Grenadier Divisions, respectively, committed suicide rather than surrender to the Russians.[56]

On June 25, 4th Army also faced an impossible situation. Its center (XXXIX Panzer Corps) was penetrated and overwhelmed, and the armies to its north and south—3rd Panzer and 9th—were collapsing. General von Tippelskirch took matters into his own hands and ordered a retreat to the Berezina River, without informing Army Group Center. Busch countermanded the order as soon as he learned of it, gave Tippelskirch a heated dressing-down, and instructed 4th Army to stand fast where it was, but Tippelskirch ignored this order as well. He instructed Generals Voelkers and Martinek, the commanders of the XXVII Army and XXXIX Panzer Corps, respectively, to post rearguards in their present positions and to continue the retreat with their main forces. He also warned them to be careful what they said in dispatches to army group. Clearly Tippelskirch was contravening his orders, but both corps commanders elected to obey him rather than Busch and his chief of staff, General Krebs. "It was Hitler's destructive orders to hold firm that . . . brought about the collapse of the principle of order and obedience," General Gerd Niepold wrote later. "To the commanders in the field, loyalty to their troops meant more than obedience to these nonsensical and pigheaded orders."[57]

In addition to exhibiting great skill in deception, Tippelskirch also demonstrated considerable tactical ability during his retreat, despite the fact that the Red Air Force launched a rare carpet-bombing raid on its headquarters during the night of June 26–27, destroying most of its communications equipment in the process. He fell back in the direction of Minsk and had the Benezina River bridges wired for demolition. Tippelskirch had no choice but to make a stand east of Minsk, however, or he would have to write off the XXXIX Panzer and XXVII Corps. As he prepared to defend the city with security troops and whatever odds and ends he could find (including five police regiments and the remnants of the 31st and 267th Infantry Divisions), the first—and the best—of Hitler's reinforcements reached the battlefield. Map 1.5 shows the situation in the zone of Army Group Center at nightfall on June 26.

The Red Army began to close in on Minsk on June 27, just as the 5th Panzer Division arrived in the city. It was greeted by a scene that could have demoralized any division. Complete pandemonium reigned. The roads were jammed with stragglers, many of them unarmed, fleeing in a disorganized mob, just trying to get out of Russia. The 5th Panzer, however, did not panic. Exceptionally well led by Lieutenant General Karl Decker,[58] it was one of the best units in the Wehrmacht. Its men had fought in Poland, Belgium, and France and had spent three years on the Russian Front. It was also very strong by 1944 standards, boasting seventy Panthers and fifty-five PzKw IVs. Also attached to the division was the 505th Heavy Panzer Battalion, which had twenty-nine ultramodern Tigers (PzKw VIs). Although its men were startled by what they saw in Minsk, they were by no means demoralized.

Tippelskirch assigned the task of defending Minsk and maintaining contact with the 3rd Panzer Army to a tough, highly decorated, and highly competent East Prussian, Lieutenant General Dietrich von Saucken. The thin, dark-haired Saucken had already distinguished himself as commander of the 4th Panzer Division and until recently, had served as deputy commander of the III Panzer Corps. Originally a cavalry officer, he habitually wore both a sword and a monocle.

Around himself, Saucken formed Group von Saucken, an ad hoc corps headquarters drawn largely from staff officers serving in the rear area of the XXXIX Panzer Corps. (After the XXXIX Panzer broke up, Group von Saucken was upgraded and became the Staff, XXXIX Panzer Corps.) He posted the 5th Panzer Division at Krupki Station, northeast of the city and east of the Berezina, where he expected the main Soviet blow to fall. The objective of the 5th Panzer Division was clear: keep the escape routes across the Berezina open as long as possible.

Map 1.5
Army Group Center, Nightfall, June 26, 1944

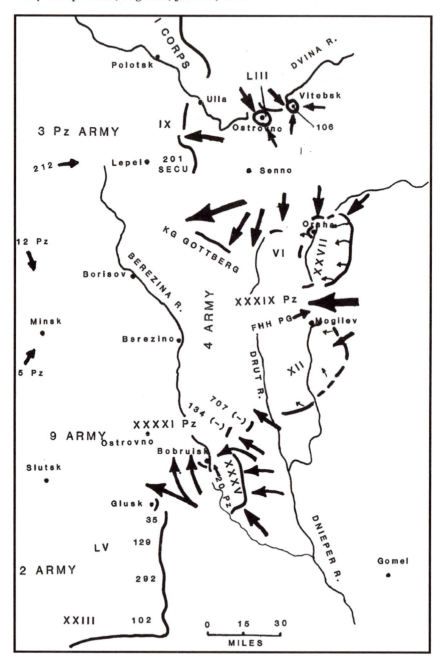

Saucken and Decker positioned the 5th Panzer Division perfectly, just as the 3rd Guards Tank Corps—the spearhead of the 3rd Belorussian Front—approached Krupki Station. Unfortunately for Decker, the division's 31st Panzer Regiment (which was coming by rail) had not yet arrived, but he did have the 505th Heavy Panzer Battalion, the 5th Panzer Reconnaissance Battalion, the 89th Panzer Engineer Battalion, and the 13th and 31st Panzer Grenadier Regiments in position when the first blow fell.

The 3rd Guards Tank ran into an inferno near Krupki Station on the evening of June 28; it was slaughtered by the Tigers of the 505th Heavy Panzer. Although they were vastly superior in numbers, the Russians were equipped with M4A2 Sherman tanks, which had little chance against the more heavily gunned Tigers, whose 88 mm guns had a longer range than the 75 mm main gun on the American-made tanks. The Soviets, however, continued to attack all night, largely because darkness neutralized the superior range of the Tigers. The Reds finally captured Krupki Station about 7 A.M. on June 29, but at the cost of dozens of AFVs. An entire corps had been decimated by a reinforced battalion.

With Krupki Station in their hands, the Russians tried to push on to the Berezina at Borisov and outflank the 5th Panzer Division. Instead, they ran into an ambush prepared by the 89th Panzer Engineer Battalion. Again checked, the Soviets tried farther north, where they committed the 29th Tank Corps. They reached the Berezina at Studenka but found the crossing sites defended by the 5th Panzer Reconnaissance Battalion. Once more, the Russians were checked.

By this point, five motorized rifle divisions from the 11th Guards Army had caught up with the Soviet vanguards. General Pavel Rotmistrov, the commander of the 5th Tank Army, threw them into action near the village of Kostritsa, which was stubbornly defended by the 31st Panzer Grenadier Regiment. The Reds were halted again in heavy fighting.

If Tippelskirch had had five or six divisions of the strength and quality of the 5th Panzer, he might have won the Battle of Minsk. But he did not, and the 5th could not be everywhere at once. By nightfall on June 29, the Soviet 29th Tank Corps and 3rd Guards Mechanized Corps had outflanked the 5th Panzer Division and had crossed the Berezina north of Borisov. South of that town, two rifle divisions from the 11th Guards Army had defeated Tippelskirch's police regiments and were fording the river. South of that, the Soviet 31st Army had brushed aside the remnants of the 31st and 267th Infantry Divisions and was crossing the river at several points. That was enough for General Decker. He ordered the 31st Panzer Grenadier Regiment to retreat to Borisov, and then he fell back across the river with most of his division. (Group von Saucken, reinforced with elements of the 5th Panzer Division, managed to hold a bridgehead on the east bank near Shukovets until the night of July 2–3.) As the Germans retreated, an aggressive Soviet vanguard pursued them and tried to capture the bridge intact. The panzer engineers waited until most of them were on the bridge and two Shermans were actually across it; then they blew it up, trapping the tanks and a few infantrymen in the process.

As the 5th Panzer Division prepared for the next onslaught, the Soviet command inadvertently paid it perhaps the highest compliment imaginable from an enemy. It signaled its units: "If you meet the 5th Panzer, try to go round them."[59]

On June 28, Busch signaled Tippelskirch to fall back behind the Berezina. He was already there by this time, but he had lost 130,000 of his 165,000 men.[60] He had been forced to leave behind XXVII and XII Corps, which were trapped in a large pocket that was forming east of Minsk. Due to Hitler's orders, 4th Army also left behind Lieutenant General Hans Traut's 78th Assault Division, at Fortified Place Orsha, where it was surrounded and forced to surrender on June 27.[61] Ninth Army also had to leave behind a division, Lieutenant General Rudolf Bamler's 12th Infantry, at Fortified place Mogilev,[62] to reinforce the city garrison, which was led by Major General Gottfried von Erdmannsdorff. After a determined resistance, both the garrison and the division were destroyed. Bamler and Erdmannsdorff capitulated on June 30 (Stalin later had Erdmannsdorff hanged.)[63] Had Tippelskirch obeyed Busch, as Busch obeyed Hitler, 4th Army would have been completely wiped out. As things were, 4th and 9th Armies were mere shells, and 3rd Panzer Army was down to three understrength divisions with a total of only seventy guns.[64]

The full extent of the disaster can be seen by comparing Table 1.1 with Table 1.2. Even though Army Group Center had received massive reinforcements by July 15 (Table 1.2), it is clear that it had been smashed. Several ad hoc battle groups had been formed under men like Lieutenant General Hermann Floerke and Major General Friedrich Stephan, the commanders of the virtually defunct 14th and 267th Infantry Divisions, respectively.[65] They controlled the shattered remnants of various commands and tried to restore them to some combat value, but with mixed results. Note also that four full corps, including fifteen infantry, two security, two Luftwaffe Field, and three panzer or panzer grenadier divisions, were simply listed as "whereabouts unknown" as late as July 15.[66] By any measurement, the disaster was enormous. Table 1.3 shows the senior commanders killed, captured, or missing from Army Group Center alone; it gives the reader an idea of the magnitude of the disaster.

Among the units caught up in 4th Army's disaster was the 60th Panzer Grenadier Division, which was needlessly sacrificed. On the evening of June 25, about a hundred Russian tanks broke through the division at Sukhari, on the Dnieper. General Steinkeller managed to escape across the river with the remnants of his command but was captured later, near

Table 1.2
Order of Battle, Army Group Center, July 15, 1944

ARMY GROUP CENTER: Field Marshal Model
2nd Army:
XX Corps:
    Corps Detachment E (−)[1]
    137th Infantry Division
    251st Infantry Division
    3rd Cavalry Brigade
    7th Infantry Division (−)
    203rd Security Division
    Elements, 7th Infantry Division[2]
    Elements, 35th Infantry Division[2]

XXIII Corps:
    292nd Infantry Division
    102nd Infantry Division
    Group Major General Stephan
    Group Lieutenant General Harteneck
    4th Panzer Division
    4th Cavalry Brigade
    Elements, Corps Detachment E
    129th Infantry Division (in remnants)

LV Corps:
    KG 28th Jaeger Division
    367th Infantry Division
    12th Panzer Division
    20th Panzer Division (in remnants)
    Group Major General von Ziehlberg

Army Reserves:
    II Hungarian Reserve Corps
        5th Hungarian Reserve Division
        23rd Hungarian Reserve Division
        1st Hungarian Cavalry Division
    52nd Security Division

4th Army:
Group Weidling
    50th Infantry Division
    Group Lieutenant General Floerke
    Group Count von Gottberg
    5th Panzer Division
    Elements, 3rd SS Panzer Division

XXXIX Panzer Corps:
    Elements, 221st Security Division
    170th Infantry Division

Table 1.2 (*continued*)

131st Infantry Division
7th Panzer Division

3rd Panzer Army:
XXVI Corps:
    Group General von Rothkirch
    201st Security Division
    KG 6th Panzer Division
    69th Infantry Division (−)
    Elements 196th Infantry Division[2]

IX Corps:
    Corps Detachment D (in remnants)[3]
    212th Infantry Division
    252nd Infantry Division (−)
    Panzer Grenadier Brigade von Werthern

Army Reserves:
    Corps Detachment G
    95th Infantry Division (in remnants)
    197th Infantry Division[2]
    256th Infantry Division[2]

Army Group Reserves:
    Headquarters, 9th Army
    5th SS Panzer Division "Viking"

"Not Available":
    299th Infantry Division (in remnants)
    134th Infantry Division (in remnants)
    383rd Infantry Division (in remnants)
    337th Infantry Division (in remnants)

"Whereabouts Unknown":
XXVII Corps:
    25th Panzer Grenadier Division
    260th Infantry Division
    78th Assault [Sturm] Division
    20th Panzer Grenadier Division

XII Corps:
    18th Panzer Grenadier Division
    12th Infantry Division
    31st Infantry Division
    57th Infantry Division
    110th Infantry Division
    267th Infantry Division
    296th Infantry Division
    6th Infantry Division
    45th Infantry Division
    36th Infantry Division

Table 1.2 (*continued*)

XXXV Corps:
    390th Field Training Division
    707th Infantry Division

LIII Corps:
    206th Infantry Division
    246th Infantry Division
    4th Luftwaffe Field Division
    6th Luftwaffe Field Division
    14th Infantry Division
    286th Security Division

Notes:
KG = *Kampfgruppe* (at regimental strength)
[1]"Minus," indicates major element detached
[2]In transit
[3]With elements of the 291st Security Division attached

Source: Kurt Mehner, ed., *Geheimen Tagesberichte*, vol. 10, pp. 504–5.

the Berezina.[67] Only a handful of FHH survivors escaped the disaster. General Martinek went up to the front on June 28 and was killed in action that afternoon. He was replaced by Lieutenant General Otto Schuenemann of the 337th Infantry Division, who tried to break out to the west, but it was too late by then. The next day, near Pagost, Schuenemann was also killed, the XXXIX Panzer Corps disintegrated, and its divisions ceased to exist.[68]

Hitler sacked Busch later on June 28 and replaced him with Field Marshal Model. The unemployed army group commander took up temporary residence at the Neuhammer Training Camp, where, on the orders of OKH, he was visited on or about July 9 by Captain Alexander Stahlberg. The captain unfolded a current situation map and placed it on a large table. When Busch "saw what had become of his Army Group in the few days since his dismissal," Stahlberg recalled, "he clapped both hands to his face, gave a loud cry and flung his massive body across the map."[69]

Busch was deeply hurt by his dismissal, for he had just been obeying orders. This was true enough, but in the process he had lost more than 300,000 men and twenty-eight divisions, as well as 215 tanks and more than 1,500 guns.[70] Naturally, most of the units that escaped were noncombat service-support and rear-area units. Army Group Center had been virtually eliminated as a combat force. It was the greatest disaster Germany ever suffered on the Eastern Front. It was now up to Walter Model, the "Fuehrer's Fireman," to save something from the wreckage.

Table 1.3
Senior Officer Casualties in Army Group Center, Summer 1944

3rd Panzer Army
14th Panzer Grenadier Division: Lieutenant General Floerke, Killed in Action
95th Infantry Division: Major General Michaelis, Killed in Action
LIII Corps: General of Infantry Gollwitzer, Captured
246th Infantry Division: Major General Mueller-Buelow, Captured
4th Luftwaffe Field Division: Lieutenant General Pistorius, Killed in Action
6th Luftwaffe Field Division: Lieutenant General Peschel, Killed in Action
206th Infantry Division: Lieutenant General Hitter, Captured
VI Corps: General of Artillery Pfeiffer, Killed in Action
197th Infantry Division: Colonel Hahne, Missing in Action
299th Infantry Division: Major General von Junck, Missing in Action
256th Infantry Division: Major General Wuestenhagen, Killed in Action

4th Army
XXXIX Panzer Corps: General of Artillery Martinek, Killed in Action
110th Infantry Division: Lieutenant General von Kurowski, Captured
337th Infantry Division: Lieutenant General Schuenemann, Killed in Action
12th Infantry Division: Lieutenant General Bamler, Captured
31st Infantry Division: Lieutenant General Ochsner, Captured
XII Corps: Lieutenant General Vinzenz Mueller, Captured
18th Panzer Grenadier Division, Lieutenant General Zutavern, committed suicide
267th Infantry Division: Lieutenant General Drescher, Killed in Action
57th Infantry Division: Major General Trowitz, Captured
XXVII Corps: General of Infantry Voelckers, Captured
78th Assault Division: Lieutenant General Traut, Captured
260th Infantry Division: Major General Klammt, Captured

9th Army
9th Army Engineer Commander: Major General Aurel Schmidt, Captured
XXXV Corps: Lieutenant General Baron von Luetzow, Captured
134th Infantry Division: Lieutenant General Philipp, committed suicide
6th Infantry Division: Major General Heyne, Captured
383rd Infantry Division: Major General Hamann, Killed in Action
45th Infantry Division: Major General Engel, Captured
XXXXI Panzer Corps: Lieutenant General Hoffmeister, Captured
36th Infantry Division: Major General Conrady, Captured

2nd Army
3rd Cavalry Brigade: Colonel Baron Hans von Wolff, Killed in Action
3rd Cavalry Brigade: Lieutenant Colonel Baron Georg von Boeselager, Killed in Action

Reserves
707th Infantry Division: Major General Gihr, Captured
60th "Feldherrnhalle" Panzer Grenadier Division: Major General von Steinkeller, Captured

Table 1.3 (*continued*)

Reserves
Commandant of Brest-Litovsk: Lieutenant General Walter Scheller, Killed in Action
Commander, 3rd Panzer Army Weapons School: Colonel Baron Constantin Digeon von Monteton, Killed in Action
Sources: Paul Carell, *Scorched Earth*, pp. 596–97; Wolf Keilig, *Die Generale*, ff. 1; Alex Buchner, *Ostfront 1944*, pp. 241–43; Gerhard von Seemen, pp. 27, 90.

NOTES

1. Stephen Mansfield, *Never Give In: The Extraordinary Character of Winston Churchill* (Elkton, Md.: 1995; reprint ed., Nashville, Tenn.: 1996), pp. 32, 40, 102–6.

2. Between the day Hitler became chancellor (January 30, 1933) and the day he committed suicide (April 30, 1945), the German Army's General Staff had no less than six chiefs of staff: General of Infantry Wilhelm Adam (1930–33), Colonel General Ludwig Beck (1933–38), Colonel General Franz Halder (1938–42), Colonel General Kurt Zeitzler (1942–44), Colonel General Heinz Guderian (July 21, 1944–45), and General of Infantry Hans Krebs (April 1–May 2, 1945). Guderian and Krebs both served as "acting" chiefs only.

3. Paul Carell, *Scorched Earth: The Russian-German War 1943–1944* (Boston: 1966; reprint ed., New York: 1971) p. 596.

4. Louis L. Snyder, *Encyclopedia of the Third Reich* (New York: 1976), p. 47; Robert Wistrich, *Who's Who in Nazi Germany* (New York: 1982), p. 35; Otto E. Moll, *Die deutschen Generalfeldmarschaelle, 1939–1945* (Rastatt/Baden: 1961), pp. 34–35.

5. Wistrich, p. 35; Moll, pp. 34–35; Snyder, p. 47.

6. Fabian von Schlabendorff, *Revolt against Hitler,* ed. Gero von S. Gaevernitz. (London: 1948), p. 127.

7. Telford Taylor, *Sword and Swastika: Generals and Nazis in the Third Reich* (New York: 1952; reprint ed., Chicago: 1969), pp. 386–87.

8. Richard Brett-Smith, *Hitler's Generals* (San Rafael, Calif.: 1977), p. 196; Taylor, *Sword*, pp. 386–87; Snyder, p. 47.

9. Robert M. Kennedy, *The German Campaign in Poland (1939)*, U.S. Department of the Army Pamphlet 20–255 (Washington, D.C.: 1956), ff. 74, maps 7, 9, and 10.

10. *Kriegstagebuch des Oberkommando des Wehrmacht (Wehrmachtfuehrungstab)* (Frankfurt-am-Main, 1961) [hereafter cited as *Kriegstagebuch des OKW*], vol. 1, p. 1123.

11. Ibid.

12. Erich von Manstein, *Lost Victories* (Novato, Calif.: 1982), p. 248; Carell, *Scorched Earth*, pp. 249–51.

13. As of January 2, 1942. *Kriegstagebuch des OKW*, volume 2, p. 1356.

14. Albert Seaton, *The Russo-German War, 1941–1945* (New York: 1970), pp. 244–45; Carell, *Scorched Earth* pp. 371–418.

15. *Kriegstagebuch des OKW*, vol. 3, p. 1157, report dated October 4, 1943.

16. Earl F. Ziemke, *Stalingrad to Berlin: The German Defeat in the East* (Washington, D.C.: 1966), p. 113.

17. Werner Haupt, *Army Group Center: The Wehrmacht in Russia, 1941–1945*, trans. Joseph G. Welsh (Atgleif, Penn.: 1997), p. 187. The 87th Infantry Division was a unit with high morale; would break out singing "Deutschlandlied" (The Song of Germany).

Georg-Hans Reinhardt was one of the earliest panzer generals and was a highly capable army commander. Born in 1887, he joined the army as a *Fahnenjunker* (officer cadet) in the infantry in 1907. Later he served as commander, 1st Rifle Brigade (a motorized unit) (1937–38); 4th Panzer Division (1938–40), XXXXI Panzer Corps (1940–41), and 3rd Panzer Group (October 5, 1941). Third Panzer Group was upgraded to 3rd Panzer Army on January 1, 1942, the same day Reinhardt was promoted to colonel general. He fought in Poland, France, and Russia. He became commander in chief of Army Group Center on August 16, 1944. Hitler relieved him of his command for retreating without orders on January 25, 1945. Reinhardt, however, had been critically wounded when a bullet struck him in the head some hours before; word had not yet reached Fuehrer Headquarters. General Reinhardt recovered from his wound, retired to Tegernsee, and died on November 22, 1971.

18. Zeimke, p. 193.

19. David Irving, *Hitler's War* (New York: 1977), p. 674; Ziemke, pp. 311–12.

20. Gerd Niepold, *Battle for White Russia: The Destruction of Army Group Center. June 1944*, trans. Richard Simpkin (London: 1987), pp. 30–32.

21. Ibid., pp. 28–33.

22. March, or replacement (*Ersatz*), battalions were formed in Germany by the *Wehrkreise* (military districts) of the Replacement (or Home) Army in Germany. They were then sent to the field armies, where they were broken up and their men sent to individual units. They were formed for security purposes (partisans infested much of the German rear by 1942), but they could fight as units in emergencies.

23. Steven Zaloga, *Bagration, 1944: The Destruction of Army Group Center* (London: 1996; reprint ed., Danbury, Conn.: 1997), p. 26.

24. Ziemke, p. 313.

25. Ibid., p. 15.

26. Hermann Gackenholz, "The Collapse of Army Group Center," in H. A. Jacobsen and J. Rohwer, eds. *Decisive Battles of World War II: The German View* (New York: 1965), p. 360; Ziemke, pp. 313–14.

27. Ziemke, pp. 314–15; Niepold, p. 57.

28. Niepold, p. 58.

29. Hans Krebs was an infantry officer who spent the entire war in staff positions, most notably as chief of staff of VII Corps (1939–42), 9th Army (1942–43), Army Group Center (1943–44), and Army Group B (1944). He was chief representative of the Fuehrer at OKH (1944–45) before being named acting chief of staff of OKH (March 29, 1945). At the end of the Battle of Berlin he committed suicide, probably on May 2. Krebs was promoted to general of infantry on August 1, 1944.

30. Ziemke, pp. 205, 315–16.

31. Christopher Chant, ed., *The Marshall Cavendish Illustrated Encyclopedia of World War II* (New York: 1972), vol. 6, p. 1640.

32. Gackenholz, p. 361.

33. Schlabendorff, p. 126.

34. Niepold, p. 12.

35. Friedrich Gollwitzer joined the Bavarian 13th Infantry Regiment in 1908 and was a colonel when World War II began. He successively commanded the 41st Infantry Regiment (1935–39), the 193rd Replacement Division (1939–40), 88th Infantry Division (1940–43) and LIII Corps (assumed command June 22, 1943). Wolf Keilig, *Die Generale des Heeres* (Friedberg: 1983), p. 111.

36. Paul Voelkers was born in Kiel in 1891 and entered the service as an officer cadet (*Fahnenjunker*) in 1910. A colonel in 1939, he served as commander of the 113rd Infantry Regiment (1937–39), commander of a rifle brigade (1940–41), as German general to the Bulgarian army high command (1941–42), as commander of the 78th Infantry (later Assault) Division (1942–43), and as commander of the XXVII Corps, beginning June 8, 1943 (Kielig, p. 355).

37. Gackenholz, p. 365.

38. Chant, vol. 6, p. 1639.

39. Brett-Smith, pp. 196–97.

40. Haupt, *Center*, p. 193.

41. Kurt von Tippelskirch was born in Berlin-Charlottenburg in 1891. He entered the Imperial Army as a *Fahnenjunker* in 1910 and was on the staff of OKH when the war began. He later served as commander of the 30th Infantry Division (early 1941–42); German liaison officer to the Italian 8th Army on the Eastern Front (1942–43); Commander, XII Corps (1943); and acting commander, 4th Army (June 4–July 18, 1944).

42. Gackenholz, p. 369.

43. Carell, *Scorched Earth*, pp. 575–77.

44. The 2nd Security Regiment was overrun by sixty Russian tanks near Smolyany on June 26 and fled to the southwest, where it soon ceased to exist.

45. Gackenholz, pp. 368–69.

46. Carell, *Scorched Earth*, p. 581.

47. The VI Corps lost contact with 3rd Panzer Army on June 25 and was transferred to the control of 4th Army. Georg Pfeiffer fought in World War I and, like many officers of his era, spent the years 1920 to 1935 in the police. He commanded the 37th Artillery Regiment (1937–39), the 105th Artillery Command (1939–40), the 94th Infantry Division (1940–43), the 306th Infantry Division (1943–44), and VI Corps (assumed command, May 20, 1944). He was promoted to general of artillery on May 1, 1944 (Keilig, p. 255).

48. Haupt, *Center*, p. 196.

49. Seaton, p. 436; Carell, *Scorched Earth*, pp. 583–86, 596. According to Soviet sources, LIII Corps lost twenty thousand killed and ten thousand captured. Gollwitzer stated after the war that LIII Corps lost five thousand killed and twenty-two thousand captured at Vitebsk. Soviet sources are, of course, notoriously unreliable. Zaloga, *Bagration*, p. 53.

50. Zeimke, p. 321.

51. The 20th Panzer Division had not had a panzer regiment for some time. Because of high casualties during the Soviet winter offensive of 1941–42, the I and II Battalions of the 21st Panzer Regiment (the tank regiment of the 20th Panzer Division) were dissolved in early 1942. Their survivors were incorporated into the III Battalion, which became the 21st Panzer Battalion. The 21st Panzer Regiment was dissolved.

52. For reasons not made clear by the records, General Jordan had relieved Weidling of the command of the XXXXI Panzer Corps on June 20 and replaced him with Hoffmeister. Now Weidling replaced the man who had replaced him.

53. Hans Jordan, a holder to the Knight's Cross with Oak Leaves and Swords, held no further commands until April 1945, when he was placed in charge of the German defenses in the Tyrol (Alpine Italy). He lived in Munich after the war. An artillery officer, Helmuth Weidling had commanded the 56th and 20th Artillery Regiments (1939–40), the 128th Artillery Command (1940–41), and the 86th Infantry Division (1942–43) before taking charge of the XXXXI Panzer Corps. In April 1945, he was named commander of the LVI Panzer Corps and battle commander for Berlin. He surrendered the capital of the Reich to the Russians on May 3, 1945, four days after Adolf Hitler shot himself. Weidling died in a Soviet prison in the 1950s. Nikolaus von Vormann was a West Prussian. He served on the Fuehrer Headquarters staff (1939), was chief of staff of the XXVIII Corps (1940–42), commander of the 23rd Panzer Division (1942–43) and commander of the XXXXVIII Panzer Corps (1943–44). At the end of the war, Vormann was named commander of the famous Alpine Redoubt, which hardly existed. He lived in Berchtesgaden after the war.

54. Gackenholz, pp. 370–71.

55. The son of an ancient Prussian military family, Baron Kurt-Juergen von Luetzow entered the service in 1914. During World War II, he served as the commander the 89th Infantry Regiment (1939–42), the 12th Infantry Division (1942–44), and the XXXV Corps (from June 25, 1944, until the surrender). He was not released by the Russians until 1956.

56. Carell, *Scorched Earth*, pp. 580, 597.

57. Niepold, p. 106. Gerd Niepold was Ia of the 12th Panzer Division during the Battle of White Russia. A War Academy graduate and a member of the General Staff, he fought in Poland and France and served almost four years on the Eastern Front before being transferred to the War Academy staff near the end of the conflict. Returning to school after the war, he qualified as a construction engineer and spent several years as an architect in Frankfurt-am-Main before joining the West German Armed Forces (Bundeswehr) in 1956. Here he commanded a panzer brigade, a mechanized division, and III Corps at Kolbenz. His *Battle for White Russia* is a major source on this campaign. Niepold was born in Stargard, Pomerania (now part of Poland), in 1913 and joined the 11th Infantry Regiment as a *Fahnenjunker* in 1932. He has a son (a lawyer and civil servant) and a daughter (an art and design teacher).

58. Karl Decker was born in Pomerania in 1897 and entered the army as a *Fahnenjunker* a few weeks after World War I broke out. An excellent panzer officer and combat leader, he commanded the 1st Anti-Tank Battalion (1936–40), I/3rd Panzer Regiment (1940–41), 3rd Panzer Regiment (1941–43), 21st Panzer Brigade (1943), 5th Panzer Division (1943–44), and XXXIX Panzer Corps (1944–45). He was promoted rapidly: to lieutenant colonel (1939), colonel (1942), major general (1943), lieutenant general (June 1, 1944), and general of panzer troops (January 1, 1945). Trapped in the Ruhr Pocket and despairing over the fact that Germany had lost the war, General Decker took his own life on April 21, 1945, rather than surrender to the Americans.

59. Paul Adair, *Hitler's Greatest Defeat: The Collapse of Army Group Center* (London: 1994), p. 132.

60. Brett-Smith, p. 197.

61. Hans Traut entered the Imperial Army in 1914 as a *Fahnenjunker*. After serving in the First World War and the Reichswehr, he commanded I/90th Infantry Regiment (1st Battalion, 90th Infantry) (1937–40), 40th Infantry Regiment (1940–42), and 263rd Infantry Division (1942–43). He led the 78th Assault (Sturm) Division from April 1 to November 1, 1943, when he was wounded. He resumed command on February 15, 1944, and was captured on July 12. Traut was released from prison in 1955 and settled in Darmstadt (Keilig, p. 348).

62. Rudolf Bamler had served as chief of staff of Wehrkreis VII (1939), XX (1939–40), XXXXVII Panzer Corps (1940), and the Army of Norway (1942–44). The 12th Infantry Division was his first command of the war. He assumed command on June 1 and surrendered on June 27. Angry over being needlessly sacrificed and motivated by ambition, he promptly went to work for the Russians. From 1946 until his retirement in 1962, he was an officer in the East German Police. General Bamler died in 1972. He was an artillery officer and commanded the 74th Artillery Regiment before the war.

63. Gottfried von Erdmannsdorff had previously commanded the 171st Infantry Regiment (1939–42) and the 465th Replacement Division (1942–44). He assumed command of Mogilev in April and was hanged in Minsk in 1946. Walter Heyne was a "retread." Born in Hanover in 1894, he entered the service as a *Fahnenjunker* in 1913 and was discharged as a *Rittmeister* (captain of cavalry) in 1928. He returned to active duty as a territorial officer in late 1933. During World War II he commanded the 754th Heavy Artillery Battalion (1939–40), I/217th Artillery Regiment (1940–42), the 182nd Artillery Regiment (1942–43), and the 82nd Infantry Division (1943–44). He assumed command of the 6th Infantry Division on June 1, 1944. Heyne was released from Soviet captivity in 1955 and died in Bolmengern in 1967.

64. Chant, vol. 6, p. 1646.

65. Hermann Floerke was named acting commander of LXVI Corps in 1945. Friedrich Stephans was born in Danzig in 1892. He commanded the 467th Infantry Regiment (1939–42) before taking charge of the 267th Infantry Division (January 1942). He was later given command of the 104th Light Infantry [*Jaeger*] Division (1945) but was reported missing in action later that year.

66. Kurt Mehner, ed., *Die Geheimen Tagesberichte der deutschen Wehrmachtfuehrung im Zweiten Weltkrieg 1939–1945* (Osnabrueck: 1993), vol. 10, pp. 504–5.

67. Friedrich-Carl von Steinkeller entered the army as a cavalry *Fahnenjunker* in 1914. He was discharged in 1919 but returned to active duty as a *Rittmeister* (captain of cavalry) in 1934. He spent the entire war in panzer or motorized positions, including tours as commander of the 7th Motorcycle Battalion (1939–42) and the 7th Panzer Grenadier Regiment (1942–44). He was promoted to major general on June 1, 1944. He spent the eleven years following his capture in Soviet prisons.

68. Robert Martinek was born in Austria in 1889 and entered the Austro-Hungarian Army in the standard manner (as a *Fahnenjunker* or officer cadet) in 1907. He was in the Austrian Army when its country was annexed by the Third

Reich in 1938. Accepted into the Wehrmacht, he was artillery commander for Wehrkreis XVIII when the war broke out. Later he commanded Arko 7 [the 7th Artillery Command] (1940–41), the 267th Infantry Division (acting commander, late 1941), the 7th Mountain Division (1942), and XXXIX Panzer Corps (from December 1, 1942). Otto Schuenemann joined the army in 1906 as a private. He earned a battlefield commission in 1915 but was not accepted into the hundred-thousand-man army. He joined the police in 1920 but reentered the service as a major in 1936. During World War II he was commander of the 184th Infantry Regiment (1939–42) and the 337th Infantry Division (1942–44) before becoming acting commander of the XXXIX Panzer (Keilig, pp. 218, 314).

69. Alexander Stahlberg, *Bounden Duty*, trans. Patricia Crampton (London: 1990), p. 355. Ernst Busch slowly worked his way back into the Fuehrer's good graces and on March 20, 1945, was named Commander in Chief of OB Northwest. His area of operations included the North Sea coast, Schleswig-Holstein, and the eastern fringe of the Netherlands. Although he tried to hold his front together by flying courts-martials and by issuing impossible orders, he simply did not have the forces to halt the British and Canadian armies under Field Marshal Sir Bernard Law Montgomery. He surrendered to "Monty" on May 4, 1945. Taken to the United Kingdom as a prisoner of war, he died on July 17, 1945.

70. Seaton, p. 442; Chant, vol. 6, p. 1653.

CHAPTER **11**

The Loss of
the Ukraine

MODEL TAKES CHARGE

Otto Moritz Walter Model was the most effective of the Nazi generals, and the one Hitler called him upon time and time again, sending him to critical spots in his crumbling empire to salvage apparently hopeless situations. Other field marshals are generally associated with particular places: Paulus, for example, is associated with Stalingrad, Rundstedt with the Western Front, Bock with Moscow, Weichs with the Balkans, Kesselring with Italy, Dietl with the Far North, Rommel with the Western Desert and Normandy, Manstein with southern Russia, and so on. Model is associated with the second half of the war. He received only the most difficult and dangerous assignments.

Model was a Prussian and certainly looked the part: tough, shorter-than-average height, somewhat thickset, close-cropped "whitewall" haircut, and of course the indispensable monocle, which he wore constantly. His background, however, was lower middle class, not military—and certainly not aristocratic or *Junker*. He was born in Genthin, near Magdeburg, on January 24, 1891, the son of a music teacher at the local girls' school. His antecedents were among schoolmasters, schoolteachers, peasants, and innkeepers, not officers. Because he ordered his private papers destroyed in the closing days of World War II, little is known about his childhood, but it appears to have been more or less normal. He grew up in a family of devout Lutherans who attended church frequently, lacked money constantly, and moved often. (Apparently his father had difficulty keeping a job.) Young Model, however, was a good student. He attended a liberal arts school in Erfurt, for example, where he excelled in Greek, Latin, and history and was a member of the local literary society.[1] Why he decided to join the Imperial Army is not known. On February 27, 1909, however, he entered the 52nd (6th Brandenburger) Infantry Regiment as a *Fahnenjunker*, (officer-cadet), largely due to the help of his uncle, an influential banker. He attended the Kriegsschule (War School) in Neisse and—although he nearly quit—was commissioned *Leutnant* on August 22, 1910.[2]

Young Model was known as a competent, ambitious officer and an uncomfortable subordinate, because he had no tact and did not hesitate to express his opinions, even to his superiors. He worked hard, displayed almost incredible energy, and formed no close friendships. These characteristics endured throughout his life. During World War I, he served on the Western Front and as regimental adjutant, was severely wounded near Sedan in 1915. After his return from the hospital, his divisional commander, Prince Oskar of Prussia (one of the Kaiser's six sons), recommended him for the abbreviated General Staff course. He returned to the front in 1916 and served as a brigade adjutant and later as a company commander. He was wounded several times (once badly) and received the Iron Cross, First Class, for bravery, among other decorations.[3] He ended the war on the Greater General Staff in Berlin.

Model was chosen for the Reichsheer in 1919 and was assigned to the 2nd Infantry Regiment at Allenstein, in East Prussia.[4] The following year he found himself commanding security troops and helped suppress Communist revolts and general strikes. During one of these assignments (at Eberfeld-Barmen [now Wuppertal] in the Ruhr), he quartered in the home of Herta Huyssen; they married the following year. This union produced three children, including a future West German general. Strangely, Model hated war stories and never discussed war or politics at home or with his wife.[5]

Unlike some officers, Model did not and would not involve himself in politics in any way. He felt his profession was a noble calling and believed that it was an officer's duty to remain aloof from politics and to involve himself in one pursuit only: service to the state. Personally incorruptible, he embodied the typically German values of family, religion, and service, and combined them with technical competence, drive, and ambition; this combination enabled him to achieve a reputation as the quintessential Prussian officer during the Weimar era. Later, however, during the Hitler regime, he came to accept the Nazi worldview more and more and his ruthless ambition, conservatism, love of order, and belief in the subservience of the individual to the state combined with Hitler's policies to pervert his military skill into something that was anything but noble. But this is getting ahead of our story.

Between the wars, Model became known as an expert on technical matters and even visited the Soviet Union to study the technical aspects of rearmament. He served as chief of the Training Department of the Defense Ministry in the early 1930s and, after commanding the 2nd Infantry Regiment in 1934, became chief of the Technical Department of the Army in 1935.[6] Despite his infantry background, Model became an early advocate of motorization, air support, and the blitzkrieg ideas of Heinz Guderian, who later praised him as "a bold inexhaustible soldier."[7]

In March 1938, he was named chief of staff of IV Corps (headquartered in Dresden), where he made himself extremely unpopular. Historian Carlo d'Este wrote later that Model "was a restless and impatient master who drove his subordinates with a heavy hand."[8] Throughout his career, Model was disliked by his staff and immediate subordinates, but his enlisted men appreciated his courage and forcefulness; in addition, he treated his men better (and with much greater respect) than he did his officers, with whom he was often harsh, arbitrary, overbearing, and obnoxious.

During the late 1930s, Model made his first contact with the Nazis. He met and impressed Dr. Joseph Goebbels, who introduced him to Hitler, who was also impressed. In 1938 he was promoted to major general and was earmarked to be chief of staff of an army during the invasion of Czechoslovakia, until the Munich accords made this campaign unnecessary. He was chief of staff of IV Corps during the Polish campaign and of 16th Army during the French campaign of 1940. (Ironically, this army was commanded by Ernst Busch.) Promoted to lieutenant general in November 1940, Model led the 3rd Panzer Division into Russia on June 22, 1941, as part of Guderian's 2nd Panzer Group. Here, on the Eastern Front, Walter Model came into his own. He crossed the Bug, then the Berezina and Dnieper, captured Bobruisk, and took part in the battles of encirclement at Bialystok, Minsk, and Smolensk. He also spearheaded Guderian's panzer army during the encirclement of Kiev. When he linked up with the 9th Panzer Division at Sencha on September 15, he completed the largest encirclement of the Second World War. Obviously capable of great things, he was given command of the XXXXI Panzer Corps in October 1941 and took part in the final push on Moscow.[9] During this drive, he was promoted to general of panzer troops.

On January 12, 1942, 9th Army (on the northern wing of Army Group Center) was on the verge of being overwhelmed and was threatened with encirclement. Its commander, Colonel General Adolf Strauss, gave up his post for reasons of health. To the surprise of virtually everyone, Walter Model—a divisional commander only three months before and a rather junior one at that—was named his successor.

"It is a strange thing," Paul Carell wrote later, "but the moment Model assumed command of the Army the regiments seemed to gain strength. It was not only the crisp precision of the new C-in-C's orders—but he also turned up everywhere in person. . . . He would suddenly jump out of his command jeep [*sic*] outside a battalion headquarters, or appear on horseback through the deep snow in the foremost line, encouraging, commending, criticizing and occasionally even charging against the enemy penetration at the head of a battalion, pistol in hand. The live-wire general was everywhere. And even where he was not his presence was felt."[10]

When Model took command, 9th Army seemed doomed. Its XXIII Corps was cut off southeast of Lake Volga, west of Rzhev; Model rescued it by counterattacking and cutting off the Soviet 39th Army. Meanwhile, he checked five other Soviet armies, which had hurled themselves at German lines in human-wave attacks in temperatures as low as minus 37 degrees Fahrenheit. During this battle, he had his first run-in with Hitler, who sent him reinforcements but wanted them committed nearly a hundred miles south of the spot selected by Model. After what General F. W. von Mellenthin called an "acrimonious argument," Model coldly stared at Hitler through his monocle and asked: "Who commands the 9th Army, my Fuehrer—you or I?" Without waiting for the startled dictator to answer, Model informed him in no uncertain terms that he knew the situation at the front far better than Hitler, who only had maps to go by. Taken aback, Hitler let Model have his way. The next Russian attacks came exactly where Model had predicted; they were slaughtered by the fresh German troops.[11] "Did you see that eye?" Hitler remarked after their argument. "I trust that man. . . . But I wouldn't want to serve under him."[12]

This incident established a precedent that continued throughout the war. "Model stood up to Hitler in a way hardly anyone else dared," General Baron Hasso von Manteuffel remarked later.[13]

Meanwhile, Model's divisions finished off the Soviet 39th Army, killing twenty-seven thousand men and capturing another five thousand in the process. Stalin's winter offensive met a decisive and totally unexpected defeat at Rzhev, and Walter Model had saved Army Group Center. He was promoted to colonel general (*Generaloberst*), his fourth promotion in three years, and Hitler personally decorated him with the Oak Leaves to his Knight's Cross.[14]

Stalin was still determined to destroy the 9th Army, which occupied a salient only 112 miles from Moscow. He launched major offensives in March, April, and from late July through mid-October. Model checked them all. After Stalingrad fell, he brilliantly evacuated the Rzhev salient in March 1943, in the face of ten Soviet armies, freeing virtually his entire force for Operation Citadel, Hitler's Kursk offensive. He persuaded Hitler to delay the offensive until a new-model assault gun—the Ferdinand—was delivered to his panzer divisions. This turned out to be a fatal mistake, for the Russians used the time well to build dense minefields and to reinforce the threatened sector, and the Ferdinand fell far short of expectations. Hitler's last major offensive in the East (and the greatest tank battle in history) resulted in a decisive German defeat.

Model's standing with Hitler diminished very little after his Citadel defeat. The Fuehrer gave him command of the 2nd Panzer Army (in addition to the 9th) and even allowed him to conduct an "elastic defense" in the Orel sector, during which he was attacked by eighty-two Soviet infantry divisions and fourteen tank corps, supported by a dozen artillery divisions. Model's superior rearguard tactics, aided by heavy cloudbursts, enabled him to contain a Red Army breakthrough. As he retreated, Model conducted a "scorched earth" policy, burning Russian crops (which were ready for harvest) and herding together 250,000 civilians with whatever they could carry and forcing them to trek to the west. He also confiscated their livestock and laid waste to anything he could not carry with him.[15] In accordance with Hitler's instructions, Model was undeniably harsh in his dealings with the Russian civilians and also apparently cooperated with the SS murder squads against the Jews, although sources do not agree on this issue.

Model was energetic, innovative, and courageous, but he also tended to oversupervise and to meddle in the internal affairs of subordinate units—affairs that were really none of his business. He could also be quite selfish and occasionally pirated units from other commanders. On March 28, 1944, for example, he had just written a report stating that his command (Army Group North) might be able to spare two divisions for Army Group South, which was under heavy attack. At that point General Rudolf Schmundt, the chief of the army Personnel Office, called to tell him that he would be named C-in-C of Army Group South within a few days. Model promptly revised his estimate, stating that Army Group North could give up five divisions and a corps headquarters immediately, and also the 12th Panzer Division as soon as two assault gun brigades and a panzer battalion arrived. The next day he raised the total to six divisions and ordered his chief of staff, Lieutenant General Eberhard Kinzel, to begin the transfer immediately. Only the intervention of General Zeitzler, the chief of the General Staff of the Army, prevented the rape of Army Group North.[16]

Model (who was promoted to field marshal on March 1, 1944) continued to act as Hitler's troubleshooter in the East throughout 1943 and well into 1944, successively commanding Army Group North, Army Group South (subsequently Army Group North Ukraine), and Army Group Center. He was a recognized master of the defense and was generally considered a tactical genius. Model, General Niepold wrote later, "was a peerless master of the large-scale defensive battle. Always present himself at critical points, he asked a great deal of his troops. Often he was harsh, sometimes ruthless. But he always found the answer to the trickiest of situations, never leaving his men in the lurch."[17]

When Model assumed command of Army Group Center on 28 June 1944, he retained Hans Krebs as chief of staff of the army group. They knew each other well. Krebs had been chief of staff of 9th Army during the battles of the Rzhev salient.

Judging from past experience, Model assumed that the Soviets would experience supply difficulties after an advance of a hundred miles or less; they would then halt to regroup and resupply. This time, however, the Red Army was showing that it had improved logistically as well as tactically. By the end of the first week of July it had advanced 125 miles and was still driving forward; in fact, it was moving too fast for the remnants of Army Group Center which was unable to fall back, concentrate, dig in, and make a stand.

When Model assumed command, his forces were in almost complete disarray. The 3rd Panzer Army was in full retreat and controlled only one, very weak corps (Wuthmann's IX) and the 201st Security Division, which had only two understrength infantry regiments and no artillery. The combat battalions of Corps Detachment D were down to forty to fifty men each, although each had fifty to eighty more with bad feet in the service support zone. Lieutenant General Walter Melzer's 252nd Infantry Division, IX Corps reported, had been "just about taken apart" by the last Russian attacks and reported an effective strength of only three hundred men. It was unable to hold Lepel on the Essa River and, to make matters worse, failed to blow up the bridges there before the Russians arrived. The 3rd Panzer Army, which had only forty-four pieces of artillery left, would have no choice but to continue to retreat.[18]

Group von Saucken had the mission of holding the front between the 3rd Panzer and 4th Armies, but everyone knew this was an impossible task. As we have seen, Saucken had one excellent unit, the 5th Panzer Division, but other than that all he controlled was Group von Gottberg, an ad hoc formation made up of police battalions, security units, stragglers, and other odds and ends. Led by SS Lieutenant General Curt von Gottberg, it did not amount to much; still, it was a start.[19]

Model was trying to stabilize the left flank. Once this was accomplished, he would perhaps be in a position to stabilize the center and bring the Soviet offensive to a halt. The right flank, which was covered by 2nd Army, was already more or less secure, at least for the moment. The problem was the center. On June 28, the day both he and Model assumed command, General of Panzer Troops Nicolaus von Vormann, the new commander of 9th Army wrote in his diary, "9 Army has virtually ceased to exist as a fighting force. It has not a single battleworthy formation left."[20] Its sister army, the 4th, was no better off. To defend the hundred miles of front that constituted its southern flank, it had just four security battalions and a few ad hoc Alarm (Emergency) units, backed by a handful of assault guns. The 12th Panzer Division, however, was on the way.

Model's tasks were simple and yet at the same time horribly complicated. He had to stop the Soviets as far forward as possible in hopes that the bulk of the encircled 4th and 9th Armies could fight their way back to German lines. The problem was that he did not have nearly enough extant combat units to accomplish this mission. Simultaneously, he had to prevent the

Russians from reaching East Prussia, keep the 3rd Panzer Army from being encircled, and keep the Red Army from trapping Army Group North. At the moment, the roads to Lithuania, Riga, and the coast of the Baltic Sea were virtually undefended, and Army Group North (the 16th and 18th Armies and Army Detachment Narva) was in danger of being cut off and isolated in Latvia.

When Field Marshal Model assumed command of Army Group Center, the Russians were only eight miles southeast of Minsk, the capital and largest city of Belorussia and the site of the army groups headquarters. Model energetically tried to keep the lines of retreat open for the 9th Army, but the situation was totally disorganized; both the front and rear areas were in chaos, and for the first time in the Russo-German war, entire German armies were disintegrating.

Much of the 4th Army, meanwhile, tried to escape over the Berezina via the bridge at Berezino, but the Red Air Force knocked a thirty-foot span out of it on June 29. After that was repaired, another Soviet air raid struck the bridge and blew away a forty-five-foot span. Greim's 6th Air Fleet was unable to intervene, as it only had fewer than forty fighters left, and its flak batteries were being used in a ground-support role as antitank weapons. German truck columns trying to escape to the east were lined up two and three abreast for thirty miles and were being blasted by Russian aircraft. Most of the 4th Army was trapped the next day, June 30, when the Soviet spearheads pushed to within artillery range of the Berezino bridge. In the meantime, 9th Army tried to keep open the road south of Minsk, as demoralized troops and shattered units streamed back to the west. Many of them had already destroyed or abandoned their heavy weapons.

North of Minsk, the main burden of the defense fell to General Decker and the 5th Panzer Division, which was under heavy attack from the 5th Guards Tank Army, now across the Berezina. By now, however, the 31st Panzer Regiment had come up, and the 5th Panzer Division fought the entire Soviet tank army to a standstill, although it lost most of its tanks in the process. By July 8, the division and the attached 505th Heavy Panzer Battalion had knocked out 295 Russian tanks but had lost 117 of its 125 panzers, including all twenty-nine of its Tigers. (Most of these tanks, however, were recovered and taken to maintenance shops, where they were eventually repaired.)

Radio communications were reestablished between 9th Army and XXXXI Panzer Corps during the night of June 27–28. General Hoffmeister, the acting corps commander, signaled that he had met with the commanders of the 20th Panzer Division and the 36th, 45th, 134th, and 707th Infantry Divisions. He requested full freedom of maneuver for the purpose of breaking out of Bobruisk. Permission was granted by 9th Army at 8:35 A.M. on June 28. Later that morning, it was modified. Hitler insisted that one division remain in the city. The 383rd Infantry Division—which Hoffmeister himself had commanded until a few days before—was selected for this suicide mission. (It was now under the command of Lieutenant General Adolf Hamann, who retained his previous position as city commandant of Bobruisk.)[21] General Hoffmeister was informed that he was on his own—no help could be expected from the outside, other than a few supply drops and limited air support from 6th Air Fleet.

Meanwhile, west of Bobruisk, in the rear of the 9th Army, the first of fifty-three trains carrying the 12th Panzer Division arrived. It had a strength of 12,300 men (including seven-hundred Hiwis, Russians who had volunteered to serve as auxiliaries or "helpers" with the Wehrmacht), but not all of its units had made the trip to Army Group Center. Its I/29th Panzer Regiment (that is, I Battalion, 29th Panzer) was back in Germany, re-equipping with Panthers, and it had only one tank battalion, equipped with thirty-five PzKw IVs and nine PzKw IIIs. Only one company of the division's antitank battalion was aboard the trains, and the division's panzer reconnaissance battalion, its antiaircraft battalion, and part of its engineer battalion were missing—most of them still in the Baltic States. In addition, only one of the division's four panzer grenadier battalions was outfitted with armored personnel carriers (SPWs); the other three were equipped with trucks and were therefore much less mobile. Even the division commander, Lieutenant General Baron Erpo von Bodenhausen, was missing. He was on leave in Germany and had been temporarily replaced by Colonel Gerhard Mueller, a highly decorated veteran of the Afrika Korps. Mueller had lost an arm in the El Alamein campaign and would prove to have lost much of his previous effectiveness as a commander.[22]

When Lieutenant Colonel Gerd Niepold, the Ia of the 12th Panzer Division, arrived at 9th Army Headquarters, he was greeted by an old friend, Major General Helmut Staedke, the chief of staff, who had been one of his instructors at the War Academy. "Good to see you!" Staedke cried. "Ninth Army no longer exists!"[23] Niepold learned from Staedke that the 12th Panzer was the only intact division in the army and that its primary mission was to keep the Berezina River bridges east of Bobruisk open for as long as possible so that as many men as was possible could escape. By this time, however, there was only one intact bridge over the Berezina leading to Bobruisk, and that was a railroad bridge, although the remnants of the 20th Panzer Division (which had already lost most of its tanks) were valiantly trying to recapture a wooden road bridge.

As the 12th Panzer Division approached the Berezina, it found chaos. "All semblance of order ceased," one tank officer recalled. "All over the place vehicles were being blown up and guns spiked. It was simply a confused column of men streaming over the railway bridge into Bobruisk. With the enemy pouring in shells and bombs, the chaos reached its climax."[24] With the Reds crossing the river and establishing bridgeheads north and south of Bobruisk, the 12th Panzer Division was not able to keep the bridge open for long.

During the night, XXXXI Panzer Corps launched its breakout. The 20th Panzer Division formed the spearhead, followed by the 36th Infantry Division and then the other infantry divisions. They had no choice but to leave 3,600 wounded men behind. (The Russians later murdered them all, in a very brutal manner). The breakout was successful, and by morning they had reached the woods northeast of Sychkovo; unfortunately, they were still thirty miles from German lines.

Meanwhile, to the northwest, panic broke out in Minsk on July 1 and the roads were filled with service and support troops trying to get out of Russia. The headquarters staff of the 9th Army tried to organize a scratch defense force at Marina Gorka, a few miles southeast of Minsk, but failed. Stragglers—officers and men alike—disappeared as quickly as the staff could assemble them. The "fortified place" of Minsk was defended by only 1,800 disorganized troops, and there were eight thousand wounded and fifteen thousand unarmed stragglers inside the city. The remnants of the 31st and 267th Infantry Divisions were able to hold Beresino but were unable to prevent the 2nd Tank Army from crossing the river north of the city on July 2. By nightfall, Tippelskirch's five police regiments were virtually surrounded, although there were now only three of them. That evening, Hitler finally authorized the evacuation of Minsk.[25]

After an all-day battle with Tippelskirch's rearguard inside Minsk, the Red Army's 1st and 2nd Guards Tank Corps finally recaptured the White Russian capital during the night of July 2–3. Meanwhile, to the south, the last of the survivors of the Bobruisk Pocket were rescued by Major Gustav-Adolf Blancbois's I Battalion, 25th Panzer Grenadier Regiment, of the 12th Panzer Division; it had attacked toward the Svisloch River near the town of the same name and had made contact with Group Hoffmeister (XXXXI Panzer Corps). Between fifteen thousand and twenty thousand "Bobruiskers" escaped through the I Battalion's corridor, though most of them were in no shape to fight. "It was a shattering experience to see how these soldiers plodded on to Marina Gorka, higgledy-piggledy, in rags and unarmed," the Ia (operations officer) of the 12th Panzer Division recalled. A few battleworthy units did escape, most notably *Kampfgruppe* 20th Panzer Division, led by General von Kessel, the divisional commander, which promptly joined forces with the 12th Panzer Division. Meanwhile, the Russians counterattacked the panzer grenadiers from three sides and forced them back, severing the last connection between 9th Army and its trapped legions. There would be no second chance. In the confusion of the battle, General Hoffmeister, the corps commander, and Major Generals Alexander Conrady and Joachim Engel, the commanders of the 36th and 45th Infantry Divisions, respectively, missed connections with the I Battalion and were captured shortly thereafter.[26]

In the meantime, von Tippelskirch's 4th Army Headquarters relocated to Molodechno, northwest of Minsk, to try to keep open the railroad bridge there. All of its efforts were in vain; there were simply not enough troops available to hold the place. On July 2, Soviet spearheads cut the 9th Army's railroad at Stolbtsy, southwest of Minsk, sealing the doom of most of that army. The 9th had been decimated; only thirty-five thousand of its soldiers had escaped. The headquarters staff had gotten out at the last moment, but it had to abandon most of its signals equipment. The army was forced to route its messages through the communications network of the 2nd Army. Map 2.1 shows Army Group Center's predicament as of nightfall on July 3.

Meanwhile, during the morning of June 29, General Zeitzler, the chief of the General Staff, met with the acting chief of staff of Army Group North and Field Marshal Model at the latter's headquarters in Lida. Zeitzler promised to reinforce the shattered army group with new divisions, including the 170th and 132nd Infantry Divisions from Army Group North (which were ordered to Minsk) and the 28th Light and 7th Panzer Divisions from Army Group North Ukraine, which were transferred to Baranovichi, on Model's southern flank. The next day, after Model returned to Russia, the Soviets again pushed deep into the left rear of 4th Army, threatening the communications and supply center of Molodechno. The field marshal ordered General of Cavalry Count Edwin von Rothkirch und Trach, the rear-area commander for Army Group Center and the commander of the White Ruthenian Military District, to send his 221st Security Division to Molodechno, along with any other forces he could lay his hands on.

The VI, XII, XXVII, and XXXIX Panzer Corps were all trapped in the huge pocket east of Minsk and were under pressure from several Soviet corps, which were trying to cause the pocket to collapse. When dawn broke on June 29, elements of the XXXIX Panzer Corps were still fighting their way west, hampered by almost incessant Red Air Force attacks. The Feldherrnhalle Division, followed by elements of the 12th and 337th Infantry, fought its way across the Berezina and broke up several Soviet counterattacks in the process. But it was still fifteen miles from the nearest German position and was low on ammunition and supplies. Some of its men had not eaten for three days.

Most of the encircled force headed for the Berezina River bridge at Berezino. A column forty-miles long and two or three vehicles abreast slowly made its way west, along the Berezino road. It was pulverized by the Red Air Force. General Schuenenmann, the acting commander of the XXXIX Panzer Corps, was killed later that day, and Vincenz Mueller, the commander of the XII Corps, ordered the destruction of the vehicles as well as any supplies that could not be moved. The gunners fired their last rounds, destroyed their guns, and formed ad hoc cavalry units, using the artillery

Map 2.1
Army Group Center, Nightfall, July 3, 1944

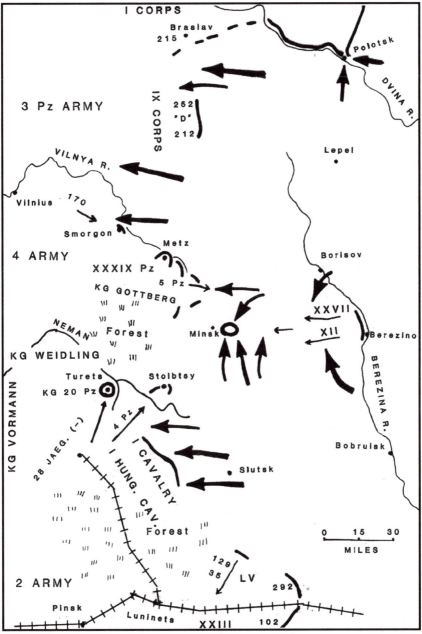

horses as mounts. Along the main road from Berezino to Cherven, on the west (left) bank of the river, Mueller posted the 17th Grenadier Regiment (of the 31st Infantry Division) and the 675th Security Battalion on the right. Both units were reinforced by stragglers.

General Tippelskirch, the commander of the 4th Army, realized that the encircled forces needed to be placed under a single commander. His choice was General Mueller, the commander of the XII Corps. He was a good officer, but he could not perform miracles. By July 1, Group Mueller was out of ammunition, and most of it was out of rations. The Russians broke through the Feldherrnhalle Division that day, but it managed to pull back about five miles and restore the situation. By evening, Mueller had the 31st, 267th, and 286th Infantry Divisions across the Berezina River, in spite of their exhaustion. He also signaled for air drops, which 6th Air Fleet executed. The retreat continued.

In the meantime, the Reds continued to attack at the front, pushing 4th Army farther away from Group Mueller. During the morning of July 4, Mueller met with General Voelckers, the commander of the XXVII Corps, as well as with the commanders of the 78th Assault Division, 25th Panzer Grenadier Division, and the 260th, 31st, and 57th Infantry Divisions. Despite their desperate situation the generals were positive, although witnesses later recalled that Voelckers seemed nearly exhausted. General Mueller was confident. Even now, there was no talk of surrender.

The plan called for XXVII Corps to attack first, heading west. The XII Corps would follow, heading northwest. The breakout began on the evening of July 4 and succeeded in overrunning the first Soviet line in heavy fighting. By noon on July 5, however, XXVII Corps had been stopped by strong resistance. Voelckers went over to the defensive, which, he told his divisional commanders, would inevitably lead to capitulation. All five of them disagreed with his decision, so Voelckers simply told them that they were free to decide for themselves whether to break out or surrender.

They all opted to break out in battle groups during the night of July 5–6.

At first, the breakout was a success, but under the pressure of combat the survivors broke into smaller and smaller groups and became more and more exhausted. General Voelckers joined the battle group led by Colonel Kurt Walter, the commander of the 11th Grenadier Regiment of the 14th Infantry Division; Voelckers was captured on July 9.[27] Some of the breakout parties managed to hide, however, and eventually made good their escape. By the end of October, some eighty officers and 838 men had made their way from the Minsk Pocket to German lines. Some of them had traveled 250 miles, all the way to the East Prussian border. The only divisional commander to make it back was Major General Paul Schuermann of the 25th Panzer Grenadier. He had thirty men with him when he arrived; he had started out with a thousand.[28]

General Mueller joined the 18th Panzer Grenadier Division, but after his

Table 2.1
Soviet Losses in Operation Bagration

Front	Strength	Killed and Missing	Wounded	Total
1st Baltic	359,500	41,248	125,053	166,301
3rd Belorussian	579,300	45,117	155,165	200,282
2nd Belorussian	319,000	26,315	91,421	117,736
1st Belorussian	1,071,100	65,779	215,615	281,394
Dnieper Flotilla	2,300	48	54	102
Totals	2,331,700	178,507	587,308	765,815

Source: Adair, *Center*, p. 177, citing G. F. Krivosheyev, ed., "The Losses of the Armed Forces of the USSR in Wars, Combat Actions, and Military Conflicts" (Moscow, 1993), p. 203 [secret classification removed].

chief of staff was seriously wounded, he decided that the attempt was hopeless. He surrendered on July 8 and apparently issued a call for all German troops in the pocket to lay down their arms.

Resistance in the Minsk Pocket ended on July 8. All three of the surrounded corps had ceased to exist, and Army Group Center had been decimated. By July 9, twenty-eight of its thirty-seven divisions had been destroyed or reduced to remnants. It had lost 215 tanks, more than 1,300 guns, and more than 300,000 men killed or captured.

About half of the men trapped in the Minsk Pocket had been killed in action or were now turned over to the partisans, who murdered them, often in the most inhuman manner. (Guerrillas are frequently very brave when fighting against unarmed prisoners, the wounded, defenseless women, small children, and babies. They usually exhibit much less enthusiasm when asked to fight men who are capable of defending themselves.) Roughly half of the 160,000 prisoners were murdered on their way to the prisoner of war camps or died of overwork, malnutrition, or disease, either in the camps or in Soviet *gulags*. (This statement is not to imply that Stalin's POW camps were any worse than Hitler's—they were not. About 65 percent of all Soviet soldiers captured by the German Army died in the prisons. French and Anglo-American prisoners, however, were accorded better facilities.) Most of those who did survive did not return to Germany until 1955.

Soviet losses were also relatively enormous. Moscow admitted 178,507 casualties,[29] but losses were actually much higher, as Table 2.1 shows. Stalin, however, could afford these losses. Nazi Germany could not.

Meanwhile, Hitler and Model attempted to solidify the German front. To close the gap between Army Groups Center and North, the Fuehrer ordered Colonel General Georg Lindemann, the commander in chief of Army Group North, to counterattack to the south and close the gap between it and 3rd Panzer Army. Model, who had commanded Army Group

North until a few weeks before, knew that this was an impossible assignment and said so. The Fuehrer, however, insisted that Lindemann attack. After the army group commander again declared that he could not, Hitler sacked him on July 3 and replaced him with General of Infantry Johannes Friessner, who was simultaneously promoted to colonel general. He could not counterattack either. The gap remained as large as ever.

On the far south side of the battlefield lay Army Group Center's only stable position, which was held by the 2nd Army. The Soviets began attacking it in strength in late June. This offensive was, in a sense, a spoiling attack, for Model had planned to assemble the 4th Panzer Division west of Slutsk to attack the Soviet flank, and the Reds must have gotten wind of it. Only about half of the division had arrived in the 2nd Army's zone of operations by July 1.

The Slutsk sector was defended by the German I Cavalry Corps under Lieutenant General Gustav Harteneck.[30] Initially it had only the 4th Cavalry Brigade and the 1st Hungarian Cavalry Division. Both units fought well, but again the enemy was simply too strong. During the night of July 1–2, Harteneck pulled his southern flank behind the Moroch River. Model responded by assigning the 28th Jaeger Division (with the 209th and 1028th Assault Gun Brigades attached) to 2nd Army and ordering Colonel General Weiss, the commander of the 2nd Army, to attack the Russian flank the following day. The 4th Panzer and 1st Hungarian Cavalry Divisions, along with the 28th Jaeger, were to clear the railroad line from Baranovichi to Dzerzhinsk. Weiss, however, canceled the attack, on the grounds that 4th Panzer Division did not have enough fuel to launch it. Model was furious at Weiss when he heard the news: The attack went forward on July 3. After some initial success, the Russians counterattacked in strength and almost cut off 4th Panzer Division. They overran the German defenses at Kletsk and pushed forward eight miles before Harteneck was reinforced with the 118th Panzer Battalion (sixty-two *Sturmpeschuets*, or StuG, assault guns). With this force he contained the offensive, but the Soviets had accomplished their objective. The threat to Zhukov's southern flank had been neutralized.

During the Battle for White Russia there appeared for the first time turncoat German soldiers. Captured earlier in the war—often at Stalingrad—they had been converted to Communism or at least into active anti-Nazism, under the influence of the National Committee for a Free Germany. Posing as messengers, they tried to misdirect units, especially escaping supply or transport columns, into partisan ambushes or into concentrations of regular Soviet troops. They produced hysteria similar to that later experienced by American soldiers during the Battle of the Bulge, when German *Soldaten* in U.S. fatigues changed road signs, seized bridges, misdirected traffic, and generally created havoc and confusion in the American rear. They were dealt with in the same way those who were caught were shot.

At Fuehrer Headquarters, General Heusinger, the chief of operations of the High Command of the Army, appreciated the gravity of the situation and was doing everything he could to reinforce Army Group Center.[31] On July 2, he informed Model's Ia that OKH was transferring the 50th Infantry Division from Army Group North to Center. Five march battalions and five of the new "Valkyrie" regiments (without artillery or heavy weapons) were also earmarked for Army Group Center, as well as the 6th Panzer Division from Germany, the 18th SS Panzer Grenadier Division from Hungary, the 367th Infantry Division from Army Group North Ukraine, and an unspecified division from Norway. (Later, the 3rd SS Panzer Division "Totenkopf" was substituted for the 18th SS.) Even with these divisions, however, Model would have only eight major formations, plus a few *kampfgruppen,* to defend a 220-mile front against 116 Soviet rifle divisions, six cavalry divisions, forty-two tank brigades, and sixteen motorized rifle brigades.[32]

To the north, 3rd Panzer Army was separated from both Army Groups North and Center and was fighting its own war. On July 3, the Russians nearly cut off the 212nd Infantry Division. Major General Franz Sensfuss, the divisional commander, personally led a fighting retreat along the road west of Glubokoye. He had only four battalions left when the battle began, and one of his regiments lost three hundred of its four hundred men in this battle. The average battalion in the 212th Division now had only 150 men. The 252nd Infantry Division was hardly better off. It had a combat strength of a thousand men, of which 150 were security troops. General Reinhardt, the army commander, signaled Model that his men had little fight left in them. "There's hardly a major general's command left," he said. "We can't do a thing, we're powerless." He fell back toward the Dunilovichi line, a defensive position built during World War I, but he doubted if he could hold even that.[33]

That same day, Model created Group Weidling and gave it the mission of closing the gap between the 4th and 9th Armies. For this purpose it was given the 50th Infantry Division, the 1057th Army Anti-Tank Battalion, the 92nd Tank Destroyer Battalion, and a pair of assault gun batteries from the 20th Panzer Division. General Weidling had no chance of accomplishing his mission. The 50th Infantry and 1057th Anti-Tank had not even arrived at the front.

The disasters continued to mount. On July 3, the 390th Field Training Division (most of which had been sent into combat near Stolbtsy as the ad hoc Group von Bergen) was smashed.[34] Only remnants of the division escaped. The 5th Panzer Grenadier Regiment of the 12th Panzer Division also suffered heavy losses in this battle. In the town of Stolbtsy itself, General von Kessel and the 20th Panzer Division were surrounded for the second time in two weeks. Kessel fought his way out, but the 20th Panzer was now a burned-out *kampfgruppe*. Other units suffered serious losses as well. The 505th Heavy Panzer Battalion, for example, lost its last five operational Tigers on July 8. A dozen had been completely destroyed, and another seventeen were in the workshops. The 5th Panzer Battalion, which had been equipped with assault guns, did not have a single gun left. The 742nd Tank Destroyer Battalion was in the same boat, while the 185th Assault Gun Battalion had lost twenty-five of its original thirty guns.

In addition, Headquarters, 9th Army, was no longer functional. It had lost too much of its signal equipment and was trying to issue orders through the communications network of 2nd Army. On the morning of July 3, Field Marshal Model sent it off the field to reorganize. Its forces were taken over by Group von Vormann, which was subordinate to 2nd Army. Vormann was given command of the I Cavalry Corps (4th Panzer Division, 1st Hungary Cavalry Division, and 4th Cavalry Brigade), 28th Jaeger Division, 12th Panzer Division, the garrison of Fortified Place Baranovichi, and any stragglers it might find. Its missions were: check the Russians in the Slutsk area; mount a converging attack on Stolbtsy with its two panzer divisions and the 28th Jaeger; and restore the road and railroad line from Baranovichi to Minsk.

On the northern flank of 2nd Army (Army Group Center's southern flank), the next few days were characterized by attack, counterattack, and heavy losses. By July 8, 12th Panzer Division had only one operational tank left. The attack on Stolbtsy failed, Baranovichi was lost, and Group Harteneck (I Cavalry Corps) was pushed back in heavy fighting and only narrowly prevented another Soviet breakthrough. Vormann reported having knocked out 507 Russian tanks since June 24 but that his own tank units were down to 10 percent of their initial strength. Group von Saucken, meanwhile, was renamed XXXIX Panzer Corps, but it received no reinforcements.

Meanwhile, in the zone of 3rd Panzer Army, the Russian advance finally began to slow. General Niepold later commented that the performance of Reinhardt's troops was "beyond all praise."[35] They were exhausted, understrength, on inadequate rations, and without sleep, but they still fought well. Behind them they left minefields and booby traps, which forced the Soviets to advance more cautiously. Also, after a spectacular advance, the Soviets were finally beginning to experience supply difficulties.

To the amazement of Colonel Erich Dethleffsen, the chief of staff of the 4th Army, the Russians slowed the pace of their advance in his zone as well. They were becoming, in fact, almost cautious, which was very odd, since there was very little left with which to stop them. "The enemy appears to be afraid of his own boldness," Dethleffsen concluded.[36]

Model tried to make a stand on the Vilnius-Lida-Baranovichi line but on July 8 reported to OKH that he could not hold this position; in fact, by this time Vilnius was surrounded, and Lida and Baranovichi had already been lost. (Most of the 52nd Security Division was destroyed when Baranovichi fell.) Model reported that he could not hold the Russians anywhere and asked for a meeting with the Fuehrer the next day. General Johannes Friessner, the commander of Army Group North, was also asked to attend.

In the meantime, one of Hitler's troubleshooters, Luftwaffe Major General Reiner Stahel, flew into Vilnius by a Storch light reconnaissance aircraft. He took charge of the defenses of the Lithuanian capital, which were very weak. They included the 761st Grenadier Brigade, an ill-equipped, static unit of only two battalions. The 16th Parachute Regiment, which had been ordered into Vilnius by Hitler—"too late," as usual—had not received its orders in time to land at the airport before the Russians brought it under fire. Only its vanguard—the regimental staff and two parachute infantry companies—had been able to land. The elite Fuehrer Escort Unit (also known as the von Werthern Brigade), which Hitler had sent forward from East Prussia, had also arrived in the battle zone too late. It was blocked by the Russians six miles west of the city. In all, Stahel had only eight battalions. He nevertheless managed to beat off several Soviet attacks. By nightfall, however, the Soviet 39th Army had taken the airfield. Staehl signaled that the defense would probably disintegrate by noon the next day; he requested permission to break out that night. Model agreed and forwarded his recommendation to Fuehrer Headquarters, but Hitler turned down the request. He ordered Kampfgruppe Tolsdorff to launch a counterattack and relieve the city. This unit consisted of the 1067th Grenadier Regiment—four newly formed battalions under the incredibly brave Colonel Theodor Tolsdorff.[37] It was a Valkyrie unit; which meant it had no artillery or heavy weapons, Naturally, its attack came to nothing.

At noon on July 9, Model conferred with Adolf Hitler and General Friessner at Berchtesgaden. Model wanted Army Group North to conduct a major retreat to the Riga-Dvinsk–Dvina River line, while he conducted his own retreat to the south; Hitler, however, refused to consider it, on the grounds that Grand Admiral Karl Doenitz affirmed that such a retreat would ruin the navy, which could not do without its training areas in the Baltic Sea. All the dictator could do was make promises: he would give Model a panzer division from Germany and two divisions from Army Group North; these would be followed by two more later. With these units, 3rd Panzer Army could counterattack and close the gap.

The Fuehrer, as usual, was one or two steps behind the course of events. Had he made these decisions two weeks before, they would have had an impact on the course of the battle, but not now. Model bluntly responded that he could not count on receiving any significant reinforcements for at least eight days, and he could not halt the Russians until they arrived. Hitler responded by ordering the transfer to two more divisions from Army Group North to Center. (These were to be the 69th and 93rd Infantry Divisions.) He also ordered that Kampfgruppe von Gottberg be reinforced with two police regiments and two "Brunhilde" regiments (replacement or "Home Guard" formations, similar to the Valkyrie units). He would, however, make no further concessions.

Without firm leadership at the top, Army Group Center could only continue to retreat. It fell back past the Neman River, in the direction of Grodno and Bialystok. On July 9, General von Saucken reported that the 5th Panzer Division had been reduced to a strength of six PzKw IVs, a dozen Panthers, six towed heavy antitank guns, and six self-propelled guns. The 7th Panzer Division, which had recently arrived in the zone of XXXIX Panzer Corps, had twenty-six PzKw IVs, six assault guns, twenty heavy antitank guns, and thirteen 88 mm guns. Saucken also declared that the 170th Infantry Division had suffered so many casualties and lost so many of its heavy weapons that it was no longer capable of defending itself.

Enemy losses were also very high. Since June 27, the 5th Panzer Division alone had destroyed 486 Soviet tanks, eleven assault guns, 119 antitank guns, a hundred trucks, against a loss of 107 tanks—and some of these were in the workshops and would soon be back at the front.[38]

Surprisingly, the Russians did not attack Vilnius in strength on July 9. By July 10, however, the city was in flames, Staehl was under attack from the 39th and 5th Soviet Armies, and General Reinhardt had stated in no uncertain terms that he did not have the strength to relieve it and would not try again, even if Hitler ordered him to do so. "Constantly acting against my better judgment is more than I can do," he declared.[39]

On July 11, Hitler finally relented. Staehl, he said, had permission to break out. This he did on the night of July 12–13, supported by a diversionary attack from the 6th Panzer Division. He saved three thousand men from capture, but more than twelve thousand were lost. The Russians took Vilnius the next day.[40]

The divisions Hitler promised to Field Marshal Model did not come. Army Group North was itself under heavy attack from the 2nd Baltic and the 3rd Baltic Fronts, and the 1st Baltic Front broke through General Paul Laux's 16th Army near Dvinsk, south of the Dvina. Friessner had no divisions to spare. On July 12, he informed Hitler that he refused to attack to the south to link up with 3rd Panzer Army, since even if he succeeded in doing so, it would be impossible to maintain it. He urged Hitler to allow him to pull his army group and 3rd Panzer Army back to the Riga-Kaunas Line and to give him freedom of maneuver; failing that, he said, he asked to be relieved of his command.[41]

Hitler emphatically rejected all of Friessner's proposals and again spoke of assembling five panzer divisions at Kaunas, to counterattack and close the gap. General Heusinger, the chief of operations at OKH, pointed out that the battle was moving too quickly for that, but Hitler refused to listen. The next day, Model said that he would try to halt the Russians forward of the Kaunas-Grodno-Brest line but would have to have fresh tank divisions to do it. Finally, on July 14, Hitler backed down somewhat. Model's first mission, he decided, was to halt the Soviet advance; then he would counterattack and regain contact with Army Group North. Friessner, on the other hand, was to hold his present forward positions at all costs and at the same time attack into the gap with two self-propelled assault gun brigades, supported by strong air units, which were to be supplied by Hermann Goering, the commander of the Luftwaffe. Even the Reichsmarschall worked up enough courage to object to this outrageously unrealistic strategy, but Hitler refused to reconsider his orders. To retreat again, he contended, would lose him the oil of Estonia, the Swedish iron ore, and the nickel from Finland. Zeitzler tried one last time to make the Fuehrer see sense on July 18 and called upon him to allow Army Group North to retreat to the Dvina line. When Hitler stubbornly refused to reconsider, Zeitzler submitted his resignation. Hitler refused to accept it, so the chief of the General Staff reported himself sick. The Fuehrer countered with an order which forbade officers to voluntarily relinquish their posts.[42] Three days later, however, he sacked Zeitzler and replaced him with Heinz Guderian, the Inspector General of Panzer Troops. This occurred the day after the Stauffenberg assassination attempt.

THE JULY 20 ASSASSINATION ATTEMPT

On the morning of July 20, 1944, Colonel Count Claus von Stauffenberg, the chief of staff of the Replacement Army, appeared at Fuehrer Headquarters in Rastenburg with a bomb in his briefcase.

An aristocratic officer and a Christian, Count von Stauffenberg had initially welcomed the rise of Hitler, because he promised to restore the economy and free Germany from the hated Treaty of Versailles.[43] Nazi excesses, however, soon converted him into a critic of the regime, although he was not initially prepared to overthrow it. After joining the Organization Section of OKH, however, and learning of Hitler's mass murders of Slavs and Jews, and of the full extent of his anti-Christian bigotry, he joined the anti-Nazi opposition. "Men are not guaranteed a civilized existence by a state without religious background," he correctly proclaimed.[44] He called for a national policy conducted on the basis of "morality firmly rooted in religion. A people which does not know how to pray is not fit to live." He added that "Christianity should again become the overriding spiritual force of the future."[45] He found a great many men in the Officer Corps who shared his beliefs and who were willing to risk their lives for their principles. Among the senior generals, however, he found many more who were willing to sacrifice their principles and ideals for promotions, career advancement, and medals.

Disgusted with the blatant careerism he found in Berlin, Stauffenberg went to the North African front in early 1943 as Ia of the 10th Panzer Division. Here, on April 7, his Volkswagen staff car was attacked by an American fighter-bomber. He was so badly wounded that he was not at first expected to live. He lost his right hand (amputated above the wrist), his left eye, and the third and fourth fingers on his left hand. After a period of temporary blindness and a series of head, eye, and knee operations, he emerged from the hospital convinced that the Fuehrer was the anti-Christ and that God had spared him (Stauffenberg) for one reason: to rid the world of Adolf Hitler and his henchmen.

Stauffenberg's bomb exploded at 12:35 P.M. on July 20, mortally wounding General of Fliers Guenther Korten, the chief of the General Staff of the Luftwaffe, and Lieutenant General Rudolf Schmundt, the Fuehrer's chief adjutant and chief of the powerful Army Personnel Office (AHA). Several senior officers were also wounded, including Alfred Jodl, the chief of operations of the High Command of the Armed Forces; his deputy, General of Artillery Walter Warlimont; and Lieutenant General Adolf Heusinger, the deputy chief of the General Staff of the Army. Both of Hitler's eardrums were ruptured by the explosion, his hair was burned, and his legs and right arm were painfully injured. Although he never was quite the same, Hitler survived the blast and put down "Operation Valkyrie," the Stauffenberg-directed military revolt against him. Colonel von Stauffenberg was summarily executed on the orders of his commander, Colonel General Friedrich Fromm, just before midnight on July 20.

From the Nazi point of view a frightening picture emerged within the next few days. The list of the men involved (to one degree or another) in the anti-Hitler conspiracy read almost like a Who's Who of the German Army. They included:

Field Marshal Erwin Rommel, the "Desert Fox" and one of the premier military geniuses of the twentieth century

Colonel General Ludwig Beck, the former chief of the General Staff

Colonel General Erich Hoepner, the former commander of the 4th Panzer Army

Colonel General Fritz Fromm, the commander in chief of the Replacement Army, who was on both sides of the conspiracy

Field Marshal Hans von Kluge, the OB West (i.e., the Supreme Commander of the Western Front)

General of Infantry Georg Thomas, the chief of the Economic Office at OKW

Admiral Wilhelm Canaris, the former chief of the Abwehr, the military intelligence agency of the armed forces

Major General Hans Oster, Canaris deputy

Field Marshal Erwin von Witzleben, the former C-in-C of OB West and former commander in chief of Army Group D

General of Infantry Friedrich Olbricht, chief of the General Army Office and deputy commander of the Replacement Army

Major General Helmuth Stieff, chief of the Organizations Section of OKH

General of Signal Troops Erich Fellgiebel, the chief signal officer for both the army and entire Wehrmacht, and several of his principle subordinates

Lieutenant General Hans Speidel, the chief of staff of Army Group B in Normandy

Colonel Eberhard Finckh, deputy chief of staff of OB West

General of Artillery Eduard Wagner, the quartermaster general of the army and deputy chief of the General Staff of OKH

General of Artillery Franz Lindemann, the chief of the Artillery Directorate of OKH and commander-designate of the 17th Army

General of Infantry Carl-Heinrich von Stuelpnagel, the military governor of France

Lieutenant General Paul von Hase, the military commandant of Berlin

Major General Henning von Treschow, the chief of staff of 2nd Army and former chief of operations of Army Group Center

Colonel Georg Schulze-Buettger, the chief of staff of 4th Panzer Army

Lieutenant Colonel Hans-Alexander von Voss, the Ia (operations officer) of Army Group Center

Major General Hans-Ulrich von Oertzen, the chief training officer of Army Group Center

Major General Erwin Lahousen, the head of the Sabotage Branch of the Abwehr

Colonel Ritter Albrecht Mertz von Quirnheim, the chief of staff of the Army General Office in the Replacement Army.

And there were dozens of others.

Further confirming the army's "disloyalty" in Hitler's eyes were the officers who did not join the conspiracy but knew about it and did not report it. Among others, they included Field Marshals Erich von Manstein, Walter von Brauchitsch (the commander in chief of the Army until late 1941), Ewald von Kleist, Georg von Kuechler, and Fedor von Bock.[46] Another officer who must have known was Colonel General Kurt Zeitzler, the chief of the General Staff. Certainly Zeitzler's deputy, General Heusinger, was convinced he knew. (Heusinger never forgave Zeitzler for leaving him inside the briefing hut with Hitler when the bomb went off.) In any case, the Fuehrer sacked Zeitzler on July 21 and replaced him with Colonel General Heinz Guderian.[47] Among others, Hitler had General Fromm, the C-in-C of the Replacement Army, arrested and later had him shot for cowardice.[48] In his place, Hitler appointed Heinrich Himmler, the Reichsfuehrer-SS. General Schmundt was replaced as personnel officer by a murderous Nazi,

Lieutenant General Wilhelm Burgdorf, who would soon earn the nickname "the Gravedigger of the Officer Corps."

Guderian, in fact, was not Hitler's first choice and was an "acting chief of staff, OKH" only. The Fuehrer's first choice was General of Infantry Walter Buhle, a rabid Nazi, but he had been wounded by Stauffenberg's bomb and had not yet recovered.[49] Hitler never completely forgave Guderian for "failing" him during the Battle of Moscow in 1941, but for now at least Guderian was one of the few generals in OKH who was not under suspicion of being a conspirator; on July 20, he had turned back a panzer battalion that had formed up to seize the SS headquarters on the Fehrbelliner Platz. He had also made it clear that German generalship on the Eastern Front had been poor since his removal, and he had frequently charged the General Staff with defeatism.

After July 20, with a few exceptions, Hitler confronted his generals and field marshals with an attitude of suspicion, paranoia, and outright hatred. More than ever, the dictator looked upon his army generals and General Staff officers as his enemies. He tolerated them only so long as they exhibited subservience and unquestioning obedience. General Guderian recalled that after July 20,

the deep distrust [Hitler] already felt for mankind in general and for General Staff Corps officers and generals in particular, now became profound hatred. . . . [W]hat had been hardness became cruelty, while a tendency to bluff became plain dishonesty. He often lied without hesitation and assumed that others lied to him. He believed no one any more. It had already been difficult enough dealing with him; it now became a torture that grew steadily worse from month to month. He frequently lost all self-control and his language grew increasingly violent.[50]

Contrary to what he implies in his rather self-serving postwar autobiography, however, Heinz Guderian sought from his first day in office to curry favor with Hitler, to disassociate himself from the image of his predecessors, and to furnish proof of his total loyalty to the Fuehrer and the regime. He demanded that the officers of the General Staff exhibit a pro-Nazi attitude on all political questions or ask to be removed from the General Staff. He also commanded that all General Staff officers attend National Socialist political lectures and take part in National Socialist leadership discussions.[51]

On July 24, Guderian agreed with Goering and passed on the order that the "Hitler salute" would now be officially adopted by the Army, in place of the old-style salute. This was a controversial order within the service, and it was generally greeted with distaste and disdain. Many officers read it aloud to their commands then dismissed their men with the traditional salute. The Army, at least, maintained a semblance of its former corporate independence, but that independence was more symbolic than tangible.

THE RETREAT CONTINUES

Meanwhile, back at the front, the agony of Army Group Center continued. Its retreat was covered mainly by the 5th, 12th, and 20th Panzer Divisions, which were often aided by antiaircraft (flak) units operating in an antitank or ground support role.

One unit that distinguished itself during the destruction of Army Group Center and emerged from the disaster somewhat intact was General of Flak Artillery Job Odebrecht's II Flak Corps.[52] Formed in Bobruisk in October 1943 from the defunct Headquarters, III Luftwaffe Field Corps, it included the 12th Flak Division (Major General Werner Prellberg) in the Bobruisk area; the 18th Flak Division (Major General Adolf Wolf) at Orsha; the 23rd Flak Division (Colonel Hans-Wilhelm Fichter) in the Minsk sector; and the 10th Flak Brigade (Colonel Guenther Sachs) around Vitebsk. Between them, these four units knocked out hundreds of Soviet tanks and AFVs but suffered very heavy losses themselves. The 10th Flak Brigade supported the 3rd Panzer Army and fought at Vitebsk, where much of the brigade it was destroyed. It suffered so many casualties that it was pulled out of the battle in August and sent to Warsaw, where it was disbanded on October 1. Its remnants were used to form the 116th Motorized Flak Regiment, which was soon on its way back to the front to support the 4th Army.

The 18th Flak Division also supported the 4th Army. Like the other flak units, it was broken into *kampfgruppen* scattered throughout the army's zone of operations and fought in all of the major battles. It too suffered so many casualties that it had to be withdrawn from the battle. It was sent to East Prussia, hastily rebuilt, and returned to the front to support the 3rd Panzer and 4th Armies.

The 23rd Flak Division (whose headquarters had been formed from the staff of the defunct 22nd Luftwaffe Field Division on October 10, 1943) lost so many men and guns that its remnants also had to be pulled out of the battle. It was sent to the Radom-Posen region of Poland (near Warsaw) to rebuild. It did not have to return to the front; the front came to it. The 12th Flak, on the other hand, supported the 2nd Army and suffered relatively few casualties.

Even with so many guns lost, the Luftwaffe reinforced Army Group Center with Colonel Alexander Nieper's 11th Flak Brigade. It had been formed in Koenigsberg on June 1, 1944, and only had two regiments; it was nevertheless sent to the front to support 3rd Panzer Army. It was used to form the 27th Flak Division in September 1944, but with no increase in strength.[53]

After July 14, Hitler allowed Model to evacuate a number of "fortified places" (some of them after Guderian ordered them held at all costs), but at considerable loss of territory. Pinsk (on the Pripet River) fell on July 14, Grodno was lost on July 16, and the Russians reached the new Russo-Polish frontier (established at the Teheran Conference) on July 18. Lublin fell on July 23, Bialystok was given up on July 27, and Brest-Litovsk was lost on July 28. The Soviets reached Praga, just across the Vistula River from Warsaw, on July 31 and on August 1 took Kalvariya, fifteen miles from the Prussian border. After that, the pace of the advance against the 4th and 9th Armies slowed, partly because of Soviet supply difficulties and partly because Model had received significant reinforcements.

Later, when he wrote about the summer campaign of 1944, Major Gerhard Friedrich, the commander of the 13th Panzer Grenadier Regiment, 5th Panzer Division, recalled:

The fighting was the heaviest we had ever experienced. We fought by camouflaging ourselves, firing everything we had, withdrawing, and then attacking again from a different direction. This meant that everyone . . . had to give of their utmost. Sleep was totally out of the question. These days of heroism, sacrifice and privation cannot be described in words. It would be wrong to mention individuals or units because all gave of their best.[54]

To the north, in the Kaunas sector, Reinhardt's 3rd Panzer Army faced eighteen Soviet rifle divisions, three tank corps, a mechanized corps, and three independent tank brigades. Reinhardt had four understrength infantry divisions and one panzer division. On July 18, he was attacked by the 2nd Guards Army, the 5th Guards Tank Army, and the 33rd Army. By July 22, 3rd Panzer Army was down to a combat strength of 13,850 men. Reinhardt requested permission to retreat, but Model ordered him to hold on for two or three more days; Hitler, however, refused to allow him to retreat at all. On July 30, the left flank of the 3rd Panzer Army finally collapsed. Reinhardt personally gave the command to retreat, in direct violation of Fuehrer orders. The Russians poured through the gap and on July 31 reached the Gulf of Riga, cutting off Army Group North and isolating it in the Courland pocket. It could now be resupplied only by sea. Third Panzer Army, meanwhile, fell back to the East Prussian border. The staff set up in Schlossberg, within the borders of the Reich. The army war diarist found headquartering in an "orderly little German city almost incomprehensible after three years on Soviet soil." Reinhardt, however, was horrified when he discovered that Erich Koch, the *Gauleiter* of East Prussia and the man responsible for civil-defense measures, did not even have an outline of a plan for evacuating women and children from the areas near the combat zone. Major General Otto Heidkaemper, the panzer army's chief of staff, told his commander that he had been protesting this state of affairs on a daily basis and had been ignored every time; apparently Koch was following a Fuehrer directive, he concluded.[55]

He was. It would cost tens of thousands of people their lives and would be responsible for untold numbers of rapes in the weeks ahead.

Meanwhile, to the south, Model had retained his post as commander of Army Group North Ukraine, although his deputy commander, General of Panzer Troops Josef Harpe, handled the day-to-day operations.[56] Model therefore came as close as anyone ever would to becoming a supreme commander of the Eastern Front. From June 22 to the middle of July, "the Fuehrer's Fireman" transferred three panzer and two infantry divisions from Army Group North Ukraine to Army Group Center, although Harpe was reinforced with several untested divisions. (Table 2.2 shows his order of battle on July 15.) Then, on July 6, the Soviets extended their offensive into the zone of Army Group North Ukraine, which was struck east of Kovel and Lvov (Lemberg) by the 1st Ukrainian Front. This front controlled ten armies (including the 1st and 3rd Guards Tank and 4th Tank Armies) and included seven tank corps, three mechanized corps, seventy-two rifle divisions, and six cavalry divisions: more than a million men, supported by 1,500 tanks, more than sixteen thousand guns, and about 450 assault guns, supported by more than three thousand airplanes. Army Group North Ukraine faced the onslaught with nine hundred thousand men, nine hundred tanks and assault guns, six thousand guns, and seven hundred airplanes,[57] almost none of which were fighters.

The first Soviet attacks came against Kovel, on the army group's northern flank. Six major roads converge on the city, which was defended by the 26th, 342nd, 131st, and 253rd Infantry Divisions (north to south).[58] They had been reinforced with Group Obersturmbannfuehrer Muehlenkamp, which was led by SS Lieutenant Colonel Johannes Rudolf "Hannes" Muehlenkamp, the handsome, cigar-smoking commander of the 5th SS Panzer Regiment of the 5th SS Panzer Division "Viking."[59] This division had just finished reforming and reequipping in the Heidelager Maneuver Area in Poland, where it had been upgraded from a panzer grenadier division to a panzer division. General Hossbach, the corps commander, concentrated the reinforced SS tank regiment at the village of Maciejow, because Muehlenkamp had convinced him that the Reds would attack through the marshes north of the Kovel-Lublin rail line and drive toward the Bug. (These marshes were normally impassible but had largely dried out in the hot summer of 1944.) Their goal, Muehlenkamp predicted, would be the Bug River bridge west of Luboml.

The Red Army's first attack began in the afternoon—an unusual time for the Russians—and took the SS by surprise. SS First Lieutenant Lichte, another lieutenant, and a sergeant were taking a dip in a nearby pond when the Reds hit. Dressed only in their bathing suits, they managed to run back

Table 2.2
Order of Battle, Army Group North Ukraine, July 15, 1944

4th Panzer Army
XXXXVI Panzer Corps:
    340th Infantry Division
    291st Infantry Division
    17th Panzer Division
    16th Panzer Division
XXXXII Corps:
    88th Infantry Division
    72nd Infantry Division
    214th Infantry Division
LVI Panzer Corps:
    1st Ski Jaeger Division
    342nd Infantry Division
    26th Infantry Division
VIII Corps:
    5th Jaeger Division
    211th Infantry Division
    12th Hungarian Reserve Division

1st Panzer Army
LIX Corps:
    1st Infantry Division
    20th Hungarian Infantry Division
    208th Infantry Division
XXIV Panzer Corps:
    254th Infantry Division[1]
    371st Infantry Division
    75th Infantry Division
    100th Jaeger Division
XXXXVIII Panzer Corps:
    359th Infantry Division
    96th Infantry Division
    349th Infantry Division
III Panzer Corps:
    1st Panzer Division
    8th Panzer Division
XIII Corps:
    Corps Detachment C[2]
    361st Infantry Division
    454th Security Division
Army Reserve:
    20th Panzer Grenadier Division[3]
    14th SS Grenadier Division (Galician)

Table 2.2 (*continued*)

1st Hungarian Army
VI Hungarian Corps
    27th Hungarian Light Division
    Elements, 2nd Hungarian Mountain Brigade
    1st Hungarian Mountain Brigade
XI Corps:
    25th Hungarian Infantry Division
    101st Jaeger Division
    18th Hungarian Reserve Division
    24th Hungarian Infantry Division
VII Hungarian Corps:
    68th Infantry Division
    16th Hungarian Infantry Division
    Elements, 168th Infantry Division[3]
Army Reserve:
    2nd Hungarian Mountain Brigade (−)
    19th Hungarian Reserve Division
    2nd Hungarian Panzer Division
    Kampfgruppe, 19th SS Panzer Grenadier Division[3]

Notes:
[1]Excluding some elements still in transit
[2]Including Divisional Groups 183, 217 and 339
[3]In transit

Sources: Mehner, vol. 10, p. 504; Keilig, ff. 1.

to their command post, only to find it burning and under heavy artillery fire. They dove into a foxhole but abandoned it when three T-34s came within fifty yards. Fortunately for them, the Russian tank commanders had stopped and were standing on their turrets in a conference, so they did not see the nearly naked SS men, who managed to escape—no doubt to the delight and amusement of their comrades. The T-34s pressed on and blundered into the gunsights of a pair of well-camouflaged Panthers, which promptly blew all three of them to pieces.

The main Soviet attack was delivered the next day, July 7, and was spearheaded by several hundred tanks. The Russians' early probing attacks had failed to detect KG Muehlenkamp (near the village of Maciejow), so the SS had not been attacked by the fighter-bombers of the Red Air Force. Just as Muehlenkamp had calculated, the Soviets now rushed down the road in column formation, presenting the sides of their tanks to hidden German gunners. The initial broadside was devastating. Within moments, dozens of Soviet tanks were destroyed. "Everywhere were burning steel hulks and smoldering wreckage!" Peter Strassner recalled.[60] The battle lasted ninety minutes. By the time the Russians retreated, more than a hundred of their tanks had been completely destroyed, and dozens of others had been damaged. One Panther platoon, led by SS Sergeant Alfred Gross-rock, knocked out twenty-six tanks by itself. Finnish First Lieutenant Olin's platoon knocked out a dozen more.[61]

Undeterred by their losses, the Russians threw ten rifle divisions, a tank corps, and two tank brigades into the Battle of Kovel. They were checked in four days of bloody defensive fighting, in which KG Muehlenkamp, the Rhineland-Westphalian 26th Infantry Division (Colonel Frommberger), and the Rhine-Mosel 342nd Infantry Division (Lieutenant General Heinrich Nickel) particularly distinguished themselves. By the time the Soviets abandoned their attacks on July 11, they had lost 295 tanks.[62]

The victory at Kovel led to a promotion for General Hossbach, who succeeded Kurt von Tippelskirch as commander of the 4th Army on July 18.[63] It is unclear whether Tippelskirch was wounded, was injured in an accident, or fell ill, but he would not return to active duty until winter. In any case, Hossbach was also a good field commander, although he was a man of extremely independent temperament. He had stood up to Hitler as early as 1938 and even as a colonel told the Fuehrer off.[64] He was a knowledgeable officer and a gifted tactician, but he was too opinionated; he sometimes ignored even rational orders from excellent commanders like Reinhardt and was difficult for any superior officer to work with.

The Soviets were, of course, undeterred by their defeat at Kovel. On July 13, they attacked Kovel again and launched another major offensive east of Lvov (Lemberg), in the zone of Breith's III Panzer Corps, whose front was held only by the weak 349th and 357th Infantry Divisions. Major General Werner Friebe tried to counterattack with his 8th Panzer Division, but it was slaughtered by the Red Air Force.[65] By July 14, it was clear that the Red offensive had two centers of gravity against Kovel, in the zone of General Harpe's own 4th Panzer Army on the right; and against Ternopol, in the zone of General of Panzer Troops Erhard Raus's 1st Panzer Army, on the left. There was also a major secondary (frontal) attack against Lvov itself. The bulk of Army Group North Ukraine more or less held its positions until July 17, when it gave way and began withdrawing to the so-called Prinz Eugen position, which was still unimproved and little more than a line on a map.

At this point let us digress to tell the story of the Ukraine in World War II and the Eastern European volunteers in the German Wehrmacht, in the context of the 14th SS Grenadier Division "Galicia 1."

THE UKRAINE IN WORLD WAR II

Modern Ukraine has a torrid and complex political history. When the twentieth century dawned, the Ukraine was divided into two parts: Western Ukraine (also called Galicia), which was part of the Austro-Hungarian Empire, and the much larger eastern Ukraine, which was occupied by Czarist Russia. During World War I, the area was overrun by the soldiers of the Imperial German Army, who were greeted as liberators. Both sections of the Ukraine, however, wanted the same thing: a free and united Ukraine. In 1918, the Austro-Hungarian Empire collapsed and, with the Soviet Union in turmoil, the Ukrainians had a chance to establish exactly that: a free and independent Ukraine. They promptly declared their independence. The international geopolitical situation, however, mitigated against the new nation, and it was soon under attack from both Russia and a regenerated Poland, which was backed by the Western allies, especially the French. In 1920, the independent Ukraine ceased to exist. Poland annexed Galicia, while the Bolsheviks conquered the larger eastern Ukraine. Galicia was subjected to a series of ruthless "pacification" campaigns, in which the Poles sought to suppress the Ukrainian culture and national identity. They committed a number of brutal atrocities and even set up a pair of concentration camps for Ukrainian political prisoners, at Bereza Kartuska and Biala Podlaska.

What the Poles did, however, seemed mild when compared to Soviets behavior in the eastern Ukraine. Although it is never popular among American pro-Socialist apologists and other confused people to have an author criticize communists—their intellectual brethren—it must be pointed out that the mass murders and artificially induced famines caused by the Reds were directly responsible for the deaths of millions of people. In numbers and in brutality, the atrocities the Bolsheviks committed in the Ukraine in the early 1930s rival the Holocaust in their horror. When the Red Army overran eastern Poland in September 1939, Stalin's reign of terror was extended to Galicia as well. Churches were closed, farms were confiscated, and leaders and members of the upper class were murdered. In barely two years, more than six hundred thousand Ukrainians were "deported," never to be seen again. Even as they retreated in the face of Hitler's invasion of 1941, the Soviets continued to murder the defenseless. When the German soldiers entered the jail at Lvov in June, they found the partially burned bodies of 2,400 Ukrainians, all shot in the scruff of the neck. "The weeping widows and orphans of these victims stood around the partially burned corpses of their fathers and husbands—a dreadful sight!" Dr. Hans Frank, normally a hard-boiled Nazi, recalled.[66]

Similar atrocities were committed in Stryi, Stanyslaviv, Ternopil, Sambir, Zolochiv, Lutsk, and other places. Small wonder the Ukrainians greeted the Germans as liberators when Hitler invaded Russia in 1941. "In every village we're been showered with bouquets of flowers, even more beautiful ones than we got when we entered Vienna," one soldier wrote in June, 1941. General Guderian (then commander of the 2nd Panzer Army) was virtually taken prisoner by the residents of one happy Ukrainian village, which refused to let him go until they felt he had been properly honored. The villagers and peasants greeted the German troops in their native costumes and carrying bread and salt (the traditional Ukrainian welcome for honored guests), serenaded them with balalaika music, offered them food and drink, and erected arches bearing such slogans as: "The Ukrainian peoples thank their liberators, the brave German Army. Heil Adolf Hitler!"[67]

That was before they met Erich Koch, the new *Reichskommissar* for the Ukraine. Koch, a former railroad clerk from the Rhineland and a close friend of the insidious Martin Bormann, had been a member of the Nazi Party since 1922 and had been appointed gauleiter of East Prussia in 1928, on the recommendation of the notorious Jew baiter Julius Streicher. Koch was already known for his ruthlessness, sadism, and corruption when Hermann Goering nominated him for the post of *Reichskommissar* prior to the invasion. Koch was theoretically subordinate to Alfred Rosenberg, the newly appointed Reich Minister for the Eastern Territories, but he made it clear long before the invasion began that he intended to ignore Rosenberg completely. Rosenberg had opposed his appointment with all of his might, but to no avail.

Koch's first official act upon taking charge of the Ukraine was to close the local schools, declaring that "Ukraine children need no schools. What they'll have to learn later will be taught to them by their German masters."[68] He quickly launched an anticultural campaign, destroying or plundering Ukrainian museums and libraries, including every university library and the library of the Ukrainian Academy of Sciences at Kiev. The gauleiter made it clear to everyone that he had nothing but contempt for Slavic *Untermenschen* (subhumans) and in his inaugural speech told his subordinates: "Gentlemen: I am known as a brutal dog. Because of this reason I was appointed *Reichskommissar* of the Ukraine. Our task is to suck from the Ukraine all the goods we can get hold of, without consideration of the feeling or property of the Ukrainians. Gentlemen: I am expecting from you the utmost severity toward the native population."[69] Later he declared, "We are a master race, which must remember that the lowliest German worker is racially and biologically a thousand times more valuable than the population here."[70]

The first crisis occurred on June 30, when the OUN/B (Organization of Ukrainian Nationalists/Bandera faction) staged an unexpected coup in Lvov, the capital of Eastern Galicia, which had just been captured by the Wehrmacht. It declared an independent state under the leadership of Yaroslav Stetsko, the loyal lieutenant of Stephen Bandera, a long-time leader of the Ukrainian nationalists, then in exile in Paris.[71]

Presented with a fait accompli, the German army considered the coup "premature and awkward" but not dangerous. It had been impressed that the OUN/B's Nightingale Battalion had staged a revolt shortly after Operation Barbarossa began (in places, being savagely repressed by the NKVD

[People's Committee for Internal Affairs—that is, the "organs of state security"] and the retreating Red Army) and had conducted purges, pogroms, and excesses against communists, Russians, Poles, and Jews. Koch and the Security Police, however, took a much dimmer view of the whole business. On July 2, the SD began arresting Bandera's supporters, and three days later the Stetsko government was dispersed. Stetsko was arrested on July 12, and Bandera was placed in a comfortable jail cell in Berlin. In mid-September, however, he and his principal lieutenants were tossed into the concentration camp at Sachsenhausen.[72] As if to emphasize the point that the Ukrainians would have no say in the governing of the Ukraine, Koch drove thousands of villagers out of the Zuman district, which he converted into a 175,000-acre private hunting estate for himself.

Koch agreed with Goering that "the best thing would be to kill all men in the Ukraine over fifteen years of age, and then to send in the SS stallions."[73] He soon made an informal deal with the *Reichsmarschall* and Himmler whereby the SS would be given a free hand in its extermination program, in return for the allocation of economic resources and "general loot" to Goering. Both, in turn, would support Koch against his archenemy, Rosenberg. They made a very effective unholy triumvirate. Koch's particular forte was to have prisoners whipped to death in public squares or parks, to encourage the Ukrainians to be obedient. Naturally, such acts had the reverse affect. Due to his policies of repression, "Germanization," murder, and exploitation, his region was soon infested with partisans. Koch's contempt extended to the German Army, which in turn refused to protect his hunting lodge from guerrillas, who eventually burned it down; in fact, in September 1942 a gunman fired at Koch, but missed and then made good his escape—in an army Mercedes. Koch was later charged with responsibility for murdering four hundred thousand Poles, as well as tens of thousands of Jews and Ukrainians.

Koch's administration of the eastern Ukraine was so brutal that General Richard Gehlen, the chief of West German military intelligence, later accused him of being a Soviet agent.[74] Although this is extremely unlikely, no paid agent could have done a better job at completely alienating the people of the eastern Ukraine than did Erich Koch.[75]

Once again, the western Ukraine was luckier than the east (unless, of course, one happened to be Jewish). Hitler made it a part of the "Generalgouvernment" (formerly Poland), which was administered by Hans Frank. As governor of Galicia the Hitlerites appointed Dr. Otto Waechter, who was much more astute and sympathetic than the typical Nazi official.[76] As a result of his rule, when 1943 began conditions in Galicia were much better than elsewhere in Nazi-occupied Europe and might even be described as peaceful.

THE FORMATION OF THE UKRAINIAN DIVISION AND THE
BATTLE OF BRODY

The racial doctrine of the Third Reich held that the people of the East were subhuman and were only fit for annihilation or semislavery under the whip of their German masters. The Battle of Stalingrad and the subsequent surrender of the 6th Army, however, shook the Nazis to the bottom of their souls. Some of them even began questioning their core beliefs vis-à-vis the people of the East. Perhaps the most outspoken was Gunter d'Alquen, the editor of the SS's house organ, *Das Schwarze Korps* (The Black Corps), who argued that the only secret weapon the Reich had left was the disaffection of the former residents of the Soviet Union. Among those who agreed with d'Alquen was Dr. Waechter. When Dr. Volodymyr Kubijovyc wrote him a letter five weeks after the capitulation of the 6th Army and suggested an armed Ukrainian force might be recruited for use against Communism, Waechter jumped at the idea. "He met with Ukrainian leaders in Galicia and then took the idea of a Ukrainian volunteer division directly to the SS Main Leadership Office (SS-FHA). Its chief, SS-Obergruppenfuehrer Gottlob Berger, had long been an outspoken advocate of recruiting non-Germans as military allies, and he proposed the idea to Heinrich Himmler, the Reichsfuehrer-SS, who was always anxious to expand his empire. Hans Frank, who was by now disillusioned with Nazism, also endorsed the proposal.[77] Opposition to the plan was led by the intransigent Erich Koch, always a racial hard-liner, but the pragmatists received the Fuehrer's reluctant approval, no doubt because of the deteriorating military situation and Germany's growing manpower shortage. (Hitler did insist that the division be dubbed "Galician" instead of "Ukrainian," which was a sore point with the Slavs from then on.)

Colonel Alfred Bysanz, a former Austro-Hungarian officer and a man with both German and Ukrainian ancestors, was placed in charge of recruiting. By the first week in June 1943, he had signed up eighty-two thousand volunteers. About thirty-two thousand of these were culled for various reasons (age, physical fitness, etc.), leaving Bysanz enough men for eight infantry regiments, even after the division's artillery regiment and all of its support battalions (engineers, antitank, reconnaissance, signal, medical, etc.) were fully manned. Since the division was to have only thirteen thousand men, in three infantry regiments, the SS formed five new Ukrainian police regiments (the 4th, 5th, 6th, 7th, and 8th Galician SS Volunteer Regiments) out of the excess personnel. The following month, the first two thousand Ukrainians were put on trains and sent to the Heidelager SS Training Grounds near Debica, Poland, to begin their basic training. Here they were designated the 14th SS Volunteer Division "Galacia." Later, the unit became the 14th SS Grenadier Division "Galicia Nr 1." Initially, the divisional commander was SS-Brigadefuehrer Walter Schimana, a police major general.[78] He was an organizer, not a combat officer, and was re-placed by SS-Oberfuehrer Fritz Freitag, the division's permanent com-mander, on October 20.

Fritz Freitag was an East Prussian (born in Allenstein on April 28, 1894), the son of a railroad official. He enlisted in the 1st (East Prussian) Gren-adier Regiment as soon as he passed his *Abitur* (high school) examinations. World War I broke out a few months later, and Freitag served on both the Eastern and Western Fronts. Commissioned second lieutenant of reserves in 1915, he spent three years as a company commander and was wounded four times. After the war, he spent 1919 with the Freikorps, before joining the East Prussian *Schutzpolizei* in 1920. A relatively late recruit to the Nazi Party, Freitag was a captain of police when Hitler came to power. He was a police lieutenant colonel when World War II began. In the Polish cam-paign, Freitag was Ia (chief of operations) of the 3rd Police Regiment and later served as chief of staff to the Senior Order Police (*Ordnungspolizei*) commander attached to the 14th Army in southern Poland. He did not join the SS until September 1940. Freitag was assigned to Himmler's staff the following year. That fall, he was named Ia of the 1st SS Motorized Infantry Brigade, a combat unit on the Eastern Front. In December 1941 he became commander of the 2nd SS Police Infantry Regiment on the Russian Front. After distinguishing himself in command of a battle group in the Volchov Pocket, he was promoted to SS colonel. On January 13, 1943, he assumed temporary command of the SS Cavalry Division but fell ill and was replaced by August Zehender. Freitag went on to command the remnants of the 2nd SS Motorized Brigade (April–August 1943) and the Kampfgruppe SS Police Division (August–October 1943), before being sent to Heidelager to com-mand the Ukrainians.

Although brave, experienced, and tactically competent, Fritz Freitag was a poor choice to command the Ukrainian division. He had no knowledge of the Ukrainians' culture, history or language, did not particularly care to learn about them, and did not understand Ukrainians generally. He was in fact highly prejudiced against them. He classified his men into three cate-gories: Prussians, Germans, and Ukrainians, in rapidly descending order. He assigned German officers to senior positions whenever possible, even when more capable and experienced Ukrainians were available. This nat-urally caused a great deal of resentment among the Ukrainians. In addition, he did not get along with his First General Staff Officer (Ia), Major Wolf-Dietrich Heike, who described Freitag as "self-seeking, unpleasant and bu-reaucratic" and as "a preening bureaucrat who did not trust anyone."[79] A member of the Army General Staff and the son of a Prussian military fam-ily, Heike was born in 1913 and had served in the Polish, Western, and Russian campaigns. Young Heike was given the rank of *Sturmbannfuehrer* (major) in the Waffen-SS, but he at first refused to wear an SS uniform—much to Freitag's outrage. Even later, Heike wore it only very rarely. For that reason, Freitag twice blocked his promotion to lieutenant colonel, but he would not approve his transfer out of the division. Naturally, this led to a great deal of resentment and not a great deal of cooperation.

The quality of the divisional staff was further weakened by the way it was formed. With the Waffen-SS expanding rapidly, the SS Main Leadership Office drew upon the established divisions for men of all ranks, to be used as cadres for new divisions. Naturally, the older divisions selected for transfer men they did not care to keep, or at least did not care if they lost. The staff of the 14th SS, therefore, was not up to the standards of the older SS divisions.

The Ukrainians nevertheless progressed in their training, and in January 1944 Freitag was sent to a special division commanders' course in Hirschberg, Silesia. He was temporarily replaced by his senior regimental commander, SS Lieutenant Colonel Friedrich Beyersdorf, commander of the 14th SS Artillery Regiment. Beyersdorf led a *kampfgruppe* of the division in its first combat operation, against partisans in the Kholm area, northwest of Lvov. It did well enough to earn praise from Field Marshal Model, who was not a man to give credit where none was due.[80]

In February 1944, the 14th SS was sent to the Neuhammer Maneuver Area, a more up-to-date training facility than Heidelager. Here it was organized into three infantry regiments, the 29th, 30th, and 31st Waffen Grenadiers, each with three battalions. The 14th SS Artillery Regiment and the 14th SS Fusilier (Reconnaissance), 14th SS Engineer, 14th SS Signal, and 14th SS Field Replacement Battalions completed the divisional organization.

On June 28, the still incompletely formed division was put on trains and sent to the central sector of the Eastern Front, which had collapsed almost completely. (The III Battalion of each grenadier regiment had not completed its formation and remained behind.) During the first two weeks of July, it was deployed behind the front a few miles due west of Brody (in the zone of the 1st Panzer Army) and about fifteen miles behind Hauffe's XIII Corps. From left (north) to right, it deployed the 31st, 30th, and 29th Regiments. The 14th SS Field Replacement Battalion, about fifteen miles west of the division's main battle line, constituted the division's only significant reserve.

General of Infantry Arthur Hauffe was a veteran General Staff officer with thirty two years' service;[81] he made it clear from the beginning that he had bad feelings about this battle. His corps had been surrounded earlier in 1944 in this same sector (from the end of March until mid-April) but had been rescued by the panzer divisions, which had forced the Russians to retreat. Hauffe clearly felt that to run the risk of a second encirclement was to tempt fate, yet it was also clear that the Russians were building up on the flanks of XIII Corps for another double envelopment. It was also obvious that Hitler was not going to allow a timely retreat; this is why the Ukrainian Division had been sent to the Brody sector.

The XIII Corps consisted (north to south) of Major General Johannes Nedtwig's 454th Security Division, which held the corps's left wing, northeast of Stanyslavchyk, on both sides of the Styr River; Major General Gerhard Lindemann's 361st Infantry Division, north and northwest of Brody; Lieutenant General Wolfgang Lange's Corps Detachment C (the remnants of the 183rd and 217th Infantry Divisions and the survivors of Lange's own 339th Infantry Division), holding Brody itself and extending south to Boratyn; and Lieutenant General Otto Lasch's 349th Infantry Division, on the southern flank, holding the towns of Lytovytsi, Peniaky, and Markopil. The 14th SS Grenadier Division "Galician Nr. 1" was in reserve, behind Corps Detachment C. All four frontline divisions were considerably understrength. The 361st Infantry was the best of the lot.

On Hauffe's left (northern) flank was General of Infantry Friedrich Schulz's XXXXVI Panzer Corps (of the 4th Panzer Army), and on his right was General of Panzer Troops Hermann Balck's XXXXVIII Panzer Corps (part of the 1st Panzer Army).[82] Both held their frontline sectors with infantry divisions, and both had two tank divisions in reserve. All four of the panzer divisions in the area were at *kampfgruppe* strength.

While the Ukrainians dug in west of Brody, the Russians concentrated two armies with five tank and mechanized corps, two cavalry corps, sixteen rifle divisions, and twenty-nine independent tank brigades on the northern flank of XIII Corps, at the junction of the 1st and 4th Panzer Armies (which was also at the junction of the XIII and XXXXVI Panzer Corps). To the south, at the junction of the XIII Corps and XXXXVIII Panzer Corps, Soviet Marshal Ivan Stepanovich Konev assembled four armies with five tank and mechanized corps, twenty-nine rifle divisions, and twenty-four tank brigades.[83] In all, the Russians had 1,700 to 1,800 tanks, against forty to fifty in the entire 4th Panzer Army.[84]

It is a time-honored military tactic to launch major attacks at the junction of major units because it inevitably results in confusion in enemy headquarters, and it is more difficult for the defender to launch coordinated counterattacks. On the Western Front during World War I, the Imperial German Army had often posted special counterattack forces—often entire divisions—at the junctions of major units, but this was not possible on the Eastern Front in World War II. The Soviets were especially adept at striking at these vulnerable spots.

The Russian offensive began at 3:45 A.M. on July 13 with a tremendous artillery bombardment that did not end until 9:30 A.M. Then the divisions of the left and right flanks of XIII Corps were subjected to massive attacks. Survivors later stated that they had never seen such concentrations of men, tanks, artillery, and aircraft.[85] By nightfall, the Russians had achieved deep penetrations both north and south of Brody. The next day, they routed Major General Oskar Eckholt's 291st "Elk" Infantry Division of the XXXXVI Panzer Corps near Lopatyn, north of the XIII Corps.[86] The 16th and 17th Panzer Divisions, led by Major General Hans-Ulrich Back and Lieutenant General Karl-Friedrich von der Meden, respectively, launched immediate counterattacks but were met by wave after wave of Soviet T-34 tanks, supported by mechanized infantry, artillery, and fighter-bomber aircraft. They were quickly stopped and then swept back to the west, along with the rest of XXXXVI Panzer Corps.

To the south, the Red Army broke through at the junction of the XIII and the XXXXVIII Panzer Corps, where the 349th Infantry Division had loose contact with Colonel Norbert Holm's 357th Infantry Division. Meanwhile, a third major Soviet attack struck XIII Corps at the junction of the 361st Infantry and 454th Security Divisions, but it was turned back in heavy fighting. Seeing that an encirclement of the XIII Corps was in the offing, General Harpe, the commander of Army Group North Ukraine quickly committed Balck's XXXXVIII Panzer Corps to the counterattack southwest of Brody.

The XXXXVIII Panzer's mobile reserve consisted of the 1st and 8th Panzer Divisions, which were led by Major Generals Werner Marcks and Werner Friebe, respectively. The 1st Panzer struck just as it had been instructed to do and brought the Soviet 38th Army to an abrupt halt near Oliiv (about twenty miles northwest of Ternopol). General Friebe, however, totally disregarded Balck's orders (to advance only through forests or on roads that went through forested areas) and moved the 8th Panzer down an open road. It was quickly pounced upon and slaughtered by the Red Air Force, which flew almost two thousand sorties against it on July 15 alone. Absolutely furious, Balck relieved Friebe of his command and temporarily replaced him with Colonel F. W. von Mellenthin, the chief of staff of the XXXXVIII Panzer.

As a result of Friebe's blunder, the Soviet 60th Army continued to expand the breach in the German line south of Brody. Realizing that a major opportunity was presenting itself, Marshal Konev, the 1st Ukrainian Front commander, committed the 3rd Guards Tank and 4th Tank Army into the breach that evening.

Konev's move was a risky one, for the XXXXVIII Panzer Corps was still offering fierce resistance, but it paid off. On July 17, the 357th Infantry Division finally collapsed, and Balck retreated with his two panzer divisions. On the morning of July 18, after smashing the 14th SS Field Replacement Battalion (the remnants of which escaped to the west), two of the Soviet spearheads met on the Bug River near Busk, thirty miles west of Lvov, encircling XIII Corps in the Brody Pocket, about sixty miles northeast of the Galician capital. Map 2.2 shows the Brody battlefield.

Later that day, General Harpe signaled XIII Corps and ordered it to

Map 2.2
The Brody Pocket

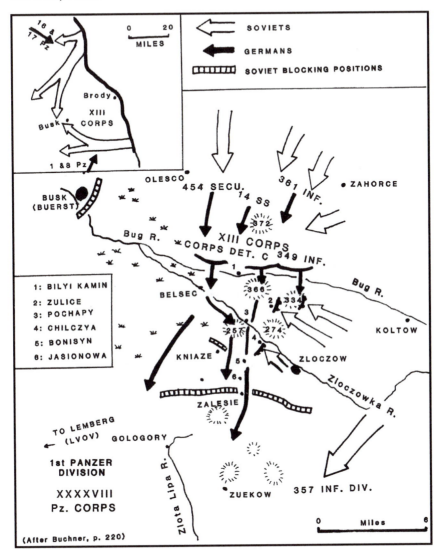

break out. Hauffe, however, had made no preparations and apparently no contingency plans for such an attempt. He seems, in fact, to have fought this entire battle under a cloud of hopelessness and depression, which significantly slowed the German reaction. In any case, valuable time had been lost.

The Battle of the Brody Pocket was fierce. More than thirty thousand

Germans and Galicians were surrounded, and it was only a matter of time before the pocket collapsed. On the afternoon of July 18, plans for a breakout were finalized. Since the Soviets were exerting heavy pressure to the north and east, and the terrain to the west was marshy and heavily forested, it was decided that XIII Corps would attack to the south while the two tank divisions of the XXXXVIII Panzer Corps attacked to the north, to link up with them. The chief of staff of the XIII Corps, Colonel Baron Hans-Werner von Hammerstein-Gesmold, told the divisional chiefs of operations that the Russian blocking forces south of the Zloczow-Lemberg Highway were relatively weak; XXXXVIII Panzer Corps was still holding a solid front, the 1st and 8th Panzer Divisions were already launching a successful drive from the south, and they (XIII Corps) would only have to push about three miles south of the highway to reach safety. All four assumptions were wrong. Before XIII Corps could reach its linkup point, it would have to traverse fourteen to eighteen miles of heavily wooded and swampy terrain, and also ford the West Bug and Zloczowka Rivers. The breakout attempt was scheduled to begin at 3:30 A.M. on July 20. Preparations began immediately.

The breakout was to be spearheaded by Lasch's 349th Infantry Division and Lange's Corps Detachment C. On July 19, after those two formations pulled out of the line and assembled for the attack, the 454th Security Division defended the northern perimeter, the 361st Infantry (with the 249th Assault Gun Brigade attached) and the corps troops held the southern sector, while the Ukrainians defended the eastern perimeter. The Soviets, seeking to collapse the pocket, attacked the inexperienced 14th SS, no doubt thinking it was the easiest target. The 29th and 30th Waffen Grenadier Regiments (WGRs), supported by most of the 14th SS Artillery Regiment, put up unexpectedly fierce resistance, and the castle and town of Pidhirtsi changed hands several times. The commander of the 29th, SS Lieutenant Colonel Friedrich Dern, was wounded, and command devolved on SS Captain Wilhelm Allenkampf, but the regiment's will to fight was undiminished. At Olesko, several miles to the west-northwest, the 14th SS Fusilier and 14th SS Engineer Battalions repulsed a major attack by T-34 tanks and destroyed several of the forty-six-ton monsters in heavy fighting.

"The Reds," SS Lieutenant Herman of the II/29th SS WGR recalled, "sprouted like mosquitoes. Although suffering ten times our losses, their lines seem to be endless. The Red Army looks like a huge advancing steamroller. Without new troops we can't even think of making an effective counterattack."[87]

Late that afternoon, the 29th WGR was overwhelmed. The regimental staff and headquarters company—275 men—made a last stand near the village of Pidhirtsi. After the battle, only seven of these men could be accounted for. The survivors of the regiment were incorporated into the 30th and 31st WGRs.

At dawn the next morning, July 20, General Lange assumed command of the XIII Corps because General Hauffe was missing. (For whatever reason, General Hauffe apparently did not make his way back to headquarters until July 22 and thereby effectively abdicated command to the highly capable General Lange, who directed the entire breakout operation.) Lange attacked at 7 A.M. (an hour and a half behind schedule), with his own Corps Detachment C acting as the spearhead in the center and on the right (west) flank while the 349th Infantry Division (with Division Group 339 of Corps Detachment C attached) formed up on the left. Initially the corps detachment made good progress. On Lange's right flank, the 183rd Divisional Group crossed the Bug about 7 A.M. and reached the village of Belsec at 7:25 A.M. In the center, Division Group 217 captured the critical Hill 366 in heavy fighting, and broke through the Russian line at 9 A.M. The Soviets countered by throwing twenty tanks at the 217th. The German infantry promptly destroyed them all. By noon, they had pushed even farther south and fought a fierce house-to-house battle for the village of Pochapy, which they captured at 3 P.M. Meanwhile, Division Group 183 took Hill 257, and on the left flank, the 349th Infantry Division captured Hill 334 and then Hill 274 but could not take the town of Zloczow. Lange's spearheads were now only five to six miles from the left flank of the XXXXVIII Panzer Corps—but Soviet resistance was stiffening.

Early in the morning of July 20, Marshal Konev had realized that Lange's counterattack constituted a significant threat to the integrity of the encircling Soviet ring, so he recalled several regiments from the north, south, and west, launched a series of hurried attacks against the perimeter of the XIII Corps, and committed his huge air forces into close air attacks against every unit in the pocket. The air attacks were constant and featured a new tactic: the Russians used their new eighty-pound shrapnel bombs tied into bundles. This method was highly effective, destroying all horses, wagons, and guns within a hundred-square-yard area—as well as any men who did not hurl themselves into foxholes or failed to take cover in time.

Meanwhile, at the front, Konev's reinforcements made their presence felt on the afternoon of July 20. The 183rd Divisional Group was checked in front of the village of Kniaze, and the 217th Group was halted near Boniszyn. On the left (southeastern) flank, heavy Soviet counterattacks struck the 349th Infantry Division and the 339th Divisional Group. The Russians stormed the critical Hill 334 and forced the 349th and 339th toward the center. General Otto Lasch, the commander of the 349th Infantry, organized an immediate counterattack and retook the hill, but the Russians were far from finished. They threw more tanks and fresh infantry units into the struggle, and Hill 334 changed hands several more times before the Soviets captured it for good that evening. Lasch's troops fell back to the village of Zulice, which they held in heavy fighting. As night fell, however, it was clear that Lange's first breakout attempt had been checked.[88]

Meanwhile, to the southwest, the 8th Panzer Division fouled up again.

On July 18, General Balck had reinforced the 8th with elements of the 20th Panzer Grenadier Regiment and ordered it to attack to the northeast the following day, to rescue the XIII Corps. Colonel Friedrich Wilhelm von Mellenthin, the acting divisional commander, naturally passed the orders down to his regimental commanders.

Colonel von Mellenthin was an experienced panzer officer. He had served as Rommel's chief intelligence officer in the desert and had been wounded leading an ad hoc battle group during the First battle of El Alamein. Laid low by amoebic dysentery in the fall of 1942, he had been chief of staff of the XXXXVIII Panzer Corps since the Stalingrad relief attempt in late 1942. He was not a man who was easily shocked; nevertheless, he was stunned on the morning of July 19 when he learned that several of his commanders were not advancing. Instead, they had taken it upon themselves to retreat! Mellenthin relieved all of the offenders of their commands, including the commander of the 10th Panzer Regiment. Mellenthin promptly began reorganizing the division for another attack, but valuable time had been lost. No rescue attempt could be launched on July 19;[89] and the panzers were unable to gain much ground on the 20th. Meanwhile, the Soviets continued to pound the pocket with fighter-bombers, artillery fire, and an occasional ground attack. The XIII Corps repulsed them only with difficulty.

Lieutenant General Wolfgang Lange was a brave, highly capable, tough, and resourceful commander. He realized that the XIII Corps was nearing exhaustion and was running out of options. Early on the evening of July 20, he assembled his principal commanders in a small wooded grove and told them that he intended to launch another breakout attempt that very night. Once again, Corps Detachment C would spearhead the attack. Lange acknowledged that a night's rest would do everyone good, but this had to be balanced against the fact that the encircling forces were growing stronger every hour, and the Soviets would not be able to use their fighter-bombers against a night attack. All of the commanders nodded their agreement. Lange then set the objective of the main attack as the Lvov (Lemberg) Highway, near the town of Liatske (Lackie). He also ordered General Lasch to launch a major secondary attack and capture Zloczow. Lange then asked the other commanders to report on their current situations. When SS General Freitag's turn came, he said that he was unable to report: "I believe the division is no longer under my control." He then offered his resignation as divisional commander. Lange did not bother to hide his disdain and contempt as he immediately accepted the resignation. He replaced Freitag with Major General Gerhard Lindemann.[90]

Russian efforts to crush the pocket continued, meanwhile, and the 31st SS Grenadier Regiment was destroyed north of Sasiv. After its commander,

SS Lieutenant Colonel Paul Herms, was killed in action, along with most of his staff, the regiment largely disintegrated. The survivors who could be rounded up were temporarily assigned to neighboring units. Chaos was beginning to make its appearance everywhere. Ukrainian First Lieutenant Lubomyr Ortynski later wrote in his diary, "Another 10 tanks could be seen firing into the II Battalion [of the 29th WGR] column on the road, while in the field the Soviet infantry were advancing like a swarm of bees. The air was full of the thunder of tank guns and the noise of engines. . . . [M]ore tanks were appearing. . . . What could we do, attack the tanks with rifles?"[91]

The second breakout attempt began at 1 A.M. on July 21 and reached the Lvov Highway four hours later. Dawn, however, brought trouble. The 349th Infantry and Corps Detachment C had lined up all of their vehicles on the few narrow roads heading south, and they were promptly strafed by fighter-bombers from the Red Air Force. General Lange later wrote that they should have simply pushed their vehicles and supply wagons off the roads and abandoned them to begin with; more of the troops would have been saved, and the vehicles were lost anyway. Now, however, the few roads were clogged by burning debris, and chaos reigned even in the German units.

The 183rd Divisional Group was quickly checked north of Kniaze and was pushed back to Hill 257. In the center, however, the 217th Group struck a weak spot in the Soviet encirclement near Jasionowca and pushed into the hills to the south. The German troops they expected to find there, however, were nowhere to be seen. After some deliberation, the officers of the divisional group decided to keep heading south on their own. (The 249th Assault Gun Brigade had been attached to the 217th, but all of its guns and vehicles had already been destroyed, so it was now of little value.) Without artillery or armored support, Group 217 nevertheless continued its advance and reached German (1st Panzer Division) lines near Zuekow (Zhukiv), about 8.5 miles south of the Lvov Highway, that afternoon.[92]

About ten miles to the west, meanwhile, Colonel Karl Neumeister, the commander of the 1st Panzer Grenadier Regiment of the 1st Panzer Division, broke through the Russian lines and reached XIII Corps positions west of Liatske.[93] About 3,400 men from various divisions, including four hundred Ukrainians from the 14th SS, were rescued. Neumeister could not keep the door open long, however, because that afternoon the Russians crossed the Zlota Lipa River to the south and captured the town of Lipowece. Neumeister, who was now threatened with encirclement himself, was ordered to turn south, counterattack, and recapture the town, which he promptly set out to do. Soon embroiled in heavy fighting to the south, he would never be able to return.

Inside the pocket, the 14th SS also lost its unit cohesiveness on the 21st. The Ukrainians had certainly fought bravely enough, but retreating under pressure and simultaneously trying to save their vehicles in the face of Russian aerial attacks (a task that turned out to be impossible) was too much for them. Captain Dmytro Ferkuniak recalled that the first of the Soviet wings (forty to fifty airplanes each) "bombed and machine-gunned the leaderless column that was headed for Bilyi Kamin. No words exist to describe such an inferno. At half-hour intervals the defenseless column was strafed and bombed. . . . Not one German plane appeared to halt these merciless attacks." The single flak battery provided by the division "fired continuously, knocking down about 25 enemy planes . . . until it too was finally bombed and put out of action."[94]

The Ukrainian Division was also hampered by very bad communications. Although many of the Ukrainians could speak some German and could communicate (with some effort) in face-to-face situations, it was soon discovered that they could not do so adequately over radio or field telephone in the heat of battle. The inevitable loss of signals equipment and key personnel further complicated matters. Also, exhaustion and ammunition shortages were now dictating tactics within the rapidly shrinking pocket.

That night, General Freitag assessed that the division was no longer intact and decreed that everyone would be on his own during the breakout. Freitag and his staff promptly formed a battle group and headed south, leaving most of the division behind. Some of the Ukrainian assault parties remained intact, while others joined the 361st Infantry Division, and others simply melted away and fled.

July 21 also saw the end of most of the 454th Security Division, which collapsed under repeated air, ground, artillery, and rocket attacks. Its few extant elements were transferred to the right flank, near Belzec, while its stragglers joined other XIII Corps units or simply wandered off on their own, where they were almost all killed or captured by the Russians.

Late that afternoon, the assault guns of the 8th Panzer Division (now under Major General Gottfried Froelich) broke through the Soviet perimeter from the south, linking up with the survivors north of Gologory and saving another remnant of the corps.[95]

To the north, the Ukrainian 14th SS Fusilier Battalion formed the rearguard of the entire XIII Corps. It held the town of Bilyi Kamin, which was on the northern bank of the Bug, and thus held open a door for any unit or straggler seeking to escape to the south. It continued to hold in spite of several Russian attempts to overwhelm it. By the evening of July 21 the town was in flames, and the 14th SS Fusilier was the only intact unit north of the river.

"Mama! Mama! I can't see!" the little girl screamed as she stepped out of a burning cottage into the street. No more than five years of age, she again screamed in agony as blood poured down her cheeks.

All shooting stopped immediately. The silence was eerie. All that could be heard was the crackling of the burning wood. The child cried out once more.

Suddenly, an SS medic could stand it no longer. "I'll get her!" he cried. Leaving his position of safety, he dashed forward, grabbed the child in his arms, and turned to run back. It seemed for a moment as if humanity might prevail for once. Then Soviet submachine guns opened up, and several bullets blew open the back of the young Ukrainian corporal. They exited through his chest and snuffed out the life of the little girl as well.[96]

In the early morning hours of July 22, the 14th SS Fusiliers abandoned Bilyi Kamin. There were now no Axis units north of the Bug. By morning, the pocket was only about four to five miles north to south and about the same distance east to west. Within the pocket, the survivors prepared for the last attempt. Their ammunition was almost gone, and some of them had not eaten or slept for days. Communications within the pocket had virtually ceased to exist. The breakout procedure in this situation was simple: no positions were to be held; every unit was to attack with everything it had and once it started moving, continue forward until it reached safety, broke up, or was destroyed.

As the 1st Company, 31st WGR prepared to break out, its commander, SS Captain von Zalzinger, lay wounded on the ground. Realizing that he would be a burden and a threat to his men if they carried him with them, and knowing that they were planning to do so, the young officer drew his pistol and shot himself. After he heard the shot, one of the Ukrainians gently covered Zalzinger's body with a poncho.[97] Many wounded Ukrainians and German soldiers would follow Zalzinger's example in the next forty-eight hours.

The battle of July 22 was fierce in the extreme. The Red Air Force flew no less than 2,340 sorties: the Germans and Ukrainians were desperate. Summoning the last of their strength, they surged southward toward the XXXXVIII Panzer Corps, and soon dozens and even hundreds of men were escaping. Realizing that his prey was escaping Konev committed the 91st Independent Tank Brigade "Proskurov," supported by infantry, into the escape corridor to seal it off. The brigade was immediately swamped by escapees, who wiped out the Soviet infantry in savage, hand-to-hand combat and blew up scores of T-34 and KV heavy tanks with *Panzerfausts*, grenades, Molotov cocktails, or whatever else was available. By nightfall, the Proskurov Tank Brigade no longer existed.[98]

SS Lieutenant Colonel King Danylko, the commander of the 14th SS Fusilier Battalion, was a true combat leader. Dressed in a camouflaged uniform and armed with a MG42 machine gun, he "actually looked like a God of War," a survivor recalled. "We're going forward!" Danylko told his last two hundred men. "We're going to where there is life, freedom and love!" And forward they went. Soon their path was blocked by a mechanized NKVD police battalion, which they promptly tore apart. "They shot, bayoneted, clubbed, stabbed and killed with their bare hands," Michael Logusz wrote later.[99] Because of this kind of determination, many of the Ukrainians did, in fact, manage to escape.

General Lange also managed to escape. With Divisional Group 217 gone and the 183rd destroyed, he joined General Lasch, who had Divisional Group 339 and one surviving regiment from his own 349th Infantry Division. They headed out for the south about 3 A.M., while it was still dark, followed by more than five thousand men—perhaps as many as ten thousand. They were pounded by Soviet mortar, artillery, and machine-gun fire, but they kept going forward. "Without order and organization, lacking coordination and contact with one another, wave after wave of German soldiers stormed forward," Buchner wrote later.[100] Screaming "Hurray!" they overran Jasionowce and Zalesie, destroyed several Russian tanks, and broke through to the southwest. This was the largest force to escape.

The fact that any significant portion of the corps escaped at all was due to the skill and courage of Generals Lindemann and Nedtwig of the 361st Infantry/14th SS and 454th Security Divisions, respectively. They held the shoulders of the breakout open, which allowed a great many men to escape. Although they saved others, they were not able to save themselves. By keeping the road to freedom open for others as long as possible, they passed up their own chance to get away. Both were wounded before they were captured; Nedtwig suffered a serious head wound;[101] Lindemann was less badly wounded.

The XIII Corps simply had too far to go against too many Russians. By the evening of July 22, it was "every man for himself." Pressed by strong Soviet forces from the north, the pocket essentially collapsed. Many ad hoc battle groups were simply wiped out by Russian artillery, tanks, "Stalins organs," heavy machine guns, and fighter-bombers. Colonel von Hammerstein placed himself at the head of a battalion and died at the forefront of the battle. General Hauffe was killed north of Kniaze.

With the death, capture, or escape of the senior officers, centralized command authority in the pocket vanished completely. The Russians continued to pound the shrinking pocket with mortars, artillery, Stalin's Organs and low-level air attacks. One survivor recalled that there were now so many burning German vehicles that the smoke—coupled with the dust thrown up by exploding Soviet bombs and shells—blotted out the sun. Then the Soviet infantry and armor mopped up what was left. One by one, each German and Ukrainian company, platoon, battalion or battery ceased to exist. Some men surrendered, others fought until the bitter end, and still others used their last bullet on themselves.[102] The Germans who surrendered were sent to the interior of Russia, which often meant Siberia. Some of them returned in the 1950s, but many were never heard from again. Most of the Ukrainian prisoners were simply murdered.

Only about twelve thousand men escaped. Seventeen thousand were captured; few of these ever returned. Between twenty-five and thirty thousand German soldiers were killed. Many of these were wounded men who were captured and then "finished off" by the Russians. These losses exclude those suffered by the 1st, 8th, 16th, and 17th Panzer Divisions, which were also severe. In July 1944, for example, the 8th Panzer lost 2,361 men, eight tanks, seventy-seven armored personnel carriers, and twenty four guns.[103]

With the XIII Corps gone, there was nothing left to bar the Russians' path to Lvov (Lemberg). It fell on July 27. The next day, the fortress-city of Przemysl was also lost.

As we have seen, Wolfgang Lange escaped the disaster. His corps detachment—which was now a disorganized remnant—was taken out of the line and in August was dissolved. Lange was given a new command (the 564th Volksgrenadier Division) on September 1.

Otto Lasch also managed to reach German lines. After being given a month's leave to recover, he was given command of the LXIV Corps on September 1. He was promoted to general of infantry two months later, when he was named commander of Wehrkreis (Military District) I (East Prussia). The Russians would not capture him until the last weeks of the war, when they overran his headquarters in Koenigsberg. Hitler would sentence him to death in absentia for surrendering the city.

Brigadefuehrer Freitag also escaped but lost seven thousand of his 10,400 men. Not all of these losses, however, were permanent. Hundreds of young Ukrainians who could not reach friendly lines hid out and later made their way back to the division over a period of weeks. This trickle eventually grew to a total of more than 2,300 men. Some of them actually joined the Red Army, deserted at the first opportunity, and asked to be sent back to their division. A sizable number of survivors made their way to their homes and back into civilian life, while others joined the UPA—the anticommunist insurgency movement in the Ukraine—and fought for an independent Ukraine into the 1950s. This number may have been as high as three thousand.

Unlike the case with Lange, Lindemann, and Nedtwig, Freitag's conduct of the battle was the subject of severe criticism, and Galician leaders appealed to Himmler to replace the unpopular commander, but the Reichsfuehrer-SS decorated him with the Knight's Cross instead. In writing the citation for the decoration, Himmler displayed his racial bigotry in almost every paragraph. Among other things, he asserted that.

Ukrainians are soft inside and fickle, and they lack much in comparison to fighting German soldiers. . . .

[During the Battle of Brody] numerous volunteers of the division fled due to their inner cowardice. . . . During this crisis, it was again the decisive presence of the divisional commander, who was there in person to reestablish the situation by inflicting the required brutal measures against any whiners, that saved the situation.

Ukrainians . . . with very few exceptions . . . are not fighters. . . .

[Whenever the division achieved success] it can only be attributed to the service of the German leaders who were led by their divisional commander.[104]

Himmler went on to describe how Freitag was one of the last to escape the pocket and was the last general to leave the field after Gerhard Lindemann had been killed. Neither of these "facts" were true, and Lindemann was not dead. In fact, very little in Himmler's report was accurate. In justice to Freitag, it must be pointed out that he acknowledged that he was not a good commander of non-German troops. He had even told Himmler that he was not the right man to lead the Ukrainian division, but his view had been ignored. After he received his Knight's Cross, Freitag showed an uncharacteristic amount of class, and went out of his way to thank his Ukrainians for the part they had played in winning the decoration for him. It was the first time he had ever officially commended them. Even so, Freitag learned little from his mistakes. He continued to fill every important position within the division with Germans even if there were older, more experienced, and clearly better qualified Ukrainians available. Freitag commanded the 14th SS until the end and eventually surrendered it to the British near Radstadt on May 8, 1945. Shortly thereafter, he was placed in the American POW camp near Graz, Austria, where he learned that he was to be handed over to the Russians. Knowing that his doom was sealed, Fritz Freitag took his own life on May 20, 1945.

NOTES

1. Carlo D'Este, "Model," in Correlli Barnett, ed., *Hitler's Generals* (London: 1989), pp. 319–20.

2. Keilig, p. 228.

3. Friedrich Wilhelm von Mellenthin, *German Generals of World War Two* (Norman, Okla.: 1977), p. 147.

4. John D. S. Eisenhower, *The Bitter Woods* (New York: 1969), ff. 16; Wistrich, p. 210; Moll, p. 137.

5. D'Este, p. 321.

6. Wistrich, p. 210; Keilig, p. 174.

7. Heinz Guderian, *Panzer Leader*, trans. Constantine Fitzgibbon (New York: 1957; reprint ed., New York: 1967), p. 175.

8. D'Este, p. 322.

9. Paul Carell, *Hitler Moves East* (Boston: 1965; reprint ed., New York: 1966), p. 393.

10. Ibid., p. 398.

11. Mellenthin, pp. 149–51.

12. Walter Goerlitz, *Walter Model: Strategie der Defensive*, 2nd ed. (Weisbaden: 1975), pp. 25–26.

13. B. H. Liddell Hart, *The Other Side of the Hill* (London: 1978), p. 102.

14. Mellenthin, pp. 393–406; Wistrich, p. 210; Carell, p. 406.

15. Ziemke, pp. 139–41; Hermann Plocher, "The German Air Force versus Russia, 1943," *United States Air Force Historical Studies*, no. 155 (Maxwell Air Force Base, Ala.: unpublished manuscript written about 1965).

16. Ziemke, pp. 265–66.

17. Niepold, p. 257.

18. Ibid., pp. 139–40.

19. Curt von Gottberg was born near Koenigsberg, East Prussia, in 1896 and entered the Imperial Army as a war volunteer in 1914. He initially served in a cavalry regiment on the Eastern Front. Transferred to Potsdam in 1915, he completed his officer training and received a commission. In 1917, while serving in the 1st Guards Regiment on the Western Front, he was seriously wounded. Apparently he saw no further action and was discharged in 1920 as a first lieutenant. He was employed in agriculture after the war. A Nazi from the 1920s, Gottberg joined the SS-Verfuegungstruppe (the forerunner of the Waffen-SS) as a battalion commander and captain of SS in 1933. An SS colonel by 1937, he was chief of the Race and Resettlement Office in Berlin until 1939, when he was transferred to Prague, where he held a similar position. Recalled to Berlin in 1941, he was promoted to *brigadefuehrer* and major general of police on April 20, 1941. He volunteered for the front in early 1942 and served in and directed antipartisan operations the East.

Gottberg, who was a *Gruppenfuehrer* by 1944, was also Higher SS and Police Leader for Russia-Center, with headquarters in Minsk. He was awarded the Knight's Cross on June 30, 1944, and on July 11, 1944, was promoted to General of Waffen-SS and Police. Three weeks later, von Gottberg returned to Germany and assumed command of the XII SS Corps, which was then forming. He led his new command on the Eastern Front and later on the Dutch-German border. He was relieved of his duties on October 18, however, for reasons of health, and spent two months in the hospital. Apparently he suffered from a thrombosis. After his release from the hospital, Himmler named him deputy commander of the Replacement Army, although he never fully recovered his health. He ended the war with Field Marshal Busch's OB Northwest in northern Germany and died at Grundhof, Schleswig-Holstein, on May 31, 1945 (Ernst-Guenther Kraetschmer, Die Ritterkreutztraeper der Waffene SS, 3rd ed. [Preussisch Oldendorf: 1982], pp. 722–23).

20. Niepold, p. 143.

21. Adolf Hamann was born in Mecklenburg in 1885 and entered the Imperial Army as a *Fahnenjunker* in 1901. A colonel when World War II broke out, he commanded a frontier defense sector on the Polish border (1939), the 3rd Infantry Replacement Regiment (1940–41), and the 327th, 523rd, and 660th Infantry Regiments (1941–42). Perhaps because of his advanced age, he was then given a series of rear area assignments, including commandant of Orel, Bryansk, and Bobruisk. He was hanged in Bobruisk in 1945.

22. Gerhard Mueller commanded the 33rd Anti-Tank Battalion (1938–39), the I/33rd Panzer Regiment (i.e., 1st Battalion, 33rd Panzer) (1941), and the 5th Panzer Regiment (1942). He was later given command of the 116th Panzer Division on the Western Front and was promoted to major general on September 1, 1944. A few days later, his staff revolted against him, and he was relieved of his command. He ended the war as deputy commandant of Pilsen. He was a Silesian (Keilig, p. 232).

23. Adair, p. 135.

24. Ibid., p. 136.

25. Zaloga, *Bagration*, pp. 65–70.

26. Niepold, pp. 176–78; von Seemen, p. 87.

27. Paul Voelckers died in a Soviet prison in 1946.

28. Adair, p. 155. Paul Schuermann was promoted to lieutenant general on September 1, 1944. He commanded a rebuilt 25th Panzer Grenadier Division until February 25, 1945, when he either was relieved of his command, fell sick, was wounded, or was otherwise injured. (German World War II military personnel records are often unclear on this point.) In any case, he saw no further service, and he settled in Wiesbaden after the war. He had joined the service as an infantry officer cadet in 1914 and had served on the staff of OKH (1937–40), as commander of the 11th Infantry Regiment (1940–42), and on the staffs of OKH and Army Group Center (1942–44). He held an advanced degree in engineering (Keilig, p. 314).

29. Zaloga, *Bagration*, p. 71.

30. Gustav Harteneck entered the Bavarian Army as a cavalry *Fahnenjunker* in 1914. During the Hitler era, he served successively as commander of the 9th Cavalry Regiment (1938), Ia of the 1st Army (1939), chief of staff of XXVII Corps (late 1940), chief of staff of 2nd Army (late 1941), and commander of the Division General Government (1944) and 72nd Infantry Division (1944). He assumed command of the I Cavalry Corps on June 10, 1944, and led it for the rest of the war. He was promoted to general of cavalry on September 1. General Harteneck surrendered to the Western Allies at the end of the war. Released from prison in 1947, he died at Grosshesselohe (near Munich) in 1984.

31. Adolf Heusinger was born in Holzminden in 1896, joined the army as an infantry *Fahnenjunker* in 1916, and was captured on the Western Front. Selected nevertheless for the Reichswehr, he joined the operations department at OKH in 1937 and became chief of operations on October 1, 1940. He held the post until July 20, 1944, when he was severely wounded in the attempt to assassinate Adolf Hitler. By that time his relationship with the dictator had become strained, and he was never reemployed. He joined the West German Army as a lieutenant general (three-star general under the new rank configuration) in 1955. He was somewhat bitter about having spent six years of his life in Allied prison camps. General Heusinger retired in 1964 and died in Koeln on November 30, 1982.

32. Niepold, pp. 192–93, 202.

33. Ibid., p. 194.

34. Lieutenant General Hans Bergen (1890–1957) had commanded the 390th since May 1943. He had previously commanded the 179th and 187th Infantry Regiments (1939–41) and the 323rd and 299th Infantry Divisions. Later he commanded the 526th Replacement Division (1944–45) (Keilig, p. 29). Following this defeat, the remnants of the 390th were reorganized as a special purposes security division (Mehner, ed., vol. 5, p. 331).

35. Niepold, p. 206.

36. Ibid., p. 245. Erich Dethleffsen held several important staff positions on the Eastern Front during World War II, including chief of staff of XXXIX Panzer Corps (1943–44). He was promoted to major general on November 9, 1944. He was named chief of staff of Army Group Vistula shortly before Hitler committed

suicide. He was also chief of the operations branch of the OKW staff in the Doenitz government. A British prisoner of war until 1948, Dethleffsen died in Munich on July 4, 1980.

37. During World War II, Theodor Tolsdorff rose from lieutenant to lieutenant general and was wounded fourteen times. He ended the war commanding the LXXXII Corps on the Western Front.

38. Adair, *Center*, p. 132. The 5th Panzer Division was soon reinforced to a strength of twenty-five PzKw IVs, twenty-five Panthers, and fifteen Tigers.

39. Niepold, p. 257.

40. Reiner Stahel was born in Bielefeld on January 15, 1892. He entered the army as a *Fahnenjunker* in 1911 and commanded an infantry platoon, an infantry company, and a machine-gun company in World War I. He was discharged from the German Army as an honorary captain in early 1918 and joined the newly established Finnish Army as a major. Promoted to lieutenant colonel shortly thereafter, he commanded the Finnish 27th Jaeger Battalion and the Finnish 2nd Jaeger Regiment and was chief of staff of the 1st Finnish Division. He was a Finnish reserve officer until 1934, when he rejoined the German armed forces as a captain in the clandestine Luftwaffe. Here he was primarily associated with the flak branch and specialized in light anti-aircraft artillery. After holding staff positions in the Army Weapons Office and the Aviation Ministry (1934–38), Stahel commanded a battery in the 73rd Light Flak Battalion (1938–39). Later he commanded the 731st Light Reserve Flak Regiment (1939–40), the 226th Reserve Flak Battalion (1940), and the 151st Reserve Flak Battalion (1940). After serving on the staff of the French Control Commission (1940–41), he commanded the 34th Motorized Flak Regiment in Russia (1941–42), the 99th Flak Regiment (1942), the 4th Luftwaffe Field Division (1942–43), and the 22nd Flak Brigade (1943). He commanded flak and security forces in northern Sicily (1943) and a special battle group in Rome before returning to Russia. He was promoted to major 1936, lieutenant colonel 1939, colonel 1942, and major general 1943. He was promoted to lieutenant general on July 1, 1944. Karl Friedrich Hildebrand, *Die Generale der deutschen Luftwaffe, 1935–1945* (Osnabrueck: 1992), vol. 3, pp. 336–38. His next assignments would be in Warsaw and Rumania (see chapters 3 and 5).

41. Seaton, *Russo-German, War,* p. 442.

42. Ibid., p. 329; Ziemke, p. 329.

43. Claus von Stauffenberg was born in Bavaria in 1907, the son of the senior marshal to the court of the king of Wuerttemburg. He could trace his ancestry back to 1262. His ancestors included Gneisenau and Yorck, major Prussian military heroes of the Napoleonic Wars. He enlisted in the 17th Cavalry (the family regiment) in 1927, was commissioned in 1933, and underwent General Staff training from 1936 to 1938. He served with the 1st Light (subsequently 6th Panzer) Division in Poland and France, and was on the Organizations Staff at OKH from 1940 to 1943. His immediate superior here was General Buhle.

44. Gerry S. Graber, *Stauffenberg* (New York: 1973), p. 116.

45. Joachim Kramarz, *Stauffenberg* (London: 1967), p. 133.

46. Kleist (the commander in chief of Army Group A) had been forced into retirement in April 1944. Bock, the former commander of Army Groups Center and South, had been placed in Fuehrer Reserve in July 1942.

47. Kurt Zeitzler was born in Cossmar on June 9, 1895, and entered the army

as a *Fahnenjunker* in March 1914. Commissioned in the infantry later that year, he fought in World War I and served in the Reichsheer. He was chief of staff of the General von Kleist's XXII Corps in Poland when World War II began. He remained Kleist's chief of staff when he commanded Panzer Group von Kleist in France (1940) and 1st Panzer Army in Russia (1941–42). He was promoted to major general on February 1, 1942, and returned to France two months later as chief of staff of Army Group D (later OB West). Despite Zeitzler's low rank, Hitler named him chief of the General Staff of the German Army (OKH) on September 24, 1942, and promoted him to general of infantry, Zeitzler skipped the rank of lieutenant general altogether. He was promoted to colonel general in early 1944. Hitler hoped Zeitzler would be a willing tool for himself and OKW, but he (Zeitzler) was not, and their relationship was severely strained by July 1944. General Zeitzler was never reemployed and was dismissed from the army in early 1945. He retired to Hamburg after the war and died on September 25, 1963.

48. Hitler's agents were unable to prove General Fromm knew about the plot, because Fromm had executed the potential witnesses against him on the night of July 20–21. These included Generals Beck and Olbricht and Colonel von Stauffenberg. Fromm was convicted of cowardice instead and was executed on March 12, 1945.

49. Walter Buhle was chief of the organizational branch at OKH (1938–42) and chief of the army staff at OKW (1942–44). After recovering from his wounds, he became chief of Wehrmacht equipment (1945). A POW until 1947, he died in Stuttgart on December 28, 1959. He was definitely pro-Nazi.

50. Anthony C. Brown, *Bodyguard of Lies* (New York: 1975), p. 771.

51. Ziemke, p. 325.

52. Job Odebrecht (1892–1982) entered the service as a naval officer cadet in 1909. Commissioned ensign in 1912, he served aboard a torpedo boat and a battleship before being sent to East Africa. When World War I broke out, Odebrecht commanded a company of ad hoc naval infantry. He was captured by the Belgians in 1916, when German East Africa was overrun by the Allies. After the war, he returned to Germany and joined the police, where he rose to the rank of major. He returned to active duty with the Luftwaffe in 1935 and was promoted to lieutenant colonel by the end of the year. His prior commands included I Battalion 11th Flak Regiment (1935–36), 71st Flak Battalion (1937–38), I/34th Flak Regiment (1938), 25th Flak Regiment (1938), 8th Flak Regiment (1938–39), 5th Luftwaffe Defense Command (1939–40), 6th Luftwaffe Defense Command (1940–41), 6th Flak Division (1941–42), Division Meindl (later 21st Luftwaffe Field Division) (1942), and the III Luftwaffe Field Corps (1942–43). He led II Flak Corps until the end of the war and was promoted to general of flak artillery on December 1, 1942. Hildebrand, *Luftwaffe Generale*, vol. 3, pp. 3–5.

53. Colonel Nieper was superseded as commanding officer by Lieutenant General Walter Kathmann when the 27th Flak Division was created. He, in turn, was succeeded by Colonel Oskar Vorbrugg on October 24.

Guenther Sachs (1903–62), the former commander of the 10th Flak Brigade, replaced Adolf Wolf as the commander of the 18th Flak Division on October 2. He was promoted to major general and named Luftwaffe Commander, East Prussia, on December 1, 1944. Wolf (1899–1973) went on to command the 13th Flak Division on the Western Front. Werner Prellberg (1896–1960), the commander of the 12th Flak Division, was promoted to lieutenant general on August 1, 1944 (Rudoph Absolom, *Rangliste der Generale der deutschen Luftwaffe nach dem Stand vom 20. April 1945* [Freidburg: 1984], p. 68; Haupt, *Center*, p. 220).

54. Adair, *Center*, p. 132.

55. Ziemke, p. 340. Otto Heidkaemper was an engineer officer who spent almost the entire war in staff positions. Born in 1901, he was commissioned in 1922 and was only forty-four years old when the war ended. He served on the General Staff of Frontier Command Eifel (1938) and 2nd Light Division (1939), was Ia of 2nd Light/7th Panzer Division (1939–40), chief of operations of 4th Panzer Division (1940–42), and chief of staff of XXIV Panzer Corps (1942–43) before becoming chief of staff of 3rd Panzer Army (May 1943). Heidkaemper was briefly placed in Fuehrer Reserve after Reinhardt was sacked by Hitler at the end of January 1945. He was given command of the 464th Infantry Division at the end of the war (late April 1945). Heidkaemper also commanded 4th Panzer Division for a month (March–April 1942) while he was a lieutenant colonel and was acting commander of XXIV Panzer Corps for a month (January–February 1943). He was promoted to lieutenant general on November 9, 1944. He surrendered to the Americans at the end of the war but was released on May 25, 1945. He died in Bueckeburg in 1969.

56. Josef Harpe joined the army as an infantry *Fahnenjunker* in 1909 and by 1935 was commander of the 12th Cavalry Regiment. He subsequently commanded, in succession, the 3rd Panzer Regiment (1935), 1st Panzer Brigade (1939), the Panzer Troop School (1940), 12th Panzer Division (1940), XXXXI Panzer Corps (late 1942), 9th Army (November 1943) and 4th Panzer Army (May 18, 1944). Promoted to colonel general on April 1, 1944, he was relieved of the command of Army Group A (formerly North Ukraine) on January 27, 1945, after the Soviets broke out of the Bavarov bridgehead. He was given command of the 5th Panzer Army on the Western Front on March 9, 1945, and was forced to surrender to the Americans in the Ruhr Pocket in April, 1945. He was liked, respected, and highly thought of by the senior German officers, in spite of his pro-Nazi views. General Harpe held the Knight's Cross with Oak Leaves and Swords. An American prisoner until 1948, General Harpe died in Nuremberg in 1968.

57. Zaloga, *Bagration*, p. 74.

58. Mehner, vol. 10, S.V. *Tafelteil, Dislokation*, Heeresgruppe Nordukranie, 2.7.44.

59. Hannes Muehlenkamp was born in Metz (then part of Germany) on October 9, 1910, the son of a civil servant. He joined the SS in 1934 and attended the Junkerschule at Brunswick. After training with the army's 2nd Panzer Division, he returned to the SS in 1938 as a platoon leader in the motorcycle company of the Germania Regiment. He commanded a company in Poland and France, served briefly as adjutant to General of Waffen-SS Paul Hausser, and led the Das Reich Reconnaissance Battalion (later 2nd SS Panzer Reconnaissance Battalion) in Yugoslavia and Russia. He assumed command of the 5th SS Panzer Battalion in 1942 and remained its commander after it was upgraded to a regiment in 1943 (Kraetschmer, pp. 329–30).

60. Peter Strassner, *European Volunteers*, trans. David Johnston (Winnipeg: 1988), pp. 165–69.

61. Ibid., p. 169.

62. Ibid. Grossrock, who was born in Ludwigsburg, Wuerttemberg, on January 2, 1918, was awarded the Knight's Cross. He was captured (and apparently wounded) in the Hungarian campaign and died in Soviet captivity on April 5, 1945.

63. Kurt von Tippelskirch returned to duty at the end of October as deputy commander of 1st Army in France (1944). Later he served as deputy commander of 14th Army in Italy (1944–45) and as commander of the 21st Army (1945). He was briefly acting commander of Army Group Vistula (1945). General von Tippelskirch died in Lueneburg in 1957.

64. Friedrich Hossbach entered the service in 1910 and was Hitler's army adjutant until 1938, when he was dismissed for informing Colonel General Baron Werner von Fritsch, the commander in chief of the Army, that the SS and SD were conspiring to have him relieved on trumped-up charges of homosexuality. He later served as commander, 82nd Infantry Regiment (1938–39); chief of staff, XXX Corps (1939); commander of the 82nd Infantry again (1939–42); acting commander, 31st Infantry Division (1942); commander, 82nd Infantry Division (1942–43); commander, 31st Infantry Division a second time (1943); deputy commander, LVI Panzer Corps (1943); commander, LVI Panzer Corps (1943–44); and commander, 4th Army (1944–45).

65. Friebe's permanent successor, Major General Gottfried Froelich, arrived on July 21. Friebe later served as chief of staff of Wehrkreis III (September 1944–April 1945) and died in Stuttgart in 1962.

66. Richard Landwehr, *Fighting for Freedom: The Ukrainian Volunteer Division of the Waffen-SS* (Silver Spring, Md.: 1985), p. 17, citing Frank, *In the Face of the Gallows*, p. 406.

67. Nichols Bethell and the editors of Time-Life Books, *Russia Besieged* (Alexandria, Va.: 1980), p. 78.

68. Ibid., p. 83.

69. Ibid.

70. Ibid.

71. Stepan Bandera was an outspokenly patriotic Ukrainian revolutionary and anti-Communist. Certainly no Nazi and not a collaborator, he was arrested by the Gestapo in September 1941 for refusing to revoke the proclamation of June 30. He spent most of the rest of the war in the Gestapo's infamous Prince Albert Place prison or in Sachsenhausen concentration camp. Both of his brothers perished in Auschwitz. Bandera was eventually murdered a Soviet agent on October 15, 1959. Michael O. Logusz, *Galicia Division: The Waffen-SS 14th Grenadier Division, 1943–1945* (Atglen, Penn.: 1997), pp. 421–22.

72. Chant, vol. 16, p. 2178.

73. Peter Padfield, *Doenitz: The Last Fuehrer* (New York: 1984), p. 433.

74. Landwehr, *Freedom*, p. 16.

75. Koch fled East Prussia in 1945, when the Russians overran the province. He then disappeared, but someone recognized him in May 1949 and informed the British, who arrested him. He was extradited to Poland in early 1950 but was not put on trial until 1958. Sentenced to death in 1959, he was not executed; his sentence was commuted to life imprisonment on the grounds of his "poor health." He lived a comfortable life in Barczewo, Poland, until his death on November 12, 1986 (Logusz, p. 414).

76. Dr. Otto Waechter was born in Austria on July 8, 1900. His father was an Austro-Hungarian general.

77. Hitler's lawyer during the Nazi rise to power, Hans Frank (born 1900), was responsible for the murder of tens of thousands of Jews and Poles. He became disillusioned with the Nazi movement in late 1942, when the Nazis arrested and executed his close friend, Dr. Karl Lasch, the former president of the German Law Academy. When Frank angrily called for a retreat to constitutional law, Hitler stripped him of all of his Nazi Party honors and positions, though he retained him as governor general of Poland. Frank confessed his guilt at Nuremberg, denounced Hitler, and pled for mercy on the grounds of his recent conversion to Christianity. He was nevertheless executed on October 16, 1946, along with Rosenberg, Streicher, Keitel, Jodl, and several others.

78. Walter Schimana was born in Troppau, in Austrian Silesia, on March 12, 1898, the son of a German newspaper editor. He joined the Austro-Hungarian army during World War I and fought on the Eastern and Italian Fronts. He moved to Bavaria in 1919, joining the Nazi Party in 1926 and the Order Police in the early 1930s. He conducted antipartisan operations in central Russia in 1941. After he left the Galician Division, Schimana directed SS District "Danube" (Donau) and was promoted to lieutenant general of police in 1944. He was arrested by the Americans after the war and was charged with war crimes but was released when it was decided that the charges could not be proven. In 1948, however, he was informed by a former police official that the Americans were preparing to arrest and try him. Shortly thereafter, Schimana shot himself. Ironically, the information his "friend" had given him was a false rumor. No Allied action was being contemplated against Schimana at the time of his suicide. Ibid., pp. 40–42.

79. Landwehr, *Freedom*, p. 16.

80. Roger James Bender and Hugh Page Taylor, *Uniforms, Organization and History of the Waffen-SS* (Palo Alto, Calif.: 1984), vol. 4, p. 25.

81. Arthur Hauffe was born in 1891 and joined the army as an infantry *Fahnenjunker* in 1912. His duty assignments included (successively) chief of operations of Group Command III (1937), chief of staff of Frontier Guard Command Upper Rhine (1939), chief of staff of XXV Corps (1939), chief of staff of XXXVIII Panzer Corps (1940), chief of staff of the German Military Mission to Rumania (1941), commander of the 46th Infantry Division (1943), and commander of the XIII Corps (September 7, 1943).

82. A Silesian, Friedrich Schulz was born in 1897 and entered the service as a war volunteer in the artillery in 1914. He was commissioned in the 58th Infantry Regiment in 1916 and was retained in the Reichsheer after the armistice. A lieutenant colonel and an OKW staff officer when the war began, he was later chief of staff of XXXXIII Corps in France and Russia (1940–42). He later served as Manstein's chief of staff at 11th Army, Army Group Don, and Army Group South. Named commander of the 28th Jaeger (light infantry) Division in the spring of 1943, he served as acting commander of the III Panzer Corps (December 1, 1943–January 1, 1944) and acting commander of the LIX Corps (early 1944) before assuming command of the XXXXVI Panzer on March 22, 1944. He was promoted to general of infantry on April 1, 1944. Later he would command 17th Army (assumed command July 25, 1944) and Army Group South (April 2, 1945–end). He was a holder of the Knight's Cross with Oak Leaves and Swords.

83. Alex Buchner, *Ostfront, 1944* trans. David Johnson (West Chester, Penn.: 1991), p. 222.

84. Landwehr, *Freedom*, p. 68.

85. Buchner, p. 223.

86. Ibid., p. 110. Oskar Eckholt, who had been promoted to major general only a few weeks before, was so badly wounded in this battle that he never returned to active duty. A major in 1941, he had distinguished himself on the Eastern Front, commanding the IV/251st Artillery Regiment (1941), the 251st Artillery Regiment (1942), the 178th Artillery Regiment (1942–43) and the 291st Infantry Division (1944). Taken prisoner by the Americans in 1945 when they captured the Hospital for Head Injuries at Heiligenstadt, he was released in 1947 and died in Bielefeld in 1982.

87. Landwehr, *Freedom*, p. 110.

88. Logusz, pp. 230–32.

89. Von Mellenthin, pp. 342–43.

90. Logusz, p. 234.

91. Landwehr, *Freedom*, pp. 111–12.

92. Buchner, p. 231.

93. Karl Neumeister previously commanded the 1st Battalion, 5th Rifle Regiment as a major (1942) (Horst Scheibert, *Die Traeger des deutschen Kreuzes in Gold: Das Heer* [Friedburg: n.d.], p. 263).

94. Buchner, p. 231; Logusz, pp. 326–37.

95. Gottfried Froelich had previously commanded the 8th Panzer Division (September, 1943–March 31, 1944) but had fallen sick, and had just recovered from his illness. He led the 8th Panzer until January 5, 1945, when he was relieved of his command due to lack of aggressiveness during the Hungarian campaign. Unemployed for ten weeks, he was given command of Corps Group von Tettau in March 1945 and ended the war as Higher Artillery Commander, 3rd Panzer Army. He had previously commanded the II/76th Artillery Regiment (1938–39) and the 78th Panzer Artillery Regiment (late 1939–43), and was acting commander of the 36th Infantry Division (August–September 1943). He was never promoted to lieutenant general. He died in Heidenheim in 1959.

96. Logusz, p. 240.

97. Ibid., pp. 240–41.

98. Ibid., pp. 243–46.

99. Ibid., pp. 252–53.

100. Buchner, p. 233.

101. Johannes Nedtwig and Gerhard Lindemann were released from Soviet prisons in 1955. Lindemann returned to his home town of Verden, but Nedtwig's native Pomerania was now in East Germany. He settled in the Rhineland.

102. Buchner, p. 234.

103. Ibid., p. 236.

104. Mark C. Yeager, *Waffen-SS Commanders* (Atolen, Penn.: 1997), vol. 1, p. 181.

CHAPTER III

Stabilizing
the Front

THE BATTLES IN POLAND AND THE BEGINNING OF THE
WARSAW UPRISING

While the XIII Corps was being slaughtered at Brody, General Harpe's 4th Panzer Army, with its twelve understrength divisions, was under attack from thirty-four Soviet rifle divisions, backed by two mechanized corps and two tank corps. The Reds also had ten rifle divisions and two cavalry corps in reserve. Harpe had only twenty operational panzers and 150 assault guns against more than five hundred Russian tanks. After gaining ground slowly for several days, Russian tanks finally broke through the 4th Panzer at Chelm on the morning of July 22 and covered the forty miles to Lublin by the following morning. Stalin lost no time, and installed a puppet Communist government under Boleslaw Bierut at Lublin as soon as the city was secure.

Farther south, the Soviet 28th, 11th, and 70th Armies struck the fortress of Brest-Litovsk on July 27. It was defended by its garrison and a weak combat group under Lieutenant General Walter Scheller, the commandant. The garrison was overwhelmed. General Scheller, the former commander of the 9th Panzer Division, was killed on July 27.[1] The last pockets of resistance in the fortress surrendered the next day.

After the fall of Brest-Litovsk, the Soviet juggernaut began to slow down. Model had by now received considerable reinforcements from the Reich, and the Russians were at last experiencing supply problems; their forward armored units were running out of gasoline. They had also outrun their air support. Still, the fortified city of Przemysl fell to the 1st and 3rd Guards Tank Armies on July 27, and Lvov fell that night, but only after most of both garrisons had escaped. The 1st Panzer Army fell back to the southwest, toward the Carpathians, relatively unmolested. The 4th Panzer Army, meanwhile, retreated behind the Vistula and beat back several Russian attempts to pursue it across the river. Field Marshal Model made the task much easier for both panzer armies: without consulting Hitler or OKH, he ordered his armies to conduct immediate withdrawals into Poland and to abandon all "fortresses" in the process.

A rebuilt Headquarters, 9th Army, returned to the battle at the end of July, with orders to defend Warsaw, hold Siedlce, and keep an escape route open to the west for 2nd Army, which was retreating from Brest. This the 9th Army was able to do, although it could not prevent the Russians from establishing two major bridgeheads across the Vistula: one south of Pulawy and the other at Magnuszew, thirty-five miles south of the Polish capital. At the same time, however, the reconstituted 17th Army (now under General of Infantry Friedrich Schulz) filled the gap between the 4th Army and 1st Panzer Army with two and a half fresh divisions.[2] Map 3.1 shows the situation in the zone of the 9th Army and Army Group South Ukraine in the summer and fall of 1944.

The German garrison, police, civil administration, and civilians began to leave Warsaw on July 21. Guderian stopped this evacuation on July 26 and ordered the military units to return to the city. Civil and police authorities followed them back to the Polish capital. On July 27, General Stahel, of Vilnius fame, took over the military command of Warsaw. Guard units were reinforced, assault guns were prominently placed at major street intersections, police and AFV patrols increased, and elements of the 73rd Infantry Division were sent to the outskirts of the city.[3]

Stahel's forces included the 4th Grenadier Regiment; the Warsaw Alarm Regiment (controlling the former 301st, 304th, and 307th Police Battalions); the 996th, 997th, and 998th Landesschuetzen Battalions,[4] the 225th Field Administrative Command Grenadier Company, the 146th Motorized Field Military Police Company, the 146th Construction Engineer Battalion, the 475th Tank Destroyer Company, and the 2nd Company, 743rd Anti-Tank Battalion. Also in Warsaw (but not under Stahel's control) were a dozen SS and police battalions under SS Lieutenant General Geibel.[5]

During the night of July 28–29, the XXXIX Panzer Corps clashed indecisively with the vanguards of the Soviet 2nd Tank Army at Wolomin. The sounds of the battle were audible in Warsaw.[6] The following day (July 29), the Russians penetrated the front of the 73rd Infantry Division south of the city (on the east bank of the Vistula) and captured its commander, Lieutenant General Dr. Fritz Franek.[7] Meanwhile, inside the city, the Poles were anxious to end five years of Nazi rule, and they were egged on by Radio Moscow, which called upon them to rebel and help the Red Army by fighting the Wehrmacht in the streets. Shooting broke out in the city on the last day of July, and on August 1 the Polish Home Army (the Armia Krajowa, or AK) staged a full-scale revolt. Led by Cavalry Lieutenant General Tadeusz Komorowski (who went by the codename "Bor"), the Home

Map 3.1
Army Group North Ukraine and 9th Army, July 14–September 15, 1944

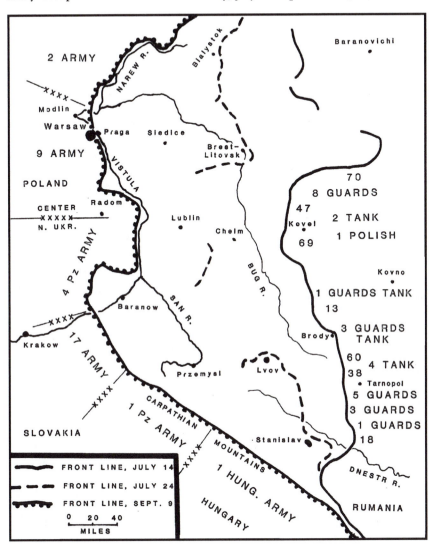

Army commander, and Major General Anton Chrusciel (codenamed "Monter"), who directed tactical operations in Warsaw, it was a well-trained, well-led, and poorly armed force of forty-four thousand men and women.

The Home Army forces inside Warsaw outnumbered the approximately sixteen-thousand-man German garrison almost three to one, but no more than 6 percent of the Poles had weapons. (Some sources put the figure as low as 4 percent.) Their arsenal consisted of machine guns, rifles, handguns, and homemade hand grenades. Their predominant antitank weapon was the Molotov cocktail, which consisted of a bottle filled with gasoline or some other explosive fuel, with a burning rag for a fuse. (Incidentally, they are not nearly as effective in reality as modern-day moviemakers think they are. Normally, it took eleven to thirteen Molotov cocktails to destroy a tank—always assuming that the weapon did not explode prematurely and immolate the attacker.) Of the more than 380,000 AK members nationwide, only thirty-two thousand were armed, and less than five thousand of these were in Warsaw. Nevertheless, they attacked with great enthusiasm and captured more than fifty square miles of territory by nightfall.

The Home Army was aided by veteran Jewish fighters from the Warsaw ghetto, which had been razed in May 1943. Remarkably, some of these freedom fighters from the leftish ZOB (Zhydowska Organizacja Bojowa, or Jewish Fighting Organization) and the more conservative ZZW (Zhydowski Zwiazeh Wojkowy, or Zionist Military Union) had so far survived the Nazi Holocaust, and now they emerged from ruined basements and sewers to join the battle. Despite their undeniable skill, they had been lucky to have lived through the first uprising; most of them would not survive the second. Hersh Berlinski, the commander of the ZZW, for example, would soon fall in battle.[8]

When night fell on August 1, most of the rebels were euphoric. Their flag flew atop the sixteen-story Prudential Building (the tallest in Warsaw) and several historic sites. Bor-Komorowski and Chrusciel, however, were less excited than their followers, because they suspected the truth: the Germans had been tipped off about the revolt. Too many important places had been converted into strongpoints and still held out, although many of them were now surrounded by the insurgents. The main police stations, for example, were still in German hands, as was the citadel, the parliament building, and the Bruehl Palace, which housed General Stahel and Governor Ludwig Fischer, the head of the Nazi civil administration. Worse still, all four Vistula River bridges—vital to any linkup with the Russians—remained in German hands, and Model's panzers had crushed the revolt east of the river (in the suburbs of Praga and Saska-Kepa) within five hours.

Model did, in fact, have prior knowledge of the uprising. He did not have the time or the resources to flood the city with troops, but he did have time to reinforce the key points. Worse still, he had time to warn the *Soldaten*. The element of surprise, so critical to rebel victory, was absent on August 1.

A cold rain began to fall on August 2, but the AK continued to attack. They managed to capture the main post office and the gas and electrical plants, but the other key positions—including all of the vital bridges—remained in the hands of the Wehrmacht. In addition to their myriad of other problems, Bor and Chrusciel were plagued by the fact that well-meaning but untrained Polish civilians often joined their trained soldiers and frequently wasted precious resources because they were ignorant of how to use them. Bor-Komorowski commented later that these civilians would acquire German weapons and "would waste a hail of bullets and hand grenades on a single German soldier. Every one of the early reports I received complained about the great waste of ammunition."[9]

On the morning of August 3, Chrusciel admitted that his limited offensive capital had been spent, and the AK went over to the defensive. The freedom fighters barricaded the streets with anything at hand, set up a military infrastructure (including field hospitals and post offices), and awaited the Germans or Russians, whoever came first.

It would be the Germans. Joseph Stalin, the Soviet dictator, had no desire for a noncommunist Poland. The Home Army had, in fact, given him an opportunity to get rid of the non-Bolshevik Poles without having to do it himself. (Not that he was unwilling to do it himself—in 1940, he had murdered more than fourteen thousand Polish officers, intellectuals, and civilian leaders in the Katyn Forest alone. This time, however, he could let the Germans do it.) On August 1, all Soviet offensive activity in the Warsaw area suddenly ceased, although it continued north and south of the city.

On the evening of August 1, the General Gouvernement signaled Army Group Center and asked it to crush the rebellion. Field Marshal Model curtly refused, stating: "This revolt is the result of the corruption and false treatment of the Polish population [by the Nazis]. My soldiers are too good for that!"[10] Model knew that he could get away with this piece of affrontry, because Hitler was already praising him as "the savior of the Eastern Front."[11] General von Vormann, the commander of the 9th Army, also refused to intervene any further, in spite of the fact that the rebellion was taking place just behind his front.[12] Hitler, predictably, was furious about the rebellion. Since Model had made his attitude clear beyond any shadow of a doubt, the Nazi dictator ordered Reichsfuehrer-SS Heinrich Himmler, his chief of security, to put down the revolt and destroy Warsaw completely. Himmler turned the operation over to SS-Obergruppenfuehrer (General of SS) Erich von dem Bach-Zelewski, his antiguerrilla expert.[13] Police and SS Lieutenant General Heinz Reinefarth was hurriedly dispatched to Warsaw with a mixed SS/police brigade; SS-Brigadefuehrer Bronislav Kaminsky was summoned with his RONA (Russian National Liberation Army) brigade, and SS Colonel Oskar Dirlewanger was called forward with his brigade of thugs and common criminals. Heinz Guderian and OKH also contributed, sending the 608th Security Regiment (Colonel Schmidt) to Warsaw.[14] The Dirlewanger Brigade (also known as SS Penal Brigade Dirlewanger, and as SS Assault Brigade Dirlewanger) went into action of August 5, though it concentrated more on raping, drinking, and shooting unarmed civilians than on fighting the Polish Home Army.

Meanwhile, back at the front, Model deployed four armies to defend central and northern Poland, East Prussia, and Lithuania. To the south, the 9th Army under Nicolaus von Vormann had been inserted between Army Group North Ukraine and 2nd Army. It defended the Warsaw sector. North of the 9th Army lay Colonel General Walter Weiss's 2nd Army. The only major Army Group Center force to survive Operation Bagration intact, it was charged with defending Bialystok and conducting a fighting withdrawal from the Pinsk-Slomin area. On Weiss's left flank lay Hossbach's 4th Army, which held the line west of Grodno. Reinhardt's 3rd Panzer Army, on the northern flank, screened East Prussia and held positions east of Vilna.

As his front line units either held their positions or withdrew very slowly. Model was at last receiving reinforcements in numbers large enough to make a difference. The 9th Army, for example, was given the 3rd SS Panzer Division "Totenkopf," the 5th SS Panzer Division "Viking," the battered 19th Panzer Division, part of the 542nd Volksgrenadier Division, the 1st Hungarian Cavalry Division, the recently rebuilt 73rd Infantry Division, the 302nd Panzer Battalion, and the Staffs, 1st Hungarian Reserve Corps and 391st Security Division. Army Group Center was also given the Headquarters, IV SS Panzer Corps when it was activated on August 10.

Despite the German reinforcements, the Russians forged ahead. They broke through 2nd Army's front on July 19, pushed back the 9th Army, and crossed the Bug near Cholm on July 22. The Viking SS Division launched several successful counterattacks and slowed them down considerably but suffered heavy losses in the process. On August 2, the Red Army pushed a large part of the Viking back against the Bug near Slezany, where there was neither bridge nor ford. The Vikings managed to escape, but only after blowing up all of their vehicles, including six panzers and two assault guns.[15]

Meanwhile, Field Marshall Model had been conserving his strength, waiting for the moment when Stalin's divisions had advanced too far and overextended themselves. At the beginning of August, he sensed that his moment had come. The Russians had gained 450 miles (720 kilometers) since June 22 and had advanced as far as Memel and the Vistula; clearly they were experiencing logistical difficulties. Many of them were also exhausted, and they had outrun their air support. Model, on the other hand, had now been reinforced by several new units, including the elite Grossdeutschland Panzer Grenadier Division and most of the grenadier divisions of Wave 29.

The German Home Army and its *Wehrkreise* (military districts) had performed brilliantly, as usual, in spite of the disruptions connected with July 20. Four shadow divisions (Wave 28) had been formed in early July but were quickly absorbed by the fifteen divisions of the 29th Wave. These divisions, numbered 541 to 553 and 558 to 562, were initially called *Sperr-*

Divisionen (blocking divisions) but were soon redesignated grenadier and then *Volksgrenadier* ("People's grenadier") divisions. The new VG divisions were looked upon almost exclusively as defensive units by OKW and OKH, so it took only six to eight weeks to train their soldiers and organize the divisions. Each division had three grenadier regiments of two battalions each (as opposed to three in most earlier divisions). Each battalion had three companies (as opposed to four in earlier days), but they were well equipped with machine pistols (called "burp guns"), and there was also a support company of medium machine guns and mortars. The division's antitank company was armed with short-range, hollow-charged weapons called *Panzerschreck*; the heavier antitank guns and assault guns were absent. (Pre-1944 divisions usually had an antitank battalion, which was often equipped with assault guns.) The Volksgrenadier divisions had fusilier companies instead of reconnaissance battalions, normally mounted on bicycles. The artillery regiment had an establishment of thirty-two guns, as opposed to forty-five in regular infantry divisions. In all, at full establishment, the new VG divisions had ten thousand men, as opposed to seventeen thousand in the old-style (Type 1939) infantry divisions and twelve thousand in the new type (n.A. 44) divisions.[16] Most of the Volksgrenadier divisions, however, never received ten thousand men; their average strength was six to eight thousand men.

The new divisions began forming on July 18 and were on their way to the front twelve days later. Of these units, Army Group Center received the 541st, 542nd, 543rd, 546th, 547th, 548th, 549th, 551st, 552nd, 558th, 561st, and 562nd Grenadier Divisions, which were upgraded to Volksgrenadier divisions in August.[17]

Model quickly put his reinforcements to good use. On August 2, he struck the III Russian Tank Corps near Wolomin (northeast of Praga) with the Hermann Goering, 4th Panzer, 19th Panzer, and 3rd SS Panzer Divisions and part of the 5th SS Panzer. The overall battle was directed by Dietrich von Saucken and the Staff, XXXIX Panzer Corps; however, Model led the way himself, riding into action at the head of the 4th Panzer Division. By August 4, III Tank Corps had been encircled. By the time the pocket was cleared on August 11, the Reds had lost hundreds of tanks and AFVs, three thousand men killed, and six thousand captured.[18] Model then retook Praga and pushed the Red vanguards back about thirty miles. At the same time, on August 3, the Hermann Goering and 19th Panzer Divisions began a series of counterattacks aimed at reducing and sealing off the Russian 2nd Tank Army's bridgehead at Magnuszew. These operations were successfully completed on August 16, killing or capturing several thousand more Russians.

Following this serious setback, the Russians tried to break through in the Grabie-Klembov sector, east-northeast of Warsaw, where they attacked the depleted 3rd SS Panzer Division "Totenkopf" on August 19, 1944. They struck from south to north, and their objective was clear: roll up the flank of the IV SS Panzer Corps, in order to encircle and destroy it, along with the Army's XX Corps.

The battle was three days of uninterrupted fury. After a five-hour artillery barrage, the Russians attacked with eight rifle divisions, a motorized rifle brigade, and elements of a tank corps, all supported by strong air forces. The tough and brutal Death's Head Division's commander, SS-Oberfuehrer Hellmuth Becker, was a former concentration camp guard and one of the more unsavory SS commanders—he had once ridden a horse to death inside an officers' club while members of his staff fornicated with French whores on the tables and floors—but he knew how to handle himself during a battlefield crisis.[19] He mobilized his last clerk-typist and supply-wagon driver and personally led them into action. Becker himself always seemed to be at the focal point of the fighting, inspiring his men with his calmness and bravery. The Russians continued to attack for eight days, but the worst was over on August 21. When the Soviets finally retreated, they left behind ninety burned-out tanks, and the field was littered with dead.[20]

The SS Viking Division, on the left (northern) flank of the 3rd SS, was also attacked on August 19, but it also held its positions. On the Viking's left flank, however, at the seam connecting the 9th and 2nd Armies, Soviet tanks managed to break through General of Artillery Baron Rudolf von Roman's XX Corps. SS Colonel Hannes Muehlenkamp, the acting commander of the division since August 10, quickly pulled back the I and II/10th SS Panzer Grenadier Regiment "Westland" and committed his former regiment, the 5th SS Panzer, to the counterattack, while General Weiss rushed Colonel Wilhelm Soeth's 1131st Grenadier Brigade into the battle.[21] A fierce struggle developed around the village of Malopole, which changed hands three times on August 22 alone. By evening, however, the Germans had prevailed.

The Soviets regrouped on August 23 and, supported by the fire of 150 batteries, struck again on August 24. The next day, they managed to penetrate the 1131st Grenadier Brigade in several places. The Vikings counterattacked on August 26, but a lucky Russian shell blew up the Bug River bridge at Czarnow, isolating the I/5th SS Panzer Regiment on the wrong side of the river. The battalion only had a dozen tanks left. SS Captain Rudolf Saeumenicht and his men defended their isolated bridgehead to the last shell. They knocked out twelve Shermans and T-34s on August 25 alone, and several others on August 26, but the defense began to fall apart after Captain Saeumenicht was killed while leading a counterattack. The surviving Vikings retreated to the downed bridge, blew up their panzers and other remaining vehicles, and scrambled across the wreckage to safety.[22]

By August 28, the front in Poland was more or less stabilized (see Map 3.2). Static, positional warfare became the order of the day and would remain so until January. The fact that the Russians had finally been stopped was gratifying to the German *feldgrau* (i.e., "field gray," the German companion in misfortune with the British Tommy and the American G.I.), whose morale, generally speaking, had remained remarkably high. His generals were less sanguine. They were cognizant of the fact that the Soviets had gained more than four hundred miles (the distance from Orsha to Warsaw) and now stood only 350 miles from Berlin. They also knew that, coupled with its defeats in Italy and the West, the Wehrmacht had lost 916,860 men between June 1 and August 30.[23]

Although the major offensive for 1944 was over in the central sector of the Eastern Front, the fighting was not yet finished. Army Group Center had two more major tasks to accomplish before it could rest: (1) it had to restore contact with Army Group North, and (2) it had to put down the Polish revolt in Warsaw. The first mission had absolute priority over the second.

At the beginning of August 1944, Army Group North was on the verge of collapse. It was badly outnumbered and outgunned by the Russians, it had been under almost constant attack since June, and it was very low in supplies of every type (see chapter 4). Due to the critical situation on 18th Army's front, Army Group Center began its relief attack in considerable haste on August 16, two days ahead of schedule. Neither of the two panzer corps taking part in the operation was completely assembled. Shortly after it jumped off, 3rd Panzer Army was attacked on the right flank by 5th, 33rd, and 11th Guards Armies, which pushed it back and retook Vilkavishkis. During the day, Model was transferred to the Western Front. Hans Reinhardt took charge of the army group, Erhard Raus (who had been promoted to colonel general the day before) replaced him as commander of 3rd Panzer Army, and Colonel General Gotthard Heinrici (the former commander of 4th Army, who had just returned from sick leave) succeeded Raus as commander of the 1st Panzer Army. General of Infantry Friedrich Hossbach, who had been acting commander of 4th Army since July 19, now filled that post on a permanent basis. Model carried his chief of staff to the West with him. Like Model, Reinhardt brought his own chief of staff, General Heidkaemper, with him from 3rd Panzer Army. On September 1, after the relief operation was over, Raus named Colonel Burkhart Mueller-Hillebrand, the former chief of the Organizations Branch at OKH and a highly capable officer, as the new chief of staff of 3rd Panzer Army.

Meanwhile, on August 17, the Soviet offensive, directed by Chernyakovskiy's 3rd Belorussian Front, continued to push back the right flank of 3rd Panzer Army until it reached the East Prussian border northwest of Vil-

Map 3.2
Situation, Eastern Front, August 23, 1944

kavishkis. One detachment actually crossed the East Prussian border and thus carried the ground war into the Third Reich for the first time, however, it was wiped out before the day was over.

Even though the situation on his right flank was serious, Raus continued to push his spearheads north, toward General Schoerner's trapped army group (see chapter 4 for the details of this battle.) On August 20, Raus reached Tukums and made contact with the southern wing of Army Group North. On Guderian's orders, two of 3rd Panzer Army's tank brigades immediately rushed to Riga, where they were put aboard trains and rushed to the front below Lake Peipus, where the 18th Army was wavering. The next day, after Raus had consolidated his gains, a major truck column headed north from East Prussia, carrying critically needed supplies to Army Group North.

Reinhardt now believed that Schoerner's two armies should be withdrawn to the south, where they would soon be desperately needed for the defense of the Reich. Guderian agreed, but the Fuehrer refused to abandon his hold on the Baltic States, for political reasons; instead, he ordered Reinhardt to continue the offensive. When the fighting ended on August 27, the corridor from Germany to Army Group North was still only eighteen miles wide and quite tenuous. Even so, Hitler reinforced Schoerner with another panzer division.

In the meantime, the Warsaw insurgents were crushed.

Both Stalin and Army Group Center looked upon this operation with distaste. Stalin did not want to help the rebels because they were non-Communists or anti-Communists and would not be willing puppets of Moscow. He, therefore, would not give them the slightest assistance and even refused to allow the Americans to use Soviet airfields in efforts to supply the Poles until the insurgency was doomed. The Soviets would not even fire on German airplanes as they dive-bombed Polish-held sectors of the city, even though the Stuka dive-bombers were well within the range of their antiaircraft batteries. When the Luftwaffe aviators realized that the Russians were not going to fire on them, they took to flying over Soviet lines as they made bombing runs on Polish positions.

Hitler and Himmler were initially delighted that the rebellion had broken out, because it gave them the opportunity to destroy the capital of a hated enemy and would provide an excellent object lesson for other occupied countries. The German Army, on the other hand, did not want to commit its already depleted units to house-to-house fighting. Himmler therefore turned the operation over to sadistic SS General Erich von dem Bach-Zelewski and SS Lieutenant General Heinz Reinefarth. Their forces included police units, the Kaminsky Brigade, the Dirlewanger Brigade, and several smaller, oddball paramilitary units. (The army initially supported these forces with a few artillery and rocket launcher units only.) The result was a battle of extreme viciousness in which the insurgents put up a stiff and prolonged resistance against the amateur police and mercenary tacticians, many of whom were not particularly interested in fighting. A good example is the Kaminsky Brigade.

THE KAMINSKY BRIGADE

The Kaminsky Brigade was one of the strangest units formed during World War II. It was initially organized in the Lokot district of the Soviet Union, between Orel and Kursk, thanks to the efforts of Colonel General Rudolf Schmidt, commander of the 2nd Panzer Army. Schmidt felt that a largely self-governing native population in Russia would police itself, fight Soviet partisans, and provide the Wehrmacht with supplies (especially food), while at the same time allowing the German Army to economize its manpower. Perhaps because Hitler had a high opinion of Schmidt in 1941, the general was allowed to conduct his experiment, in spite of Nazi racial theory, which held that Russians and all Slavs were *Untermenschen*.[24] The district was placed under the control of Mayor Ivan K. Voskoboinikov of Lokot, who was also chief of police. The district itself was predominantly agricultural and unremarkable; its only industry seems to have been its liquor distillery. Schmidt's experiment was nevertheless a complete success. When Voskoboinikov was killed by a special Soviet assassination team on January 8, 1942, he was succeeded by Bronislav Vladislavovich Kaminsky. He promptly assumed the rank of *Kombrig* (brigade commander) and *Oberburgomeister*.[25]

Kaminsky's father was a Pole who reportedly married a girl of *Volksdeutsche* (ethnic German) ancestry. He owned an estate in the Vitebsk area and did quite well until the Bolsheviks took over in 1918 and outlawed private agriculture. He nevertheless provided a good education for his son. Bronislav, who was born in St. Petersburg in 1923, was fluent in Russian, Polish, and German. A chemical engineer by profession, he ran afoul of the Bolsheviks in 1935, spent the next five years in a forced labor camp, and then was ordered by the government to settle in Lokot. He was an engineer at the liquor distillery when the war began.

Kaminsky was given all but a free hand in the administration of the Lokot district, and his performance exceeded German expectations. When it came to producing grain, for example, his peasants exceeded their quota. They also suppressed the partisan movement so effectively that the Germans—apparently with the approval of Field Marshal Guenther von Kluge, the commander in chief of Army Group Center—extended Kaminsky's jurisdiction into neighboring areas, which the partisans had taken over. Kaminsky was so successful that when he demanded the tax burden of his subjects be lightened because they were producing more rye than anyone else, both Kluge and the SS approved. Except for a small liaison group and an occasional inspection team, the Germans virtually withdrew from Lokot and let Kaminsky run his district. Kaminsky went so far as to declare Lokot a National Socialist Republic in 1943. Although it would be unwise to draw far-reaching conclusions based on the results achieved in just one district, Lokot's performance does make one wonder what would the result have been had Schmidt's experiment been adopted throughout the entire occupied area of the former Soviet Union. Conceivably it could have radically affected the entire course and even the outcome of the war.

Kaminsky was never a traditional disciplinarian. His "brigade" lived well, ate well, drank much, and partied often. Kaminsky himself lived like a king in the former estate of Grand Duke Michael Romanov, where he held many celebrations and gala performances. Since his first wife was behind Soviet lines, Kaminsky simply forgot about her and remarried; the thought of being faithful apparently never crossed his mind. When they were not fighting partisans or farming, the men of the brigade engaged in dances, parties, and drunken orgies. They were like a mercenary horde from the Thirty Years' War. The brigade orchestra alone contained more than a hundred men. The entire district remains like one of the military settlements of earlier centuries. Because so many of the district's peasants were also part-time soldiers and members of the brigade, the system worked very well. Kaminsky abolished the collective farm system, gave the peasants their own land, and protected them from the partisans. His popularity in the district was very high, and the peasants were willing to pay his taxes (usually a portion of their grain), in part because they knew Nazi or Soviet levies would have been much higher.

Acting upon a German suggestion, Kaminsky gave married soldiers higher pay than single men. As a result, the adventurers who gravitated to the Kaminsky Brigade from other parts of occupied Russia often married local women, further cementing the relationship between the brigade and the local community.

The Lokot experiment ended in August 1943, when the Red Army reentered the district. As the Soviets neared Lokot, Kaminsky evacuated the area, carrying with him about six thousand "soldiers" and twenty-five thousand civilians. One observer stated that the brigade looked like a circus. It drifted westward, raping, marauding, and looting as it went. Ziemke compared it to a sixteenth or seventeenth-century mercenary band, and it acted much like one.[26] The Germans gave Kaminsky the Lepel district of Belorussia, which was thoroughly infested with partisans. Unlike those in Lokot, however, the residents of the new district were universally hostile, looking upon the Kaminskies as outsiders. For their part, Kaminsky and his men made no attempt to win them over. Soon the brigade was able to control only the major towns, and the countryside belonged to the guerillas. In January 1944, it fought two partisan brigades near Lukomi and was severely beaten. Only the artillery battalion escaped undamaged; Kaminsky's 5th Regiment and armored battalion were smashed. Because of the brigade's outrageous behavior and military failure, General Reinhardt, then the commander of the 3rd Panzer Army, intervened in the district. Kaminsky protested loudly against Wehrmacht interference, but Reinhardt's liaison officer responded only with contempt. As a result, Kaminsky transferred his allegiance to the SS, which was initially happy to have him. Himmler had him flown to East Prussia, decorated him with the Iron Cross, First Class, promoted him to SS-Brigadefuehrer (SS major general), and redesignated his unit the 29 SS Waffen-Grenadier-Division (Russische Nr. 1).

Now that they were under the protection of the Reichsfuehrer-SS, the behavior of Kaminsky and his men became even more unrestrained. They raped, pillaged, burned, looted, and murdered almost at will. Entire villages were put to the torch and their inhabitants wiped out. The Kaminskies seized carts, wagons, and horses without compensating their owners and shot anyone who protested. When they took villages in partisan areas, they often herded the entire population into a nearby church or school and then set it on fire, shooting anyone who attempted to escape. Sometimes they shot children and threw their bodies into the local well, adding pollution to murder.

In July 1944, after Army Group Center collapsed, the Kaminsky Brigade fell back to the west, leaving former Soviet territory for Poland. German Army Major O. W. Mueller, the liaison officer between Army Group Center and Rosenberg's Eastern Ministry, suggested that this would not work. "To what extent this rather depraved group, which moves across the countryside stealing and plundering, without concern for anything, can be made to settle in the General Government [Poland] and fight against the partisans, cannot as yet be judged," he reported.[27]

Initially, the 29th SS Division was sent to Sokoow, a district east of Warsaw. It was then decided to send it to Hungary. It was on trains heading for Uzhhorod, near the border of Hungary and Carpathorussia, when the Slovak military mutiny broke out on September 5, 1944 (see chapter 7). Left on the railroad sidings, the men refused to give up their boxcars, which the German railway officials demanded back and desperately needed. They slaughtered their cattle and, when these rations ran out, took to indiscriminately robbing both German and Polish residents. The Gauleiter of Upper Silesia put an end to the situation by threatening to court-martial and shoot the SS liaison officers attached to the division if they did not immediately remove it from his province.

Meanwhile, the Polish Home Army had revolted in Warsaw. The 29th SS was posted to the area but proved so demoralized and reluctant to fight that Kaminsky sent only a regiment-sized battle group to the combat zone.

It was composed mainly of his lowest-quality soldiers, his disciplinary problems and unmarried men. In all, Kaminsky sent 1,700 of his four to five thousand combatants, as well as four captured T-34 tanks, a Soviet SU-76 assault gun, and two 122 mm guns.[28] This force, according to Dallin, "now shed the last vestiges of discipline and inhibition." The result was an orgy of rape, murder, plundering, and theft. "They returned loaded with golden watches, bracelets, even gold teeth," one witness recalled.[29] Another recalled, "There were savage orgies there [in Warsaw]. They raped nuns and plundered and stole anything they could get their fingers on. Some returned from Warsaw with five kilograms of gold. It was the most shameful episode I know of."[30] In one particularly disgusting atrocity, some of Kaminsky's barbarians entered a hospital for female cancer patients. They raped patients and staff alike and killed or savagely beat anyone who resisted.[31]

Kaminsky himself was slightly wounded in the battle but otherwise did not distinguish himself in any positive way. He refused to discipline his men or to try to exert any control over them whatsoever. At one point during the battle he was seen sitting on a balcony, drinking champagne, with a girl on each knee.[32] Neither was his current wife. He also sent three boxcars of loot to Stettin, where his civilian elements and one of his wives were now located. Kaminsky in particular refused to obey orders that did not suit him and, like his indifferently equipped and demoralized men, would not submit to any kind of discipline whatsoever. The men of the unit were notably less enthusiastic about fighting armed Poles than they were in stealing, raping, and murdering, and the behavior of the "brigade" was so outrageous that it alienated the Poles, the Wehrmacht, and even the SS. Worse still, it intensified Polish resistance. Even the brutal Bach-Zelewski was repelled by its behavior. Rittmeister (captain of cavalry) Scheidt filed an affidavit at Nuremberg stating that SS-Obergruppenfuehrer Hermann Fegelein, the SS liaison officer to the Fuehrer, told Generals Guderian and Alfred Jodl (the chief of operations of the High Command of the Armed Forces) of the atrocities committed by the Kaminsky Brigade, and Jodl took the matter to Hitler himself. Ten minutes later, Hitler ordered that the brigade be dissolved. Kaminsky himself was sent to Lodz (Litzmannstadt), obstensibly to attend an SS leadership course, but instead he was arrested on Bach's orders in connection with a truckload of stolen jewelry and other valuables that he was trying to get out of Warsaw. He was apparently taken to Lodz, where the Gestapo executed him without trial on Bach's orders. He was temporarily succeeded by a Colonel Belai. The brigade was purged and dissolved. Most of its survivors ended up in the Vlasov movement, an anti-Communist force made up largely of former Soviet prisoners-of-war and led by General Andrei A. Vlasov, formerly one of Stalin's generals. Like Vlasov, most of them were executed by the Soviets after the war.

CRUSHING THE WARSAW UPRISING

The Dirlewanger Brigade was no better than that of Kaminsky. It was led by SS Colonel Oscar Dirlewanger, a sexually perverted drunkard who enjoyed performing unnatural acts with the dead bodies of his victims, especially the younger ones. He had once been expelled from the SS for drunkenness and moral offenses but had wormed his way back into the Reichsfuehrer's good graces. Except for a few officers and a very few men, the troops of this brigade were former concentration-camp inmates. Some of them were communists, and others were political prisoners, but the great majority were thugs and common criminals. Most of the men were as brutal as their commander, who had committed dozens of atrocities and had escaped more than one court-martial only because he enjoyed Himmler's protection. One of its first acts in "suppressing the rebellion" was to gun down dozens of innocent men, women, and children in the Wola and Ochota sections of Warsaw on August 5 and 6. The Dirlewanger and Kaminsky Brigades were much less successful against men and women who were capable of defending themselves, and the battle dragged on much longer than was necessary.

On August 5, Police and SS General Reinefarth began an offensive that presented the first serious threat to the uprising. Supported by elements of the Luftwaffe's elite Hermann Goering Parachute Panzer Division, he began clearing a block at a time, building by building, killing civilians and soldiers alike. Then he moved on to the next block. At the end of the first day he reported that he had cut the defenders in half and killed ten thousand Poles. German losses were six killed and thirty-six wounded.[33]

Himmler had ordered that "every inhabitant of Warsaw is to be shot; prisoners will not be taken; the town is to be leveled."[34] It was clear that Reinefarth intended to do just that. This was too much, even for the pervert Bach. That evening, he ordered that at least women and children be spared. This order cut down on the number of atrocities committed in Warsaw, although it by no means stopped them.

Reinefarth's strategy was clear to anyone who could read a map: he intended to push from the west a little more than two miles to the Vistula bridges, opening the main west-east supply and transportation route, and freeing the governor and military commandant. Since he was supported by panzers and flamethrowers from the Hermann Goering Division, the Poles could not stop him, although they did slow him down. By August 10 Reinefarth had cut the defenders into three parts. Meanwhile, he was reinforced with new dive-bomber squadrons as well as strong battle groups from the 5th SS Panzer Division "Viking" and the 3rd SS Panzer Division "Totenkopf." He also employed remote controlled Goliath minitanks, which carried two hundred pounds of TNT; *Nebelwerfer* multiple-tube rocket launchers; and a special explosive gas called Taifun, which was used to clear sewers. Bach, meanwhile, borrowed the 122-ton "Karl," a superheavy 600 mm mortar that fired a two-ton shell, from the army.

Bach and Reinefarth next turned their attention to clearing the Old Town, which was characterized by narrow streets and ancient buildings, some of which were six centuries old. The city was, of course, completely sealed off by now, and Stalin still would not allow Allied supply airplanes to land behind his lines, even though there were now sixty operational Soviet airfields within easy flying distance of the Polish capital. Air drops by the Anglo-Americans were thus kept to a minimum. By mid-August, the Poles were very low in food and ammunition and were virtually out of medical supplies. Even drinking water was in short supply.

Increasingly, the Poles operated out of the sewers. On September 1 and 2, Bor-Komorowski and two thousand surviving AK soldiers and civilians evacuated the Old Town by wading through the sewer lines. They left behind thirty-five thousand wounded and thousands of dead. Resistance now continued only in the city center (north of the Old Town) and in the Zoliborz and Czerniakow districts to the south. Meanwhile, Stalin denounced the freedom fighters as a "handful of criminals."[35] Simultaneously, over the city, the Stukas continued to blast Warsaw; while none of the 2,400 Red Air Force aircraft within range of the city lifted a finger to intervene. Home Army soldiers on their way to Warsaw were disarmed and arrested by the Red Army. Bor Komorowski's request to establish direct contact between the AK and Marshal Konstantin Rokossovsky's 1st Belorussian Front was ignored.

On September 9, the situation had deteriorated to the point that General Komorowski sent out two delegates to negotiate the surrender of the rebels. (For once, Hitler had taken advice from General Guderian, the chief of his General Staff, and had offered the rebels regular prisoner-of-war status.) The next day, however, the Russian 47th Army attacked Colonel Kurt Haehling's weak 73rd Infantry Division, a unit that had been hastily rebuilt after being slaughtered in the Crimea.[36] No longer the reliable unit it had been before Sevastopol, it was subjected to a bombardment from 180 batteries; then it was attacked by Soviet tanks. The 73rd quickly collapsed; Colonel Haehling was replaced by Colonel Franz Schlieper, and Hitler summoned General von Vormann to Rastenburg, personally reprimanded him for the division's behavior, and stopped all leaves and promotions for the 73rd, despite the fact that it had suffered heavy losses.[37] Hitler's actions, of course, did no good: the Russians pushed the weak 9th Army back almost thirty miles. By September 13, they were back in Praga, and the next day the Germans fell back to the west bank of the river and blew up the Vistula bridges. It seemed as if the communists were about to rescue the Home Army at the last moment after all. Stalin even began to run nightly supply drops to Warsaw on September 13, no doubt to allay Western public opinion; however, since the cargos were dropped without parachutes, they were usually badly damaged when the Poles got them. The Russians also dropped ammunition to the insurgents, which made them look good to the average British or American citizen, who did not know that Russian bullets would not fit Polish weapons.

The Red Army's successes of September 9–14 gave new hope to the Polish Home Army, and the fighting resumed. The Red offensive was apparently a greater success than Stalin wanted; in any case, the Russians halted in Praga and made no attempt to rescue the insurgents. There were Poles on the Communist side as well, however, and they did make an effort.

On September 13, General Zygmunt Berling, the commander of the communist 1st Polish Army, sent his 1st Polish Infantry Division across the Vistula in an effort to rescue his embattled countrymen. Unfortunately, many of his soldiers had simply been impressed into the army when the Soviets entered Poland and were without the benefit of any military training whatsoever. They were certainly no match for the Vikings, the Death Heads or the Hermann Goerings, many of whom had spent three years on the Eastern Front. They also received absolutely no support from Marshal Rokossovsky, who was himself Polish. Apparently Berling had acted without Stalin's permission. The Polish Reds were chased back across the Vistula after suffering more than 3,700 casualties. Stalin promptly sacked Berling and several of his commanders.

Meanwhile, on the German side, it became clear that the SS units were not going to be able to suppress the revolt by themselves. Hitler relieved General von Vormann of the command of the 9th Army and replaced him with General of Panzer Troops Baron Smilo von Luettwitz,[38] who had fewer scruples about using his soldiers to put down the revolt. Luettwitz promptly committed Colonel ·Karl Britzelmayr's veteran 19th Panzer Division (a *kampfgruppe*) to the fighting. It quickly cleared the Czerniakow district by September 23. Four days later, resistance ended in the Mokotow sector. On September 29, the 19th Panzer launched a major attack on Zoliborz. All resistance there ended the next day.

On September 28, Bor-Komorowski signaled Rokossovsky that if the Soviet Army did not intervene within seventy-two hours, he would be forced to capitulate. There was no response to his message. At 8 P.M. on October 2, in an estate west of the city, he surrendered to SS General von dem Bach-Zelewski. The Warsaw Uprising—one of the most heroic episodes of World War II—was over. It had lasted sixty-three days. Even the SS had been impressed with the Poles' courage and tenacity, and the survivors were granted prisoner-of-war status. A total of 15,378 rebels marched off to the prison camps. Another twenty-two thousand lay dead in the rubble. Estimates of the number of civilians killed are all unreliable, but 200,000 to 250,000 seems to be as good a guess as we have. German casualties included ten thousand dead.[39] Since Army Group Center did not report its casualties for this battle separately, the exact numbers are not known. German equipment losses were not reported separately either, but the subsequent Polish claim that they destroyed more than three hundred panzers can be safely dismissed as a gross exaggeration.

After the battle, the Germans evacuated most of the rest of the civilians and blew up much of the rest of the city.

After the war, Stalin's secret police hunted down the remnants of the Polish Home Army, both in Warsaw and the provinces, because it was considered a threat to Communism. It was finally wiped out in 1947. Many of those captured by the Germans in 1944 chose not to return to their homeland.

With the Warsaw Uprising over and the city in ruins, something of a lull descended on the central sector of the Eastern Front. Fighting would continue, but major combat operations would not resume in this zone until 1945. In any case, since the Russian offensive stalled out on the Vistula at the end of July, the focus of the war had shifted to the Western Front, where the Wehrmacht was suffering yet another catastrophic defeat. The Anglo-American D-Day invasion was successful; they liberated Paris on August 25 and pushed to the very borders of the Reich during the first days of September. Meanwhile, in the Baltic States, Army Group North was fighting for its life.

NOTES

1. A Hanoverian infantry officer, Walter Scheller was born in 1892 and began his career as an officer cadet in 1911. After serving in World War I and the Reichsheer, he commanded the 66th Infantry Regiment (1938–39), was chief of staff of Wehrkreis X (1939–40), and commanded 8th Rifle Brigade (1940–41), 11th Panzer Division (1941–42), and the 9th Panzer Division (1942–43). He was severely wounded at the end of Operation Citadel. Not judged a successful tank division commander, Scheller was transferred back to the infantry after he recovered. He was acting commander of the 334th Infantry Division (1943), commander of the 337th Infantry Division (1943–44), and commander of Military Area Command 399 (1944). In June 1944 he was named commander of Brest-Litovsk. Haupt, p. 207; Keilig, p. 297.

2. General of Artillery Fritz Lindemann, the chief of artillery of the Replacement Army, was earmarked to command the 17th Army, but he was involved in the attempt to assassinate Hitler and had fled for his life on July 21, 1944. Eventually, he was shot by the Gestapo, captured, tried, and executed.

3. Christopher Ailsby, *SS: Hell on the Eastern Front* (Osceola, Wis.: 1998), p. 149.

4. *Landesschuetzen* units consisted of older reservists not fit for frontline service.

5. Haupt, *Center*, p. 210.

6. Ailsby, p. 149.

7. Fritz Franek was an Austrian lieutenant colonel when Hitler annexed that country in 1938. Inducted into the Wehrmacht, he commanded I/98th Motorized Infantry Regiment (1939–40), 634th Infantry Regiment (1940), 405th Infantry Regiment (1940–41), 196th Infantry Division (1942–43), and 44th Infantry Division (1944). He assumed command of the 73rd Infantry Division on June 26. Released from prison in 1948, he returned to Vienna, where he had been born in 1891 (Keilig, p. 94).

8. Wilfred P. Deac, "City Streets Contested," *World War II* 9, no. 3 (September 1994), p. 42.

9. Guderian, p. 283, citing Bor-Komorowski, *The Unconquerables* (published in *Reader's Digest*, February 1946).

10. Haupt, *Center*, p. 211.

11. Chester Wilmot, *The Struggle for Europe* (New York: 1981), pp. 265–66.

12. Haupt, *Center*, p. 211.

13. Erich von dem Bach-Zelewski was born in Lauenburg, Pomerania, in 1899. His command in Warsaw was eventually designated Corps Group von dem Bach, and he was awarded the Knight's Cross. He died on March 8, 1972.

14. Haupt, *Center*, p. 211.

15. Strassner, p. 172.

16. Seaton, *German Army* (New York: 1982; reprint ed., New York: 1982), p. 240.

17. Ibid., p. 231; Samuel W. Mitcham, Jr., *Hitler's Legions* (Briarcliff Manor, N.Y.: 1985), pp. 283–93. Some of these divisions were quickly absorbed by older divisions, but most continued to fight until the end of the war.

18. Haupt, *Center*, p. 209.

19. Helmut Becker was a protégé of Theodor Eicke, the notorious inspector of concentration camps and commandant of Dachau. Becker was born in Brandenburg in 1902, the son of a house painter, and spent twelve years as an enlisted man in the army. He joined the SS in 1933, received a commission in 1934, and transferred to the paramilitary Death's Head Regiment of concentration camp guards in 1935. He was successively company, battalion, and regimental commander in the Totenkopf (later 3rd SS Panzer) Division. The father of five children, Becker surrendered his division to the Americans in 1945, but they turned him and his men over to the Russians. Becker was executed for sabotaging a Soviet building project on February 28, 1953. His family was not notified of his death until 1973.

20. Yeager, vol. 1, pp. 74–75. Becker was awarded the Knight's Cross with Oak Leaves for this action.

21. A Valkyrie Alarm unit, the 1131st Grenadier Brigade was, in reality, a weak regiment, taken from the 542nd Volksgrenadier Division. Raised in Berlin-Spandau, it consisted of two grenadier battalions (eight companies total), an antitank company, an engineer company, and an artillery battalion of three batteries. Activated on July 27, 1944, it was assigned to Headquarters, 2nd Army. It would be dissolved in November 1944. Its commander, Wilhelm Soeth, had previously commanded the 73rd Panzer Artillery Regiment of the 1st Panzer Division. In January 1945 he was promoted to major general and given command of the 3rd Panzer Division. Georg Tessin, *Verbaende und Truppen der deutschen Wehrmacht und Waffen-SS im Zweiten Weltkireg, 1939–1945*, vol. 13 (Osnabrueck: 1976), p. 300; Keilig, p. 326.

22. Strassner, p. 176.

23. Chant, vol. 6, p. 1663.

24. Certainly Hitler had a higher opinion of Rudolf Schmidt than Schmidt had of Hitler. In the summer of 1943, the Gestapo arrested Schmidt's brother. A search of his residence uncovered several letters in which the general was highly critical of both Hitler and the Nazi Party. Schmidt was relieved on July 10, 1943, and never reemployed. A native of Berlin, Schmidt died in Krefeld in 1957. He had successively commanded the 1st Panzer Division (1937), XXXIX Panzer Corps (1940), 2nd Army (1941), and 2nd Panzer Army (late 1941).

25. The principal sources for this section are Alexander Dallin, *The Kaminsky Brigade: 1941–1944: A Case Study of German Military Exploitation of Soviet Disaffection*, Technical Research Report No. 7 (Maxwell Air Force Base, Ala.: 1952), and Antonio J. Munoz, *The Kaminski Brigade: A History, 1941–1945* (Bayside, N.Y.: 1996). Munoz in particular gives an excellent account of the brigade's anti-partisan operations 1942–43.

26. Ziemke, p. 344.

27. Dallin, pp. 44–45.

28. Munoz, pp. 40–41.

29. Dallin, p. 31.

30. Ibid., p. 129.

31. Munoz, p. 45.

32. Ibid., p. 104.

33. Deac, p. 42. Heinz-Friedrich Reinefarth was born in Gnesen, in the Posen Province of West Prussia, in 1903. An army reservist, he served in France (1940) and earned the Knight's Cross as a sergeant in the army's 337th Infantry Regiment. He was awarded the Oak Leaves for his part in crushing the Warsaw Uprising. He died in Westerland on May 7, 1979.

34. Deac, p. 42.

35. Ibid., p. 43.

36. Haupt, *Center*, p. 213. Colonel Haehling was an acting commander only. The 73rd Infantry Division's permanent commander, General Franek, had been captured earlier.

37. Ibid., p. 213.

38. Nikolaus von Vormann was named Fortress Commander, OB Southeast, in October 1944—a definite demotion. He never held another major command. Luettwitz, a holder of the Knight's Cross with Oak Leaves and Swords, had previously served as adjutant, XV Motorized Corps (1938–40); commander, 12th Rifle Regiment (1940–42); commander, 4th Rifle Brigade (1942); commander, 26th Panzer Division (1942–44); and commander, XXXXVI Panzer Corps (1944). A major in 1938, he was promoted to general of panzer troops on September 1, 1944. Later, he ran afoul of Field Marshal Schoerner, who relieved him of his command on January 20, 1945, for ordering the unauthorized evacuation of Warsaw. He was nevertheless given command of the LXXXV Corps on the Western Front on March 31, 1945, and led it until the end of the war. In the late 1950s, he was a lieutenant general (the equivalent of a U.S. three-star general in the West German Army) and commander of the III Corps of the West German Army. Luettwitz began his military career as an infantry *Fahnenjunker* in 1914. Smilo von Luettwitz was one of the best panzer officers in World War II, yet he is virtually unknown today, because almost all of his service was in the East. His more famous cousin Heinrich com-

manded the 2nd Panzer Division in Normandy and XXXXVII Panzer Corps in the Siege of Bastogne and in the Ruhr Pocket.

39. James Lucas, *The Last Year of the German Army: May 1944–May 1945* (London: 1994), p. 192.

CHAPTER IV

Into the Courland Pocket

As we have seen, Army Group Center was crushed by the huge Soviet summer offensive of 1944. On its left flank, Army Group North was also threatened with annihilation. Here the Soviets concentrated four *fronts* (army groups). From north to south (the German left to the German right), they were: the Leningrad Front (Marshal Govorov), 3rd Baltic Front (General Masslenikov), 2nd Baltic Front (General Eremenko), and 1st Baltic Front (General Bagramian). There were more than two thousand armored fighting vehicles in the Baltic fronts alone.

In all, the four fronts opposing Army Group North had at least 1,200,000 men and 2,500 tanks. Army Group North had 540,000 men and fewer than three hundred tanks and assault guns. Table 4.1 shows its order of battle on June 15, 1944.

Stalin planned for the first offensive to be launched by 1st Baltic Front. Cooperating with the 3rd Belorussian Front to the south, its job was to separate Army Group North from Army Group Center and help encircle Vitebsk. Marshal Vassilevskiy had the task of coordinating the two fronts.

The 1st Baltic Front included the 6th Guards Army, 43rd Army and I Tank Corps, supported by the 3rd Air Army. The offensive began at 3 A.M. on June 22, with a ninety-minute artillery barrage from hundreds of guns, including "Stalin organs." Then came the Russian infantry, screaming "Urrah!" and supported by dozens of fighter-bombers. Meanwhile, hundreds of other Soviet aircraft pounded the German communications zone and secondary positions.

The main target was Major General Horst von Mellenthin's 205th Infantry Division, located north of Obol, in the forests on the right flank of Army Group North, northeast of Polozk.[1] The men from Baden-Wuerttemberg fought valiantly. Despite fearful odds and the fact that the enemy had dozens of T-34 tanks, it was 6 P.M. before the Reds succeeded

Table 4.1
Order of Battle, Army Group North, June 15, 1944

ARMY GROUP NORTH:

16th Army:
I Corps:
    205 Infantry Division
    87th Infantry Division
X Corps:
    389th Infantry Division[1]
    290th Infantry Division
    263rd Infantry Division
II Corps:
    81st Infantry Division
    329th Infantry Division
    23rd Infantry Division
VI SS Corps:
    15th Waffen SS Grenadier Division (Latvian Nr. 1)
    19th Waffen SS Grenadier Division (Latvian Nr. 2)
L Corps:
    218th Infantry Division
    132nd Infantry Division
    83rd Infantry Division
Army Reserve:
    Elements, 24th Infantry Division
    69th Infantry Division
    281st Security Division
    Elements, 285th Security Division

18th Army:
XXXVIII:
    21st Luftwaffe Field Division
    32nd Infantry Division
    121st Infantry Division
XXVIII:
    30th Infantry Division
    21st Infantry Division
    212th Infantry Division
    126th Infantry Division
    12th Luftwaffe Field Division:
    300th Special Purposes Division[2]
    207th Security Division[3]
Army Reserve: none

Army Detachment Narva[4]:
XXVI Corps:
    227th Infantry Division[5]
    170th Infantry Division
    225th Infantry Division

Table 4.1 (*continued*)

Army Detachment Narva[4]:
XXXXIII Corps:
  58th Infantry Division
  11th Infantry Division
  122nd Infantry Division
III SS Panzer Corps:
  SS Panzer Grenadier Division "Nordland"
  SS Brigade "Nederlande"
  20th Waffen SS Grenadier Division (Estonian Nr. 1)
Coastal Defense Command East:
  Staff, 2nd Flak Division
  Elements, 2nd Flak Division
  5 Estonian battalions
Coastal Defense Command West:
  285th Security Division[1]
  4 Estonian battalions
Army Detachment Reserve:
  61st Infantry Division

Army Group North Reserve:
Field Training Division North
Elements, 12th Panzer Division

Notes:
[1]Minus major elements
[2]Controlled 1st and 4th Estonian Border Guards Regiments
[3]Controlled 5th Estonian Border Guards Regiment
[4]Formerly Headquarters, LIV Corps
[5]With 2nd and 3rd Estonian Border Guards Regiments attached

Source: Mehner, ed., *Geheimen Tagesberichte*, vol. 10, pp. 502–503.

in breaking contact between Mellenthin and Lieutenant General Walter Melzer's 252nd Infantry Division on the left flank of Army Group Center. But break through the Russians did. The 252nd Infantry was in remnants when it retreated to the south.[2]

Army Group North was led by pro-Nazi, Colonel General Georg Lindemann. A tactician of indifferent quality, he had been commander of the 18th Army during the Siege of Leningrad and as such had been largely responsible for the German failure to retreat from Leningrad while there was still time. As a result, 18th Army had lost thirty-one thousand men (fourteen thousand of them killed) and had been reduced to a bayonet strength of only seventeen thousand men by February. Ironically, Lindemann benefited from this serious error; Hitler saddled his predecessor, Field Marshal Georg von Kuechler, with the blame. Kuechler was sacked as C-in-C of Army Group North on January 30, 1944, and was replaced with

Field Marshal Model, who on March 1, 1944, was given command of Army Group North Ukraine. Model was, in turn, replaced by Lindemann.[3]

Although a mediocre commander, Lindemann certainly made the correct moves on June 22. By noon, he had Major General Gerhard Henke's 290th Infantry Division en route to the endangered sector, and a half an hour after the Russians broke through, he was on the telephone to OKH asking permission to send Lieutenant General Kurt Versock's 24th Infantry Division to the far right flank as well. OKH acted with unusual speed, and at 7:30 P.M. the 24th was en route to Obol. Lindemann also ordered the 909th Assault Gun Brigade forward from Polozk to help plug the gap.[4]

Unfortunately, the Soviets spent the night pouring forces through the hole in the German lines, including the XXII Guards Corps and the T-34s and KV-1s of the I Tank Corps. When dawn broke, the Saxons of the 24th Anti-Tank Battalion were in position in front of Obol, while the 24th Engineer Battalion launched an attack to the north, to rescue the 472nd Infantry Regiment of the 252nd Infantry Division, which was surrounded near Grebentsy. It was met by hordes of Russians, shouting "Urrah!" A fierce battle developed in the burning forests north of Obol, into which the 24th Infantry Division's units, the 909th Assault Gun Brigade, and the self-propelled anti-tank guns of the 519th Heavy Tank Destroyer Battalion (equipped with Hornets) were thrown as soon as they arrived. The battle lasted well into the night, but the Germans were unable to close the gap in their lines. By sunrise the next day, the left flank of Army Group Center had collapsed. On June 24, the gap south of Lindemann's flank grew to sixty miles, and Soviet vanguard was already twenty miles beyond the original front.

Elsewhere, the Soviets extended their offensive on June 23 into the zone of the 18th Army, which faced repeated attacks along a wide front. The main effort seems to have been against Lieutenant General Hellmuth Priess's 121st Infantry Division; it held its line with difficulty.[5] On June 24, the Reds shifted the focus of their attacks to the south, against Mellenthin's 205th and Major General Wilhelm Huen's 83rd Infantry Division. Both divisions held by committing the last of their reserves. But they could not help the 24th Infantry Division to the south. By nightfall on June 24, General Versock had lost contact with the divisions on both his right and left, and Soviets poured through both north and south of his positions, heading west.

On June 24, General Lindemann now committed his last reserves to plug the gap: Henke's 290th Infantry Division, a battery from the 912th Assault Gun Brigade, and the 751st Heavy Anti-Tank Battalion. It was not enough. The 24th withdrew that night, rejoining I Corps to the north. Meanwhile, Field Marshal Busch asked that Colonel Baron Rudolf-Christoph von Gersdorff, the Ia of Army Group North, attend a meeting at Army Group Center's Headquarters in Minsk that day. Also present was Colonel General Kurt Zeitzler, the chief of the General Staff of the High Command of the Army. Busch, whose army group was on the brink of disaster, asked Gersdorff what reserves he could give Army Group Center. Gersdorff said, "We have nothing to give to Center!"[6] Busch called for help again on the evening of July 25, informing Army Group North that 6th Guards Army was marching on Polozk with three divisions. Lindemann wanted to withdraw behind the Duena, but Hitler intervened. He declared Polozk a fortress and named General of Infantry Carl Hilpert, the commander of I Corps (16th Army), fortress commandant.[7] He further ordered Army Group North to transfer the 12th Panzer Division, the 212nd Infantry Division, and the 277th and 909th Assault Gun Brigades to Army Group Center.

General Hilpert was flabbergasted by this order. He had three divisions—24th, 205th, and 290th Infantry—but they were all locked in mortal combat southeast of the city against at least six divisions from the 4th Shock and 6th Guards Armies. He was not even in contact with all of his regiments. Hitler's order extended his front to a length of more than sixty miles! Hilpert and his divisional commanders formed ad hoc battle groups and rushed them to Polozk, where fourteen *fla* (light antiaircraft) and flak batteries from 1st Air Fleet reinforced the defense and provided at least some antiaircraft cover for the convoys driving for Polozk. Meanwhile, Hitler intervened again: Army Group North was to counterattack to the south and restore contact with Army Group Center.

General Lindemann knew that a counterattack to the south had absolutely no chance of succeeding, but he tried nevertheless. He formed a *kampfgruppe* under Lieutenant General Christian Usinger, the commander of the 315th Higher Artillery Command (Harko 315).[8] KG Usinger included a reinforced regiment from the Silesian 81st Infantry Division, elements of the 909th Assault Gun Brigade, the 1181st Assault Gun Battery, and nothing else. They advanced south at 2 A.M. on June 28, ran into the Soviet 90th Guards Rifle Division at 4 A.M., and were quickly checked. An hour later, the Reds counterattacked, in an attempt to destroy the battle group. They advanced in rows, as if on a parade field. The Germans waited until they were within four hundred yards and opened fire. Three 75 mm antitank guns fired a hundred rounds in five minutes. The attack stalled within a hundred yards of the German defensive positions.

As the day wore on, Usinger's men lay immobile in their positions under the hot Russian sun, while the Reds pounded them with artillery fire. Nineteen forty-four was the hottest year of the war, but they could not move. The *kampfgruppe* had no artillery of its own, so there was no counterbattery fire. As the sun passed its zenith, every assault gun and every antitank gun was knocked out. Finally, at 5 P.M., as the Soviets unleashed another attack, the order came to withdraw. It was more like a rout. By the time what was left of the battle group arrived back its original jump-off point, it had lost all its vehicles.

Meanwhile, Lindemann, Hilpert and General of Artillery Christian Hansen, the commander of the 16th Army, held up the rest of the 81st Infantry

Division from reinforcing Kampfgruppe Usinger, because they knew its attacks were doomed from the beginning to fail. Lindemann also ordered Major General Siegfried Hass's 170th Infantry Division and Lieutenant General Herbert Wagner's 132nd Infantry Division from the Narva sector to the army group's extreme right flank, even though 18th Army was also under heavy attack and could ill afford to give up any more men.[9] To defend the deep right flank of the army group—which was now completely "in the air"—the High Command of the Army created another ad hoc *kampfgruppe* under Colonel Rudolf Geiger, an officer from OKH's own engineer branch.[10] He was given the 3rd Latvian Police Regiment, the 3rd Frontier Guard Regiment, the 605th Security Regiment, and a couple of security battalions and was ordered to construct a defensive line along the Duena, under the overall command of General of Infantry Paul Laux's II Corps. KG Geiger was all Laux had (other than General Headquarters troops) until the 132nd Infantry arrived a few days later. By the end of the month, the 226th Assault Gun Brigade and the 290th Infantry Division had also arrived on the Duena. They, however, could do nothing about the chasm between Army Groups North and Center. The hole had grown so large that the troops were already calling it the "Baltic Gap."

Hitler was not only facing defeat in the East in the fall of 1944; the Western Front was on the verge of collapse as well. In fact, on July 14, even as the situation in Normandy grew critical, Hitler moved his headquarters from Berchtesgaden to Rastenburg, East Prussia, because of the desperate situation on the Eastern Front.[11]

KG Usinger (which now included two infantry regiments and many of the support troops of the 81st Infantry Division) and Lieutenant General Vollrath Luebbe with the rest of the 81st defended Polozk against repeated Soviet attacks. They were gradually pushed back, however, and it was clear that they could not hold the vital communications center indefinitely.

By now, the entire region was in chaos. To the rear, the roads were clogged with civilians who did not care to be "liberated" by the Soviets. All around the front, the forests were on fire, adding to the already intense heat. In both front and rear, the Red Air Force bombed and strafed at will, attacking refugee columns and German Army columns alike. On July 1, one of their bombs must have hit the ammunition depot in Polozk, because nine hundred tons of ammo blew sky high. All along the line, Army Group North defended a two-hundred mile front with nineteen divisions against 180 Soviet divisions. Meanwhile, at Berchtesgaten, in Upper Bavaria, Hitler again ordered Lindemann to attack south, to close the Baltic Gap. Lindemann duly passed the command on to Hilpert, who designated assembly areas for the Thueringian 87th Infantry Division (Major General Baron Mauritz von Strachwitz), which was trying to come up to the front on the damaged railroad system.[12] Elements of the battered 24th Infantry Division were also earmarked for the attack, even though Hilpert, Hansen, and Lindemann all agreed that it was hopeless.

On July 2, the Soviet 51st Guards Division reached the edge of Polozk, which was now engulfed in flames. As the 87th Infantry had still not reached the front, Hilpert attacked with all he had available: part of the 24th Infantry Division. Then, on his own initiative, Hilpert suspended the attack on the grounds that it was suicide. Lindemann approved. That night, he informed OKH that he had not only canceled the attack but ordered the evacuation of Polozk. Hitler was stunned. The following morning, the rearguard of the 81st Infantry Division blew up the last bridges and fell back to the west, leaving the Russians with a field of ruins.

Meanwhile, south of the Duena, the Soviet 6th Guards Army advanced on Duenaburg, almost without opposition. Another *kampfgruppe* was established to deal with the latest threat. This one consisted mainly of construction engineers, other support personnel, and a few training units under the leadership of Lieutenant General Johann Pflugbeil, the commander of Field Training Division North, who was named commandant of Duenaburg.[13] Since Pflugbeil would not be able to hold out for long with the forces available, another battle group was formed under Major General Bernhard Pamberg, the commander of the 56th Infantry Division. The 56th itself was just a *kampfgruppe* and had been assigned to Corps Detachment D as Division Group 56. Pamberg nevertheless hurried to Duenaburg with two understrength infantry battalions, an ad hoc alarm battalion, a weak assault gun battalion, and an antitank battalion. Meanwhile, a third combat group, consisting of a regiment of the 215th Infantry Division and the 393rd Assault Gun Brigade, was ordered to close the gap between Army Group North and 3rd Panzer Army, but it advanced only ten miles before it was surrounded near Vydziai. It broke out with heavy losses. The Baltic Gap was now eighteen miles wide.

Even now, Hitler insisted that Lindemann launch a counterattack. This Lindemann could not do and, even though he was a loyal Nazi, Hitler sacked him a few minutes after midnight on July 4 and replaced him with General of Infantry Johannes Friessner, who had distinguished himself as commander of Army Detachment Narva on the northern wing of Army Group North. Friessner was simultaneously promoted to colonel general, effective July 1. General of Infantry Anton Grasser, the commander of the XXVI Corps, succeeded him in command of the army detachment.[14]

When Friessner arrived at army group headquarters at Segewold that afternoon, he was optimistic, like almost all new commanders. It took him only one staff conference and a conversation with Field Marshal Model to convince him that Fuehrer Headquarters had deceived him as to the true situation. He had taken over a sector that was on the verge of destruction. He was outnumbered eight to one (by his own estimation), the Russians had reached the Latvian and Lithuanian borders, and there was almost nothing between their spearheads and the Baltic Sea.

Friessner's first priority was to try to save his right flank and prevent the Soviets from turning north, into his rear. The best way to accomplish this, Friessner believed, was to hold the key communications center of Duenaburg and simultaneously strike the 6th Guards Army in the flank. He quietly withdrew the II Corps (205th, 225th, and 263rd Infantry Divisions) to positions west of Lake Dissna and threw them into the attack. Although initially surprised, the Soviets reacted quickly, and were just too strong. They soon pushed II Corps back to its starting point. Meanwhile, General Hilpert reported that the Russians were building up opposite his front and were about ready to launch another major offensive against his I Corps. On July 6, Friessner decided to pull back his battered southern flank to Latvia before the Reds broke his lines again.

Friessner's order was countermanded by Hitler. Every unit in Army Group North was ordered to stay where it was, and Army Group North was to launch an immediate counterattack, to regain contact with 3rd Panzer Army; furthermore, since the Russian attacks against 18th Army had been repulsed, Friessner was ordered to immediately transfer the 69th and 93rd Infantry Divisions to Army Group Center.[15]

July 9 was another disastrous day for the Wehrmacht on the Eastern Front. In the zone of Army Group North, eight Soviet rifle divisions pushed I Corps back to the west, while the formations of the 6th Guards Army marched deeper into Latvia, opposed only by three construction engineer battalions and some Latvian police. Later that day, Hitler—always looking for someone to blame—relieved General of Artillery Christian Hansen, the commander of the 16th Army. He was replaced by the highly competent General of Infantry Paul Laux. Lieutenant General Wilhelm Hasse was named commander of the II Corps.[16]

Paul Laux, who was born in Weimar in 1887, was fifty-six years old when he assumed command of 16th Army. He had joined the army as a *Fahnenjunker* in 1907 and had been commissioned into the infantry. He earned his General Staff stripes, fought in World War I, and served in the Reichsheer. During Hitler's initial military expansion of 1935, he had been given command of a regiment (the 24th Infantry). This was followed by a steady advancement: commander of the 10th Infantry Command and deputy commander of the 10th Infantry Division (1938–39), quartermaster general of 1st Army in the West (1939–40), commander of the 126th Infantry Division (1942), and commander of the II Corps (1942–44). He had been primarily responsible for II Corps's successful evacuation of the Demyansk Pocket in 1943, one of the most brilliant tactical operations of the war. Laux carried it off without a hitch, saving a hundred thousand men. He was, in short, a superbly trained General Staff officer and tactician, and his skills had been honed by experience, including three years on the Eastern Front. In the fifth year of the war, it would have been hard to find a better commander for 16th Army.

Laux got his first test as an army commander two days later, on July 11, when Eremenko's 2nd Baltic Front launched a major offensive against the left flank of 16th Army. The attacks came along a hundred mile section of the front, against the VI SS and X Corps, and centered on Novosokolniki. The divisions under heavy attack were (from left to right) the 93rd Infantry, 19th SS, 15th SS, 23rd Infantry, 329th Infantry, 281st Security, and 263rd Infantry. (The 15th SS and 19th SS were Latvian divisions.) The 263rd was commanded by Major General Rudolf Sieckenius, the former commander of the 16th Panzer Division. Sieckenius's brilliant career in the armored branch had been cut short after the Allies landed on the mainland of Italy, and Hitler needed a scapegoat for the German defeat at Salerno. Sieckenius was relieved of his command and was used as a replacement division commander despite his experience and seniority, and despite the fact that he held commands designated for lieutenant generals, Sieckenius was never even considered for further promotion. He nevertheless performed very well, as usual, and turned back a series of major Russian attacks aimed at separating General of Infantry Friedrich Kochling's X Corps from I Corps.[17] The 912th Assault Gun Battalion also distinguished itself in this battle. Captain Richard Engelmann, commander of the 1st Battery, personally destroyed seventeen Russian tanks on that one day. The 2nd Baltic Front, however, continued to attack. To the south, meanwhile, the Russians were beginning to reinforce the 6th Guards Army in the Baltic Gap with the 2nd Guards Army and 51st Army, which was driving into eastern Lithuania.

On July 14, 3rd Baltic Front joined the offensive, striking the right wing of 18th Army in the thick, pathless forests. It focused against General of Infantry Wilhelm Wegener's L Corps, with the objective of separating the 16th and 18th Armies. To the south, in the zone of X Corps, the Russians finally managed to break through the 15th and 19th SS (Latvian) Divisions. General of Artillery Herbert Loch, the commander of the 18th Army, immediately committed his main reserve—Major General Gotthard Fischer's 126th Infantry Division—to plug the hole in his neighbor's flank, but it was too late. Russian tanks were behind the 93rd Infantry Division; it retreated without informing 18th Army, which had effectively been outflanked. Loch, however, checked the Russians at Opochka on July 16 by throwing in his last reserves.

By this point, Army Group North had suffered about fifty-thousand casualties since June 22. On July 18, Friessner estimated that only two of 16th Army's divisions (the 61st and 225th Infantry) were fully combat effective. Four divisions were listed as partially effective, seven as exhausted, and one (the 23rd) as combat ineffective. The 18th Army was in somewhat better shape, with five fully combat effective divisions (30th,

32nd, 121st and 126th Infantry, and 12th Luftwaffe Field). Two divisions were classified as exhausted (218th Infantry and 21st Field), the 93rd was partially combat effective, and the 83rd Infantry was classified as combat ineffective.[18]

That same day, Friessner met with Hitler at Rastenburg. Even Goering was impressed with the losses Army Group North had suffered and the odds it was facing. He suggested a retreat to the Duena River. Hitler, however, would have none of it. He ordered Friessner to restore contact with Army Group Center via counterattack. If necessary, Army Detachment Narva was to be stripped bare. He offered Friessner nothing in the way of reinforcements; instead, he ordered him to pull the 58th Infantry Division, 202nd and 261st Assault Gun Brigades, and 11th SS Reconnaissance Battalion out of the line, place them under XXXXIII Corps, and counterattack through Lithuania to the 3rd Panzer Army. Friessner must have been astonished. This order was unrealistic in the extreme.

Meanwhile, back at the front, the situation continued to deteriorate. The Soviets were nothing if not persistent. They extended their offensive to the north, pinning down General of Artillery Kurt Herzog's XXXVIII Corps (83rd Infantry, 21st Luftwaffe Field, and 32nd Infantry Divisions) in front of the Velikaya River.[19] The fighting was extremely hard and bitter; the Germans simply had too long a front to defend against too many opponents. The 21st Field collapsed on the evening of July 20, and XXXVIII Corps was forced to evacuate Ostrov the following day in order to prevent being encircled. The Soviets, with fifteen rifle divisions and five tank brigades, broke through XXXVIII Corps at its junction with General of Infantry Hans Gollnick's XXVIII Corps. In this situation, Gollnick could no longer hold his well-prepared positions south of Lake Peipus without being encircled. He gave the order to retreat on July 20.[20] Hitler was in no position to countermand these orders, because he was still in shock over the assassination attempt earlier that day. By nightfall, the entire army group was in full retreat, except for Army Detachment Narva on the far left flank of 18th Army.

"We are exhausted," a member of the 290th Infantry Division wrote. "One cannot recognize another; over the tanned, dusty faces are sweat encrusted furrows. Stubby beards are pasted with sweat and dirt. The wide open field shirts are covered in a layer of yellowish-brown powder. Thus we plod through ankle deep sand, one behind the other. . . . We haven't slept for days. . . . Our tongue and gums are like wood. No one speaks."[21]

Meanwhile, after a devastating aerial and artillery bombardment, the Soviets attacked Duenaburg on July 19 with five infantry divisions, a tank brigade, and a mechanized brigade. The city was defended by the 81st Infantry Division (Colonel Franz-Eccard von Bentivegni), the 132nd Infantry Division (General Wagner), the 393rd Assault Gun Brigade (Captain Paul Pelikan), and the remaining Tigers of the 502nd Heavy Panzer Battalion. During this attack, the Soviets threw their superheavy Stalin tanks into action. This was their first appearance in the zone of Army Group North, and they were superior to every German tank yet developed, including the Tiger. The 502nd fought back bravely, with many of the officers and NCOs drawing on five years' experience in armored warfare. The 1st and 3rd Companies (Lieutenants Johannes Boelter and Otto Carius, respectively) knocked out twenty-two Soviet tanks, including seventeen of Stalin's, on the first day.

Meanwhile, Lieutenant General Eberhard Kinzel, the chief of staff of Army Group North, reported to Colonel General Guderian, the new chief of the General Staff of OKH. "Before long," Kinzel declared, "the army group will be destroyed! Therefore, the Fuehrer will not only lose two armies, but the entire East!" Guderian responded with harsh and angry words. The Fuehrer's orders were to be obeyed! There would be no withdrawals! Army Group North was to fight and die where it stood! Kinzel's career, for the moment at least, was over.[22]

The fighting in and around Duenaburg raged day and night for a week, almost without letup. By July 25, the two infantry divisions were in remnants, the 393rd Assault Gun Brigade had lost most of its guns, the 502nd Panzer no longer existed, and Duenaburg was nearly surrounded. The next day, the army group ordered the city abandoned. The order, however, did not come from Friessner but from the new commander, Colonel General Ferdinand Schoerner.

On July 22, Friessner signaled Fuehrer Headquarters and categorically demanded permission to retreat. The next day, at the suggestion of Heinz Guderian, Hitler ordered Friessner to swap commands with Ferdinand Schoerner, the C-in-C of Army Group South Ukraine. (Guderian made this suggestion in order to save Friessner's career. After his dispatch of July 22, his days in command of Army Group North were clearly numbered.)[23] General Kinzel (who had argued with Guderian earlier and who had earned the Fuehrer's displeasure) was sacked and was replaced by Major General Oldwig von Natzmer, the Ia of the Grossdeutschland Panzer Division.[24] Schoerner arrived at Segewold on July 24. Map 4.1 shows the situation he faced.

Ferdinand Schoerner was the most brutal of Hitler's army generals. Author Robert Wistrich later wrote that he "shot privates and colonels with equal zeal for the smallest infractions."[25] He dealt as harshly with his own men as he did with the Russians, whom he considered subhuman.

Schoerner was born into a lower-middle-class family in Munich in 1892. His father was a police officer. He joined the army as a private in 1911 and by 1914 had obtained a commission as a second lieutenant in the reserves. He was studying to become a primary schoolmaster when World War I erupted in 1914. Schoerner rejoined his regiment and spent most of

Map 4.1
Army Group North, July 23, 1944

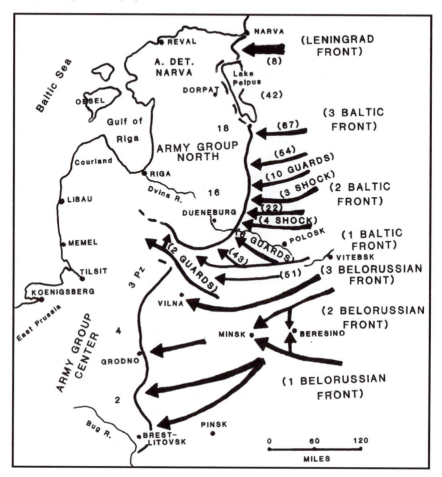

the war in the German Alpine Corps. He fought on the Italian Front (1915), in the Verdun battles (1916), and in Romania and the southern Carpathians (1917), where he stormed the fortress on Monte Kolonrat and earned the Pour le Mérite, Imperial Germany's highest decoration. Sent back to the Western Front in 1918, he was seriously wounded near Rheims. He was holding a staff position in Serbia when the war ended.

In 1919, Schoerner (now a first lieutenant) joined Freikorps von Epp (under Major General Ritter Franz von Epp, the future Nazi governor of Bavaria) and helped put down Communist insurrections in the Ruhr. He also fought the Poles in Upper Silesia. The following year, he was selected for the Reichsheer, largely because he held the "Blue Max." He spent most of his interwar career in the mountain units and was an early supporter of the Nazi movement.

Schoerner applied for admission to the General Staff, but (like 85 percent of the applicants) failed his entrance exam. This, coupled with his humble origins and his family's lower social standing, caused him to bear great resentment—indeed hatred—toward the aristocratic gentlemen on the General Staff, who tended to look down on him. The fact that they were mostly Prussians and he was Bavarian only intensified his feelings. Hitler shared Schoerner's hatreds, which caused the two to be drawn to each other.

Colonel Schoerner commanded the 98th Mountain Regiment in Poland and distinguished himself by capturing the critical Zbolska Heights near Lvov and then repulsing several desperate Polish counterattacks. He led his regiment in Belgium and France in 1940. (After the war, the Belgians tried to extradite him for war crimes but failed; there were too many in line ahead of them.) In any case, Schoerner went on to command the 6th Mountain Division (1940–42), which he led in the conquest of the Balkans, in the last stages of the Battle of Crete, and in northern Finland and northern Russia against the Soviets. During the Russian winter of 1941–42, Ferdinand Schoerner did very well in the brutal environment and held his positions despite frequent attacks by better equipped and numerically superior Red Army formations. This led to his promotion to general of mountain troops and command of Mountain Corps Norway.

Schoerner came into his own in October 1943, when he was transferred from this backwater theater of operations to the southern sector of the Eastern Front—and the focal point of the war. He was given command of the XXXX Panzer Corps, despite the fact that he had no tank training. He had impressed Hitler with his loyalty and brutality, and that was enough.

The XXXX Panzer Corps was almost immediately redesignated Group Schoerner and given control of the XXX, XVII, and IV Corps in the Nikopol bridgehead, on the east bank of the Dnieper. Stalin's forces made attempts to crush Schoerner's group, but as usual, he held his positions. By February 1944, however, Group Schoerner was almost surrounded. The general broke through Russian lines and led his men out through knee-deep Ukrainian mud—a brilliant tactical achievement. This led to his appointment as chief of the National Socialist Leadership Corps at OKW, where his job was to spread Nazi doctrine throughout the armed forces. Then, at the recommendation of Heinrich Himmler, he was promoted to colonel general and named commander in chief of Army Group A (soon Army Group South Ukraine), effective April 1, 1944.

Schoerner did not do well in his first army group command. Hitler had decreed that the 17th Army hold the Crimea peninsula at all costs. Schoerner agreed with this strategy and instituted draconian measures to try to increase German resistance. His severity had little effect. The Soviets attacked the Crimea on April 8, and the naval fortress of Sevastopol, the last bastion of defense on the peninsula, fell on May 13. Only 26,700 of the 64,700 Germans trapped in the fortress escaped. Another 26,700 Romanians were lost. Even though he knew that the true responsibility for the disaster lay with the Fuehrer, Schoerner joined with Hitler in blaming the calamity on Colonel General Erwin Jaenecke, the veteran commander of the 17th Army, for his lack of faith. Jaenecke was relieved of his command, placed in Fuehrer Reserve, and never reemployed.

When Schoerner arrived in the Baltic States, Army Group North (16th and 18th Armies and Army Detachment Narva) had a strength of about seven hundred thousand men. Seven of its divisions were fully combat effective: the 11th, 21st, 30th, 58th, 61st, and 227th Infantry, and the 12th Luftwaffe Field. Six of its divisions were still partially effective: the 126th, 225th, 263rd, and 389th Infantry, 20th Estonian SS, and 21st Luftwaffe Field. The 24th, 32nd, 81st, 83rd, 87th, 93rd, 121st, 132nd, 205th, 215th, 218th, 290th, and 329th Infantry and 281st Security Divisions were exhausted, and the 23rd, 15th Latvian SS, and 19th Latvian SS were listed as ineffective.[26] He inherited a gap of more than thirty miles between the 16th and 3rd Panzer Army to the south, on the northern flank of what was left of Army Group Center. By July 25, Army Group North was under attack by the Soviet 2nd Baltic, 3rd Baltic, and Leningrad Fronts—twelve armies with more than eighty divisions. The main focus of the attack (which began on July 24) was now in the sector around the Estonian town on Narva, which was defended by General of Waffen-SS Felix Steiner's III (Germanic) SS Panzer Corps (III. [germanisches] SS Panzerkorps), which consisted of pan-European volunteers—Danes, Dutch, Estonians, Flemish, Norwegians, Swedes, Walloons, and Germans.[27] The veteran East Prussian 11th Infantry Division and the inexperienced 4th and 6th Estonian Border Guards Regiments were also attached to the corps.

Except for its Luftwaffe Field and Estonian border guard units,[28] the III Panzer had fought well during the vain attempt to maintain the Siege of Leningrad and in the subsequent retreats, although the 23rd SS Volunteer Grenadier Division "Nederland" had suffered heavy casualties, and the Dutch 48th SS Volunteer Grenadier Regiment "General Seyffardt" and the 23rd SS Volunteer Reconnaissance Battalion had been virtually destroyed.[29]

The overextended corps included the Nederland Division (SS Major General Baron Juergen Wagner), the 11th SS Volunteer Panzer Grenadier Division "Nordland" (SS Lieutenant General Fritz von Scholz), and the 20th SS Volunteer Grenadier Division "Estonia Nr. 1" (SS Major General Franz Augsberger).[30] It had little in reserve, other than the 27th SS Tank Destroyer Battalion and SS Lieutenant Colonel (SS-Obersturmbannfuehrer) Conrad Schellong's 6th SS Volunteer Sturm Brigade "Langemarck" (6. SS-Freiwilligen Sturmbrigade "Langemarck"), a Flemish unit. Formed in April 1941, as an SS regiment, it had served in the East since November 1941, and had suffered severe casualties. A brigade in name only, it had only two grenadier battalions, along with an infantry gun company, an assault gun company, and two flak companies—one heavy and one light. Because he had insufficient troops, Steiner divided the 6th SS and ordered Schellong to send a battle group to hold Orphanage Hill, a critical position in the center of the German line. The Soviets attacked the hill for four days, beginning on July 26. The Schellong battle group suffered 90 percent casualties but held its positions. During the first two days of the battle, SS Private First Class Remy Schrynen knocked out five T-34 and two KV-2 tanks with a 75 mm "PAK" antitank gun before his weapon was destroyed by a Soviet tank on July 27. Schrynen survived a direct hit and, although badly wounded, was rescued by his comrades and evacuated to Germany, where he was awarded the Knight's Cross. He was still alive in 1997.[31]

The battered German line held, but only barely. It was saved a number of times by the last-minute intervention of SS Lieutenant Colonel Paul-Albert Kausch's 11th SS Panzer Battalion "Hermann von Salza"[32] and the 27th SS Tank Destroyer Battalion, which was led by SS Captain Ekkehard Wangemann. Ironically, Wangemann held a degree in theology and had been a pastor in Mecklenburg before the war.[33]

By the time the Russians suspended their attacks in the Narva sector on July 29, the III SS Panzer Corps had destroyed 113 Soviet tanks—many of them with *Panzerfausts* and PAKs. It had not lost a yard of ground, but German losses were nevertheless heavy. Among the dead were SS Lieutenant General von Scholz and three SS regimental commanders: SS Colonel Count Hermenegild zu Westphalen, SS Lieutenant Colonel Hans Collani, and SS Major Arthur Stoffers.

Meanwhile, to the south, the 6th Guards Army was marching on Shaulen (Slaulyay) in central Lithuania. On the morning of July 26, the vanguards of the III Guards Mechanized Corps reached the city, which was defended by Colonel Hellmuth Maeder. Maeder was nominally the commandant of Army Group North's Weapons School and Demonstration (Lehr) Brigade North, but most of his units had already been committed to combat elsewhere. At age thirty-six, Maeder was also one of the best young combat officers in the German Army. He had only a few training and security companies, but under Maeder's command they put up a good fight, tying down an entire guards mechanized corps for three days.[34] By the night of July 28–29, however, KG Maeder was virtually surrounded. Schoerner ordered it to break out to Libau, which it did. But this was the last ditch. Army Group North had nothing left to throw in front of the Russian armor.

On July 29, Soviet motorized units passed through Slaulyay, turned north, advanced fifty miles, captured Jelgava, and cut the last rail link between Army Groups North and Center. Schoerner ordered 16th Army and the right wing of 18th Army to pull back to the so-called Marienburg Positions and to prepare to evacuate Riga, which was threatened by Eremenko's 2nd Baltic Front. His only way to communicate directly with OKH was over the public telephone line that ran from Segewold to Helsinki to Oslo and Berlin-Zossen. All female Wehrmacht personnel (about 1,500 of them) were evacuated from Riga by sea that same day.

On August 1, the Russians reached the Gulf of Riga west of the city of Riga, cutting off Army Group North (thirty divisions) in Estonia and Latvia. They were eighty miles behind Soviet lines.

Meanwhile, elements of the 16th Army, including the 81st, 215th, and 290th Infantry Divisions, marched rapidly to the west, covering the rear of Army Group North. They attacked to the south, captured Mitau, and severed the main supply line of the Soviet vanguards. This robbed the Soviet units of their momentum and temporarily imposed stalemate on the southern flank.

Even though Hitler was still clamoring for a counterattack, it was highly doubtful that Army Group North had enough men to even survive. Since June 22, it had received only individual replacements, the number of which had been far exceeded by their casualties. The only reinforcements they had received were some two thousand airmen from Colonel General Kurt Pflugbeil's 1st Air Fleet, which was hardly big enough to justify its impressive title. Contrary to earlier practices, these men were not grouped into Luftwaffe Field units but were sent to the infantry divisions as replacements. Schoerner also dissolved the 394th and 395th Field Administrative Commands (rear area headquarters) on August 4. Hitler did order the transfer of the 122nd Infantry Division from Finland to Army Group North, and the Home Army contributed ten march (replacement) battalions early in the encirclement.

Between Duena and Lake Peipus, the 2nd and 3rd Baltic Fronts resumed their offensives on August 5. Fighting was very heavy all along the 18th Army's front. A regiment of the 126th Infantry Division was surrounded but fought its way out. One battalion (II/257th) of the 83rd Infantry Division lost all of its officers and was reduced to a strength of one NCO and thirty men. "The divisions no longer existed," Werner Haupt wrote later, "only individual combat groups, which marched, fought, and died in isolation."[35]

On August 5, the Russians lost 125 tanks in the Army Group North area alone, bringing the total destroyed by the army group since June 22 to 1,325. But still they kept coming. The Russians finally broke the German line at the junction of the VI SS and X Army Corps, again separating the 16th and 18th Armies. A counterattack by elements of Major General Hero Breusing's 122nd Infantry Division, which had just arrived from Finland, failed to restore the front. Then the 2nd Baltic Front hit the 81st Infantry

Division near Birsen with ten rifle divisions, reinforced by the I and XIX Tank Corps.

The Upper Silesians of the 81st Infantry Division had been in combat since 1941. They had suffered heavy losses at Polozh and now amounted to no more than a regimental combat group. Against such odds, the Silesians could not hold, but—remarkably—they fell back intact and denied Soviets their breakthrough. General Gollnick also reacted quickly and threw the 912th Assault Gun Brigade into the battle. It destroyed fifty-three Soviet tanks—about twice its own strength. The primitive nature of the road network and the sandy, forested terrain worked for the defenders and slowed the Soviet drive; a retreat was nevertheless clearly in order. Schoerner ordered the flanks of the 16th and 18th Armies to fall back to the Bauske-Memele-Trentelburg line. Army Group North still blocked Stalin's road to Riga.

On August 10, the Russians struck again, launching massive attacks against the 18th Army below Lake Pskow and north of Dvina. With heavy artillery support and complete domination of the air, they sent wave after wave of bombers to blast the XXVIII Corps. Then they attacked with their tanks and infantry. General Gollnick's troops fought back tenaciously, but the odds were simply too great. Lieutenant General Hans von Basse's 30th Infantry Division alone was attacked by four rifle divisions, a tank division, and a mechanized brigade. The Red Army broke through in both places that same day.

With no reserves to speak of, Schoerner resorted to his talent of squeezing the last drop of effort out of his troops. For Schoerner, this involved flying court-martials, summary executions, and other high-handed acts of unfairness and/or brutality. Hans von Basse, for example, was relieved of his command the day the Soviets broke through for failing to halt five Soviet divisions (one of them armored) with a weak infantry division. He was replaced by Colonel Otto Barth.[36] When the veteran 23rd Infantry Division (one of the best in the Wehrmacht) lost a position, Schoerner sent a message to the 18th Army concerning the divisional commander, a veteran of more than three years on the Eastern Front: "Lieutenant General Chales de Beaulieu is to be told that he is to restore his own and his division's honor by a courageous deed or I will chase him out in disgrace. Furthermore, he is to report by 9 P.M. which commanders he has had shot or is having shot for cowardice." He also demanded "draconian intervention" and "ruthlessness to the point of brutality" from General Loch, the army commander.[37]

Walter Chales de Beaulieu was the former chief of staff of the XVI Panzer Corps and the 4th Panzer Army and was already under suspicion by the Nazis (including Schoerner) for his previous close association with Colonel General Erich Hoepner, a prominent leader in the anti-Hitler conspiracy.

In January 1942, after Hitler sacked Hoepner and retired him in disgrace for retreating against orders, Chales was named commander of the 394th Panzer Grenadier Regiment—a definite demotion. He then staged a fine professional comeback, successively commanding the 26th Panzer Grenadier Brigade and the 168th Infantry Division, both on the Eastern Front, while earning promotions to major general and lieutenant general. But he would not shoot loyal subordinates for failing to hold their positions against overwhelming odds. He was relieved of his command on September 11. Never reemployed, he was dismissed from the service on January 31, 1945.[38]

In this battle, Hitler helped (for a change) by giving Schoerner freedom of action, placing him in charge of all branches of the service in his zone of operations, and airlifting the newly formed 31st Infantry Division (Major General Hans-Joachim Stolzmann) from Koenigsberg to Courland. He had sent Schoerner a specially equipped antitank Stuka group, led by the famous Major Hans Rudel, who had destroyed his three hundredth Russian tank a few days before.

By this time, the Soviet juggernaut was running out of steam. With the pressure temporarily off in the II Corps zone, Schoerner transferred it to the left and inserted it into the line between XXVIII and XXXVIII Corps, with the 31st Infantry Division, followed quickly by 87th. A major Soviet breakthrough was again frustrated. Field Marshal Model, the C-in-C of Army Group Center, was desperately trying to form a defensive line in Poland and to organize a counterattack, to restore contact with Army Group North. The question was: could Army Group North hold out until help reached it, or would it be destroyed? On August 6, Schoener informed Hitler that his line would hold, provided "not too much time elapsed" before Army Group Center restored contact with it and reinforced it. He also stressed the fact that his troops were exhausted and the Russians were attacking relentlessly, often throwing fourteen-year-old boys and old men into the battle, trying to find any weak point in the German line. The thickly forested nature of the front made the situation even more difficult for the defenders.[39]

Meanwhile, a daring panzer raid temporarily took the wind out of the Soviet sails and lifted the spirits of every soldier in Army Group North.

It was led by Major General of Reserves Count Hyazinth Strachwitz von Gross-Zauche, one of the boldest officers in the history of the German Panzerwaffe (tank force). A cavalryman by profession, he was the descendent of a family of wealthy Silesian landowners who could trace their aristocratic genealogy back to the Middle Ages. Born in 1893, Count Hyazinth was educated at Gross-Lichterfelde (Imperial Germany's West Point) and commissioned into the elite Guards Cavalry Corps in 1914. During the drive on Paris, he led a number of bold raids behind enemy lines. The last one led to his capture—eighty miles behind enemy lines.

Finally released in 1919, he was not selected for the Reichsheer, so he joined the Freikorps and took part in the famous Battle of Annaberg, in which the Freebooters defeated the Polish Army.

Count Hyazinth spent the years 1921 to 1934 managing the family estate—a boring activity for a man of his bold and reckless temperament. In 1934, during Hitler's secret military buildup, Strachwitz's application to return to active duty was finally accepted, and he was gazetted into the 2nd Panzer Regiment.

Strachwitz fought in Poland (1939) and France (1940), where his bold raids earned him fame throughout the Reich as the "Panzer Count." The following year, he added to his reputation as a battalion commander in the 18th Panzer Division on the Eastern Front. He and his men destroyed three hundred Soviet soft-skinned vehicles and the several artillery battalions on the first day. At one point during Operation Barbarossa, a Russian bullet lodged in his body. Realizing that the wound was not life threatening, Strachwitz cut it out himself and continued fighting. In another battle, he rushed out of his damaged tank and engaged Soviet infantry with machine pistols and hand grenades.

Promoted to lieutenant colonel and transferred to the 16th Panzer Division, Strachwitz led the German penetration to the Volga and destroyed 158 Russian airplanes at an airfield north of Stalingrad. Seriously wounded shortly thereafter, he was flown to a military hospital at Breslau. After he recovered, the Panzer Count was promoted to colonel and was given command of a Tiger battalion in the elite Grossdeutschland Division. After fighting at Kharkov and in several other battles, he was again wounded. Strachwitz was promoted to major general of reserves on April 1, 1944, and was named senior panzer officer of Army Group North.

Although Strachwitz was promised he would have three panzer divisions and a tank destroyer brigade to work with, not one had actually arrived by late summer, nor was one likely to, given the situation of the Eastern Front at that time. All Strachwitz had available for his personal employment was ten panzers and fifteen armored troop carriers.

Strachwitz's first act was to plan an attack. Before he launched it, however, he signaled the Soviets, telling them exactly where and when he was going to strike. They set up an ambush for him—just where Strachwitz expected it. He carried out his attack successfully, pushed on to a point a hundred miles behind the Russian front, then looped around the enemy concentration and overran it from the rear. He returned to base without losing a single vehicle.

Shortly thereafter, it became obvious that the Reds intended to attack Riga again, using the recently captured town of Tuccum as a base. General Schoerner ordered Strachwitz to recapture the place. Strachwitz led his ten panzers in a raid south of the town, which he bypassed to the east; finally, he descended on Tuccum from the north, overrunning several Red infantry formations in the process. On the outskirts of the city, he discovered forty-eight Soviet tanks, lined up in parade formation. The Panzer Count radioed the cruiser *Luetzow* off the coast, and it blew away the Soviet tank battalion with its 280 mm guns. Strachwitz barreled into the rear of the Soviet assault group, whose general drew the wrong conclusion—that he was surrounded—so he surrendered immediately. Strachwitz's raid resulted in the capture of eighteen thousand men, twenty-eight artillery batteries (about a hundred guns), several intact tanks, and a mass of other weapons and equipment.[40] His victory earned him the Knight's Cross with Oak Leaves, Swords, and Diamonds: a decoration equal to the U.S. Congressional Medal of Honor.

During the short lull in the fighting, the 18th Army created a new formation, Combat Group General Wegener, on or about August 12. Under the command of General of Infantry Wilhelm Wegener, it included L Corps, X Corps, and VI SS Corps and was responsible for the defense of the right flank of 18th Army.[41] In the south, 16th Army created Combat Group General Kleffel (under General of Cavalry Philipp Kleffel), which controlled the ad hoc Blocking Verbaende Riewald and the 225th Infantry Division, to protect the southern flank of the army group along the Baltic Sea coast.[42]

The Soviets attacked again on August 15, focusing on the remnants of the 81st Infantry Division and the 290th Infantry Division near Bauske. They spearheaded their advance with heavy tanks. Again the 912th Assault Gun Brigade saved the day and knocked out another forty tanks.

It was clear that the Soviets wanted to break through I Corps and capture Riga. They attacked the 81st Infantry again on August 16, but again the Silesians held their positions. Since it was clear they were nearing exhaustion, however, General Loch reinforced them with the 438th Infantry Regiment and 132nd Fusilier Battalion of the 132nd Infantry Division that day. The Russians did not succeed in capturing Bauske until August 19, and again there was no decisive breakthrough.

Bauske was not the only place the Soviets attacked in strength in mid-August. Some of the heaviest fighting took place in the Narva sector around Tartu (Dorpat), where the I Battalion of the 5th SS Assault Brigade "Walloon" faced virtual human-wave attacks for days on end. By the time the battle was over, the I Battalion of the Walloon had lost all of its antitank guns and 228 of its 260 men, but it still held its positions. Every surviving Belgian was decorated with the Iron Cross, and SS General Felix Steiner, the commander of the III (Germanic) SS Panzer Corps, who personally shook hands with every survivor, declared, "One Wallonian is worth a thousand ordinary soldiers!"[43]

Personal courage was the salvation of Army Group North and the III SS Panzer Corps in the summer of 1944. On August 23, for example, an

Estonian unit collapsed under heavy attack, exposing the entire German flank west and southwest of Dorpats. At that point, SS Colonel Leon Degrelle, the commander of the SS-Sturmbrigade, was traveling down the road to visit his heavy weapons company, which was engaged farther to the southwest.

Leon Dregelle was the most famous foreign SS volunteer. Born in Belgium in 1906, he studied law before becoming head of a publishing company and then founding his own newspaper. In 1935, he became founder of the Belgian Rexist movement, which very much resembled the Nazi Party. It won several seats in the Belgian parliament in 1936, but this did not prevent the government from arresting the controversial Dregelle in 1940, when Germany invaded Belgium.

Dregelle was freed by the Germans after the Wehrmacht conquered the Low Countries. A firm anti-Communist with Fascist leanings, he enlisted in the German Army as a private in the infantry (at age thirty-five) when the Wehrmacht invaded Russia. Although a leader of great propaganda value, he refused to meet with Hitler until he could wear the Knight's Cross. This occurred in 1944, after the Battle of Cherkassy. Hitler later remarked that if he ever had a son, he would want him to be like Leon Dregelle. The Belgian Rexist leader, in fact, survived 130 close combats on the Russian Front, earned a battlefield commission, and by August 1944 had risen to the rank of major in the Waffen-SS. He also held the Wounded Badge in Silver for being wounded in action on four different occasions (he would be wounded at least once more). He may also have found time to murder his wife's lover—or at least Ernst Kaltenbrunner, the chief of the Reich Main Security Office (Reichssicherheitshauptamt, or RSHA) and head of the secret police, thought he did.[44] Dregelle had succeeded to the command of the SS-Storm Brigade "Walloon" on February 13, 1944, during the Battle of Cherkassy, when SS Colonel Lucien Lippert died of a bullet through the chest.[45]

On August 23, Dregelle saw the Estonians fleeing and immediately grasped the seriousness of the situation. He quickly assumed command of a weak German alarm unit that happened to be nearby and pulled many of the Estonians together by deliberately exposing himself to enemy fire. He convinced them to occupy some trenches at a strong point in the Lemmatsi Hills and then directed the battle standing above them, calmly issuing orders to the men below. Dregelle thus restored the situation by his personal example.[46] Miraculously, he was not hit by Soviet fire.

Another such incident occurred east of Opotschka, in the zone of the 15th SS Grenadier Division "Latvia" (15 Waffen-Grenadier-Division der SS [lettische Nr. 1]). On July 11, its neighboring division, the 19th SS Grenadier, collapsed under the pressure of heavy attacks from vastly superior Soviet infantry and tank forces, and the panic infected the 15th SS as well. The division commander of the 15th SS, Oberfuehrer Nikolaus Heilmann, along with a few officers and NCOs, "forced the fleeing Latvian grenadiers and their leaders back to the front, partly by threatening them with violence, partly by words." The Latvians rallied and checked the threatened breakthrough, averting another potential disaster.[47]

It was the general opinion of the Soviet generals after the war that except for a handful of units (such as the 5th Panzer Division), Army Group North simply fought better than did Army Group Center in 1944. A good example was the case of Second Lieutenant Wolfgang von Bostell of the 23rd Infantry Division.

Bostell was born in Heiningen in 1917, and after matriculation enlisted in the 48th Artillery Regiment in 1935. The following year, he transferred to the anti-tank branch of the artillery and became a member of the Pomeranian 12th Anti-Tank Battalion. He was promoted to corporal in 1937 and sergeant in 1938. After fighting in Poland and France, he became a staff sergeant. His division (the 12th Infantry) crossed into Russia on June 22, but Bostell was seriously wounded a month later. Upon recovery, he was part of the Demyansk relief effort of 1942, in which he was again wounded. Following his recovery, he fought at Volchov and then was transferred to the 1023rd Assault Gun Battalion of the new 23rd Infantry Division as a *Fahnenjunker-Feldwebel* (sergeant/officer cadet). (The original 23rd Infantry Division had been merged into the 26th Panzer Division in 1942.) Bostell attended the officer's training course at Wischau and a panzer-troops school near Berlin (August 1943–March 1944), after which he was promoted to *Leutnant* (second lieutenant). After attending the Assault Gun School at Mielau, Poland, he returned to his unit as a platoon leader in the 2nd Company.

The standard German assault gun (Sturmgeschuetz or StuG) was a self-propelled weapon featuring a high-velocity 75 mm main battle gun, mounted on a PzKw III chassis. It had no turret, and its gun could only traverse twenty-four degrees; the driver often had to turn the vehicle so the crew could aim at their target. The assault gun had the advantage of a low superstructure, which made it difficult to hit. It was also much cheaper and quicker to make than a tank. By January 1944, the StuG had destroyed twenty thousand enemy tanks on the Eastern Front.

On August 11, 1944, Second Lieutenant von Bostell's battalion was near Modohn, Latvia, supporting the division's riflemen. He saw Major General Ernst Wisselinck, the commander of Army Noncommissioned Officers' Schools, East,[48] with rifle in hand, bringing back several Russian prisoners. Shortly thereafter, the Soviet armor counterattacked, and Bostell's assault gun shot up six T-34s in a matter of minutes.

Early the next morning, the Russians attacked again. Bostell rolled out looking for Soviet tanks and found himself in the middle of a camouflaged Russian position. The Soviets were assembling to attack the German line again. Fortunately for Bostell, the Reds thought his self-propelled gun was a Russian weapon and waved him forward. Bostell, whose field-gray uniform appeared to be brown after days of fighting, calmly waved back and joined the Soviet advance. Near the forward German positions, two T-34s raced past Bostell's *Sturmgeschuetz*. He let them get about sixty yards beyond him before he opened fire, striking both tanks in the rear, where their armor was thinnest. Both blew up immediately. Simultaneously, Bostell's crewmen threw open their hatches and fired their machine pistols and machine guns into the ranks of the shocked Russian infantry. Suddenly, two more T-34s emerged from a copse nearby. Bostell quickly knocked them out. Then he threw a track. A moment later, Bostell spotted another T-34, partially hidden by a small hill. With only one track, the lieutenant's assault gun could not maneuver; it could only turn in circles. Ignoring his own vulnerability, Bostell turned until his gun was fixed on the Soviet tank, which he promptly blew away. Wolfgang von Bostell and his crew had knocked out eleven enemy tanks in two days. Fortunately for them, nearby German riflemen realized that the assault gun was in serious trouble. They surged forward, chased off the surviving Russian infantry, and rescued the crew.

Bostell received the Knight's Cross for this action on September 24. It was placed around his neck by the senior surgeon at the military hospital at Quedlinburg. The lieutenant had been severely wounded on August 22. He would soon be back in action, however. Before the war was over, he would knock out another seventeen Russian tanks.[49]

Even the arrogant and murderous SS-Obergruppenfuehrer and General of Police Friedrich Jeckeln got into the act and contributed to the salvation of Army Group North. A short-tempered, cruel, and irrational moral coward, Jeckeln would later meet the fate he so richly deserved when he was hanged as a war criminal in 1946. A Nazi since the 1920s, he had made a name for himself as a brawler and a street fighter. Hitler named him to the Reichstag in 1932. Rising rapidly in the Allgemeine-SS (the General SS), he became an *Obergruppenfuehrer* (General of SS) in 1936 but, due to his relative lack of education and military training, was only offered a battalion command in the Totenkopf (Death's Head) Division in 1940. This unit was made up largely of former concentration camp guards. Jeckeln accepted the post and participated in the Western campaign of 1940, without earning any special distinction. Named Higher SS and Police Commander West after the fighting ended, he was on Himmler's personal staff in 1941 and helped plan the *Einsatzgruppen* (murder squad) operations in Russia. On June 23, 1941, he became Higher SS and Police Leader for South Russia, where he was responsible for the mass murder of tens of thousands of Jews and Slavs, including the mass execution of thirty-three thousand Jews in the Kiev ravine (September 29–30, 1941). Shortly afterwards, Jeckeln exchanged commands with Hans-Adolf Pruetzmann and became Higher SS and Police Leader for the Baltic States and Northern Russia (1941–45). In this post, he combined mass murders with antipartisan operations, but he longed to be a successful combat commander.

He got his chance in the summer of 1944, when Army Group North was in constant danger of collapse and would use any and every formation offered to it—even Jeckeln's collection of motley police and half-trained Latvian replacement battalions. Despite the desperate situation, the army would not thrust Kampfgruppe Jeckeln with front line duty, but it did post his men near the front, no doubt hoping that if the Soviets did break the thin gray line, Jeckeln might at least slow them down.

On August 16, the contingency became reality when the Russians broke through Herzog's XXXVIII Corps. To the obvious amazement of the army generals, Jeckeln's men not only held their positions but launched a bold counterattack, personally led by Jeckeln himself. The Latvian Fascists— who were, after all, fighting for their homes—turned the Soviets around and sealed off the breakthrough, saving the 122nd Infantry Division from a potentially deadly situation in the process. Even General of Artillery Herbert Loch the non-Nazi commander of the 18th Army, praised Jeckeln's "shining example of personal bravery" and "lack of regard for his own person." He recommended Jeckeln for the Knight's Cross. The commander in chief of Army Group North, Ferdinand Schoerner, was a rabid Nazi whose personality was very similar to Jeckeln's. He promptly endorsed the recommendation, and Jeckeln received the award.[50]

While Army Group North was fighting for its life, General Raus, the commander of the 3rd Panzer Army, took advantage of the lessening Soviet pressure and organized two major forces in East Prussia: the XXXIX Panzer and XXXX Panzer Corps. Their mission was to advance into Lithuania and reestablish contact with Army Group North. The XXXIX Panzer Corps assembled around Libau, near the Baltic Sea, while XXXX organized around Tauroggen. Table 4.2 shows the Order of Battle of Raus's relief forces.

Raus launched his relief attack, which he dubbed Operation Doppelkopf, on August 16. The inland attack of XXXX Panzer Corps was unlucky. Generals Henrici, von Manteuffel, and others ran into ten Soviet infantry divisions, which were backed by three artillery divisions and four antitank brigades. They gained very little. In the zone of Dietrich von Sauchen's XXXIX Panzer Corps, however, the Germans were more fortunate.

The attack of the XXXIX Panzer Corps was spearheaded by an ad hoc panzer formation led by General Count Hyazinth Strachwitz, who was flown to East Prussia for this purpose. His new command included the SS Panzer Brigade "Gross" and the 101st Panzer Brigade.

The hastily organized relief attack began on August 18. Panzer Formation (Verbaende) Strachwitz on the extreme left flank was very well supported by the German Navy, which contributed the II Battle Group, commanded by

Table 4.2
Order of Battle, 3rd Panzer Army's Relief Forces, August 16, 1944

3rd Panzer Army: General of Panzer Troops Erhard Raus
XXXIX Panzer Corps: General of Panzer Troops Dietrich von Sauchen
    4th Panzer Division: Major General Clemens Betzel
    5th Panzer Division: Lieutenant General Karl Decker
    12th Panzer Division: Lieutenant General Baron Erpo von Bodenhausen
    Panzer Verbaende Count Strachwitz: Major General of Reserves Count
      Hyazinth Strachwitz von Gross-Zauche
    52nd Security Division: Major General Albert Newiger
XXXX Panzer Corps: General of Panzer Troops Sigfrid Henrici
    1st Infantry Division: Lieutenant General Ernst Anton von Krosigk
    7th Panzer Division: Major General Dr. Karl Mauss
    14th Panzer Division: Lieutenant General Martin Unrein
    Grossdeutschland Panzer Grenadier Division: Lieutenant General Baron
      Hasso von Manteuffel

Vice Admiral August Thiele.[51] It included the heavy cruiser *Prinz Eugen* (which had survived the cruise of the *Bismarck* in 1941) and the destroyers *Z-25* and *Z-28*. On August 20, the *Prinz Eugen* fired more than a hundred 203 mm shells on Soviet positions, and the destroyers fired more than 150 smaller shells. Strackwitz reached Army Group North's outposts near Tuckum at noon, completing the linkup. Verbaende Strackwitz was followed by the 52nd Security Division, which temporarily screened the narrow corridor while badly needed supply convoys headed for Army Group North. Along the Baltic Sea coast, the security units found ten abandoned Soviet tanks, twenty-three guns, eleven antitank guns, and assorted other equipment.

The next day, Reinhardt recommended to Guderian that Army Group North be withdrawn into East Prussia for the defense of the Reich. Hitler, however, rejected this suggestion for political reasons—he was concerned that Finland was about to defect. By this time, Army Group Center had reinforced Schoerner with a panzer division. Stalin, however, had also reinforced the three fronts attacking him; Army Group North was now facing 130 Soviet divisions.

Meanwhile, against the wishes of OKH, General Schoerner took charge of Panzer Formation Count Strachwitz, attached an artillery battalion and an engineer company to it, and sent it on to Estonia, where he expected the next Russian attack. He did not have long to wait. The next day, August 21, the 3rd Baltic Front struck again with three armies, between Dorpat and Walk. They wanted to break through and link up with the Leningrad Front to the north, encircling Hasse's II Corps. The Germans, however, gave ground very slowly, and Schoerner had time to reinforce II Corps with elements of Army Detachment Narva. There was no major breakthrough, although the Soviets did manage a minor penetration in the zone of the 87th Infantry Division on August 23. By this time, Panzer Formation Count Strachwitz was arriving in the rear of II Corps. Schoerner ordered it to counterattack that evening.

Unfortunately, everything went wrong for the Verbaende that night. Count Strachwitz went forward on a reconnaissance, which ended in a car crash. His head, legs, arms, and hands were severely injured, and he was not expected to live at first. He did pull through, but it would be months before he would be able to return to duty.[52] Lieutenant General Gottfried Weber, the commander of the 12th Luftwaffe Field Division, took temporary command of the formation and organized it for the battle but refused to actually lead the attack, on the grounds that he was a stranger to the unit.[53] Schoerner instead gave this mission to Lieutenant General Walter Chales de Beaulieu, the commander of the 23rd Infantry Division, in spite of their intense mutual dislike. Perhaps he made this move because Chales, the former chief of staff of the 4th Panzer Army, had experience in armored operations. It any case, the Verbaende gained a little ground before it was counterattacked by large Soviet formations and forced over to the defensive. By the time Chales de Beaulieu retreated that night, his two brigades combined had only three operational tanks and a hundred men left. Schoerner chalked up another black mark against Chales and replaced him with Colonel Meinrad von Lauchert.[54] Chales de Beaulieu returned to his division, at least for the moment; Schoerner would relieve him of his command and end his military career in less than three weeks.[55]

The Soviet attacks continued. On August 24, they separated Army Detachment Narva from 18th Army. The next day, the Soviet 67th Army attacked Dorpat, which was defended by the 11th Infantry Division and a few other elements of II Corps. The Reds pounded the city and German positions with heavy artillery and fighter-bombers. Then they advanced into the built-up area, where the veteran East Prussian division met them with *Panzerfausts* and other antitank weapons. The fighting was house to house and hand to hand in the streets. The city was in flames when the Prussians finally evacuated it that night.

By now, Army Group North's casualties exceeded seventy thousand. It was down to a strength of 570,000 men, augmented by 43,000 "Hiwis"— Eastern volunteers. They were supported by 1st Air Fleet, which had fewer than three hundred airplanes. The Soviets had 125 infantry divisions, five tank corps, and a mechanized corps. Their infantry was supported by 3,080 tanks, 17,480 guns, and 2,640 aircraft.

To the south, Stalin renewed his efforts to capture Riga, the capital of Latvia. To defend the city, 16th Army created Combat Group General of Infantry Boege. It included Corps Group Lieutenant General Risse (58th, 205th, and 225th Infantry Divisions), the 389th Infantry Division, X Corps (24th Infantry Division and a few GHQ units), and Corps Group Lieutenant General Wagner (121st and 329th Infantry Divisions). Meanwhile, on August 29, the brilliant commander of the 16th Army, General of Infantry Paul Laux, was shot down on a reconnaissance flight and severely burned. His operations officer, Colonel Kurt Hartmann, was killed. Laux died of his wounds on September 2. He was succeeded by Carl Hilpert, the commander of the I Corps, who led the army until March 1945. Lieutenant General Theodor Busse, the brother-in-law and close friend of Lieutenant General Wilhelm Burgdorf, the murderous pro-Nazi chief of the Army Personnel Office, was promoted to the command of I Corps, despite the fact that he had less than two months experience as a divisional commander. Colonel Werner Rank succeeded Busse as commander of the 121st Infantry Division.[56]

Meanwhile, Schoerner's other army commander, General Loch, appears to have come under suspicion of being an anti-Nazi. Certainly Schoerner did not think he commanded his army with sufficient brutality. He was relieved on September 2 and replaced by General of Infantry Ehrenfried Boege, the commander of the XXXXIII Corps, who would lead the 18th Army for the rest of the war.

By August 27, Raus's 3rd Panzer Army had established a corridor eighteen miles wide to Army Group North. In early September, a lull descended upon most of the Eastern Front, as Stalin's armies regrouped for their next onslaught. In the political and diplomatic fronts, however, things were much more active.

Hitler was right to be concerned about Finland. On August 17, Field Marshal Wilhelm Keitel, the commander in chief of the High Command of the Armed Forces (OKW), arrived in Helsinki.[57] He awarded the Finnish president, Marshal Carl Gustav von Mannerheim, with the Oak Leaves to the Knight's Cross and decorated his chief of staff with the Knight's Cross. He tried to present as optimistic a picture of Germany's military situation as was possible (which was very difficult, under the circumstances) and asserted that the Third Reich could fight on for ten more years, if necessary. The old Finnish marshal diplomatically replied that this was probably true—a nation of ninety million might be able to. Then he cleared the air telling Keitel that the Ryti-Ribbentrop agreement, which made Finland a German ally, had been nullified by Prime Minister Rysto Ryti's resignation. Keitel lamely replied that he could not accept this statement, as he was not authorized to receive political communications. Mannerheim informed Keitel that he had agreed to combine civilian and military power under himself and that Finland would henceforth act in its own interests. Keitel left Helsinki with the knowledge that the Finnish-German alliance was at an end and that Mannerheim intended to take Finland out of the war.

Helsinki accepted Soviet armistice terms on September 2 and formally declared a cease-fire two days later. Stalin's bargain was harsh, and Helsinki was left with a crushing reparations debt, but at least Finland avoided Soviet annexation. Shortly thereafter, Dr. Lothar Rendulic's 20th Mountain Army (whose two hundred thousand men were outnumbered two to one by the Finns alone) began to withdraw slowly from northern Finland to Norway.[58] The Red Army showed little interest in pinning down this army, and relations between the German and Finnish military remained quite good, in spite of the tense geopolitical situation. Then the German naval staff persuaded Hitler to agree to the seizing of the Finnish naval base at Suursaari. The Germans did not expect the Finnish garrison to resist, but it did, driving the Germans off with heavy losses. A few days later, the individualistic Finnish General Siilasvuo provoked a battle for the Baltic coast town of Tornio, which was destroyed in heavy fighting.[59]

Hitler's attack on Suursaari played into Soviet hands and relieved Mannerheim of an embarrassing situation. He was now in a position to demand that Colonel General Rendulic accelerate his withdrawal and promptly did so. Rendulic, however, realized that the Finnish demand had been made in order to satisfy the Soviets; he continued to withdraw slowly, shadowed by the Finns, but there were no further incidents. Twentieth Mountain Army brought off all of it's heavy equipment and most of its munitions and was out of Finland by the end of October (except for a small strip of that country that it held until April 1945). It would now be able to meet either a Soviet or Anglo-American invasion of Norway with at least a reasonable chance of success. Despite Hitler's fears, however, no such invasion was launched. Almost half a million German troops were left idle in Norway for the next few months, awaiting an attack that never came, while the Wehrmacht—at the end of its manpower reserves—bled to death on both the Eastern and Western Fronts. Table 4.3 shows the order of battle of the 20th Mountain Army and the Army of Norway on September 16, 1944.

By December 1944, it was clear that an invasion of Norway was unlikely, and Hitler began to move troops from Norway to the mainland of Europe, where the Third Reich was in imminent danger on invasion from both east and west. There was obviously no longer any need to have two German army headquarters in Norway; the Army of Norway was dissolved, and its commander, Colonel General Nikolaus von Falkenhorst, the non-Nazi Wehrmacht Commander in Norway, was retired. Falkenhorst, who had opposed the brutal occupation policies of Joseph Treboven, Hitler's Commissioner of Norway, was replaced by the Austrian Rendulic, who was an enthusiastic National Socialist. The last months of the German occupation were not happy ones for the Norwegian people. On January 17, 1945, Rendulic was succeeded as commander of the 20th Mountain Army and Wehrmacht Commander of Norway by General of Mountain Troops Franz Boehme, another Austrian. Like Rendulic, Boehme tended to cooperate

Table 4.3
Order of Battle, 20th Mountain Army and the Army of Norway,
September 16, 1944

20th Mountain Army
XVIII Mountain Corps:
    7th Mountain Division
    6th SS Mountain Division
    140th Special Purposes Division
XXXVI Mountain Corps:
    163rd Infantry Division
    169th Infantry Division
XIX Mountain Corps:
    6th Mountain Division[1]
    2nd Mountain Division
    210th Infantry Division (Static)
    Division Group Rossi[2]

Army of Norway
LXXI Corps:
    230th Infantry Division (Static)
    270th Infantry Division (Static)
    199th Infantry Division
XXXIII Corps:
    14th Luftwaffe Field Division
    702nd Infantry Division
    295th Infantry Division (Static)
LXX Corps:
    280th Infantry Division (Static)
    269th Infantry Division
    274th Infantry Division (Static)
    710th Infantry Division
Army Reserve:
    560th Infantry Division[2,3]

Notes:
[1]With the 388th Grenadier Brigade attached
[2]Included 193rd and 503rd Grenadier Brigades
[3]In transit

Source: Mehner, ed., *Geheimen Tagesberichte*, vol. 11, p. 340.

with Treboven and his thugs. He ended his own life on May 29, 1947, in a Nuremberg jail cell, where he was awaiting trial as a war criminal.[60]

The defection of Finland left Schoerner in a strategically useless and tactically dangerous position. His forces held a front more than four hundred miles long, with their backs to the sea. Meanwhile, Stavka was obviously preparing to annihilate his army group. The Soviet buildup proceeded slowly enough for Schoerner to follow it. North to south, the Russian Leningrad Front faced Army Detachment Narva with the 8th and 2nd Shock Armies and was in a position to encircle and destroy it. Converging for an attack on Riga and the 18th Army were the 3rd Baltic Front (67th, 1st Shock, and 6th Armies), the 2nd Baltic Front (10th Guards, 42nd, 3rd Shock and 22nd Armies), and the 1st Baltic Front (4th Shock, 43rd, 51st, and 5th Guards Tank Armies), while the 6th Guard Army (of the 1st Baltic Front) and 3rd Belorussian Front (39th, 5th, 11th Guards, and 31st Armies) were preparing to attack the 16th Army and break Army Group North's tenuous link with the 3rd Panzer Army and East Prussia.

Not even Schoerner believed that the Riga corridor in the east could be held. Army Detachment Narva in Estonia was 120 miles away at the nearest point, and 220 miles away at the farthest. The Soviets, on the other hand, were within thirty-five miles of the city. Hitler and OKH (Guderian), however, believed that it could be held and would not allow Schoerner to withdraw. Hitler wanted to keep Estonian oil and other raw materials, while General Dankers, the head of the Estonian government, gave his full support to the German defense. This did not prevent thousands of Estonians, including entire police battalions, from deserting to the Russians.

Events proved Schoerner right. On the morning of September 14, following an artillery barrage of an hour and a half, the Russians launched a massive offensive with all three Baltic *fronts*. The Luftwaffe's 54th Fighter Wing, the only fighter formation in the Baltic States, particularly distinguished itself by shooting down seventy-six Russian airplanes in one day—more than its own strength. It had no impact on the overall air battle, however, the Russians maintained aerial supremacy. On the ground, the German troops responded magnificently and held the attackers to a maximum advance of four miles, but the relentless attacks continued. Map 4.2 shows how the situation developed between September 14 and October 10.

The focus of the 3rd Baltic Front's offensive was in the zone of the XXVIII Corps of the 18th Army. The combat strengths of its divisions—the 21st, 30th, 31st, and 227th Infantry and the 12th Luftwaffe—had already declined to dangerous levels, and now they suffered more casualties every hour. The 12th Luftwaffe Field repulsed thirteen Russian attacks but could not hold under the weight of the fourteenth. The last reserves had to be committed to seal off the penetration. The other divisions checked the Soviet attacks in their sectors, although some did so in their third (and final) trench line, having lost the first two.

The major effort of the 2nd Baltic Front came around Ergli, west of Modohn, in the zone of the X Corps of the 16th Army. It also was repulsed. The attack of the 1st Baltic Front, however, was more successful. Here two Soviet armies, with eighteen rifle divisions and two tank brigades, struck

Map 4.2
Army Group North, September 14–October 10, 1944

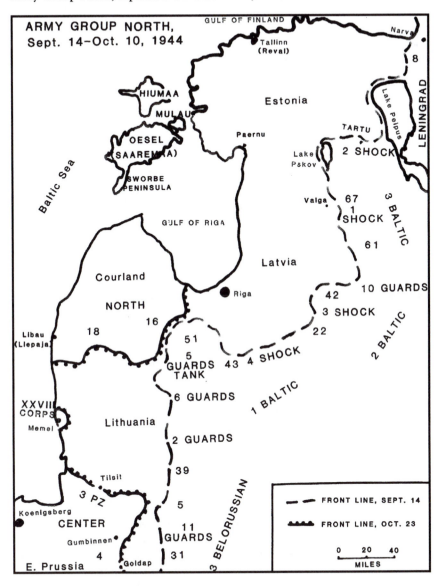

the I Corps and its four understrength divisions—the 58th, 215th, and 290th Infantry and 281st Security.

The initial artillery bombardment knocked out most of the German supporting artillery, including the 636th Army Artillery Battalion (equipped with 210 mm mortars) and the 814th Army Artillery Battalion (heavy howitzers). Then the Russian infantry came in waves, centering on the 215th and 290th Infantry Divisions. The two divisions were routed. The Russians poured into the German rear and captured Bauske. General Hilpert, the 16th Army commander, committed his reserve—the 101st Panzer Brigade under Colonel von Lauchert—to the sector. It ran into the III Guards Mechanized Corps, which pinned it down in heavy fighting. By nightfall on September 15, the Russians were only about twenty-five miles south of Riga, and Schoerner was calling for the evacuation of Estonia, stating that this was the last possible moment to escape. Receiving no reply, Schoerner flew to Fuehrer Headquarters in person the next day to argue with the Fuehrer. Another commander might have been sacked for this, but not Schoerner, who was known to be strongly pro-Nazi. Hitler put up a whole series of objections but in the end agreed to a retreat if Schoerner would wait two days and if the order could be canceled in the meantime. Raus's 3rd Panzer Army was due to attack the next day, to relieve the pressure on Army Group North, and Hitler apparently wanted to await the results of this battle.

Raus's attack was made with the three divisions of von Saucken's XXXIX Panzer Corps. They destroyed sixty-two Russian tanks, twenty-nine assault guns, 147 antitank guns, and thirty-seven field artillery pieces. The attack failed, however; the Russians were simply too strong. Meanwhile, Schoerner dissolved musical bands and supply units. He threw literally everything he had into the battle—except Colonel Geiger's 3rd Higher Engineer Command. He ordered it to begin constructing positions at Aa and Tuckum to defend Courland (Kurland) in case the army group had to retreat into the last-ditch position—as Schoerner obviously expected.

On September 16, the 18th Army continued to hold its line, but the I Corps (of 16th Army) could not. By nightfall, Russian tanks had pushed to within fifteen miles of Riga. On September 17, the 2nd Shock Army pushed passed Army Detachment Narva and finally took Tartu, unhinging its northern flank. That night, to save his southern flank, Schoerner ordered elements of Steiner's III SS Panzer Corps, including the veteran East Prussian 11th Infantry Division, to make the retreat from the Narva River to Paernu on the Gulf of Riga (120 miles) by September 20. The rest of the SS corps would be evacuated by sea from Reval (now Tallinn), the capital of Estonia. Army Detachment Narva was now dissolved, and General Grasser was named commanding general, Wehrmacht Command East, with authority over all branches of the service, the SS, the police, the civil administration and the RAD (Reich Labor Service.)

As the 18th Army's southwestern flank was finally beginning to buckle under the incessant attacks, it seemed as if the East Prussians and III SS had little chance of reaching their destination before 18th Army collapsed. If they failed to arrive in time and keep the Riga corridor open, the entire

18th Army would be lost. Schoerner rushed every motorized unit, self-propelled antiaircraft gun, and assault gun unit he could lay his hands on to the 18th Army at Vortsjaerv. This desperate measure enabled the German line at Vortsjaerv to hold—but just barely.

Meanwhile, to the south, 3rd Panzer Army attacked again and this time made progress. By September 18, it had pushed a ten-mile salient in the Soviet flank, freezing the Russian reserves, which might have otherwise been used at Riga. Even so, on September 19, the Red spearheads reached a point near the Dvina, only ten miles south of Riga. Here they were finally halted. On September 20, the III SS Panzer Corps arrived at Paernu, while the II Corps (General Hasse) pivoted 180 degrees and continued the retreat to the south, forming the rearguard for 18th Army. Although this retreat was an undeniably skillful tactical maneuver on the part of Schoerner and his subordinates, northern Estonia was lost, and the survival of Army Group North was still by no means assured.

On September 17, a German naval force under Vice Admiral Theodor Burchardi, the Commanding Admiral, East Baltic, began evacuating battle groups of the III SS Panzer Corps and the motorized elements of the 11th Infantry Division, as well as Estonians loyal to the Reich, Estonian police, and the 20th Estonian SS Division. The evacuation was completed on September 22, when the Red Army entered Reval. Burchardi had evacuated fifty thousand soldiers (more than thirteen thousand of whom were wounded), twenty thousand civilians, and almost a thousand prisoners.[61]

Hitler, meanwhile, transferred 3rd Panzer Army (Raus) to Army Group North and ordered Schoerner to regroup and counterattack with his panzer divisions on the south and his infantry on the north, encircling and destroying the entire 1st Baltic Front in its salient southwest of Riga. The Russians, however, did not give Schoerner enough time to attempt this doubtful maneuver. On September 18, using the six reserve divisions freed by the halt of 3rd Panzer Army's counterattack, they struck again all along the line. In the zone of the 18th Army, the XXVIII Corps turned back every attack, but for once the L Corps could not stop the Soviet heavy tanks, which broke through at the seam connecting the East Prussian 21st Infantry Division with the 31st Infantry. The 31st Division fell back into Wolmar, where it fought on for hours, finally retreating after sunset. The 21st Infantry Division was virtually destroyed. Among those killed was the division's most distinguished officer, Colonel Herbert Schwender, the commander of the 45th Infantry Regiment. He was posthumously awarded the Knight's Cross with Oak Leaves and Swords—the equivalent to the Victoria Cross or the Congressional Medal of Honor. He was thirty-two years old. Also dead was General of Infantry Wilhelm Wegener, the commander of the L Corps. He fell fighting at the front as the Russians overran his corps.

The 18th Army was near collapse. General Boege reported that since

September 14 his army had been attacked by seventy Russian divisions, as well as two tank corps and several independent brigades. His troops had knocked out 622 tanks, but ten of his eighteen divisions were now *kampf-gruppen.*

The next day, September 19, was another disastrous one for Army Group North. The Soviets managed to surround the 205th Infantry Division near Misa. General von Mellenthin launched an immediate breakout attempt and reached the 215th Infantry Division at Vecmuiza, but his division was no longer battleworthy. The Russian 43rd Army pushed even closer to Riga, Lieutenant General Hermann Foertsch's X Corps was smashed west of Madona, and the 3rd Baltic Front broke through and passed Valga. The 11th SS Panzer Grenadier Division "Nordland" (now commanded by SS Major General Joachim Ziegler) force-marched 250 miles in four days and arrived south of Riga on September 22, just in time to shore up X Corps and prevent a disaster.

Schoerner, meanwhile, continued preparing to move the army group into the Courland bridgehead. On September 24, he moved his command post from Segewold to the Pelci Palace near Goldingen, in Kurland. By September 26, the 11th, 30th, 31st, and 218th Infantry Divisions and the SS Divisions "Nordland" and "Niederlande" were either in Courland or en route there, along with the remnants of the 21st Infantry. Schoerner also ordered Major General Otto Rauser, the senior quartermaster of the army group, to quietly begin the evacuation of Riga.

Summer had now given way to autumn, and the Russian winter was not far off. The rains had come, and they were both cold and continuous. The wind blew, chilling the men to the bone as they marched toward what would soon be known as the Courland Pocket. The Latvians felt another kind of cold, however, and that was fear. They knew that they were about to be abandoned to the tender mercies of the Red Army, which would be followed by Stalin's secret police.

By September 27, the retreat was over, as least for the moment. The frontage of the 16th and 18th Armies had been reduced from 240 to seventy miles. The Soviets could attack this tighter front now only with greater difficulty and less chance for profit. On September 27, 16th Army reported heavy enemy traffic heading southwest, away from its front. Schoerner therefore reinforced 3rd Panzer Army with Panzer Verbaende Colonel von Lauchert (i.e., the 303rd Assault Gun Brigade and SS Panzer Brigade "Gross"). He also returned the 25th Panzer Regiment and the II/6th Panzer Grenadier Regiment to the 7th Panzer Division for employment farther south.

Stavka, in fact, had decided to strike due west toward Memel (Klaypeda) with the 3rd Belorussian and 1st Baltic Fronts, while the 2nd and 3rd Baltic Fronts pursued Army Group North into Courland. Hitler on the other hand, was determined that Army Group North launch a counterattack. On

September 30, Schoerner told Hitler that to attack, Army Group North would have to pull its front east of Riga back to positions nearer the city; start the evacuation of Riga as a precaution; absorb thirty thousand replacements (which Hitler had not yet sent); and conduct an extensive regrouping. Schoerner did not believe he could accomplish all of this before November 3.

Schoerner also did not believe that the 1st Baltic Front could redeploy for a drive against 3rd Panzer Army before October 16. In late September, Guderian sent him a directive (approved by Hitler) allowing him to send a tank-strong detachment from 3rd Panzer Army to the north, to block the approaches to Memel. Schoerner did not believe Memel was in any danger, so he ignored Guderian's warning. He was wrong. On October 5, Ivan Bagramian's 1st Baltic Front struck the 3rd Panzer Army along a sixty-mile front west of Shaulyay with twenty-nine rifle divisions, an armored corps with more than five hundred tanks, and four independent tank brigades. The focus was against Colonel Siegfried Verhein's 551st Volksgrenadier Division, which was responsible for a twenty-four-mile sector—a zone so long that it could only be manned at strong points. By the end of the day, the 551st VG was smashed, and the 1st Baltic Front had achieved its break-out and was more than ten miles in the rear of XXVIII Corps. On October 6, Bagramian committed the 5th Guards Tank Army to the rush to Memel, while the Russian 39th Army (on the right flank of the 3rd Belorussian Front) began a drive toward Tilsit, and the Leningrad Front began an amphibious attack on Saaremaa, a Baltic Sea island less than twenty miles from the tip of Courland. (The island would be cleared of German forces by the middle of the month.) Schoerner, however, was too busy elsewhere to pay much attention to Saaremaa. He ordered 3rd Panzer Army to reinforce the XXVIII Corps in the Memel sector with the Grossdeutschland Panzer Grenadier Division. He also sent the 14th Panzer Division south, along with the 502nd Heavy Panzer Battalion and two heavy artillery battalions—but it was too late.[62]

On October 7, 3rd Panzer Army's front broke completely. The 5th Guards Tank and 43rd Armies reached the coast north and south of Memel on October 9, while other elements of the Red Army reached the East Prussian border on the evening of October 7. There were no combat divisions available to defend here—only the training units of the II Field Jaeger (Light Infantry) Corps under General of Infantry Karl von Oven. Fortunately for the province of East Prussia, the Soviets did not know this. Meanwhile, the 3rd Panzer Army's command post was overrun by the Russians. General Raus and his staff had to break out of an encirclement and fight their way into Memel, where Gollnick's XXVIII Corps formed a beachhead around the port with the remnants of its divisions—the 58th Infantry, the 7th Panzer, the Grossdeutschland, and what was left of the 551st Volksgrenadier—as well as the 6th Flak Regiment, the 502nd Heavy

Panzer Battalion, the 217th and 227th Naval Flak Battalions, four security battalions, and a couple of *Volkssturm* (home guard) companies. Army Group North, which now had twenty-six divisions (two of them panzer), was cut off for the second and final time.

On October 9, Schoerner signaled Hitler that he would attack toward Memel and rescue XXVIII Corps; however, to get enough divisions for this operation and to defend northern Courland against possible amphibious attacks, he would have to evacuate Riga. Hitler delayed a decision on Riga until October 11. The German Navy, on the other hand, reacted quickly to save the Memel garrison. It sent in the 14th Security Flotilla, the 15th, 16th, and 22nd Minesweeper Flotillas, the 24th U-Boat Flotilla, and finally the air defense ship *Hans Albrecht Wedel*. The operation was conducted from October 7 to 12; the garrison was rescued, but only a small fraction of the thirty thousand civilians could be gotten out. Many of the rest were raped and/or murdered by the Russians.[63] Also, four German divisions—including the elite Grossdeutschland and the 7th Panzer, which had become famous as Rommel's "Ghost Division" in the French campaign of 1940—lost all of their tanks, guns, and vehicles. They would have to be completely rebuilt.

On October 10, the Soviets pushed even closer to Riga and brought the city under artillery fire. Meanwhile, OKH returned 3rd Panzer Army to the control of Army Group Center. It had one corps surrounded at Memel, with its back to the sea, and one corps cut off to the north, where it joined Army Group North. This left it with an effective operational strength of only one corps, and it was pinned down, defending Tilsit against the Soviet 39th Army.

One after another, the defeated divisions of the 18th Army retreated silently through Riga, which resembled a city of the dead. Lieutenant General Werner Anton's 6th Motorized Flak Division guarded the route of retreat with dozens of antiaircraft (AA) batteries, including thirty-three batteries of 88 mm AA guns. Major General Maximilian Wengler's 227th Infantry Division and Captain Barths's 393rd Assault Gun Brigade formed the rearguard of the army. After the last assault gun crossed the Duena, the engineers blew up the last bridge, shortly before 2 A.M. on October 13.

Riga was captured by General I. I. Maslennikov's 3rd Baltic Front on October 13, and five days later three Soviet armies attacked into East Prussia. On October 21, Hitler decided that Schoerner's idea for a counteroffensive by Army Group North was no longer feasible and ordered him to go over to the defensive. Ten days later, he rejected another Schoerner plan to reestablish contact to the south and began to take divisions away from Army Group North, via the Baltic Sea route.[64] He turned a deaf ear to Guderian's repeated pleas that the entire army group be evacuated back to Germany. Army Group North spent the rest of the war isolated in Courland, where it performed no strategic purpose whatsoever.

Map 4.3
Army Group North, October 10, 1944

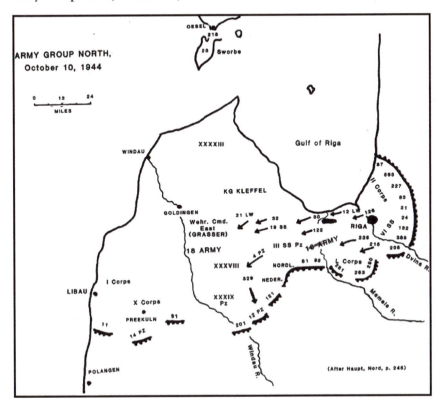

Despite their desperate situation, the morale of the German troops and their allies remained remarkably high. When Reval (Tallinn) and Riga fell, for example, it would have been reasonable to expect demoralization and desertions from the Estonian and Latvian battalions. Instead, as they evacuated Riga, the 19th Latvian Fusiliers marched out of town singing.

On October 15, the Soviets launched their first major attempt to crush the Courland Pocket, when they struck the 19th SS Grenadier Division "Latvian No. 2" and the German 504th Grenadier Regiment near Dzukste. In a week of heavy fighting, the Latvians and the 504th Grenadiers held their positions, shooting up two Russian tank brigades and a rifle division in the process.[65] By the time the battle ended on November 7, Schoerner's regiments had knocked out 522 Russian tanks; their own losses totaled only twenty field pieces and antitank guns.[66] The Reds gained only about a mile of territory in this, the First Battle of the Courland Pocket. There would be five more in the next eight months. Map 4.3 shows Army Group North's initial position in the Courland pocket.

Meanwhile, in late September and early October, the Russian 8th Army—using American-made landing craft—began conducting amphibious attacks against the Baltic Sea islands in the Gulf of Riga. These were defended by the 23rd and 218th Infantry Divisions (led by Lieutenant Generals Hans Schirmer and Viktor Lang, respectively). They held off six Russian divisions for eight weeks; then they were evacuated to Courland by the German Navy, without losing even their heavy equipment. The operation, however, further intensified the isolation of the German 16th and 18th Armies in the Courland region of eastern Latvia. Meanwhile, the focus of the war had long since shifted south, to Rumania, where Hitler's Wehrmacht had suffered yet another disastrous defeat.

NOTES

1. Horst von Mellenthin had been educated at cadet schools and entered the service as a *Faehnrich* (senior officer cadet) in 1915. During the Hitler era, he was chief of the attaché branch at OKH (1937); commander, 677th Artillery Regiment (1940); commander, 67th Infantry Regiment (1943); acting commander, 23rd Infantry Division (1943); acting commander, 93rd Infantry Division (1943); commander, 205th Infantry Division (December 1, 1943); deputy commander, XVI Corps (1944); and commander, XXXVIII Panzer Corps, XI Corps, and VIII Corps (1945). He was promoted to lieutenant general on July 1, 1944, and to general of artillery in 1945. His younger brother, F. W., was Rommel's chief of intelligence in Africa and later became a major general and chief of staff of Army Group G and the 5th Panzer Army in the West.

2. Walter Melzer, *Geschichte der 252 Infanterie-Division* (Bad Nauheim: 1960), pp. 201–204. The division's 472nd Grenadier Regiment was forced into the zone of the 24th Infantry Division.

3. Georg Lindemann was born at Osterburg in Altmark on March 8, 1884, and entered the army as a *Fahnenjunker* in 1903. Commissioned in the 6th Dragoon Regiment the following year, he transferred to the *jaegers* (light infantry) and, as a first lieutenant, was involved in the drive on Paris in 1914. Then he finished his General Staff training and spent the rest of the war in staff positions, mostly on the Western Front. Selected for retention in the Reichswehr, he was a colonel commanding the 13th Cavalry Regiment in 1931. During World War II, he led the 36th Infantry Division (1936–40), L Corps (1940–42), 18th Army (1942–44), and Army Group North (1944). He owed the last three promotions more to political intrigue and the fact that he ingratiated himself with the Nazis than to any other factor. See Samuel W. Mitcham, Jr. and Gene Mueller, *Hitler's Commanders* (Latham, Md.: 1992), pp. 58–62.

4. Kurt Versock had been wounded in the retreat from Leningrad and had only recently returned to his division. On September 3, 1944, he assumed command of the XXXXIII Corps and in 1945 was promoted to general of mountain troops. Gerhard Henke later commanded the 11th Luftwaffe Field Division. After the war, he spent seven years in Yugoslav prisons.

5. Hellmuth Priess was born in 1896 and entered the service in 1914, when

World War I broke out. Initially a *Fahnenjunker* in the infantry, he was a lieutenant colonel on the staff of OKW when the war began. Priess served successively as quartermaster of 1st Army (1940); commander, 671st Infantry Regiment (1942); and commander of the 121st Infantry Division (1942). He was succeeded by Lieutenant General Theodor Busse on July 7, 1944. Priess rebuilt the XXVII Corps (which had been destroyed in Operation Bagration) and commanded it from July 27 to October 21, 1944, when he was killed in action near Hasenrode, East Prussia. He had been promoted to general of infantry on October 1 (Keilig, p. 262).

6. Werner Haupt, *Heeresgruppe Nord, 1941–1945* (Bad Nauheim: 1966), p. 199. A cavalry officer and a Silesian, Baron von Gersdorff was only thirty-nine years old in 1944. He spent the entire war in various staff positions. He was also a prominent anti-Hitler conspirator and even volunteered to become a "human bomb" and blow himself up with the Fuehrer. He managed to get into Hitler's presence and activate the timing mechanism on the bomb, but Hitler left suddenly. Fortunately for Gersdorff, he was able to get to a restroom and disarm the bomb. Gersdorff's part in the anti-Hitler plot was never discovered by the Gestapo, suggesting that he benefited from divine protection. He was struck by lightning during the Battle of the Falaise Pocket, but survived that as well. He ended the war as a major general and chief of staff of 7th Army on the Western Front. An American prisoner of war until 1947, he died in Munich in 1980.

7. Carl Hilpert was born in Nuremberg in 1888 and entered the Bavarian Army as a *Fahnenjunker* in 1907. He later served as commander of the 35th Infantry Regiment (1935), chief of staff of IX Corps (1937), chief of staff of Army Detachment A on the Western Front (1939), chief of staff of Frontier Guard Sector South in Poland (1939), chief of staff of 1st Army (1940), and chief of staff of Army Group B in France (1940). A furious Hitler unjustly relieved him of his post after a successful British commando raid on St. Nazaire. Three months later, Hilpert went to the East and began a fine professional comeback, serving as acting commander of LIX Corps (1942), commander of XXIII Corps (1942), commander of LIV Corps (1943), commander of I Corps (January 1, 1944), and commander of 16th Army. On March 3, 1945, he became the last commander of Army Group Courland (formerly North). He was promoted to colonel general effective May 1, 1945. He died in a Moscow prison in 1946.

8. A higher artillery command (*Hoeherer Artillerie-Kommandeur*) was a staff normally charged with providing artillery support for an army. It is translated "higher artillery commander" when referring to the commanding general only. The *Arko (Artillerie-Kommandeur)* provided support for a corps. The 315th Higher Artillery Command (Harko 315) was charged with supporting 16th Army (Tessin, vol. 9, p. 76). Christian Usinger entered the service as an eighteen-year-old war volunteer in 1914 and earned a reserve commission in the artillery. He was a police officer from 1920 to 1935, when he reentered the army as a major. He successively commanded an artillery battalion (1935), an artillery regiment (1939), Arko 146 (1941), Arko 110 (1942), the 223rd Infantry Division (1942), Harko 315 (1943) and I Corps (April 20, 1945). He died in a Russian prison in 1949.

9. At the end of the war, Herbert Wagner was Higher Artillery Commander 302 in East Prussia.

10. Rudolf Geiger was promoted to major general on December 1, 1944. He was later sent to the Balkans, where he surrendered to the Yugoslavs. Sentenced to

twenty years in prison, he was amnestied in 1951 and returned to his native Austria, where he died in 1972.

11. Walter Warlimont, "From the Invasion to the Siegfried Line," *ETHINT 1* (European Theater Historical Interrogation 1). Historical Division, U.S. Army 1945, U.S. Army Institute of Military History, Carlisle Barracks, Penn.

12. Baron Mauritz von Strachwitz was also a Silesian and apparently distantly related to Count Hyazinth Strachwitz. He was the former chief of operations for the 18th Infantry Division (1938), VIII Corps (1939), and 18th Army (1940). He became chief of staff of the X Corps in early 1942 and commander of the 87th Infantry Division in November 1943. He led the 87th until the end of the war. Baron von Strachwitz died in a Soviet prison in 1953.

13. Johann Pflugbeil was a "retread," having retired in 1938 after thirty-two years' service. Recalled to active duty in 1939, he commanded the 221st Infantry (later Security) Division (1939–42) and the 388th Field Training Division (later Field Training Division North and Division Kurland) in 1942–45. He apparently returned to Germany in the last days of the war. He died in Stuttgart in 1951.

14. Johannes Friessner was born in Chemnitz on March 22, 1892. He joined the army as a *Fahnenjunker* in the 103rd Infantry Regiment in 1912, fought in World War I, and served in the Reichsheer. He was chief inspector of the war schools in 1938 and was on the staff of the Replacement Army when the war broke out. Promoted to major general in 1940, he commanded the 102nd Infantry Division (1942–43), the XXIII Corps (1943–44), and Army Detachment Narva (from February 2, 1944).

A former police officer, Anton Grasser earned a reserve commission in the infantry during World War I. He had previously commanded the 25th Infantry Division (1942), LVI Panzer Corps (1943), and XXVI Corps (January 1, 1944). He was commander of the West German Border Guards in the early 1950s.

15. Haupt, *Nord*, p. 207.

16. After forty-one years of service, Christian Hansen retired to Garmisch and was never reemployed. He had previously commanded the 10th Artillery Regiment (1933), 25th Infantry Division (1936), and X Corps (1939). He assumed command of 16th Army in November 1943. General Hansen died in Garmisch in 1972.

Wilhelm Hasse was promoted to general of infantry, effective August 1, 1944. He was named commander of the 17th Army on March 30, 1945, and surrendered it to the Soviets on May 8, 1945. Later that day he was mortally wounded. He died in Soviet captivity on May 21.

17. Kochling's predecessor, General of Infantry Thomas-Emil von Wickede, had been killed in an accident on June 23, 1944.

18. Haupt, *Nord*, p. 211.

19. A veteran artillery officer, Kurt Herzog had been in the army since 1907. During the Nazi era, he commanded the 31st Artillery Regiment (1935), Arko I (1938), I Engineer Command (1939), Arko 108 (1939), and the 291st Infantry Division (1940). He had commanded the XXXVIII Corps (later Panzer Corps) since June 1942. General Herzog died in a Soviet prison in 1948.

20. Hans Gollnick (born 1892) joined the army as an infantry officer-cadet in 1912. He spent the entire World War II period in command positions, leading the 76th Infantry Regiment (1939), the 36th Panzer Grenadier Division (1941), the

XXXXVI Panzer Corps (1943), and the XXVIII Corps (May 20, 1944–end). Released from British captivity in 1946, he retired to Hamburg.

21. Haupt, *Nord*, p. 210.

22. Eberhard Kinzel spent the war in higher staff positions, successively serving as chief intelligence officer, East, at OKH (1938); chief of staff of XXIX Corps (1942); and chief of staff of Army Group North (from January 22, 1943). Sacked by Guderian, he was unemployed for more than eight months. He returned to active duty as chief of staff of Army Group Vistula in March, 1945. He was promoted to general of infantry on April 20, 1945, and named chief of staff of OKW Operations Staff North two days later. Part of the Doenitz government, he committed suicide in Flensburg in May 1945.

23. Guderian, p. 281.

24. Oldwig von Natzmer was a former cavalry officer who joined the army as a *Fahnenjunker* in 1925. A major in 1939, he was promoted to lieutenant general in 1945. Highly capable, he spent the entire war in staff positions and was highly thought of by Schoerner, who even sometimes let his young chief of staff reverse his decisions—such as the summary execution of a private or a captain. Schoerner carried Natzmer with him when he was given command of Army Group Center in February 1945.

25. Wistrich, p. 277.

26. Haupt, *Nord*, p. 214.

27. Felix Steiner was born in Ebenrode, East Prussia, in 1896. He entered the army as an infantry *Fahnenjunker* in 1914 and was severely wounded in the Battle of Tannenburg. He spent four years on the Eastern Front in World War I. Demobilized in 1919, he joined the Freikorps and later the Reichsheer. A major in 1933, Steiner transferred to the SS as an SS lieutenant colonel in 1935. Here he commanded a battalion in the Deutschland Regiment (1935–36), the regiment itself (1936–40), and the SS Division "Viking" (later 5th SS Panzer Grenadier Division "Viking") (1940–43). After commanding the III SS Panzer Corps (1943–44), he directed the 11th Army during the Berlin campaign. He surrendered to the Americans and was released from the POW camps in 1948. A lifelong bachelor, he died in Munich on May 12, 1966.

28. About a thousand Estonian border guards deserted to the Soviets in July 1944 alone.

29. Allen Brandt, *The Last Knight of Flanders* (Atglen, Penn.: 1998), p. 115.

30. SS General Franz Augsberger commanded the 20th SS until March 19, 1945, when he was killed in action near Neustadt, Silesia.

31. Schrynen was promoted to sergeant later that year (1944).

32. The 11th SS Panzer Battalion was part of the 11th SS Volunteer Panzer Grenadier Division "Nordland." Paul-Albert Kausch was Steiner's former adjutant with the 5th SS Panzer Division "Viking." He was captured by the Soviets during the Battle of Berlin and spent ten years in Soviet prisons. After the war, he was an executive purchaser for a major pharmaceutical firm. He was still alive in 1981 (at age seventy). Brandt, p. 241.

33. Ibid., pp. 210–15. Wangemann, who had led the 2nd SS Tank Destroyer Battalion "Das Reich" in Normandy, led the 27th SS Tank Destroyer Battalion for the rest of the war. As of 1997, he was living in Kiel.

34. Hellmuth Maeder later served as acting commander the 7th Panzer Division (October–November 1944), took a divisional commanders' course, and was commander of the elite Grossdeutschland Panzer Grenadier Division at the end of the war. Maeder held the Knight's Cross with Oak Leaves and Swords and was promoted to major general in 1945. He spent ten years in Soviet prisons. Returning to West Germany, he joined the Bundeswehr as a brigadier general in 1958.

35. Haupt, *Nord*, p. 220.

36. Hans von Basse was an older officer. Born in 1887, he joined the army as a *Fahnenjunker* in 1902 and retired as a major in 1928. Recalled to active duty as a territorial officer in 1933, he assumed command of the 60th Infantry Regiment as a lieutenant colonel in 1935. Later he commanded the 182nd (1940) and 225th Infantry Divisions (1941), retiring again in January 1943. He was recalled to active duty once more that summer, as a special advisor on the staff of the 18th Army. He assumed command of the 30th Infantry Division in March. The fact that he was sacked by Schoerner had no impact on his career. OKH promptly named him German commander in west Hungary. An artillery officer, Otto Barth was promoted to major general in November. In February 1945 he was named commander of the 21st Luftwaffe Field Division. Like many German officers in the East, he spent the period May 1945 to October 1955 in Soviet prisons. He died in Baden-Baden in 1979.

37. Ziemke, pp. 342–43.

38. Keilig, p. 59.

39. Ziemke, p. 342.

40. James Lucas, *Hitler's Enforcers* (London: 1966), pp. 173–74.

41. Wilhelm Wegener had been educated at cadet schools and entered the service as an infantry *Faehnrich* in 1914, when World War I broke out. In 1939, he was a lieutenant colonel and adjutant of the II Corps. Later he commanded the 94th Infantry Regiment (1940–42) and 32nd Infantry Division (1942–43). A very brave officer, Wegener held the Knight's Cross with Oak Leaves and Swords. He assumed command of L Corps on September 12, 1943.

42. Philipp Kleffel had previously commanded 1st Infantry Division (1940), L Corps (1942), I Corps (1942), a special staff at OKH (1944), and XVI Corps (1944). He later led XXX Corps (1944), and he was deputy commander of the 25th Army at the end of the war.

43. Richard Landwehr, Jean-Louis Roba, and Ray Merriam, "The 'Walloon': The History of the 5th SS-Sturmbrigade and 28th SS Volunteer Panzergrenadier Division," *Weapons and Warfare/Siegrunen Series No. 1* (Bennington, Vt.: 1984), p. 2.

44. See Peter R. Black, *Ernst Kaltenbrunner* (Princeton, N.J.: 1984), p. 125. Frau Degrelle's apparent lover, a Luftwaffe officer named Helmuth Pess, was stationed in Brussels. On April 12, 1943, he was found in an alley with a bullet in his heart. Shortly thereafter, Degrelle told Gestapo investigators in Brussels that Pess had expressed a wish to commit suicide. Kaltenbrunner, whose RHSA controlled the Gestapo, did not believe the story for a moment but wrote to Himmler that he was suspending the investigation for "political reasons" and because "the moral right" lay with Degrelle.

45. Ironically, many of the members of the Walloon Brigade were Spaniards. In 1941, the Spanish dictator Francisco Franco sent the "Blue" Division, a unit of Spanish volunteers, to the Eastern Front, where it took part in the siege of Leningrad as the 250th Infantry Division. Seeing the writing on the wall (that Germany was going to lose the war), Franco recalled it in late 1943, but many of its men wanted to keep fighting. About a thousand of these formed a "Blue Legion," and most of them joined the Walloon Brigade after a personal appeal from Leon Dregelle. Landwehr et al., "Walloon," p. 2.

46. Yeager, vol. 1, pp. 112–14. Dregelle later commanded the 28th SS Volunteer Panzer Grenadier Division "Wallonien," from January 30, 1945, until the end of the war. He was promoted to SS lieutenant colonel (January 1, 1945) and colonel (April 20, 1945—Hitler's last birthday). After the dictator committed suicide, it was clear that Degrelle would be hanged by the Belgian government if he fell into Allied hands. He left Germany and fled to Denmark and then Norway. Here he borrowed Albert Speer's private airplane and flew toward Spain, crashing just off the Spanish coast. He managed to reach shore, and Madrid quickly granted him political asylum. He changed his name to Leon José de Ramirez Reina and became a Spanish citizen in 1954. He died in Spain on April 1, 1994. He had, in the meantime, fathered several children and had been sentenced to death in absentia by a Belgian court. His last wish—that his ashes be buried on Belgian soil—was denied. (The author has it on reliable authority, however, that he secretly visited Belgium in disguise some years after the war.)

47. Yeager, vol. 1, pp. 265–66. Born at Gundhelm on April 20, 1903, Nikolaus Heilmann was a schoolteacher by profession. He joined the SS in 1925 and received his commission in 1929. He joined the 3rd Police Rifle Regiment when it was formed in October 1939 and later was Ia of the Police Division (later 4th SS Panzer Grenadier Division "Police") (1940–43), chief of staff of the IV SS Panzer Corps (1943), chief of staff of the VI SS Volunteer Corps (Latvian) (1943–44), and commander of the 15th SS Division (1944). Later, Heilmann was General Gille's chief of staff at IV SS Panzer Corps (1944) and commander of the 28th SS Panzer Grenadier Division "Walloon." He was killed in action at Mittwalde, west of Schweibus, on January 30, 1945. Nervous and short-tempered, Heilmann was a less than perfect choice to command foreign troops, although he certainly had physical courage and his corps commanders were satisfied with his performance. He left behind a wife and two children.

48. Keilig, p. 373.

49. Gordon Williamson, *Infantry Aces of the Reich* (London: 1989), pp. 116–18. All of Bostell's crewmen were awarded the Iron Cross, 1st or 2nd Class, for the action of August 12. Bostell was promoted to first lieutenant on May 1, 1945, and went into Soviet captivity a week later. He remained in communist prisons until October 1955.

50. Yeager, vol. 1, pp. 272–76. Friedrich Jeckeln was born in 1895, the son of a factory worker. He served in the artillery in World War I, became a pilot, and was discharged as a second lieutenant in 1920. He married but abandoned his family. When his wife protested to Hitler that Jeckeln was not providing financial support for his three children, Jeckeln justified his actions on the grounds that his

father-in-law was a Jew—thus branding his own children as partially Jewish in the most anti-Semitic state the world has ever known. Jeckeln later commanded the V SS Volunteer Mountain Corps on the Eastern Front (1945). Captured by the Russians at the end of the war, he was tried at Riga on February 3, 1946, and was hanged the same day. In all, Jeckeln fathered nine children.

51. August Thiele was one of the better naval officers in the Third Reich. He was born in Berlin-Charlottenburg in 1893 and entered the navy as a cadet in 1912. Commissioned in 1915, he spent most of his career alternating between staff assignments and cruisers. During World War II, he was fortress commander on the Pomeranian coast (1939), captain of the heavy cruiser *Luetzow* (1939–40), admiral of the Norwegian north coast (1940–41), chief of staff to the commander of the High Seas Fleet (1941–43), and commander of the fleet training command (1943–44). He was named commander of the II Battle Group in July 1944 and in that capacity supported the effort to relieve Army Group North. He ended the war as Commanding Admiral Eastern Baltic; after Hitler's suicide he evacuated as many men from Courland as he could. He surrendered to the British at the end of the war. Released from prison in 1946, he died in Moelin in 1981. Hans H. Hildebrand and Ernest Henriot, *Deutschlands Admirale, 1849–1945* (Osnabrueck: 1988), vol. 3, pp. 438–39.

52. Count Hyazinth Strachwitz recovered in time to fight in the last battles of the Third Reich. After the surrender, he led an ad hoc formation through Czech partisans to Bavaria, where he surrendered to the Americans. When he was released from prison, he found his estates had been confiscated by the communists and that his wife and younger son were dead. He went to work for Syria and reorganized that nation's agriculture and army. When a coup overthrew the Syrian government, Strachwitz was a wanted man. He and his new (young) wife escaped, and the Panzer Count returned to Germany in 1951. He died in poverty shortly thereafter. Lucas, *Hitler's Enforcers*, p. 174.

53. A Silesian and a veteran infantry officer, Gottfried Weber was acting commander of the XVI Corps at the end of the war. He was named inspector of infantry for the Bundeswehr in 1958 but was killed in a traffic accident on an autobahn later that year.

54. Meinrad von Lauchert later commanded the 2nd Panzer Division in the Battle of the Bulge. He was promoted to major general in 1945. He was not yet forty years old when the war ended.

55. Chales de Beaulieu was succeeded as commander of the 23rd Infantry Division by Lieutenant General Hans Schirmer, who would lead it for the rest of the war. A native of Stettin, Schirmer was released from the Soviet prison camps in October 1955 but died before the year was out. Chales de Beaulieu died at Kressborn/Bodensee on August 26, 1974.

56. Theodor Busse was born in Frankfurt/Oder in 1897 and joined the army as an infantry *Fahnenjunker* in 1915. He was a lieutenant colonel on the staff of OKH when the war began. During the war, he was Ia, 11th Army (1940); Ia, Army Group Don (later South) (1942); chief of staff of Army Group South (1943); commander of the 121st Infantry Division (July 10, 1944); and commander of I Corps. On January 9, 1945, because of his influence with Burghoff, he was given command of the 9th Army and charged with defending Berlin. Although his army was de-

stroyed and most of it ended up in Soviet captivity, Busse escaped to the West. He was promoted to general of infantry in late 1944; he died in Wallerstein in 1986.

Werner Rank was thirty-nine years old in 1944. He entered the service as a private in 1924 and was commissioned in the 6th Artillery Regiment in 1927. A major when the war broke out, he was Ib (Chief Supply Officer) of X Corps (1939), Ia of the 290th Infantry Division (1942), chief of staff of X Corps (1943), and commander of the 366th Infantry Regiment (1944). He was captured in September 1944. Nevertheless, OKH promoted him to major general in October 1944 and to lieutenant general in April 1945. He spent eleven years in Soviet prisons.

57. A notorious yes-man, Wilhelm Keitel was commander in chief of the High Command of the Armed Forces (OKW) from 1938 to 1945, but he had no real authority. Held in contempt by most of the senior commanders, he was hanged in Nuremberg in 1946.

58. An Austrian lawyer, Dr. Lothar Rendulic was born in Wiener-Neustadt in 1887. He fought with the Austro-Hungarian Army in World War I and remained with the Austrian Army until it was annexed by the Third Reich in 1938. A strong Nazi, Rendulic was named chief of staff of Wehrkreis XVIII (1938) and chief of staff of XVIII Corps (1939). He was in command positions for the rest of the war, successively leading 14th Infantry Division (1940), 52nd Infantry Division (1940), XXXV Corps (1942), 2nd Panzer Army (1943), 20th Mountain Army (1944), Army Group Courland (1945), and Army Group South (March 25, 1945–end). Rendulic distinguished himself in the defensive fighting in the East. He died in Seewalchen in 1971.

59. Seaton, *Russo-German War*, pp. 464–65.

60. Boehme had previously commanded the 32nd Infantry Division (1939–40), XVIII Mountain Corps (1940–43), and Wehrkreis XVIII (1943–44) and had been acting commander of the 2nd Panzer Army in the Balkans (1944). He had been in Fuehrer Reserve since July 1944 (Keilig, p. 41). Theodor Burchardi was born in Homburg in 1892 and entered the Imperial Navy as a sea cadet in 1911. He spent most of World War I in torpedo boats. In the interwar years, he was in various assignments involving minesweepers, supply ships, naval artillery and cruisers. The captain of the cruiser *Koeln* (1937–40) when the war broke out, he was Naval Commander, East (1941–44) and Commanding Admiral, Eastern Baltic (1944–45). Promoted to full admiral in 1945, he was released from prison in 1946 and died at Gluecksubrg on the Baltic Sea in 1983. Hildebrand and Henriot, vol. 1, pp. 192–93.

61. Haupt, *Nord*, p. 234.

62. Siegfried Verheim was not held responsible for this disaster; he retained command of his division (or what was left of it) for the rest of the war. He was promoted to major general later that year and to lieutenant general in 1945. He spent the next ten years in Soviet prisons. Keilig, p. 354; Mehner, ed., vol. 12, p. 457.

63. Haupt, *Nord*, pp. 241–44.

64. Schoerner ended the war commanding Army Group A (formerly North Ukraine) in Czechoslovakia and East Germany. On April 28, 1945, Hitler named Schoerner commander in chief of the army upon his (Hitler's) death. Two days later, Hitler shot himself. Schoerner himself either deserted his army or tried to make his way to the Alpine Redoubt; in any case, he was arrested by members of the 1st Panzer Division on May 18 and handed over to the Americans, who trans-

ferred him to the Russians. He was sentenced to twenty-five years' imprisonment but was released in 1955 and moved to Munich. Here he was convicted of manslaughter and sentenced to four and a half years' imprisonment. He lived in Munich after his release and died in poverty on July 6, 1973, at the age of eighty-one.

65. Lawrence M. Greenberg, "Army with No Way Out," *World War II* 6, no. 1 (May 1991), p. 26.

66. David Irving, *Hitler's War* (New York: 1977), pp. 730–31.

Colonel General Eduard Dietl, the commander of the 20th Mountain Army on the Far Northern sector of the Eastern Front, early 1942–1944. Following a visit to Fuehrer Headquarters, General Dietl was killed when his airplane crashed on the way back to his headquarters on June 23, 1944 (U.S. Army War College).

Alfred Rosenburg, the "philosopher" of the Nazi Party and head of the Eastern Ministry, 1941–1945. With little actual power, Rosenburg was unable to influence Hitler's disastrous policy in the occupied East. Convicted as a war criminal, he was hanged at Nuremberg in October 1946 (U.S. Army War College).

Luftwaffe Colonel General Ritter Robert von Greim (left), commander of the 6th Air Fleet on the Eastern Front, shown here with two of his top aces, Major Walter Oesau (center) and Lieutenant Colonel Guenther von Luetzow, both of the 3rd Fighter Wing, 1943. The 6th Air Fleet was charged with the task of supporting Army Group Center. By mid-1944, Greim's aviation forces had been depleted to the point that he had only 60 operational fighters and was completely defeated by the Red Air Force in Operation "Bagration." Major Oesau, meanwhile, was promoted to lieutenant colonel and given command of the 1st Fighter Wing in the West. He was shot down and killed by five U.S. Lightning fighters near St. Vith, Belgium on May 11, 1944. Luetzow was later killed in action near Donauwoerth (on the Danube) on April 24, 1945. Oesau had 125 aerial victories at the time of his death; Luetzow had 108. Greim was promoted to field marshal and succeeded Hermann Goering as commander of the Luftwaffe in late April 1945. He committed suicide the following month (U.S. Air Force, Air University Archives).

General Ritter Robert von Greim (right), the commander of the Luftwaffe forces on the central sector of the Eastern Front, with Luftwaffe Lieutenant Colonel Stolle (the commander of a flak regiment on the Eastern Front) and General of Infantry Hans Zorn, the commander of the XXXXVI Panzer Corps, Rzhev sector, circa 1943. Zorn was later killed in action (U.S. Air Force, Air University Archives).

Luftwaffe Colonel General Alexander Loehr, the commander of Army Group E in the Balkans (1942–1945) and on the Eastern Front (1944–1945). Loehr, the commander of the Austrian Air Force until 1938, had previously commanded the 4th Air Fleet in the East. He was executed by the Yugoslavs after a "show trial" on February 16, 1947 (U.S. Air Force, Air War University).

Major General Eberhard Thunert, the commander of the 1st Panzer Division on the Eastern Front, 1944–1945. Thunert was promoted to lieutenant general on May 1, 1945, the day after Hitler committed suicide. Thunert managed to disengage his unit from the Soviets and surrendered to the Americans on May 8 and 9, 1945 (U.S. Army).

A Luftwaffe mortar crew in action in the Russian Front. Part of a Luftwaffe Field division, men such as these generally lacked proper training for ground combat and often performed poorly in the East (U.S. Army).

A German armored personnel carrier is stuck in the mud on the Eastern Front, circa 1944. This personnel carrier is towing a 88mm gun, which was often used as an antitank weapon (U.S. Army War College).

A Ju-88 aircraft. This multi-purpose airplane was used in a variety of roles during World War II and was even used to resupply the IX SS Mountain Corps in Budapest in 1945 (U.S. Air Force, Air War University).

General of Artillery Robert Martinek, the commander of the XXXIX Panzer Corps of Army Group Center, in a discussion with Luftwaffe Major General Franz Reuss, Russia, 1944 (U.S. Air Force, Air War University).

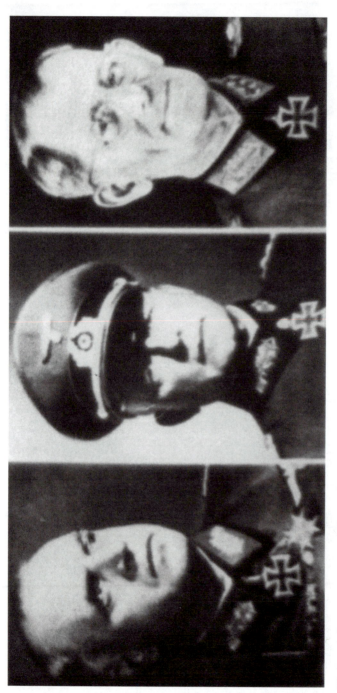

Three of the "Eastern Marshals" (left to right): Ernst Busch, the commander of Army Group Center; Ewald von Kleist, the commander of Army Group A until he was sacked by Hitler in April 1944; and Baron Maximilian von Weichs, the OB Southeast and commander-in-chief of Army Group F, 1943–1945. Along with Hitler, Busch was primarily responsible for the disaster which overtook Army Group Center. Hitler relieved him of his command on June 28, 1944 for his failure to check Operation "Bagration." Busch was given command of OB Northwest on the northern sector of the Western Front in the last days of the war. He died in British captivity in July 1945 (U.S. National Archives).

A German heavy machine gun covering a potential river crossing on the southern sector of the Eastern Front (U.S. National Archives).

German war graves in Warsaw, circa 1944. The graves in the foreground are of those men killed in World War I; the graves of the World War II dead are in the background (U.S. National Archives).

German infantry advancing through the snow (U.S. National Archives).

Franz Halder, chief of the German General Staff, 1938–1942. He conspired against Hitler and ended the war in a concentration camp (U.S. National Archives).

Ritter Robert von Greim, 1944. A World War I fighter ace, Greim shot down 28 enemy airplanes and is wearing the Pour le Merite or "Blue Max," which was normally given to German pilots who shot down 25 enemy airplanes or more. As a young man, Greim took Hitler on his first airplane ride in 1920. The Fuehrer became violently airsick and swore he would never fly again—a promise he later retracted (U.S. National Archives).

German mountain troops on skis, date unknown (U.S. National Archives).

The Big Three Allied leaders: Joseph Stalin, Franklin Roosevelt, and Winston Churchill.

The German High Command (left to right): Reichsmarshall Hermann Georing, Supreme Commander of the Luftwaffe; Adolf Hitler, Fuehrer, Supreme Commander of the Armed Forces and Commander-in-Chief of the Army; Field Marshal Wilhelm Keitel, Commander-in-Chief of the Armed Forces (OKW); Grand Admiral Karl Doenitz, the Commander-in-Chief of the Navy; and Reichsfuehrer-SS Heinrich Himmler, Chief of the SS and Commander-in-Chief of the Replacement Army after July 20, 1944. Hitler and Himmler committed suicide in 1945. Goering committed suicide at Nuremberg in 1946, about three hours before Keitel was hanged. Only Doenitz died in bed (U.S. National Archives).

The German Army dealing with suspected partisans behind the Eastern Front. Hitler's Eastern policies were a major contributing factor to his eventual defeat.

Concentration camp victims, 1945. This was the fate of much of the Hungarian Jewry.

Russian infantry in the attack (U.S. Army War College).

German infantry prepares the next defensive position.

An aging German captain of reserves directs his men in street fighting on the Eastern Front, circa 1944. By the fifth year of the war, German manpower resources had been stretched to their limits (U.S. National Archives).

A German recruiting/propaganda poster, 1944.

Marshal Ion Antonescu, the dictator of Rumania in 1944. Hitler accepted his word that Rumania would stand by Germany through thick and thin. Antonescu, however, was unaware that the vast majority of the rest of the Rumanian civil and military leadership favored defection from the Axis. When they did defect in August 1944, the German 6th Army and Meith's corps of the 8th Army were virtually annihilated. Antonescu himself was arrested and executed after the war (U.S. National Archives).

Hitler and Himmler in happier times, circa 1932. After the plot of July 20, 1944 failed, Himmler succeeded General Fromm as Commander-in-Chief of the Replacement Army (Nazi Party Photo Album).

SS Major General Helmuth Becker, the commander of the 3rd SS Panzer Division "Totenkopf," who reportedly rode a horse to death inside an officers' club, while members of his staff fornicated with French whores on the tables. A former concentration camp guard, Becker was not a great military thinker or tactician, but he did possess physical courage and distinguished himself on the northern sector of the Eastern Front in 1944. In Hungary, he was less successful. In May 1945, he surrendered his division to the Americans, who turned it over to the Russians. Becker was executed by the Soviets in 1954, allegedly for trying to conceal a hand grenade inside the wall of a building which German prisoners of war were constructing. His wife and five children were not informed of his death for another 20 years (U.S. National Archives).

Colonel General Heinz Guderian, the "father" of the Blitzkrieg and a gifted tactical commander. As chief of the General Staff of the Army, where he had to endure daily interference from Hitler, he was less effective (U.S. National Archives).

Field Marshal Walter Model (right), who successively commanded the 3rd Panzer Division (1940–1941), XXXXI Panzer Corps (late 1941–1942), 9th Army (early 1942–1944), Army Group North (assumed command January 9, 1944), Army Group North Ukraine (March 31, 1944), and Army Group Center (June 29, 1944). He became commander of Army Group B on the Western Front on August 17, 1944 and led it until it was destroyed in the Battle of the Ruhr Pocket (1945). Rather than surrender, he committed suicide near Duisburg on April 21, 1945 (U.S. National Archives).

A STUG III assault gun. Built around a PzKw III chassis, this weapon was often used against enemy armor. By early January 1944, it had destroyed 20,000 enemy tanks on the Eastern Front alone. Normally manned by members of the artillery branch, it was used to equip some of the panzer battalions by the second half of 1944 (U.S. National Archives).

Another assault gun, mounted on a Panzer Mark III chassis. This one is in a U.S. Army captured equipment facility (U.S. Army War College).

A Jagdpanzer tank destroyer. This is a well designated weapon which experienced considerable success in the last year of the war (U.S. Army War College).

A German Tiger tank, formerly part of the 504th Heavy Panzer Battalion, captured by the Americans in Sicily, July 1943. The 504th was attached to the Luftwaffe's Hermann Goering Panzer Division during the Sicilian campaign. This tank, which has apparently suffered little or no combat damage, may have broken down during the German retreat from the island. Mechanical problems plagued the Tigers throughout their existence, but they were an extremely formidable weapon when they worked properly (U.S. Army War College).

A German Panther tank. Although lighter than the Tiger, it was considered more mechanically reliable than the Tiger (U.S. Army War College).

CHAPTER V

Rumania

As incredible as it may sound, Colonel General Johannes Friessner definitely got the worst end of the deal when he exchanged commands with Ferdinand Schoerner on July 23, 1944. In July 1944, Army Group South Ukraine included the German 6th and 8th Armies and the Rumanian 3rd and 4th Armies. The Rumanians, however, were no longer willing to serve exclusively under German command. As a result, in May 1944 Schoerner had been forced to compromise. He had divided his army group (*Heeresgruppe*) into two temporary *Armeegruppen*: Armeegruppe Dumitrescu (led by Rumanian Colonel General Petre Dumitrescue, the commander of the Rumanian 3rd Army) and Armeegruppe Woehler, led by General of Infantry Otto Woehler, the commander of the German 8th Army. (The *Armeegruppe* headquarters was intermediate between the *Heeresgruppe* and army-level headquarters. It will remain untranslated throughout this book, to avoid confusion.) Armeegruppe Dumitrescu included the Rumanian 3rd Army and General of Artillery Maximilian Fretter-Pico's German 6th Army. Armeegruppe Woehler included the German 8th and Rumanian 4th Armies. For the first time in the war, German commanders came under the actual (instead of nominal) command of their foreign allies. The order of battle of both *Armeegruppen* as they stood on August 15 is shown in Table 5.1. General of Infantry Helge Auleb's LXIX Corps z.b.V. (the rear area command for Army Group South Ukraine) also came under Rumanian control.

Schoerner did not care for this arrangement and wanted to take "more energetic measures" to prepare the army group for attack. He was, however, overruled by Hitler, who was afraid that Schoerner might cause further damage to German foreign relations. As a result, the German divisions remained dependent upon Hungarian and Rumanian railroads for their supplies. Both systems were of limited capacity and plagued by inefficiency.

Table 5.1
Order of Battle, Army Group South Ukraine, August 15, 1944

ARMY GROUP SOUTH UKRAINE: Colonel General Friessner

Armeegruppe Dumitrescu: General Petre Dumitrescu
3rd Rumanian Army: Dumitrescu
    II Rumanian Corps
        9th Rumanian Infantry Division
        Several security and coastal defense battalions on the Black Sea
    II Rumanian Corps
        110th Rumanian Infantry Brigade
        2nd Rumanian Infantry Division
        15th Rumanian Infantry Division
    XXIX Corps: Lieutenant General von Bechtoldsheim
        9th Infantry Division
        21st Rumanian Infantry Division
        4th Rumanian Mountain Division
        278th Assault Gun Brigade
6th Army: General of Artillery Fretter-Pico
    XXX Corps: Lieutenant General Postel
        306th Infantry Division
        15th Infantry Division
        257th Infantry Division
        302nd Infantry Division
        384th Infantry Division
        239th Infantry Division
    LII Corps: General of Infantry Buschenhagen
        320th Infantry Division
        294th Infantry Division
        161st Infantry Division
        243rd Assault Gun Brigade
    XXXXIV Corps: General of Infantry Ludwig Mueller
        335th Infantry Division
        282nd Infantry Division
        258th Infantry Division
        62nd Infantry Division
        911th Assault Gun Brigade
    Armeegruppe Reserve:
        LXXII Corps Headquarters
        1st Rumanian Cavalry Division
        304th Infantry Division

Armee-Gruppe Woehler: General of Infantry Woehler
8th Army: General Woehler
    IV Corps: General of Infantry Mieth
        376th Infantry Division
        11th Rumanian Cavalry Division
        79th Infantry Division
        228th Assault Gun Brigade

Table 5.1 (*continued*)

    IV Rumanian Corps
        5th Rumanian Cavalry Division
        7th Rumanian Infantry Division
        102nd Rumanian Mountain Brigade
        3rd Rumanian Infantry Division
4th Rumanian Army: General Avramescu
    Group General Kirchner: General of Panzer Troops Kirchner
    VI Rumanian Corps
        76th Infantry Division
        5th Rumanian Infantry Division
        101st Rumanian Mountain Brigade
        325th Assault Gun Brigade
    LVII Panzer Corps: Kirchner
        1st Rumanian Infantry Division
        46th Infantry Division
        13th Rumanian Infantry Division
        286th Assault Gun Brigade
    V Rumanian Corps
        6th Rumanian Infantry Division
        20th Rumanian Infantry Division
    VII Rumanian Corps
        104th Rumanian Mountain Brigade
        103rd Rumanian Mountain Brigade
    XVII Corps: General of Mountain Troops Kreysing
        3rd Mountain Division[1]
        8th Jaeger Division[1]
    Armeegruppe Reserve:
        20th Panzer Division
        "Greater Rumania" Panzer Division
        8th Rumanian Infantry Division
        10th Rumanian Mountain Division
        905th Assault Gun Brigade
    Army Group South Ukraine Reserve:
        153rd Field Training Division
        10th Panzer Grenadier Division
        1st Slovanian Security Division
        97th Jaeger Division[2]
        959th Artillery Brigade

Table 5.1 (*continued*)

4th Air Fleet: General of Fliers Deichmann
    I Air Corps
    5th Flak Division
    15th Flak Division

Notes:
All units are German unless otherwise indicated.
[1]With Rumanian Frontier Units attached.
[2]En route from Army Group South Ukraine to the northwest

Sources: Buchner, *Ostfront 1944*, pp. 332–34; Mehner, ed., *Geheimen Tagesberichte*, vol. 10, pp. 499–500.

Luftwaffe reconnaissance airplanes had to sometimes fly more than a hundred miles looking for trains that had been lost. It took two to three weeks for supplies from Germany to reach the front—if they arrived at all. Most German formations (including replacement battalions) preferred to march rather than depend on the uncertain Rumanian and Hungarian railroads.[1]

Meanwhile, to the north, on the left flank of Army Group South Ukraine, Army Group North Ukraine was being defeated.

On June 29, as we have seen, Field Marshal Model became C-in-C of Army Group Center while simultaneously retaining command of Army Group North Ukraine. The day-to-day conduct of operations, however, devolved upon Joseph Harpe, the commander of 4th Panzer Army and deputy C-in-C. Harpe turned command of 4th Panzer over to General of Panzer Troops Hermann Balck, the former commander of the XXXXVIII Panzer Corps. To stabilize Model's army group and check the Russian flood, Hitler and OKH gradually transferred several units from Army Groups North Ukraine and South Ukraine. These included the Staff, XXXX Panzer Corps; Staff, XXXIX Mountain Corps; 3rd, 14th, and 23rd Panzer Divisions; the Grossdeutschland Panzer Grenadier Division; the 97th Jaeger Division; and the 304th Infantry.

In June and July, Harpe detected major Soviet concentrations, including armored forces, in the vicinity of Tarnopol, Luzk, and Kovel. Germany, however, lacked the strategic reserves to reinforce him. On July 13, Marshal Konev's 1st Ukrainian Front (1st, 3rd, and 4th Guards Tank Armies; 1st, 3rd, and 5th Guards Armies; and 13th, 18th, 38th, and 60th Armies, along with two cavalry corps and two air armies) attacked, with a major concentration at the junction of the 1st Panzer and 4th Panzer Armies. Major General Otto Beutler's 340th Infantry Division was overrun, and the Soviets poured into the German rear.[2] A second attack against Lieutenant General Otto Lasch's 349th Infantry Division (at the junction of the

XIII and XXXXVIII Panzer Corps) also produced a breakthrough. As a result, XIII Corps was encircled at Brody (see chapter 3), and the entire front of Army Group North Ukraine came unglued.

On July 18, the Soviet 1st Belorussian Front broke through Balck's 4th Panzer Army, where it linked up with the 2nd Army of Army Group Center. The 12th Hungarian Reserve Division and most of General of Infantry Gustav Hoehne's VIII Corps were smashed. Contact with Weiss's 2nd Army was soon lost as the 4th Panzer fell back toward the Bug River. The 2nd Soviet Tank Army and 8th Guards Armies led the pursuit and captured most of the city of Lublin on July 22. Even so, Hitler refused to lift the "fortified place" designation from the city, despite the fact that it was garrisoned by only nine hundred men. Not allowed to break out, the garrison surrendered the next day.

During the withdrawal to the Bug, Colonel Arthur Finger's 291st Infantry Division withdrew slowly, covering the retreat of XXXXII Corps; it launched several local counterattacks, destroying a number of Russian tanks. As it crossed the Bug near Sokal, however, the Reds cut the division off. On many occasions, the divisional historian wrote later, the men of the division "extracted themselves from tight situations, not by defense, but by surprise offensive operations."[3]

Major Harry Andree, the commander of the 505th Infantry Regiment, launched such a surprise attack, routed a Soviet anti-tank battalion and destroyed its guns. Later he ambushed an entire cavalry division and routed it as well.[4] By July 20, however, the division was isolated and loosely surrounded. Colonel Finger "put all of his eggs in one basket," the divisional history reported, "and led his entire division through a thick forest to the northwest to cross over the Wieprz near Szczebrzeszyn, where he assumed the last opportunity for withdrawal would lie. The withdrawal from the sack succeeded completely, and without a fight."[5] The division regained contact with XXXXII Corps and, after checking a Soviet attack at Zawichost, retired across the Vistula.[6]

Meanwhile, on July 23, the Reds smashed General Beregffy's 1st Hungarian Army and penetrated the right flank of the 1st Panzer Army. The Hungarians retreated into the Carpathians, while the 1st Panzer Army withdrew behind the Dnestr and was forced to abandon Lemberg (Lvov).

With the Germans in retreat, the 4th Ukrainian Front joined the offensive with fresh tank forces and pushed the 1st Panzer and 1st Hungarian Armies back to Beskiden. Simultaneously, the 1st Ukrainian Front established bridgeheads across the San. General Harpe had recently inserted General of Infantry Friedrich Schulz's 17th Army between the 4th Panzer and 1st Panzer Armies, in hopes of preventing the collapse of his army group.[7] The capable Schulz initially controlled two corps headquarters (XI SS and LIX), two of the new Volksgrenadier divisions (the 544th and 545th), and a *kampfgruppe*. Harpe soon reinforced him with the 8th Panzer, 23rd Panzer, and 371st Infantry Divisions.[8] Meanwhile, 4th Panzer Army counterattacked and destroyed the Russian vanguards in and west of Sandomir, saving Krakov and the Upper Silesian industrial region, at least for the moment. Unfortunately, the Soviets had already established the Baranow Bridgehead, which was thirty miles long and twenty miles deep, on the west bank of the Vistula and quickly reinforced it with two tank corps.[9] Colonel General Heinrici, who assumed command of the 4th Panzer Army on August 16, tried to wipe it out with a counterattack later that month but was not successful.[10]

With this battle, Harpe's Army Group North Ukraine had stabilized its front along the Vistula and in the Carpathians, but its front was only a hundred miles east of the borders of the Reich. Also, it was left in no position to come to the aid of its neighbor, Army Group South Ukraine, should it run into trouble.

The zone of Army Group South Ukraine had been quiet since the fall of the Crimea and the destruction of the 17th Army in May 1944. The German 6th Army and the right flank of the 8th Army had retreated into eastern Rumania, the area called Bessarabia, in early 1944. It was a quiet, agrarian region of cornfields and forests, with occasional villages with straw-roofed houses. Unmolested for months, the German divisions in Rumania were as well rested as any in the Wehrmacht and, after half a year in a virtually inactive sector, were almost up to strength. Each had about twelve to fourteen thousand men, six thousand horses, and four hundred motorized vehicles.[11] Most of the replacements who arrived in 1944, however, were not up to the standards of 1940. Still, there seemed to be no immediate cause for concern. During his tenure as C-in-C, Schoerner had kept his command busy with a rigorous training and physical fitness program.

The political situation and the air war in this sector, however, had been anything but quiet. On April 5, the U.S. 15th Air Force had launched its first raid against the vital Ploesti oilfields and against river traffic on the Danube. Periodic heavy raids continued, in spite of heavy losses to the B-17s. By May 20, Rumanian oil production (which had amounted to 2,400,000 tons in 1943) had been halved. Between 1942 and 1944, however, Hungarian production increased from 150,000 tons to 800,000 tons, and production in the oilfields of eastern Austria had increased from 340,000 to 1,300,000 tons. Meanwhile, German synthetic oil production increased from almost nothing when the war began to 6,300,000 tons in 1942.[12] Therefore, although the Rumanian oil production was still extremely important, the German war effort was no longer absolutely dependent on it, as had been the case in 1940.

Meanwhile, the long series of German defeats was having its effect on the political situation in the Balkans. On April 21, Turkey had stopped delivering chrome to Germany. At the same time—unknown to Nazi Germany—Soviet, American, and British representatives met with Prince Stirbey of Rumanian on April 12, to begin peace negotiations. Ion Antonescu, the Rumanian dictator, broke off these discussions on May 15, because the peace terms were unacceptable to him.[13] Most of the Rumanian people were now opposed to the continuation of the war, however, so the opposition groups (including representatives of opposition political parties, diplomats, the nobility, the intelligentsia, and most of Rumania's senior military officers) continued to negotiate behind Antonescu's back. He had no idea that they were planning, at the proper moment, to depose him and defect to the Allies.

When General Friessner arrived, he found that most of his commanders were very uneasy. They found the new attitudes of their Rumanian counterparts unsettling; even allowing for Rumanian inefficiency, it was clear that they were doing nothing to prepare their sectors for war. In the rear, nothing was being done to put the nation on a war footing, and it was obvious that Antonescu's orders were no longer being obeyed. Many of the newly appointed Rumanian commanders were openly hostile to the regime, and the German officers suspected that the Rumanians were secretly negotiating with the Allies. Friessner, who shared these fears, relayed them to Fuehrer Headquarters at Rastenburg.[14] Hitler, however, had entirely different intelligence reports from OKW. On April 2, General of Infantry Erik Hansen, the chief of the German Army Mission to Rumania and the commander of all German bases in the country, reported that both the Rumanian people and their leaders were determined to continue the war, side by side with Germany.[15] Lieutenant General Alfred Gerstenberg, the air attaché to Bucharest and commander of all Luftwaffe forces in the country (including two flak divisions), issued a similar report to Goering and told Friessner that he could quell any attempted coup with a single flak battery. Baron Manfred von Killinger, the German ambassador (and a World War I U-boat commander and a long-time brownshirt), reported to Foreign Minister Joachim von Ribbentrop that Friessner's fears were without foundation, that the entire country was loyal to Antonescu. His opinion was reinforced by a report from OKH's Foreign Armies East Department, which stated that a major offensive against Army Group South Ukraine in the foreseeable future was very unlikely. Most of the senior German generals in Rastenburg and Berlin agreed with this estimation. They believed that the Russians were withdrawing forces from the south to reinforce their successful campaign against Army Group Center.[16] Ribbentrop, however, was more suspicious; he knew that young King Michael and his mother were staunchly pro-British and that the palace was a center of anti-Axis intrigue; therefore, he asked Hitler to station a panzer division in Bucharest, to assure the security of the Antonescu regime. Guderian did not have one to spare, however; in any case, he regarded Rumania as an OKW responsibility and called upon Jodl to post the motorized 4th SS Panzer Grenadier Division "Police" from Yugoslavia to the Rumanian capital. Jodl demurred, and Hitler could not make up his mind whether to overrule him or not, so nothing was done.[17]

On August 5, Antonescu visited Rastenburg, accompanied by Mihai Antonescu, his foreign minister, and General Steflea, the chief of the Rumanian General Staff. The Fuehrer asked him point-blank whether or not Rumania would stay in the war until the end. He assured Hitler that it would and gave the impression of honesty and sincerity to both Guderian and Friessner.[18] Perhaps remembering what had happened in Italy the year before—when Mussolini was deposed and arrested during a visit to the royal palace—Hitler asked Antonescu not to visit King Michael's palace if a crisis developed. Antonescu assured the Fuehrer that he would not.

The Antonescu visit and the reports of von Killinger and Hansen allayed Hitler's mind concerning the Rumanian alliance. Both of these men were blinded by their own faith in Antonescu. Hitler and his entourage also had an excessive tendency to confuse Antonescu's personal loyalty with that of the Rumanian people and their army. This error would cost the German Army dearly in the days ahead.

The German Military Mission to Bulgaria suspected that something was up. Colonel Baron Ernst von Jungenfeldt, a member of the mission, reported to Guderian that the behavior of the Bulgarian troops indicated that something was happening beneath the surface.[19] King Boris, a staunch supporter of the Axis and an enemy of communism, had died under mysterious circumstances (apparently poisoned), and the government was shaky. Friessner was further disturbed by the fact that Hitler, OKW, and OKH looked upon his army group as little more than a reservoir of reinforcements for other fronts. When Schoerner took over, it had had nine panzer divisions. By mid-August, it had only three mobile divisions—one panzer, one panzer grenadier, and one Rumanian armored division. On August 15, Friessner had some six hundred thousand men, 340,000 of which were German. He had the equivalent of twenty-three German and twenty-three Rumanian divisions. Many of the German infantry divisions had been brought up to strength, but the quality of the replacements was by no means satisfactory; too many of them were older men who had been taken from rear-area jobs and sent to the front. There were shortages of artillery, mortars, and ammunition, and especially serious shortages of tanks, airplanes, and motorized vehicles. The main mode of transport was the two-wheeled *panje* (peasant) wagon. Of the 120 tanks in the entire army group, more than half were in the Rumanian armored division. The 13th Panzer had only forty tanks. The army group did have 280 assault guns, but Colonel General Otto Dessloch's 4th Air Fleet had only 232 operational aircraft, of which only fifty were daylight fighters (Me-109s). To make matters worse, neither of his two flak divisions had experience fighting Russian tanks, and half of their gun crews were Rumanian.[20]

In early August, Colonel Ivo-Thilo von Trotha, the chief of operations (Ia) of Army Group South Ukraine, asked Field Marshal Keitel to have

General Friessner named Wehrmacht Commander in Rumania (thus giving him control of the Luftwaffe, naval, and SS forces in the country). He also proposed that General Hansen be replaced by an officer who was less trusting of the Rumanians. Keitel was at first impressed by von Trotha's arguments, but after talks with Antonescu, he said he saw no need for any changes: Rumania would stand by the Third Reich "through thick and thin."[21] He told Trotha that Army Group South Ukraine was to hold its front without worrying about its rear.[22]

Army Group South Ukraine deployed Dumitrescu's 3rd Rumanian Army on its far right flank, nearest to the Black Sea, along the lower Dnestr (see Map 5.1). To its left lay Fretter-Pico's 6th Army, covering Kishinev, the capital of Bessarabia.[23] West of this lay the Rumanian 4th Army (General of Infantry Racovitza), in the Jassy (Iasi) sector, and on the left flank lay Woehler's German 8th Army, which extended to the lower slopes of the eastern Carpathians. In all, the army group held 392 miles of front, running generally east to west, of which 160 were held by the Rumanians. Antonescu had suggested months earlier that the Axis forces should evacuate Bessarabia and withdraw southward into Transylvania, following the line of the Carpathians–lower Sereth, Focsani, Galatz-Danube estuary. He considered the present line too long and too vulnerable, because the valleys of the Pruth and Sereth offered the Soviets easy avenues of approach into the rear of both the German 6th and Rumanian 3rd Armies. Both Schoerner and Friessner supported this suggestion, but Hitler, with his obsession for never surrendering ground voluntarily, rejected the proposal.

On August 2, Turkey severed diplomatic relations with Germany, which sent shock waves throughout eastern Europe and the Balkans. On August 8, Luftwaffe reconnaissance flights spotted large Soviet troop movements east of the Pruth in apparent preparation for a major offensive. OKH took another division from Army Group South Ukraine on August 13, and the next day a rumor that Antonescu had been overthrown almost threw the German rear area into a panic. On August 16, Armeegruppe Woehler reported that the Russians would be ready to attack in a day or two.

In mid-August 1944, General Friessner and his men faced two Soviet fronts: the 2nd Ukrainian (Marshal Rodion Y. Malinovskiy) on the north and the 3rd Ukrainian (Marshal Fedor I. Tolbukhin) to the east. Malinovskiy had six rifle armies and a tank army, an independent tank corps, an independent mechanized corps, and a cavalry corps, with the 5th Air Army in support. Tolbukhlin had four rifle armies (mainly in the large bridgehead around Tiraspol), as well as two independent mechanized corps and the 17th Air Army. The two fronts were coordinated by Marshal Timoshenko. All told, he had 920,000 men, 1,400 tanks, 1,700 airplanes, and 16,000 artillery pieces, rocket launchers, and mortars. Army Group South Ukraine faced him with 360,000 German soldiers in twenty-three divisions, of

Map 5.1
Army Group South Ukraine, August 1944

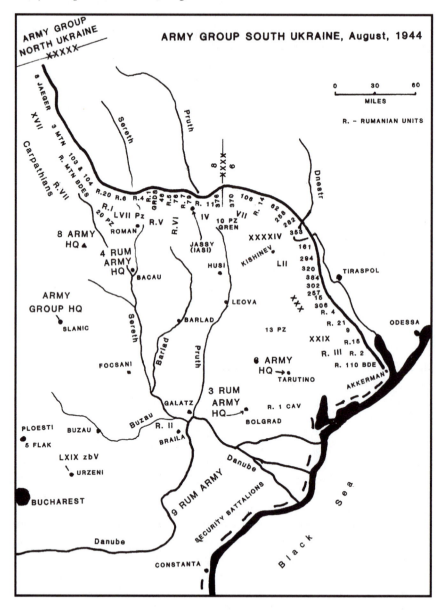

which twenty-one were infantry. All twenty-three of Friessner's Rumanian divisions had lost the will to fight.

The eastern sector of the Axis front offered the defenders the advantage of several natural obstacles, including the Dnestr (Dniester) Pruth, Barladul (Berlad), and Sereth Rivers, which flowed generally north to south. To the north, however, the stronger 2nd Ukrainian Front—which was generally facing south—faced no such obstacles.

The Soviet generals did a magnificent job of deceiving the German high command and completed their buildup without being detected. The size of the offensive would come as a complete surprise, even to Army Group South Ukraine. Map 5.2 shows the destruction of the 6th Army.

August 20, 1944—the day the Soviet offensive in Rumania began—has gone down in history as the "Black Sunday" of the German Army in World War II. It began at dawn with a one-and-a-half-hour artillery bombardment, aimed primarily at the Rumanian units, with particularly heavy concentrations in the sectors northwest of Jassy and south of Tiraspol. Several Rumanian divisions were at the point of collapse even before the Russian infantry arrived. Then the Soviet ground forces struck, advancing on a twenty-mile front. As a result of a secret agreement with the Russians, the IV and VI Rumanian Corps protecting Jassy (in the zone of Armeegruppe Woehler) abandoned their positions without firing a shot, only the German 76th Infantry Division (Lieutenant General Erich Abraham) put up any real resistance. There was fighting on the western outskirts of Jassy by 10 A.M., and by noon the Russians were across the Bahlui.

Colonel General Friessner and General Woehler both understood the situation completely and ordered an immediate counterattack by all available reserves. They realized that if the German line was not restored quickly, it never would be. They also realized that with the Rumanians not resisting, the front probably never would be restored; still, there was nothing left to do but try. The 10th Panzer Grenadier Division hurled itself at the Russians, along with the Greater Rumanian Armored Division, one of the few Rumanian units still fighting. General of Artillery Ernst-Eberhard Hell, the commander of the VII Corps (on the left wing of the 6th Army) also contributed Lieutenant General Eugen Bleyer's 258th Infantry Division to the efforts to restore the front. None of these counterattacks were successful. There was house-to-house fighting in Jassy by nightfall, and the Reds gained twelve miles on the first day.

On the eastern (Armeegruppe Dumitrescu) sector, the story on "Black Sunday" was equally dismal. A preliminary bombardment began at 4 A.M. and lasted an hour. Then, at 7 A.M., the main bombardment began. It lasted an hour and a half and was immediately followed by Soviet infantry, tanks, assault guns, and artillery, all liberally supported by fighter-bombers.

The main Soviet attack concentrated south of Tiraspol, in the zone of the 3rd Rumanian Army. The Rumanian XXIX Corps collapsed immedi-

Map 5.2
The Destruction of 6th Army, August 1944

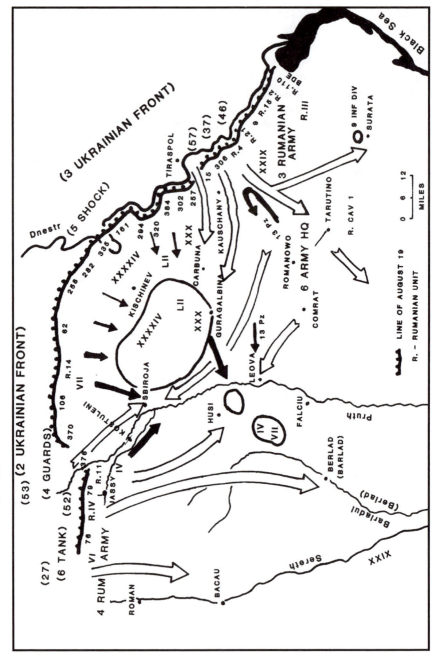

ately, leaving the entire defense to three German divisions: the 15th, 306th, and 9th Infantry (north to south). Russian armored vehicles poured through the gaps left by the Rumanians and quickly encircled the veteran 9th Infantry Division. Major General Werner Gebb quickly formed an egg-shaped defense but his division was gradually pushed back to the south, away from its comrades. Wave after wave of Russian assault forces crashed against the 15th and 306th; but they generally held their strong points. Losses, however, were heavy. Lieutenant General Rudolf Sperl's 15th Infantry Division suffered 20 percent casualties in the initial attacks, and the 306th Infantry Division was struck even harder. It lost a third of its men in the initial bombardments, and by 10 A.M. Soviet tanks were rolling beyond its command post. The Russians later reported capturing thirty-seven guns in the 306th Division's sector alone on August 20. By noon the right wing of the German 6th Army had been ripped wide open, and the roads were clogged with fleeing troops—mostly Rumanian.[24]

The 9th Infantry Division continued to retreat to the south, where it somehow broke out of its encirclement and became the only German division with the isolated and rapidly disintegrating Rumanian 3rd Army. As the Red Army overran the southern extremity of Bessarabia, it was virtually destroyed in heavy fighting. With his back to the Black Sea, General Gebb surrendered on August 29. How many of his thirteen thousand men survived long enough to capitulate is not known. Werner Gebb would die in Asbest Prison at Sverdlovsk, in the Ural Mountains, on August 12, 1952.

Like Friessner and Woehler, Lieutenant General Georg Postel, the commander of the XXX Corps, which was responsible for 6th Army's right flank, made the correct moves on August 20: he hurled his reserves into the battle with immediate counterattacks. He even signaled his predecessor, General Fretter-Pico, who was now the 6th Army commander, and got him to transfer the army's mobile reserve to XXX Corps. Just as in the Jassy sector, however, there were not enough reserves.

The only mobile unit in 6th Army's reserve was part of the 13th Panzer Division.[25] It was well led by Hans Troeger, one of the "rising stars" in the Wehrmacht. He had joined the Imperial Army as an officer-cadet in 1915 and had served with an engineer battalion in World War I. During the present war, he had successively commanded a motorcycle battalion and a motorized rifle regiment and had been temporary commander of the 27th Panzer Division in late 1942 and early 1943. He had even served nine months as commandant of the School for Panzer Troops, before assuming command of the 25th Panzer Division in late 1943. He had risen from the rank of major in 1939 to lieutenant general in 1944.[26] When he had the chance to take command of the 13th Panzer Division in May 1944, he immediately did so. It was—or had been—one of the best divisions in the Wehrmacht. Two years ago, it had pushed across the Kuban, into the Caucasus, and onto the doorstep of Asia. Now, however, due to casualties and detachments, it had only tank battalion (thirty-five tanks), two panzer grenadier battalions, and part of a panzer engineer battalion. Troeger nevertheless launched an immediate counterattack and threw the Russians back to the Dnestr—but his unit was not strong enough to close the gap. Soon fresh Soviet formations were attacking the 13th Panzer with hundreds of tanks. By afternoon, Troeger was conducting a fighting withdrawal to the west.

In the midst of this confusion arrived Marshal Antonescu, the dictator of Rumania and the commander in chief of its army. He had heard that his men had been routed, and he came to the combat zone personally to try to get them back to the front. He relieved several senior Rumanian officers, demoted others, and reportedly even resorted to summary execution, but it had no effect on the disaster.

Overhead, another disaster took place. The Red Air Force flew more than two thousand sorties, while the German Air Force could only manage 230. It was to be the Luftwaffe's maximum effort. No one at the front remembered seeing a German airplane after August 20. The Soviets had achieved complete aerial supremacy on the very first day of the offensive.

Meanwhile, Fretter-Pico's headquarters at Tarutino was too far to the rear; late that night, he was still unaware of the extent of the disaster. His headquarters knew only that the right flank was under heavy pressure. Worse still, 6th Army's staff was unaware of the Soviet breakthrough at Jassy. Had it known, it probably would have realized that a potential double envelopment was in the making.[27]

At dawn the next morning, the 2nd Ukrainian Front committed its armor to the task of expanding the breakthrough and capturing the key city of Jassy. On the other side, Friessner had organized a joint German-Rumanian counterattack to save the city. All he had left was elements of the 10th Panzer Grenadier Division: twenty tanks and a panzer grenadier regiment. During the morning, the attack was remarkably successful. Then the 10th Panzer Grenadier ran into a Soviet formation of more than a hundred tanks and was soon defeated. The Greater Rumanian Armored Division, which was well equipped with German tanks, watched the battle but did not participate in it. It then pulled back to the south and was never seen again.

It was now obvious that Jassy could not be held. About noon, Lieutenant General Friedrich-August Weinknecht, the commander of the 79th Infantry Division, pulled back to the south with the last rearguards. That afternoon, south of the city, a Russian armored corps of more than three hundred tanks descended upon and overwhelmed the 76th Infantry Division.[28] Small elements and stragglers (including its commander, Lieutenant General Erich Abraham) managed to escape to the west, but the 76th Infantry had effectively ceased to exist. To the east, VII Corps was also battered.

The task of saving the German left flank devolved upon the commander of the IV Corps, General of Infantry Friedrich Mieth, a veteran General

Staff officer with thirty-eight years of service. Mieth pulled the intact German divisions back to the Bahlui, which he held against repeated attacks. But Soviet mobile and armored units surged by his open flanks on both the right and left. By the end of the day, the Russian spearheads were thirty miles from where they had started on August 20, and there was no hope of sealing off the breakthrough. Things were still far from stabilized on the German left as night fell.

Meanwhile, except for IV Corps, 8th Army had only three divisions and had been effectively pushed off the battlefield to the west. On August 21, Friessner therefore took the corps away from 8th Army and placed it under command of the Fretter-Pico's 6th. Unfortunately, the general and his staff were on the run, with nothing except stragglers and refugees between them and the Russian tanks, and were not in much of a position to command anything.

In the Tiraspol sector, things were even worse than they were in the Jassy area. When August 21 began, General Postel's XXX Corps was fighting in a vacuum. It had been penetrated in several places, and large Soviet columns were driving south and southwest, completely unmolested. Landlines were down, and telephone contact with higher headquarters had been severed. The corps was unable to make radio contact with 6th Army or Army Group South Ukraine (probably because of Soviet jamming), and messengers could no longer get through and come back. The 9th Infantry Division had been surrounded and pushed off the battlefield to the south. It was not to be heard from again. Postel's other infantry divisions, the 15th and 306th, were under heavy attack from two Soviet armies with large tank formations; defending themselves fiercely under the hot Eastern European sun, they maintained their unit cohesion only with difficulty. The colonel commanding the 306th was killed by an enemy fighter-bomber. When General Postel's front waivered, he went forward, gun in hand, rallied two battalions, and inspired the soldiers by his personal example. Overhead, the Red Air Force bombed and strafed at will. The Luftwaffe was nowhere to be seen.

With his front crumbling, Postel had nothing with which to reestablish his flanks. In this desperate situation, he commandeered the last unit from the army group's reserve: Lieutenant General Friedrich Bayer's inadequately trained and ill-equipped 153rd Field Training Division. Bayer was ordered to take his handful of trucks and rush men into blocking positions, to seal the gaps left open by the Rumanians. But a few German platoons could not replace entire divisions, and the Red armored spearheads continued to roll west, far into the German rear.

Meanwhile, the 13th Panzer Division, reinforced by small, ad hoc battle groups from XXX Corps, tried to check the Soviet advance southeast of Kauschany, but it only had twenty tanks left when the day began. Like the infantry, it fought heroically and destroyed ninety-two Russian tanks, but it was all for nothing. They could not stop the avalanche. By the end of the day, XXX Corps's situation was desperate. On its left, the Soviet 5th Shock Army pinned down Erich Buschenhagen's LII Corps forward of Kishinev with heavy attacks; the 3rd Rumanian Army on its right had collapsed altogether. The Soviets were well beyond Postel's right flank, his front had been penetrated, the 15th Infantry was severely battered, the 306th was smashed, the 153rd Field Training Division was of little value to begin with, and every one of the 13th Panzer's tanks had been knocked out. The Soviets had broken through to a depth of thirty miles, and there was nothing left with which to stop them. The few roads still open to the west were clogged with Rumanian refugees—civilians and unarmed soldiers—so supplies could not get through to the combat units.

By nightfall, the Red spearheads were only ten miles from the 6th Army's headquarters at Tarutino, with no German combat units in between. General Fretter-Pico and his staff had no choice except to flee. German command functions at the army and army-group levels, which were already weak, now became weaker still and would soon cease.

By nightfall on August 21, Fretter-Pico's 6th Army was still holding firm, but the Rumanian forces on both of its flanks had disappeared, and Soviet tanks were in the rear of 6th Army. It was obvious that most of the Rumanian formations were not fighting; Armeegruppe Woehler reported that all five of its Rumanian divisions had fallen apart completely. Worse yet, there were reports of German liaison officers being arrested by their hosts, Rumanians cutting German telephone lines, and German orders being refused or ignored. The men of the 5th Rumanian Cavalry Division announced they had been demobilized, threw away their weapons, and left the battlefield. Hundreds of Rumanians attacked the German 3rd Mountain Division with such ferocity that the Germans suspected them of being Red Army troops in Rumanian uniforms.

With his army group collapsing and an encirclement of 6th Army already forming, Colonel General Friessner decided that he could wait no longer. On his own initiative, Friessner ordered 6th Army to retreat west of the Pruth (Prut) and sent motorized flak batteries forward to protect the crossings. That same morning, after considering the matter for more than a day, Adolf Hitler finally approved Friessner's request to withdraw the army behind the river. Word reached Fretter-Pico—who had hurriedly set up a temporary headquarters at Comrat—later that morning. He immediately signaled the trapped forces by radio: fall back behind the Pruth. Because of the Soviet command of the air, however, the withdrawal could not be carried out in broad daylight; Fretter-Pico ordered it to begin at 7:30 P.M.

He had waited too long.

August 22 was a day of continuous fighting on the Rumanian Front. The sky was cloudless and the heat oppressive; Soviet air units, which had improved considerably since 1941, bombed and strafed the columns almost at will. No one had seen a German airplane for a long time.

In the sector south of Jassy, in the zone of Mieth's IV Corps, the Rumanian 11th Division dissolved itself, despite the efforts of its commander to check its flight. The 79th and 376th Infantry Divisions struggled to keep the Pruth crossings around Kostuleni and Sbiroja open for the main body of the 6th Army, but they were pushed back in heavy fighting, and most of the bridges were in Soviet hands by nightfall. In the east, the exhausted soldiers of the XXX Corps, who had had no rest for three days, also continued to fight and fall back, fight and fall back, from burning village to burning village. Simultaneously, the remnants of the 13th Panzer Division, without any tanks, made a forced march to the Pruth, dodging Russian spearheads along the way. Here they set up two small bridgeheads on the east bank, near Leova and Falciu (southeast of Husi and the IV Corps), prepared to defend them, and awaited the arrival of the rest of the 6th Army.

The 306th Infantry Division, along with an assault gun brigade, set up defensive positions around the large airfield at Romanowo. They held it until the afternoon, when they were surrounded. Led by the assault guns, they broke out to the west. Then they were struck by a converging attack from several Russian armored units. Although individuals and small groups of soldiers managed to escape, the 306th Infantry ceased to exist.[29]

That evening, the Russians took Comrat. Fretter-Pico and the staff of the 6th Army managed to get out, just ahead of the Russian tanks. They headed for the area southeast of Berlad and would be out of touch with their disintegrating units for some time.

The next day, August 23, Dumitrescu's 3rd Rumanian Army (or what was left of it) was forced back against the Black Sea coast and surrounded. Friessner cut the Rumanians out of the command system when he ordered 6th Army to revert to army-group control. By now, the Russian plan was abundantly clear to anyone who had the facts and could read a map: they were executing a double pincer movement, aimed at Husi, a town just west of the Pruth. If it was successful, 6th Army (including IV Corps) would be encircled. Unfortunately for the Germans, the Soviet tanks were advancing rapidly through the gaps left by the Rumanians, and many of them had reached the Pruth River (forty miles in the German rear) before the 6th Army's retreat even got under way. They were followed by the Soviet infantrymen, most of which were racing into the German rear in vehicles made in Detroit. The German foot soldiers, on the other hand, could travel only as fast as their feet could carry them. (Standard infantry speed in the Vietnam era was considered to be 2.7 miles per hour.)

On August 23, the XXXXIV, LII, and XXX Corps and most of the VII were probably already doomed. There may still have been time, however, to save part of the IV Corps. But General Mieth was operating in the dark. He had received no orders and few reports, he had no contact with the main body of the 6th Army, he had no recent instructions from higher headquarters, and he did not know that 6th Army was disintegrating. Unaware that huge Soviet forces, spearheaded by the 6th Tank Army, were barreling down the west bank of the Berlad, well beyond Mieth's left flank, he decided to carry out his last instructions: hold the Pruth crossings at Sbiroja and Scoposeni for another twenty-four hours. In doing so, he unwittingly passed up his last opportunity to escape. Meanwhile, events of even greater consequence were taking place, as the political alliance between Nazi Germany and Rumania collapsed.

On the evening of August 23, Antonescu did exactly what he had promised Hitler he would not do: he reported to the royal palace to brief the king on the war situation. There he was arrested, along with War Minister Hano Pantazi and Minister of the Interior Constantin Vasiliu. Unlike the case with Mussolini, there would be no rescue of Antonescu, he would not reappear on the stage of history until after the war, when he was tried and executed as a war criminal. "Why didn't he for goodness sake listen to me?" Hitler whined that night.[30] Christescu, the chief of the Rumanian Secret Police, had been alarmed when Antonescu failed to return from his meeting and immediately reported his suspicions to the German embassy. Ambassador Baron Manfred von Killinger, however, refused to believe him until 10 P.M., when the king announced the formation of a new government under General Senatescu. They also declared the war over for Rumania; Rumanian troops were ordered to cease hostilities, and the Wehrmacht was given fourteen days to leave the country. Rumania, he said, was going to join the United Nations (i.e., the Allies) against the common enemy (the Third Reich). He also renounced the Treaty of Vienna, under which Hitler and Ribbentrop had forced Rumania to give up much of Transylvania to Hungary. This was tantamount to a declaration of war against Budapest.

At Rastenburg, Hitler and his advisors misjudged the situation entirely. Shortly before midnight, Friessner sent a dispatch to Fuehrer Headquarters recommending the evacuation of all German troops and installations to Hungary. At midnight on August 23–24, the OKH Operations Branch (under Lieutenant General Walter Wenck since Heusinger had been badly wounded by the Stauffenberg bomb) relayed an order from the Fuehrer to Army Group South Ukraine. Friessner was to smash the putsch, arrest the king and his court, and turn the government back over to Antonescu. If he were "no longer available," Friessner was to pick a pro-German general.[31] Friessner tried to pass this order on to von Killinger, Hansen, or Gerstenberg, but he discovered that all three had been arrested. He handed the order over to SS Major General Hoffmeyer instead and placed Major General Julius Kuderna's 5th Flak Division at Ploesti at his disposal. Its vanguards were soon on the way to Budapest.

That night, Friessner summoned General Dumitrescu, the commander of the 3rd Rumanian Army and the most influential Rumanian commander, to his headquarters at Slanic and almost begged him to ignore the orders from Bucharest and to continue to fight the Red Army. Dumitrescu, however, simply replied that he could not betray his oath of allegiance to the king.[32]

The political situation continued to deteriorate as the night wore on. Before dawn on August 24, General Hansen telephoned Friessner and told him that if the German measures against the new government (i.e., the move from Ploesti) were not halted within an hour, the Rumanian Army would join the battle against the Germans. He and the others were convinced that the German forces were not strong enough to capture Bucharest, Hansen added. Friessner then asked Hansen if he were under restraint; Hansen replied that he was.

Friessner transmitted a summary of this conversation to Fuehrer Headquarters. A few minutes later, Jodl telephoned to say that it would be better to force the issue and clear up the situation right away. He added that Field Marshal von Weichs, the OB Southeast, who happened to be visiting Fuehrer Headquarters, was sending a mobile group from Belgrade to Bucharest, and that Friessner was now Wehrmacht Commander, Rumania. A moment later General Gerstenberg called: the Rumanians had released him, apparently thinking that he would attempt to stop the impending German reaction. They had picked the wrong man. Gerstenberg described the new Rumanian government as a small, frightened clique, protected by very few troops. Friessner thereupon placed him in command of the Bucharest area, with orders to carry out the Fuehrer's directives. General Friessner was faced with carrying out three difficult operations at once: capture Bucharest and restore the Antonescu government; extricate the 6th Army from its impending encirclement; and conduct a retreat to Hungary through hostile territory and in the face of vastly superior Soviet forces.

Gerstenberg's attempt to capture Bucharest was a failure. Six thousand German troops from the 5th Flak Division and a few miscellaneous formations attacked the Rumanian capital at 7:30 A.M., but were facing unexpectedly stiff resistance within fifteen minutes. By 10:30 A.M., the Luftwaffe buildings within the city were surrounded and under fire, and Gerstenberg had been halted by Rumanian armored units some of which were equipped with PzKw VI Tiger tanks. Shortly before noon, Gerstenberg telephoned HQ, Army Group South Ukraine, and admitted that he had not been able to push beyond the suburbs.

At the front, the situation continued to deteriorate rapidly on August 24. Of the 6th Army's forces inside the rapidly forming pocket, the three divisions of the VII Corps (the 106th and 370th Infantry and the 14th Rumanian Infantry) had the shortest distances to march to reach the Pruth. After an exhausting forced march, the 370th reached Mieth's bridgehead near Sbiroja, linked up with the IV Corps, and crossed the river. The other two divisions of VII Corps never made it. The 14th Rumanian Infantry disintegrated, and its men disappeared. The 106th Infantry was overtaken and surrounded by Russian tanks and motorized infantry, which destroyed it in a battle that lasted two days. Only small remnants broke out, escaped, and reached the west bank of the Pruth.

The XXXXIV Corps abandoned Kishinev during the night of August 23–24, and its withdrawal continued on August 24, despite traffic jams and air strikes from enemy fighter-bombers. As the LII Corps withdrew, however, it was attacked on the march by faster-moving Soviet tank and mechanized divisions, which the frontline units beat off only with difficulty. The poor Rumanian roads could not handle the flight of four German corps, and massive traffic jams soon occurred. In places, German vehicles were lined up three and four abreast, presenting Russian pilots with most inviting targets. The main road from Kishinev to Husi was soon completely blocked. The fact that the few decent roads were often assigned to more than one division further complicated matters. Units quickly became hopelessly intermixed, and all control was lost. The retreat quickly degenerated into a disorderly rout—unthinkable for German armies just three years before.

On the southern side of the rapidly forming pocket, the 257th Infantry Division and other elements of the XXX Corps were encircled in the Carbuna area, about twelve miles east of Guragalbina. Here they were attacked by Soviet tanks and by wave after wave of bombers and fighter-bombers. Early that afternoon, Major General Friedrich Bluemke, the divisional commander, launched a breakout attempt, but it was not successful. Before he could organize another, he was mortally wounded by a Soviet fighter-bomber.[33] Panic set in, and it was "every man for himself." A few of them succeeded in escaping into the forests, but very few.

Early that afternoon, far to the southwest, about forty miles behind 6th Army's rearguards, a Soviet tank corps from the 2nd Ukrainian Front barreled into Husi. The city was full of German supply units, all of which were heading west. Complete chaos resulted. As soon as they secured the city, the Russians sent a strong column across the Pruth and linked up with the vanguard of the 3rd Ukrainian Front, surrounding the 6th Army in a giant pocket between the Dnestr and the Pruth. Trapped here were the VII, XXX, XXXXIV, and LII Corps, along with the 9th, 15th, 62nd, 106th, 161st, 257th, 258th, 282nd, 294th, 302nd, 306th, 335th, 376th, and 384th Infantry Divisions, and most of the 153rd Field Training, 10th Panzer Grenadier, and 13th Panzer Divisions, as well as seven assault gun brigades and dozens of army and corps units. This left Army Group South Ukraine with only seventy-eight assault guns and forty-five tanks. Friessner forbade General Fretter-Pico (whose Headquarters, 6th Army, was outside the encirclement) to fly into the pocket to join his troops. He, like Friessner himself, was to concentrate upon scraping together a new force for the defense of Hungary. Both men were rapidly pushed to the west by the advancing Soviet tanks. Friessner had already made the difficult decision to abandon the 6th Army to its fate; his task was to save Hungary—if he could.

That afternoon, on Hitler's orders, 150 airplanes from the 4th Air Fleet bombed the royal palace and government buildings in Bucharest. This gave the Rumanian government the pretext it needed for a complete break from Germany. It declared war on the Third Reich the next day, August 25.[34] Also on August 24, Hitler ordered the elite special-purposes Brandenburg Parachute Battalion to capture Bucharest—a clearly impossible task for a thousand men. Nevertheless, they had to try. During the night of August 24–25, they seized the airfield at Otopeni, eight miles north of the capital, before the new Rumanian government could defend it. The next day, they captured a Rumanian Army base, Forest Camp Number 1, a mile and a half away. But that was as far as they got, even though Hitler continued to reinforce them to a strength of almost three thousand men.

During the night of August 24–25, a major storm system drenched Bessarabia. The already poor dirt roads over which 6th Army was traveling quickly became all but impassable. The wet and exhausted Germans had no choice but to abandon most of their vehicles, including their artillery.

That same evening, the three commanders in the pocket—Generals Mueller, Buschenhagen, and Postel—decided to break out to the southwest. None of them were under any illusions. All three corps were in shambles, there were signs of disintegration everywhere, and masses of Soviet tanks and artillery ringed the pocket, waiting for just such an attempt. Despite the fact that he was the junior of the three, Georg Postel assumed command of the breakout, probably because his corps was closest to the Pruth. He signaled 6th Army of his intentions later that night.

It was the last message 6th Army ever received from its encircled units.

Inside the pocket, officers burned their codebooks and secret documents. The men discarded all unnecessary equipment and destroyed all the vehicles they could not take (which was most of them), as well as their heavy weapons, field kitchens, and anything else that might slow them down. The next day, August 25, the remaining soldiers of the XXX Corps massed and led by General Postel and his divisional commanders, charged the Russian lines, screaming "Hurrah!" The Russians, who were waiting for them behind hastily constructed barricades, cut them down with heavy machine guns, artillery salvos, and tank fire. George Postel and Colonel Willi Fischer, the commander of the 302nd Infantry Division, went down with serious wounds. Major General Werner von Eichstaedt, the commander of the 294th Infantry Division, and Lieutenant General Hans de Salengre-

Drabbe, the commander of the 384th Infantry, were killed outright. Although small elements of the 294th, 302nd, and 384th Infantry Divisions succeeded in penetrating the Soviet ring, it was clear that there would be no major breakout.

The pocket was ringed by four full Soviet armies and several independent corps. In reserve, between Guragalbina and the Pruth, lay another Russian army and a tank corps, positioned to make sure that any Germans who succeeded in breaking out were killed or captured before they could reach the Pruth. After Postel's breakout attempt failed, all four Soviet armies drove into the pocket from all directions, splitting it up and killing or capturing hundreds of Germans.

The end of the 6th Army's encircled divisions was not far off.

West of the pocket, from the right flank of the 3rd Mountain Division (in the mountains west of Targu Neamt) to the mouth of the Danube 250 miles to the southeast, lay a huge gap, which Army Group South Ukraine could not cover with even a screening force. Remarkably, on August 26, Hitler ordered the army group to take up a new defensive line running from the mouth of the Danube, through Galatz and Focsani, to the Carpathians. This was the same line Antonescu, Schoerner, and Friessner had advised him to take up earlier. Fretter-Pico had attempted to hold this line the day before with rear-echelon troops, but they had been rapidly pushed back or destroyed by Malinovskiy's spearheads.

By August 26, the Rumanians had Gerstenberg's assault force surrounded near Bucharest, and at Ploesti the rest of the 5th Flak Division had lost the oil refineries and half the city. Woehler's 8th Army (minus Mieth's IV Corps, which was encircled with 6th Army) was retreating from the Siret, with barely enough men to block the Carpathian Mountain passes from Oitoz to the north. This left 190 miles—from the Transylvanian Alps to the Iron Gate of Yugoslavia—completely exposed. The airplanes of Dessloch's 4th Air Fleet were using the last of their fuel to fly to new bases in eastern Hungary, and to the south, the Bulgarians (who were desperately trying to keep the Red Army out of their country) were disarming and interning all Army Group South Ukraine forces who crossed into their territory.

What was happening to the encircled forces of 6th Army?

Between the Dnestr and the Berlad, two giant pockets had formed. One (about 10 divisions) lay east of the Pruth and east of Husi, while the other (IV Corps divisions) was south of Husi and moving slowly to the west.

Despite all odds, a significant fragment of the 6th Army broke through the Soviet encirclement on the morning of August 26 and pushed on to the banks of the Pruth. There were no more bridges in German hands, however. Mieth's corps had already lost the bridges at Sbiroja and Scoposeni, and on the evening of August 24, the 13th Panzer Division had been pushed back to the west, giving up the bridgeheads around Leova and Falciu. All the fleeing and largely leaderless troops found was a small bridgehead on the east bank of the Pruth, which was occupied by an isolated battle group from the 282nd Infantry Division of the XXXXIV Corps.

Estimates of the number of 6th Army soldiers who reached the Pruth bridgehead vary from ten to twenty thousand. The rest of the 6th Army was crushed in the Guragalbina (or Kishinev) Pocket, where all resistance ended by August 30. The 6th Army had lost at least 150,000 of the 170,000 men with which it had started this campaign less than a week before.[35]

On August 26, German engineers organized a few inflatable boats and launched an assault across the Pruth. They established a bridgehead and began to ferry the rest of the survivors across the river. Only then did a reconnaissance patrol discover that they had not crossed the river at all: they were going to a low, marshy island, about three miles long and half a mile wide, in the middle of the river. The western fork of the Pruth was more like a marshy lake, three to five hundred yards wide. It turned out to be fordable, so a ground attack across it might be possible. Worse, they discovered that the Russians had already arrived on the true west bank and were waiting for them.

Throughout August 26, 27, and 28, the remnants of the XXX, LII, and XXXXIV Corps gathered on the island, including Generals Mueller, Buschenhagen, and the wounded General Postel—all three corps commanders. For three days, the island was pounded by Stalin organs, heavy artillery, bombers, and fighter-bombers. A breakout attempt set for the night of August 27–28 was aborted when the exhausted men forming the spearhead blundered into a swamp in the darkness. A final, desperate attempt took place on the evening of August 28. It was later described by Alex Buchner as "a wild charge . . . [w]ithout preparation, without orders, without any kind of order or organization."[36]

Led by their officers, an estimated ten to twelve thousand German soldiers took part in the final attack. Some drowned, others collapsed from exhaustion, and a great many were killed. Braving intense fire, however, the assault wave reached the steep western bank of the Pruth, and the desperate veterans of the Eastern Front stormed the Russian barricades in sometimes brutal hand-to-hand combat. The surprised Soviets panicked and fled in all directions. The remnants of the 6th Army had made their way across the Pruth.

It was a Pyrrhic victory. The exhausted survivors continued to march west about two miles, until they reached a large forest, where they rested for the night. The Soviets, however, had recovered quickly. On the morning of August 29 they surrounded the forest and began the task of mopping up the remnants of 6th Army. General of Infantry Ludwig Mueller, the commander of the XXXXIV Corps, tried to break out again, but he could organize only about two hundred men for the attempt. It failed, and he was captured.

The fighting was all over by September 5. Hardly anyone escaped.[37] General of Infantry Erich Buschenhagen and a small band of his men managed to evade the encirclement and headed for the Carpathians on foot. He was betrayed by a Rumanian on September 13 and was captured by the Russians.[38]

The assault forces left their wounded behind on the island in the Pruth, and it is not known whether General Postel reached the west bank or not; he was taken prisoner when the Red Army mopped up the area. He died in a Soviet prison in 1953.

THE END OF THE IV CORPS

Meanwhile, on the other side of the Pruth, General of Infantry Friedrich Mieth's IV Corps—joined by stragglers from the VII Corps—continued to try to fight its way out to the west.

Fourth Corps initially consisted of the German 370th, 79th, and 376th Infantry Divisions and the Rumanian 11th Infantry Division. The 79th Infantry began its retreat on August 21, with the other three starting out the next day. Because of recent heavy rains, a number of pieces of heavy artillery had to be abandoned; the horses could not pull them out of the mud. Mieth's retreat carried him south, parallel to the Pruth River. He had already lost contact with the units on both his flanks.

Friedrich Mieth was a highly capable officer of great physical and moral courage. A soldier since 1906, he was a major on the General Staff when Hitler came to power. He was a major general and chief of staff of the 1st Army when the war broke out. Like many generals, he was upset and appalled after the Polish campaign, when the SS and SD *Einsatzgruppen* began committing atrocities against Jews and Poles. Unlike the vast majority of his contemporaries, however, he forcefully spoke out against it. He even assembled his officers and told them that the SS was conducting mass executions and "has besmirched the Wehrmacht's honor."[39] He specifically denounced Reinhard Heydrich, the chief of the SD.

Hitler promptly became to the defense of his minions and sacked Mieth. Three weeks later, however, General of Artillery Franz Halder, the chief of General Staff from 1938 to 1942 and an occasional anti-Hitler conspirator, rescued him from professional oblivion and named him chief of the Operations Department (O Qu I) of OKH. Soon promoted to lieutenant general, Mieth helped plan and execute the Western campaign of 1940. Later that year, he assumed command of the 112th Infantry Division, which he led on the Russian Front until Stalingrad was surrounded. With the southern sector on the verge of collapse, Field Marshal Erich von Manstein named him commander of the ad hoc Corps Mieth, which he led with distinction in the battles along the Don, in the Donetz, and in the retreat to the Mius. Because he had proven himself to be an excellent field commander, he was promoted to general of infantry on April 20, 1944. Six weeks later, his headquarters was upgraded to permanent status and was redesignated IV Corps. It was named after a unit destroyed at Stalingrad.

On August 23, the Soviet mechanized and armored attacks grew stronger and bolder, and they were beaten off only with difficulty. The troops had not received supplies for days and resorted to eating their Iron Rations (a hard chocolate concoction, laced with caffeine) or lived off what little corn they could find in the poor Rumanian cornfields. The wounded, carried along in Panje wagons, were without medication or proper medical attention and died by the dozens in the scorching heat.

Although he delayed for a day at Sbiroja and Scoposeni to wait for the 6th Army, Mieth resumed his retreat on August 24. Fourth Corps was still an organized fighting force on August 25, when it reached Husi and found the place in Russian hands. General Mieth launched a series of desperate attacks against the town, but could not take it, due to the swampy nature of the terrain that surrounded the place, the stiffness of the Russian defense, and the rapidly diminishing combat strength of his exhausted units. Only the 666th Grenadier Regiment of the 370th Infantry Division fought its way into Husi; it was quickly encircled by a Russian counterattack and completely wiped out. On August 26, after a final assault failed, Mieth ordered all carts burned and all unwanted horses shot.

Without food or rest for days, IV Corps now began to disintegrate and the Soviets were clearly trying to compress the corps and isolate it in the Vutcani Valley area. Mieth tried to fight his way out by slipstepping to the west. He ordered his officers to attack across the Berlad River, destroy all remaining equipment, and break into small groups. These parties were then to head west for the German lines in the Carpathians (seventy miles away)—at least that is where Mieth hoped they were. He had had no contact with any other German unit for days and had no idea where Army Group South Ukraine was or what it was doing.

The German assault group was supposed to form up for the attack on the night of August 27–28. It was to be spearheaded by the four assault guns left in the 825th Assault Gun Brigade, followed by Lieutenant General Friedrich-August Weinknecht's veteran 79th Infantry Division and Lieutenant General Count Botho von Huelsen's 370th Infantry Division, followed by four combat engineer companies. The infantry by now was too exhausted and too low in ammunition to be of much use, the soldiers who could still walk followed behind like zombies in stupefied silence.

Weinknecht and von Huelsen could not form their assault units on time. The combat organization of the divisions was breaking down, communications were out, and the exhausted troops simply could not be roused in sufficient numbers. Headquarters, IV Corps had already been overrun the night before, and the corps chief of staff, Colonel Guenther Siedschlag, had been killed, but General Mieth escaped and was right up front with the assault unit when it crossed the river under Soviet artillery and mortar fire after daybreak on August 29. He died in close combat as the 179th Engineer Battalion overran the Soviet blocking positions and seized the Berlad River bridge at Chitcani. He fell just as his corps ceased to exist.

Once across the Berlad, IV Corps broke up into smaller groups as planned. About twenty thousand of Mieth's men managed to cross the river and pushed southwest of Husi. Almost all of them were run down and killed or captured by the Soviets. Only one member of the 79th Infantry Division reached friendly lines in Hungary, twelve days later.

Other IV Corps units distinguished themselves as well in this, their last battle. Captain Mergen's 661st Army Panzer Battalion, for example, destroyed fifty-two Soviet tanks in four days. In the end, however, only Colonel Otto-Hermann Bruecker's 76th Infantry Division (a unit originally organized in Berlin from Prussian reservists), elements of the 10th Panzer Grenadier Division (Colonel Walter Herold), and a remnant of the 13th Panzer Division (Lieutenant General Hans Troeger) were able to fight their way back to German lines. General Troeger was not with this part of his command at the time, however. After he was forced to abandon this bridgehead on the eastern bank of the Pruth, he was assigned to the XXIX Corps and ordered to establish blocking positions farther west, along the Seret.

Headquarters, XXIX Corps, which was with the 3rd Rumanian Army on August 20, had quickly lost all of its divisions. The German 9th Infantry was cut off and largely destroyed near Sarata, and its two Rumanian divisions had dissolved themselves. As a result, the XXIX (which was commanded by Lieutenant General Baron Anton Reichard von Mauchenheim gennant von Bechtoldsheim) had no units under its command; so Army Group South Ukraine pulled it back to the Berlad and on August 26 ordered it back farther west to the Seret River, where it was ordered to establish a new front. It was given command of the 13th Panzer, the 10th Panzer Grenadier, and 153rd Field Training Divisions, as well as Panzerverband Braun (Tank Formation Braun). Unfortunately, the remnant of the 13th Panzer that managed to reach the Seret had no tanks, not a single armored vehicle—only a few guns, and enough motorized infantry to equal about a regiment. The 10th Panzer Grenadier Division was in a similar condition, while the 153rd Field Training could not muster even a decent-size regiment. Only the recently formed Panzerverband Braun, which included elements of the 20th Panzer Division, twenty-one assault guns, and an assault battalion from the 8th Army, was of any significant combat value.[40]

The XXIX Corps never had a chance to carry out its mission. It was in a running fight with the pursuit forces of the Red Army that very afternoon, before it could even thinly man the Seret, and the next day, August 27, the Soviets crossed the river unopposed. On the afternoon of August 28, the corps was surrounded.

General von Bechtoldsheim met with his commanders in a small wood east of the Buzau-to-Bucharest highway on the morning of August 29. As they talked, they could see a steady procession of Soviet columns on the road, heading west. After some discussion, von Bechtoldsheim gave all the mobile elements of his corps permission to make their way south, toward Bulgaria, which was still regarded as an ally. That night, he said, the marching units of the corps—which he would personally lead—would break out to the west. Most of the marching units (including formerly mobile units which had lost their vehicles) broke out but were quickly pursued by the Russians. Most of the men were killed or captured. The general himself, however, managed to reach the Carpathians on foot, accompanied by Colonel Theodor Mehring, his chief of staff, and about a hundred of his men. Baron von Bechtoldsheim was promptly placed in Fuehrer Reserve and investigated. Cleared of any wrongdoing, he was later given another command.[41]

General Troeger and that portion of his men who still had their motorized vehicles fought their way to the Bulgarian border, where they were disarmed by the Bulgarian Army. They were interned and handed over to the Soviets. Hans Troeger did not see Germany again until 1955.[42] General Bayer also reached the Bulgarian border with a fragment of the 153rd Field Training Division and suffered the same fate.[43]

Panzerverband Braun did not make it that far. It was surrounded and scattered on August 30, before it could reach the Danube.

Of the roughly 180,000 men cut off in the pockets east and west of the Pruth, approximately twenty thousand soldiers who wanted to avoid capture at any cost decided to trek through the Rumanian forests on foot until they reached the new German front. They had, of course, no idea of the distance involved, or of the fact that the front was moving away from them every day. They endured hunger, thirst, and lack of shelter. Many were tracked down by the Russians and/or Rumanians, while others died alone in the forests of illness, wounds, or exposure. Many lived for weeks on a diet of uncooked corn and rainwater. They marched by night, hid in the woods or forest by day, avoided settlements and roads, forded or swam across streams and rivers, and constantly dodged Russian columns. After enduring great hardship and suffering, about 1,500 reached German lines.

Lieutenant Steinmeyer of the 161st Infantry Division is a fairly typical example of these men. Following a breakout from the Pruth lowlands, he and about four hundred men from the XXXXIV Corps were cut off in a wooded area south of Husi on August 28. They set out on foot that same day, with the goal of reaching the German front on the Seret. On August 30 they had their first clash with the Russians and fought daily skirmishes with the Red Army for several days thereafter. Due to casualties and men becoming separated from the main body, there were only eleven men left on September 5, the day they swam across the Seret. Disappointed that the Wehrmacht had been driven west, they nevertheless were still determined to reach German lines.

On September 6, Steinmeyer and his comrades were surrounded by elements of the Rumanian Army, which was now working with the Russians. After a seven-hour battle, the lieutenant and six of his colleagues broke out and hid in the Carpathian foothills. En route back to friendly lines, they occasionally approached Rumanian villages and were given cucumbers, corn, fruit, and raw or hastily cooked potatoes. After being betrayed several times to Russian or Rumanian patrols, however, they avoided all contact with Rumanian civilians and lived mainly on raw corn. Pursued again and again, they celebrated when they heard the roar of heavy artillery, which indicated that the front was not far off. They continued northwest for days, however, and the front got no closer, indicating that the Wehrmacht was withdrawing. Finally, after a trek of 32 days, during which they traveled more than 380 miles on foot, Steinmeyer and two other survivors reached Hungarian lines in Transylvania.[44]

Meanwhile, the Soviets mopped up the German pockets in Rumania. General Gerstenberg surrendered his battle group on August 28. Major General Julius Kuderna, the commander of the 5th Flak Division, and his chief of operations, Major Hans-Joachim Schulz, were captured in Ploesti on August 31.[45] The rest of the division surrendered on September 4. The 180th Flak, 202nd Flak, and 188th Heavy Flak Regiments ceased to exist. The few remnants of the division that managed to escape were temporarily absorbed by the 15th Flak Division.

The two pockets on either side of the Pruth were cleared by September 5. Total German casualties were not less than 250,000 and may have reached 280,000. According to estimates quoted by Alex Buchner, about 125,000 Germans were killed, and 150,000 were captured; of these, about eighty thousand died in Rumanian collection camps—most from starvation. About seventy thousand eventually returned home.[46] According to an official Soviet report dated September 13, 1944, German losses were 256,000 men, of whom 150,000 were killed and 106,000 were captured. The Soviets also claimed to have captured or destroyed 830 tanks and armored vehicles, 330 airplanes, 3,500 guns and mortars, and 35,000 vehicles.[47] The disaster left Friessner with only five divisions: the two that escaped, two that were not attacked (the 3rd Mountain and 8th Jaeger), and the 97th Jaeger, which had been en route to another sector when the offensive began but was hurriedly returned to Army Group South Ukraine. About ten thousand men from rear-echelon units also escaped.

Once the pockets were surrounded, the Soviets quickly swept over the rest of Rumania and pushed as far west as the Carpathians, accompanied by what Colonel Seaton described as "a spate of horrifyingly violent excesses, including murder, rape, and robbery, committed on the civil population by a capricious and often drunken soldiery."[48] On August 26, the Red Army spearheads reached the Danube near Galati, opening up a clear path into the Balkans. Two days later they took Oituz Pass in the Carpathians and entered Transylvania. On August 29 they occupied Constanta (the German naval flotilla had already fled) and took Ploesti and the oil-fields the next day. Only remnants of 5th Flak Division managed to escape. On August 31, the Red Army entered the Rumanian capital. About six hundred Germans, including many women and children, were surrounded in the German embassy but were ordered to vacate the buildings on September 1. Rather than surrender to the Russians, Ambassador von Killinger shot his female secretary, then himself. General Eric Hansen was captured, as was Major General Dr. Karl Spalcke, the military attaché; Lieutenant General Reiner Stahel, the commandant of Bucharest; and General Gerstenberg.[49] Table 5.2 gives a partial list of the senior German officers captured in Rumania. The Soviets overran the rest of the country so rapidly that only sixty thousand of the two hundred thousand Transylvanian Saxons and 240,000 Swabians in Rumania managed to escape to Austria.

On August 29, after an artillery bombardment, a delegation of Rumanian officers approached Forest Camp Number 1 and informed the officers of the Brandenburg Parachute Battalion that they were surrounded and would have to leave the country immediately. If they agreed to do so, they would be allowed to keep their arms and would be escorted to the Yugoslavian border. The Brandenburgers readily consented but had not proceeded far before they were halted by the Russians. The Red Army had not agreed to grant the battalion safe conduct and demanded that the Germans surrender. The Rumanians promptly joined the Russians and renounced their own armistice. Seeing that escape was impossible, the paratroopers lay down their arms. Hitler had wasted three thousand of his best men.[50]

The Red Army rounded up about 1,500,000 former Rumanian soldiers in August and early September and sent them to the Soviet Union as slave laborers. It entered Bucharest on August 31. The Rumanian government quickly put its armed forces under the command of the Soviets, including the 1st Army (General Anastasiu), the 4th Army (General Avramescu), and the 5th Army (General Mihai Racovitza). Shortly thereafter, a Soviet puppet government was installed. Many of the Rumanians who had secretly negotiated Rumania's defection from the Axis were invited to a banquet at Red Army headquarters. They were greeted with great fanfare and then disappeared behind Russian lines, never to be seen again.

Table 5.2
Senior German Officer Casualties, Rumania, 1944

Major General Stanislaus von Dewitz gen. von Krebs, commandant of Kischinev, captured August 18

Major General Walter Gleininger, commander, 586th Field Administrative Headquarters, committed suicide August 21

General of Infantry Ludwig Mueller, commander, XXXXIV Corps, captured August 23

General of Infantry Friedrich Mieth, commander, IV Corps, killed August 29

Luftwaffe Major General Julius Kuderna, commander, 5th Flak Division, captured August 31

Major General Friedrich Bluemke, commander, 257th Infantry Division, mortally wounded August 24, died September 2

Lieutenant General Friedrich-August Weinknecht, commander, 79th Infantry Division, captured August 29

Major General Hans Simon, commander, 15th Flak Division, captured August 29

Colonel Paul Kohwalt, commander, 134th Artillery Command, killed in action, August 31[1]

Lieutenant General Georg Postel, commander, XXX Corps, captured end of August

Major General Karl Stingl, Commandant of Jassy, captured end of August

Major General Dr. Karl Spalcke, military attaché, Bucharest, captured September 1

General of Cavalry Eric Hansen, captured September 1

Lieutenant General Alfred Gerstenberg, air attaché to Bucharest and Luftwaffe commander, Rumania, captured September 1

General of Medical Services Dr. August Raess, chief medical officer to the Rumanian Military Mission, captured September 1

Lieutenant General Botho von Huelsen, commander, 370th Infantry Division, captured September 3

Lieutenant General Otto Schwarz, commander, 376th Infantry Division, captured September 4

General of Infantry Erich Buschenhagen, commander of the LII Corps, captured on or about September 8

Lieutenant General Friedrich Bayer, commander, 153rd Field Training Division, captured September 11

Lieutenant General Hans Troeger, commander, 13th Panzer Division, interned in Bulgaria September

Notes:
[1]Posthumously promoted to major general.

Sources: Keilig, *Generale*; Buchner, *Ostfront 1944*, pp. 332–34.

NOTES

1. Seaton, *Russo-German War*, pp. 469–70.

2. Major General Otto Beutler, the commander of the 340th Infantry Division, was killed in action on July 21, 1944. He was previously chief of operations of IV Corps (1939), chief of staff of IV Corps (1939–42), and a staff officer at OKW (1942–43). He assumed command of the division on June 16.

3. Wernes Conze, *Die Geschichte der 291, Infanterie-Division, 1940–1945* (Bad Nauheim: 1953), p. 74.

4. Major Andree was awarded the Knight's Cross as acting commander of the 504th Infantry Regiment in May 1944. He was killed in action a few weeks later. Seemen, p. 53; Conze, p. 74.

5. Conze, p. 74.

6. In 1914, Arthur Finger joined the Imperial Army as a war volunteer. He was sixteen years old at the time. He received a reserve commission in the artillery four years later. After World War I, he was a police officer. He rejoined the army as a captain in 1935 and commanded three artillery regiments from 1940 to 1944, mostly in Norway. Promoted to major general on October 1, 1944, he was killed in action on January 27, 1945, during the Russian drive into Silesia (Keilig, p. 90).

7. Headquarters, 17th Army had been smashed at Sevastopol in May and had to be almost completely rebuilt. Friedrich Schulz assumed command of the army on July 25. A holder of the Knight's Cross with Oak Leaves and Swords, he had risen rapidly, from lieutenant colonel in 1939 to general of infantry in 1944. In the process, he had served of the staff of OKW (1937–40); chief of staff of XXXXIII Corps (1940–42); chief of staff of Manstein's 11th Army in the Crimea and the siege of Leningrad (1942); chief of staff of Army Group Don in the Stalingrad campaign (1942–43); and commander of the 28th Jaeger Division, III Panzer Corps, LIX Corps, and XXXXVI Panzer Corps, all on the Eastern Front (1943–44). Schulz commanded 17th Army until April 2, 1945, when he was named commander in chief of Army Group South in Italy. He surrendered it to the Anglo-Americans less than a month later. A native of Silesia, General Schulz retired to Freudenstadt after the war.

8. Mehner, vol. 10, p. 508.

9. Werner Haupt, *Army Group South: The Wehrmacht in Russia, 1941–1945* (Atglen, Penn.: 1998), pp. 377–81.

10. On August 15–16, 1944, a major transfer of senior personnel took place in the German Army. Field Marshal Guenther von Kluge was relieved as commander in chief of Army Group B and OB West (i.e., Supreme Commander, Western Front) and was replaced by Walter Model. Georg-Hans Reinhardt, the commander of the 3rd Panzer Army, succeeded Model as C-in-C of Army Group Center. Raus, the commander of the 1st Panzer Army, assumed command of the 3rd Panzer Army, and Gotthard Heinrici (who was returning from sick leave) succeeded Raus at 1st Panzer.

Gotthard Heinrici (1886–1971) had previously commanded the 16th Infantry Division (1937–40); VII, XII, and XXXXIII Corps (1940–42); and 4th Army (1944). A defensive genius, he directed Army Group Vistula in the defense of Berlin (1945).

11. Buchner, pp. 243, 304.

12. Johannes Friessner, *Verratene Schlachten* (Hamburg: 1956), pp. 53–54; Seaton, *Russo-German War*, p. 467.

13. Ion Antonescu was born in 1882. He served in World War I and later became chief of staff of the Rumanian Army, until King Carol II relieved him of his post because of his pro-Nazi attitude and his suspected intrigues with the Iron Guard, the Rumanian incarnation of the Nazi Party. On September 4–5, 1940, however, threatened with revolution and German intervention, Carol appointed Antonescu premier, with dictatorial powers. On September 6, 1940, Antonescu forced the king to abdicate in favor of his son, Michael. Rumania joined the Axis in November 1940. Antonescu gave Hitler virtual control of the Rumanian economy and foreign policy. He also cooperated with Hitler's Jewish policies, including the Holocaust.

14. Seaton, *Russo-German War*, pp. 469–70.

15. A native of Hamburg, Eric Hansen had entered the Imperial Army as an officer cadet with the 9th Light Dragoons. He commanded the 4th Infantry Division (1938–40), was chief of the German Military Mission in Rumania (1940–41) and commander of the LIV Corps on the Russian front (June 1941–early 1943). He was named commander of German Forces in Rumania and chief of the German Military Mission in Rumania in January 1943. A capable commander, he was not a good mission director, because he was too opinionated, saw only what he wanted to see, and tended to ignore unpleasant evidence.

16. Buchner, p. 245. Baron Manfred von Killinger was born in Lindigt in 1886. He joined the Imperial Navy, rose to the rank of lieutenant commander in World War I, and served in the infamous Ehrhardt Naval Brigade in the turbulence following the war. He joined the Nazi Party in 1927. An SA Obergruppenfuehrer (General of Storm Troopers), he served as Reichskommissar for Saxony (1933–35) and German Counsel General in San Francisco (1936–38), before returning to Berlin to head a department in the foreign ministry. He was named ambassador to Romania in 1941.

17. Guderian, p. 292.

18. Friessner, p. 44.

19. Guderian, pp. 292–93. Jungenfeld was in charge of tank training. He had previously commanded the 656th Heavy Tank Destroyer Regiment (Scheibert, p. 176).

20. Seaton, *Russo-German War*, pp. 472–73.

21. Ziemke, pp. 349–50.

22. Ivo-Thilo Trotha had been on the staff of OKW from the outbreak of the war, so he was well acquainted with Keitel. He had served as chief of operations of the 267th Infantry Division (1941) and 4th Army (1942) before becoming Ia of Army Group South Ukraine in April 1944. Later he would be chief of staff of 1st Panzer Army (October 1944), branch chief at OKH (March 1945), and chief of staff of Army Group Vistula (late April 1945–end). He was promoted to major general in 1945.

23. Maximilian Fretter-Pico was born in Karlsruhe in 1892 and entered the service as a *Fahnenjunker* in 1910. A colonel when World War II began, he was chief of staff of XXIV Corps (1939); commander, 97th Jaeger Division (1941); commander, XXX Corps (late 1941); and commander, Army Detachment Fretter-Pico

(fall 1942). He assumed command of 6th Army on July 17, 1944. His younger brother Otto (born 1893) became a lieutenant general in World War II.

24. Buchner, pp. 249–50.

25. Mehner, vol. 10, p. 506.

26. Keilig, p. 349.

27. Buchner, pp. 251–52.

28. Buchner, p. 253.

29. Ibid., p. 257.

30. Perry Pierik, *Hungary, 1944–1945* (Nieuwegein, Neth.: 1996), p. 52. Antonescu was executed in 1946.

31. Ziemke, p. 352.

32. Pierik, p. 51.

33. Buchner, pp. 260–61. Friedrich Bluemke was born in Pomerania on February 18, 1898. He joined the Imperial Army as a *Fahnenjunker* in 1916 and was commissioned second lieutenant in the 42nd Infantry Regiment the following year. After fighting in World War I, he was retained in the Reichsheer and was a captain on the General Staff when the Nazis rose to power in 1933. He was subsequently promoted to major (1936), lieutenant colonel (1940), colonel (early 1942), and to major general on August 1, 1944, the day he assumed command of the 257th. Prior to that, Bluemke had served as Ia of the 23rd Infantry Division (1938–41), chief of staff of the XIV Panzer Corps (1941–42), chief of staff of the XXXXII Corps (1942), and commander of the 347th Infantry Regiment (1942–44). Captured by the Russians when his division disintegrated, General Bluemke was taken to Odessa, where he died of his wounds on September 4.

34. Hitler had first issued the order to bomb Bucharest to General Friessner at 11 P.M. on August 23. When Friessner delayed executing the order, Hitler gave it to Goering instead. The *Reichsmarschall*, of course, made sure it was carried out.

35. Buchner, p. 273.

36. Ibid., p. 278.

37. Like General Troeger, Ludwig Mueller had risen rapidly. A lieutenant colonel when the war began in 1939, he was promoted to general of infantry in 1944. He remained in various Soviet prison camps until 1955. After escaping the Jassy catastrophe, Erich Abraham was given command of the LXIII Corps on the Western Front and was promoted to general of infantry in 1945. Released from captivity in 1947, he died at Wiesbaden in 1971. He was born in East Prussia in 1895.

38. General Buschenhagen also survived his captivity and returned home in 1955. He was reportedly still alive in 1990, but the author is unable to confirm this.

39. Irving, vol. 1, p. 77.

40. Buchner, p. 285.

41. Haupt, *South*, p. 390. In a subsequent investigation, Baron von Bechtoldsheim was cleared of all wrongdoing concerning the Rumanian disaster. Hitler obviously accepted the conclusions of the investigators, because von Bechtoldsheim was given command of the LXXI Corps in mid-December 1944 and was promoted to general of artillery on March 1, 1945. He was the former military attaché to London, Brussels, and the Hague (1937–39); Ia, 10th (later 6th) Army (1939–41); chief of staff, XXIII Corps (1941); chief of staff, XXIX Corps (1941–42); chief of

staff, 1st Army (1942–43); and commander of the 257th Infantry Division (1943–44). He was a Bavarian (Keilig, p. 219).

42. Hans Troeger was considered a "rising star" in the panzer branch and had risen from the rank of major in 1939 to lieutenant general in 1944. In the process, he had commanded the 3rd and 64th Motorcycle Battalions (1939–41), the 103rd Rifle Regiment (1941–42), the School for Battalion Commanders (1942), the 27th Panzer Division (1942–43), the School for Panzer Troops (1943), and the 25th Panzer Division (1943–44). He remained in Soviet prisons until 1955 (Keilig, p. 349).

Otto-Hermann Bruecher, a Berliner, was promoted to major general on October 1, 1944. He was later given command of the 6th Volksgrenadier Division and was promoted to lieutenant general in 1945. He survived the war. Colonel Herold was promoted to major general on November 9, 1944, but was killed in action nineteen days later.

43. Friedrich Bayer died in a Soviet prison on August 5, 1953.

44. Buchner, pp. 296–98.

45. General Kuderna also survived his captivity and was still alive in the early 1980s. He was born in 1892 (Absolom, pp. 38, 54).

46. Buchner, p. 299.

47. Ibid.; Pat McTaggart, "Budapest '45," in *Hitler's Army: The Evolution and Structure of the German Armed Forces*, by the Editors of *Command* (Conshohocken, Penn.: 1995), p. 343.

48. Seaton, *Russo-German War*, p. 485. Stahel was released from prison in October 1955 but died on November 30, 1955. He was a member of the flak branch and had, among other things, commanded the 4th Luftwaffe Field Division. He was born on January 15, 1892 (Absolom, p. 43).

49. Both Hansen and Spalcke survived their captivities. Lieutenant General Alfred Gerstenberg surrendered to the Rumanians and was handed over to the Russians. Like Hansen and Spalcke, he was released from prison in October 1955. He died on January 4, 1959 (Keilig, p. 327; Absolom, p. 38).

50. Lucas, *Last Year of the German Army*, p. 190.

CHAPTER VI

The Retreat from
the Balkans

Rumania was not the only country that wanted to break its close ties with Nazi Germany in the summer of 1944: Bulgaria and Hungary wanted out of the alliance as well. The Bulgarian leaders thought they were in a stronger position, after all, they had declared war on the United States and Great Britain but had never done so against Moscow. In addition, there were no German troop units in the country. When Turkey broke diplomatic relations with Berlin on August 2, Bulgaria began to actively seek a way out of the war. During the next two weeks Sofia reestablished consular relations with Moscow and severely restricted German troop movements through the country. Field Marshal von Weichs, the C-in-C of OB Southeast, was unable to intervene, because he lacked the troops and because the Bulgarian Army (which had not seen action since the conquest of Yugoslavia in 1941) was well equipped with German tanks and airplanes. It was, in fact, better outfitted than most of his own divisions.

On August 17, the Bulgarian premier told the Bulgarian parliament that his government was "determined to remove all obstacles to peace."[1] Field Marshal Weichs concluded that Bulgaria intended to defect and that when it did, he would have to withdraw his troops from Greece and the islands in the Aegean Sea, since his flank would be hopelessly exposed. Unfortunately for the Germans, coordination between OB Southeast (an OKW theater) and Army Group South Ukraine (an OKH force) was none too good. Friessner apparently assumed that Weichs had the Balkans (including Bulgaria) under control, while Weichs assumed that Friessner had the situation in Rumania well in hand. Both assumed that Hitler was in control of the overall political situation in southeastern Europe. All of these assumptions were wrong.

As C-in-C of Army Group B in 1942, Field Marshal Baron Maximilian von Weichs had played a major role in the Stalingrad disaster.[2] Taken unaware, his 6th Army was encircled and destroyed in the city, and after his other armies were smashed during the Soviet winter offensive of 1942–43, his headquarters was pulled out of the line and dissolved. (Most of his staff officers were later assigned to Field Marshal Rommel's new command in Italy.) In August 1943, Rommel was named OB Southeast and simultaneously C-in-C of Army Group F, but his new command lasted only one day; Italy defected, Rommel was recalled to Germany to organize the forces that eventually recaptured northern Italy, and Weichs was recalled from disgrace to succeed the Desert Fox in both of his Balkan commands.

Although he had not done well as an army group commander on the Eastern Front, Weichs's new assignment suited him better. He quickly disarmed the considerable Italian forces in the Balkans, crushed the Italian forces that did resist, and was generally successful in suppressing the partisans, who were quick to try to take advantage of the Italian defection.

Lacking the forces to decisively crush the partisan uprising that had resulted from Hitler's brutal occupation policies, Weichs took advantage of the hostility between the various guerilla forces in the Balkans. In Yugoslavia, he pitted Colonel Draza Mihailovic's pro-Royalist Chetniks against Tito's Communist partisans and bottled up the latter in western Yugoslavia, in the former Italian zone. In Greece, he pitted the Communists against the Nationalists and established a truce with the latter that lasted until the fall of 1944. By skillfully combining force and diplomacy, he was able to maintain German hegemony in the troubled Balkans. He had, in fact, performed most impressively under the circumstances.

In August 1944, Weichs's OB Southeast consisted of two major subordinate headquarters: General of Artillery Maximilian de Angelis's 2nd Panzer Army and Army Group E, commanded by Luftwaffe Colonel General Alexander Loehr.[3] In spite of its designation, 2nd Panzer Army had not been a panzer army for some time; in fact, since it had been sent to the Balkans following Kursk and the Battle of the Orel Salient, it had been commanded by two generals of the mountain branch, Dr. Lothar Rendulic and Franz Boehme. (Boehme had been replaced by de Angelis on July 18, 1944.)[4] It did not have a single panzer division or brigade, and its few tanks were captured Italian vehicles: good enough for use against poorly equipped partisans, but next to useless against regular Soviet troops.

Weichs's Order of Battle looked formidable on paper. As of August 25, he controlled nine hundred thousand men and women, many of whom were technicians, bureaucrats, police, or administrative personnel. OB Southeast included six hundred thousand men classified as combat troops in thirty-eight divisions and seven brigades. However, seven of these divisions were Bulgarian, over which he had only nominal control, and nine were collaborator divisions. Except for the 1st Mountain Division and the 22nd Air Landing Division on Crete, and perhaps the 8th SS Cavalry Division, none of his fifteen German divisions and seven fortress brigades were first-class formations, most of them lacked combat training, and most consisted of overage, limited-service troops who were not fully equipped. Half of Weichs's combat troops were in Army Group E, and ninety thousand of these were on islands in the Aegean Sea. Army Group E was supplied only by one inadequate railroad, which ran from Belgrade to Athens to Salonika. Table 6.1 shows his Order of Battle as of July 15, 1944.

Weichs was in Rastenburg when the news of Rumania's defection arrived at Fuehrer Headquarters. Hitler decided that most of Greece, and especially the Peloponnesus, would have to be evacuated if the Anglo-Americans attacked and that Army Group E would have to be withdrawn to the north, around the Belgrade-Athens-Salonika railroad. Two days later, he ordered all civilians and noncombatant military personnel out of the area, because it might suddenly become a combat zone. On August 26, Weichs moved his 1st Mountain Division out of Greece and into southern Serbia, just north of the Bulgarian zone of occupation. On August 29, OKW directed Weichs to deploy his reserves in the Belgrade-Nis-Salonika area and to begin preparation to withdraw from Greece to the Corfu–Mount Olympus line. Neither Jodl nor Weichs was in any hurry, and neither wanted to give the impression that an evacuation was under way. Even so, on August 30— certain that Bulgaria would leave the war within days—Weichs ordered a mountain division to Nis and an SS and Luftwaffe field division to move into the Bulgarian zone of occupation from Greece, to secure the important road and railroad junction at Skopie. To defend the former Yugoslavian capital, Weichs created the ad hoc Corps Belgrade, which was commanded by General of Infantry Willi Schneckenburger, the former chief of the German Military Mission to Bulgaria.[5]

On September 1, the Allied air forces began "Ratweek," a bomber offensive aimed at cutting all German exits from Greece and southern Yugoslavia and at helping Tito's partisans push into Serbia and join hands with the Soviets as quickly as possible, cutting off large parts of Army Group E in the process. On September 3, heavy air strikes severed all routes through Nis and badly damaged or destroyed all of the Danube and Sava River bridges at Belgrade. The Allied bombers disrupted German troop movements in eastern Yugoslavia and stalled all ground transport to and from Greece. Luftwaffe Command Southeast was able to do little to stop them.

The Bulgarians, meanwhile, hoped to prevent the Soviet occupation of their country by reverting to complete neutrality; they demanded the withdrawal of the German Military Mission and disarmed and interned the Germans who crossed their border following the collapse of Army Group South Ukraine in Rumania. They also tried to negotiate a military arrangement with the Turks, but like their negotiations with the Soviets, these were unsuccessful. On September 2, the day the Red Army reached the Rumanian-Bulgarian border on the Danube, a new cabinet was formed in

Table 6.1
Order of Battle, OB Southeast and Army Group F, July 15, 1944

2nd Panzer Army: General of Mountain Troops Franz Boehme[1]
LXIX Corps z.b. V.: General of Infantry Helge Auleb
    1st Cossack Cavalry Division
    98th Infantry Division
    373rd Infantry Division
XV Mountain Corps: General of Panzer Troops Gustav Fehn
    392nd Croatian Infantry Division
    264th Infantry Division
    1st and 4th Regiments, Brandenburger Panzer Grenadier Division
    92nd Motorized Infantry Regiment
V SS Mountain Corps: SS Lieutenant General Artur Phleps
    118th Jaeger Division
    369th Infantry Division
    7th SS Mountain Division
    13th SS Mountain Division
I Bulgarian Corps
    22nd Bulgarian Infantry Division
    24th Bulgarian Infantry Division
    25th Bulgarian Infantry Division
    27th Bulgarian Infantry Division
Army Reserve:
    Elements, 4th SS Police Division
    Brandenburger Panzer Grenadier Division[2]

Army Group E: Luftwaffe Colonel General Alexander Loehr
XXII Mountain Corps: General of Mountain Troops Hubert Lanz
    104th Jaeger Division
    966th Fortress Regiment
    1017th Fortress Regiment
    964th Fortress Brigade[3]
LXVIII Corps: General of Fliers Hellmut Felmy
    117th Jaeger Division
    41st Fortress Division
    11th Luftwaffe Field Division
    18th SS Police Mountain Infantry Regiment
Commandant of Crete: General of Infantry Friedrich-Wilhelm Mueller
    22nd Air Landing Division
    133rd Fortress Division
II Bulgarian Corps[4]
    7th Bulgarian Infantry Division[4]
    16th Bulgarian Infantry Division[4]
    28th Bulgarian Infantry Division[4]
    2nd Bulgarian Cavalry Division[4]
    939th Fortress Regiment[4]
    967th Fortress Regiment[4]
    968th Fortress Regiment[4]

Table 6.1 (*continued*)

Army Group E Reserve:
   963rd Fortress Regiment
   4th SS Panzer Grenadier Division "Police"

German Commanders in Western Hungary and Eastern Hungary:
22nd SS Cavalry Division[3]
73rd Infantry Division

OKW Reserve in Army Group F's Area of Operations:
1st Mountain Division
8th SS Cavalry Division[3]
18th SS Panzer Grenadier Division[3]

Notes:
[1]Succeeded by General of Artillery Maximilian de Angelis on July 18, 1944
[2]Minus major element
[3]In transit
[4]Located on island(s) in the Aegean Sea

Source: Tessin, *Verbaende*, vol. 2, pp. 88–89; Mehner, ed., *Geheimen Tagesberichte*, vol. 10, p. 506.

Sofia. Two days later, Bulgaria unilaterally declared an end to her state of war with the Allies and a return to full neutrality. This, of course, was not enough for Moscow, which declared war on Bulgaria on September 5, on the thin pretext that Bulgaria was harboring German troops. That same day, the Russian 6th Guards Tank Army reached Turna Severin (near the Iron Gate) on the eastern side of the Danube, on the Rumanian-Yugoslavia border. General of Infantry Hans Felber, Military Commander Southeast (a rear-area command under OB Southeast) set up a thin front that followed the Yugoslav border and straddled the Danube west of the Iron Gate. The Soviet tanks could have penetrated this screen at almost any point but turned north instead, in the direction of Hungary, giving Weichs a slight breathing space. This ended, however, on September 8, when the 3rd Ukrainian Front invaded Bulgaria. The Bulgarian Army did not resist. That night, Sofia declared war on Germany.

Seeing that the Bulgarians were trying to ally themselves with Moscow in order to save themselves, Field Marshal von Weichs acted quickly to neutralize the Bulgarian forces in his area of operations. In Macedonia, the Germans disarmed the I Bulgarian Corps and its four infantry divisions without much difficulty. At Skopie, three Bulgarian divisions abandoned their weapons and fled into the mountains. Only at Prilep in western Macedonia (near the Bulgarian border) did several Bulgarian regiments put up resistance, and they were crushed within twenty-four hours.

The Rumanian and Bulgarian defections had opened up a 425-mile front from the Hungarian border to the Aegean Sea, and Baron von Weichs somehow had to defend it. His immediate problem was to create a new front east of the Salonika-Skopje-Nis line, so Army Group E could escape. Weichs concentrated 2nd Panzer Army in Croatia (in case its puppet government also tried to defect) and shifted Army Group E's boundary to the north, adding Albania to Loehr's zone of responsibility and making him responsible for the most vulnerable part of his own escape route. Map 6.1 shows his withdrawal from the Balkans.

Hitler and OKW accepted the fact that Army Group E would not be able to hold Greece indefinitely, but Weichs was in no hurry to abandon it: he wanted to get his troops off the Aegean Islands, and in any case he correctly guessed that the main Russian effort would be to his north, into Hungary. Accordingly, he sent part of a division and two SS police battalions to Timisoara, Hungary (in Army Group South Ukraine's zone), to guard the southern gateway to the Hungarian plain and to cover his own rear. In the meantime, he ordered Loehr to begin evacuating the islands. Much to Weichs's surprise, the Anglo-American navies did not try to disrupt this operation. Heavy RAF-USAF raids against the airfields around Athens on September 15 did destroy a number of Ju-52 transport airplanes, which hampered the evacuation of the islands but did not stop it. During the next few days, the Royal Navy moved into the Aegean area with aircraft carriers and night fighters, and losses on flights to and from the islands began to increase, but the Allies still did not commit their surface vessels to interdiction operations against Army Group E.

During the third week of September, Weichs detected a major Soviet buildup opposite his long eastern flank. North of the Transylvanian Alps, the 53rd Army of the 2nd Ukrainian Front moved into position opposite Timisoara, the 46th Army deployed around Turna Severin, and the 57th Army (of the 3rd Ukrainian Front) was south of the Danube, moving toward the Bulgarian-Yugoslavian border. Most alarmingly, the Red Air Force entered Bulgaria in strength. About four hundred Russian airplanes were observed in the Sofia area alone.

Despite the Russian buildup, Weichs was still using his airplanes to take troops off of the islands, not to reinforce Macedonia, as Loehr advocated. The soldiers coming off the islands, after all, could not take even their few vehicles with them and were virtually immobile. Weichs was definitely taking a chance that the Russians would not advance quickly. On September 18, OKW approved Weichs's request to evacuate the island of Corfu and start moving the front back from the west coast of Greece.

On September 22, without taking the time for an orderly buildup, the 3rd Ukrainian Front tried to disrupt Weichs's strategy. It crossed the Danube bend west of Turnu Severin. The Reds gained ground slowly at first, but by the 25th Weichs was concerned enough to commit his best division, Lieutenant General Ritter Walter Stettner von Grabenhofen's 1st Mountain, to clear the bend.

Map 6.1
The Withdrawal from the Balkans, 1944

Early on the morning of September 27, Weichs's HQ in Belgrade received reports that the left flank of the 2nd Ukrainian Front was advancing between Timisoara and the Danube. Weichs had parts of two SS divisions at Timisoara and a motorized brigade north of the Iron Gate, but nothing between them except occasional patrols. He had assumed the Russians

203

would advance to the northwest, past Timisoara into Hungary. Now he correctly surmised what would happen next: the Russians were going to launch two thrusts from the east, on either side of the Danube, both aimed at Belgrade; later they would be reinforced by Tito's partisan divisions from the west. Still he did nothing, except bring up two regiments from Greece (one by air, the other by sea). He had already recalled a jaeger division from Greece on September 18, but it would not arrive in Belgrade until October 2, due to the sorry state of the Balkan railroads.

Weichs and his staff did not really become concerned about the Soviet offensive until September 30. By this time, the Russians had three corps in action north of the Danube against seven understrength German battalions. South of the Danube, Stettner was fighting at least four Soviet divisions, and the Reds had at least that many in reserve. Even so, Baron von Weichs retained his composure. He was still determined to evacuate every German soldier he could from the islands and was not going to start the evacuation of Greece and Yugoslavia until the last possible moment.

OKW became alarmed on October 2, when Jodl asked Weichs to set a date for the beginning of the evacuation of Greece. The next day, Weichs replied that everything could be ready to move by October 10. He ordered Loehr to evacuate Albania, southern Macedonia, and Greece on that date, but the flights from the Aegean islands were to continue as long as Luftwaffe Command Southeast had gasoline and airfields within range of the islands. Hitler approved these plans.

On October 4, the Russians reached Pancevo, located on the northern bank of the Danube, ten miles from Belgrade. By October 6, they had pushed the German defenders back into a small bridgehead, just across the river from the Serbian capital. Weichs evacuated his headquarters to Vukovar on the 5th; that same day he changed the designation of the Military Commander Southeast to Army Detachment Serbia and proposed to OKW that the 2nd Panzer Army be taken away from the coast to a line in the mountains. Permission was quickly granted. It was obvious already that the escape of Army Group E was going to be a near-run thing, but still Weichs did not rush the evacuation.

On October 5, the left flank of the Russian 46th Army was outside Belgrade, but the bulk of the army had turned northwest, to join the offensive across the Tisza into Hungary, just as Weichs had hoped. Three days later, however, a strong mechanized detachment from the 57th Russian Army slipped past Bor, on the Bulgarian-Greek border. It was not discovered until it cut the Belgrade railroad on the Morava River, fifty miles behind German lines. In the meantime, Tito's partisans arose, and guerilla forces pushed into the area southwest of Belgrade and west of Nis. On October 9, the 1st Bulgarian Army (under Soviet command) began to advance toward Nis.

By this time, the 2nd Panzer Army's withdrawal to the mountains was almost complete. Weichs ordered it to take charge of the defenses north of

Belgrade, while Army Detachment Serbia defended the city and simultaneously pushed troops south, to clear the Morava Valley and the railroad. (Army Detachment Serbia absorbed the remnants of Schneckenburger's Korps Belgrad; General Schneckenburger had been killed in action on October 10.) Meanwhile, the 1st Mountain Division was ordered to join it from the east. Felber's strike force entered the Morava Valley on October 12 and reached Velike Plana (where the Soviets had first cut the railroad), but it discovered that the 57th Army now had an entire mechanized corps in the sector. Soon Army Detachment Serbia was being forced back up the valley. By noon the next day, both the army detachment's strike force and the 1st Mountain Division were cut off in the Morava Valley, and Soviet armor was south of Belgrade and within six miles of the city. Weichs ordered Felber to hold Belgrade until Stettner could break out and cross the Sava (which meets the Danube at Belgrade). He also ordered de Angelis's 2nd Panzer Army to put some units on the upper Sava, in case the encircled forces had to break out farther west.

During the night of October 14, the Russians entered the southern outskirts of Belgrade. On the afternoon of the next day, they captured the central city. Army Detachment Serbia had to muster all the strength it could to hold a bridgehead around the Sava bridge. Meanwhile, Ritter Stettner was heading west and had reached Grocka, fifteen miles southeast of Belgrade. He gained ten more miles on the 16th, but his attempt to break through to Belgrade failed on October 17. He tried again the next day but again failed. Stettner von Grabenhofen was killed in this attack and was replaced by his senior regimental commander.[6]

Army Detachment Serbia was forced to evacuate its Belgrade bridgehead on October 19, and the rest the Yugoslavian capital fell to Tito and the Russians. Meanwhile, the 1st Mountain Division worked its way west of the Russian forces and crossed the Sava at Sabac on October 21, followed by the several thousand survivors of the Army Detachment Serbia's Morava Valley strike force. They had regained contact with Army Group F but had lost all of their heavy equipment.

First Mountain Division was reequipped in late October, thanks to the 1st Panzer Division, which disarmed the 13th SS Mountain Division "Handschar," an unreliable Moslem unit that was probably the worst unit of its size in the Wehrmacht. It had refused to serve outside of its own area, was plagued by desertion, and was more interested in massacring defenseless Christian villages than anything else. SS General Berger had nevertheless seen to it that it was superbly equipped. Now the *panzertruppen* saw to it that the 1st Mountain was superbly equipped. Second Panzer, of course, also took what it could use for itself.

Meanwhile, on August 23, Army Group E began the evacuation of Greece as planned. As of that date, General Loehr had four corps (at Tirane, Yanina, Athens and Salonika), ten divisions (seven on the mainland and three on the islands), and six fortress brigades. After the Rumanian defection, OKW ordered him to retreat to a line running from Corfu to Metsovon to Mount Olympus. Loehr began by pulling troops off the islands. In September, he successfully evacuated the Peloponnese, in spite of heavy attacks from Greek guerrillas, who were reinforced by British paratroopers. On October 13, General of Fliers Helmuth Felmy, the commander of the LXVIII Corps, handed over control of Athens to its mayor.[7] Still the retreat continued—aided by political factionalism in the ranks of the partisans. Major General Gerhard Henke's 11th Luftwaffe Field Division, for example, made good its escape through areas heavily infested with Communist guerrillas in a unique manner: it supplied the partisan Reds with certain heavy arms and equipment in exchange for free passage through their territory. The Reds—who were more interested in equipping themselves for the upcoming civil war with the loyalists than in fighting the Wehrmacht—took the material and allowed the Germans to depart unmolested.[8]

There was reason to hurry. As of October 15, Weichs had no front at all from Nis to Belgrade (120 miles), and he could do nothing about it. Loehr's direct escape route from Greece was therefore cut, and now he would have to go farther west. This he accomplished, but not without difficulty. On October 26, British forces landed on the island of Kithira, off the southern tip of the Peloponnesus, while Loehr's rearguards retreated to the Isthmus of Corinth. The Allied air forces now shifted their main effort to the support of the British ground forces, which eased the pressure to the north considerably, without a corresponding increase to the south.

After Belgrade fell on October 19, Field Marshal von Weichs gave 2nd Panzer Army command of the front from Belgrade north and ordered it to halt the Russians on the line of the Tisza, Danube, Sava, and Drina Rivers. Army Group E was given responsibility for keeping the Skopie-Kraljevo-Visegrad leg of the retreat route open, while 2nd Panzer Army held the door open to the north. After halting on the Metsovon Pass–Larisa line for several days, Loehr began retreating again on October 21 and evacuated Salonika on October 31. His last rearguards crossed the Greek border on November 1, leaving behind forty-five thousand troops (fifteen thousand of them Italians) on the islands. These surrendered to the Anglo-Americans at the end of the war.

It was late October before the Russians and Bulgarians pushed strong forces to the west to take Kraljevo and Skopie. By now, however, Loehr had the railroad and a three-week jump on them, as well as the forces on hand to fight them. On November 2, Army Group E checked the Soviet-Bulgarian advance near Kraljevo. Over the next several days Loehr turned back the Bulgarians east of Skopie; his worst ordeal, in fact, was the Balkan road system.

As October wore on, Ziemke later wrote, it began to look as if Weichs "had displayed a genuine feeling for timing and a talent for sure-footed retrograde movement."⁹ The German retreat would have been much more difficult had not Tolbukhin, the commander of the 2nd Ukrainian Front, turned northward toward Hungary and left the pursuit of the 2nd Panzer Army west of Belgrade and the Tisza to the partisans. On November 2, de Angelis ended his retreat. Second Panzer Army's front now followed the Drina to Vukovar, across the Vukovar gap to the Danube, and from there north to the Hungarian border, where it tied in with the 2nd Hungarian Army of Army Group South (formerly Army Group South Ukraine) near Apatin, Hungary, just west of the Serbian border. The Soviets began to attack this line in strength on November 10, and 2nd Panzer Army had to give ground in several places. Meanwhile, to the south, Army Group E's retreat was handicapped by partisans, the poor Balkans transportation network, and by the immobility of its units. Nevertheless, due to the lack of direct Allied pressure, Loehr was able to carry out his retreat successfully. He was still holding Zagreb (the capital of Croatia) and occupying positions in northern Yugoslavia on December 1, when Hitler took 2nd Panzer Army away from Weichs and gave it to Friessner. General Loehr was not compelled to give up Sarajevo until April 6, 1945. By this time, the focus of the war had long since shifted elsewhere.

NOTES

1. Ziemke, citing the *New York Times*, August 19, 1944.
2. Baron von Weichs was a Bavarian cavalry officer who had entered the service in 1900. He successively commanded the 1st Cavalry Division (1933), 1st Panzer Division (1935), Wehrkreis XIII (1937), 2nd Army (1939), Army Group B (1942), and Army Group F and OB Southeast (1943). He was promoted to field marshal on February 1, 1943. When the Russians were threatening Berlin, Guderian nominated Weichs to be commander in chief of Army Group Vistula, but Hitler rejected him because he was a devout Catholic. With the Balkans lost, Army Group F was disbanded on March 26, 1945, leaving Weichs without a job. Never reemployed, he died in 1954.
3. Born on May 20, 1885, Alexander Loehr was commander of the small Austrian Air Force when Hitler annexed that country. Inducted into the new Luftwaffe, Loehr later commanded the 4th Air Fleet on the Eastern Front (1941–43) and Army Group E (1943–end). He was never promoted to field marshal because of Hitler's prejudice against Austrians. He became OB Southeast on March 26, 1945. A capable officer but not a brilliant one, General Loehr was executed by the Yugoslavs after a show trial on February 16, 1947.
4. Maximilian de Angelis was an Austrian officer who was born in Budapest in 1889. In German service, he commanded Arko XV (1938), 76th Infantry Division (1939), XXXXIV Corps (1942), 6th Army (acting commander, late 1943), and 2nd Panzer Army, which he surrendered at the end of the war. He also spent ten years in Soviet prisons. General de Angelis died in Graz in December 1947.

5. Willi Schneckenburger was born in Tuebingen in 1891 and joined the army as a *Fahnenjunker* in 1909. A colonel when the war started, he was chief of staff of III Corps (1939), commander of the 125th Infantry Division (1940), German liaison officer to the Romanian 3rd Army (1943), commander of XVII Corps (1943), and chief of the German Military Mission to Bulgaria (1944).

6. A Bavarian, Stetten had joined the army as a *Fahnenjunker* when World War I broke out. He spent his entire World War II career commanding mountain units. He commanded I/98th Mountain Regiment (1937), the 99th Mountain Regiment (1940), the 91st Mountain Regiment (late 1940), and the 1st Mountain Division (1942). He was eventually replaced as commander of the 1st Mountain Division by Lieutenant General Joseph Kuebler, who assumed command on December 27.

7. Helmuth Felmy (1885–1965) was a leading figure in the Luftwaffe during its prewar buildup phase (1935–39). He assumed command of the 2nd Air Fleet when the war broke out but was unjustly cashiered by Hermann Goering on January 12, 1940, for a security violation. He went to work for the army on May 20, 1941, directing a special staff charged with planning the German invasion of Iraq. Eventually, he rose to corps command. Absolom, p. 19.

8. Chant, vol. 7, p. 1892.

9. Ziemke, p. 378.

CHAPTER VII

The Battle for Hungary

THE RETREAT INTO HUNGARY

On August 29, 1944, after Army Group South Ukraine had been virtually annihilated in Rumania, OKH ordered General Friessner to retreat into the Transylvanian Alps and Carpathian Mountains, there to tie in with OB Southeast at the Iron Gate on his right flank and the 1st Hungarian Army (the right flank unit of his neighboring Army Group North Ukraine) on his left, near the Czech border. Although this mountainous region unquestionably provided Friessner with his best possible defensive line, he did not have the strength to adequately man it with the six divisions he now controlled. (These included the 15th Flak Division, which he broke up to protect his retreating columns from the Red Air Force.)[1]

On Friessner's right flank, Fretter-Pico's 6th Army consisted of only twenty battalions, mainly ad hoc units thrown together from assorted stragglers, without heavy weapons or radio equipment. Fretter-Pico could not even cover the western flank or make contact with Army Group F on his right. By the end of the month, Friessner had already ordered his army headquarters to reconnoiter a line on the Muresul River—the next logical defensive position they would have to occupy if the mountain passes were lost.

Meanwhile, in Transylvania, he was reinforced with General Lajos Verres's 2nd Hungarian Army (which only had four divisions), while the reconstituted 4th Rumanian Army joined the Russians. Seeing an opportunity to attack their traditional and well-hated foes, the 2nd Hungarian struck with considerable élan and smashed the 4th Rumanian in the Cluj sector on September 5 and 6. At the same time, a 3rd Hungarian Army was being formed under General Heszlenyi on Friessner's exposed right flank. Before this process could be completed, however, the Soviets pushed into the Vulcan and Turnu Rosu passes before the Germans could muster enough troops to adequately defend them, and the Hungarian offensive was halted by the arrival of the Soviet 6th Tank Army. Friessner therefore ordered the German 6th and 8th Armies to start the withdrawal to the Muresul during the night of September 7–8.

Friessner's retreat to the Muresul was a complete success. Despite their victory in Rumania, the Russians were experiencing serious supply difficulties and could no longer attack the German rearguards with overwhelming strength. As a result, they lost nearly two hundred tanks, 150 guns, and several thousand men, without significantly disrupting Friessner's timetable.

On the political front, the situation in Budapest was very unstable. As a result, OKW moved the 8th and 22nd SS Cavalry Divisions close to the capital on August 24, in case an anti-German coup was attempted. This move had the desired effect; on August 30, Colonel General Gaza Lakaos replaced the seriously ill Doeme Sztojay as minister president, preserving the German hold on the Hungarian government.

Admiral Miklos (Nicholas) Horthy, the Hungarian regent since 1919, was an aristocrat who lived and behaved like a feudal monarch.[2] Brought up in the service of the Austro-Hungarian Empire, he had never been particularly pro-German and was certainly not pro-Nazi—especially now that Hitler was losing the war. On September 7, the Hungarian Crown Council held a secret meeting and presented OKH with an ultimatum: send five panzer divisions to Hungary within twenty-four hours. If it did not do so, Hungary reserved the right to act in its own interests (i.e., defect from the Axis). Guderian considered this demand extortion, but he agreed to send roughly the forces demanded.

Unknown to Germany, Horthy had already opened up negotiations with Moscow and, on September 11, asked the cabinet to approve this step; however, the vote went heavily against him, and the cabinet demanded his resignation. Horthy neither resigned nor dismissed the cabinet, avoiding a political crisis but gridlocking the Hungarian government. In the meantime, Hitler lost faith in the Hungarian leadership and continued to send troops into Hungary, virtually occupying the country. Henceforth, the Fuehrer would treat Hungary as if it were an occupied vassal, and the roundup and extermination of the Hungarian Jewry began.

The basis for the extermination of the Hungarian Jews had been established long before. The country had a long history of anti-Semitism, exacerbated by the perception that although the 750,000 Hungarian Jews constituted only 5.1 percent of the nation's population, they enjoyed a disproportionate share of affluence and influence in this predominantly rural, Catholic, and agricultural country. Some 49.2 percent of the country's judges were Jewish. More than 59 percent of Hungary's bankers were Jews. Jews constituted 75.1 percent of the people employed in industry, 30.4 percent of those employed in publishing, and 31.7 percent of the people work-ing in academics.[3] Social prejudice against them was already widespread in March 1944, when Hitler summoned Admiral Horthy to Klessheim and forced him to accept a larger German role in the country. Accordingly, an extensive SS presence appeared in Budapest that same month. Dr. Edmund Veesenmayer arrived as Hitler's special envoy to the Hungarian govern-ment, while Dr. Otto Winkelmann was installed as Higher SS and Police Leader in Hungary.[4] Most ominously for the Jews, SS Lieutenant Colonel Adolf Eichmann, Himmler's Jewish "expert" and chief extermination co-ordinator, installed himself in the luxurious Majestic Hotel in Budapest.

Meanwhile, on March 22, Horthy was forced to appoint Doeme Zstojay prime minister. He soon named Dr. Laszlo Endre as secretary of state for political (i.e., Jewish) affairs. A strong anti-Semitic, Endre immediately hit it off with Eichmann, and the two soon became close personal friends.[5]

On March 29, the Hungarian government prohibited Jews from em-ployment as journalists, judges, lawyers, musicians, teachers, or academic administrators, and other professional fields. Only doctors were excluded from this purge of the professions. (Had Jewish doctors been banned from practicing, the Hungarian medical system would have collapsed.) Most reg-istered companies owned by Jews were shut down. These included eighteen thousand of the thirty thousand firms operating in Budapest and about forty thousand of the 110,000 companies doing business in the entire coun-try. All Jews were required to wear the Star of David except highly deco-rated war veterans and those veterans severely handicapped due to combat injuries. More than eight thousand "dangerous" Jews were arrested, and travel by Jews was severely restricted.[6] But this was just the beginning. Before it was over, some 437,000 Jews would be deported, of whom 330,000 would be exterminated. Another 140,000 would be used as slave laborers, both inside and outside Hungary.

THE SLOVAK REBELLION

Meanwhile, antigovernment elements in the German puppet state of Slo-vakia sought to take advantage of the deteriorating German military situ-ation, Hitler's new military commitments in Hungary, and the nearness of the Red Army to overthrow the puppet regime of President (Father) Joseph Tiso and to set up an anti-Nazi government.

The Germans already knew that the Slovak Army was unreliable. In the fall of 1943, a full regiment of the 1st Slovakian Infantry Division (two thousand men), led by its officers, had deserted to the Soviets. A short time later, eight hundred members of the 2nd Slovakian Security Division—also led by their officers—had gone over to the Reds. Both divisions had been withdrawn from the front and sent home. Then, in January 1944, several

Slovak regiments defected near Odessa. "Slovak soldiers desert *en masse* whenever they had the chance," an American intelligence report stated.[7] But the anti-Nazi Slovak officer corps had not been purged. Father Tiso, Richard Landwehr wrote later, "had the personality of a genial country priest and he was altogether too trusting of his subordinates."[8]

General Ferdinand Catlos, the defense minister, headed the Slovakian plot to defect from the Axis and join the Russians. Colonel Jan Golian, the acting commander of the Slovak Army, was also in on the conspiracy.

In August 1944, the Slovak Army consisted of the I Infantry Corps (1st Infantry and 2nd Security Divisions), stationed in eastern Slovakia; the Western Army (twenty thousand troops, including eight thousand guarding the Slovak capital of Bratislava); and the Slovak Home Army, which occupied the rest of the country. I Corps had a strength of twenty-four thousand men, while the Home Army had fourteen thousand soldiers, four thousand laborers, and thirty-six thousand reservists who had not yet been called up. In all, including general headquarters and reserve units, the Slovak Army had a strength of about sixty-two thousand men.[9]

General Catlos's plan called for a diversionary partisan uprising in the center of the country. Then, on September 1, the I Corps would attack the Germans in the rear and seize the Carpathian mountain passes, opening up the way for Stalin's armies to pour into Slovakia and cutting off the German 1st Panzer Army. Unknown to Berlin, the Slovak Army had been cooperating with the partisans for some time. Although the Western Army was not in on the plot, the only forces still fully loyal to Tiso were the poorly equipped militia units of the Slovakian People's Party (the "Hlinka Guard") and a few police and gendarme units.

On August 23, Communist partisan bands began an uprising in central Slovakia. The army would not take action against them, and the rebellion spread. People's Party officials were assassinated, and ethnic Germans were killed. On August 28, twenty-two German officers on their way home from Rumania were hauled off the train at St. Martin (a town in central Slovakia) and gunned down by Slovak soldiers, who were acting under the direction of Slovak officers and Soviet-partisan advisors. This tipped off OKH as to the true threat in Slovakia. By evening, Tiso was calling for German military assistance, and the German Army replacement and training units in Bohemia and Moravia (under the 539th and 540th Special Administrative Division Staffs) had been put on alert and ordered to form mobile battle groups for immediate deployment to Slovakia. Kampfgruppe von Ohlen of the 178th Infantry entered Slovakia the next day and began advancing on the town of Sillein (Zilina) and St. Martin. When General Catlos received this news, he decided not to wait until September 1 but to put the revolt into motion immediately. This he did in a radio address at 7:30 that evening, August 29. Broadcasting from the city of Banska Bystrica in central Slovakia, he called for an armed uprising, beginning immediately.

Catlos's decision was a disaster for the conspiracy. General Malar, the commander of the I Corps, was attending a conference at Bratislava so he was unable to issue the appropriate orders. On August 30, the Germans disarmed the bulk of the I Corps; meanwhile, the Slovak Air Force (thirty-eight airplanes) flew to safety behind Russian lines, and hundreds of other Slovaks joined the partisans in the middle of the country.

On September 1, SS-Obergruppenfuehrer (General of SS) Gottlob Berger, the newly appointed Higher SS and Police Leader for Slovakia, arrived in Pressburg (as the Germans called Bratislava) and assumed command of all German forces in central and western Slovakia; he began the task of putting down the rebellion.[10] On September 2, he signaled Himmler that he would accomplish the mission in four days. His forces included a few battle groups from Bohemia and Moravia, a 1,200-man, battalion-sized battle group from the 86th Infantry Division (dispatched by Army Group North Ukraine); SS Regiment "Schill" (a *kampfgruppe* of Waffen-SS officer and noncommissioned-officer candidates, plus a few army troops, 2,200 men in all, commanded by SS Lieutenant Colonel Rudi Klotz); and SS-Kampfgruppe "Schaefer," a 1,200-man battle group from the 18th SS Panzer Grenadier Division "Horst Wessel" led by SS Major Ernst Schaefer, the commander of the 40th SS Panzer Grenadier Regiment. Elements of the 14th SS Grenadier Division "Galician Nr. 1" also participated in the operation.

The 14th SS had been rebuilt following the Brody disaster by absorbing the 4th, 5th, and 8th Ukrainian SS Police Regiments. It also now incorporated the 14th SS Field Replacement Battalion, which had escaped the debacle with relatively few casualties. In addition, it had received about a thousand more German officers, NCOs, and men. Some 60 percent of the signals battalion was now German, so the division no longer suffered from the poor communications that had plagued it at Brody. It contributed about 1,500 Ukrainian troops to the Slovakian campaign. They were led by SS Lieutenant Colonel Karl Wildner, the commander of III/29th Waffen Grenadier Regiment.

On the first day of September, fewer than two hundred German soldiers disarmed the entire Bratislava garrison (eight thousand men), which offered no resistance. The next day, Kampfgruppe Schill captured Nitra, the second-largest city in the country, again without firing a shot (because the commandant of the garrison refused to join the rebellion). The first resistance occurred at Topolcany on September 3. SS KG Schill took the town and killed a hundred Slovak defenders, with a loss of six SS killed and fifteen wounded.[11] By now, however, the rebels numbered about forty-seven thousand men (including eighteen thousand former regular soldiers, seven thousand Slovak and Soviet partisan advisors, plus the 2nd Czech Parachute Brigade, which had entered the region via airdrop on the orders of Stalin). The Slavic forces controlled about 12,500 square miles of mountainous terrain in central Slovakia, an area that contained a million people and was 30 percent larger than the state of New Jersey. Most of these rural peasants, however, were still pro-Tiso. Map 7.1 shows the Slovak military mutiny and how it was suppressed.

The rebel forces, which were grouped into six brigades under the command of Colonel Golian, generally held their positions in the mountains until September 19, despite the fact that Berger (who lacked command experience) was reinforced with the ad hoc Panzer Division "Tatra"—six thousand men under the command of Lieutenant General Friedrich Wilhelm von Loeper, mostly drawn from replacement units and the 178th Infantry Division. Under Berger's inept leadership, the Germans actually lost ground in some sectors while partisan activity spread in their rear. Only KG Schill made significant progress. In two weeks, it cleared the entire Nitra Valley, killing five hundred rebels and capturing another two hundred, and pushed to within twenty-five miles of Banska Bystrica. Elsewhere the Germans were held at bay.

On September 14, Berger was replaced by General of Police Hermann Hoefle, the tough police president of Hanover, who proceeded much more systematically and much more competently than had his predecessor.[12] Hoefle attacked on September 20. The next day, von Loeper broke through and captured St. Martin, overrunning a rebel brigade and killing or capturing about a thousand men. By October 1, German forces were within twenty miles of the rebel capital, and Hoefle ordered his final attack. The Soviet, Czech, and Slovakian defenders fought back tenaciously, however, and the German offensive was halted on October 7.

A lull now descended on the sector, during which Hoefle was reinforced with SS Penal Brigade Dirlewanger, which was led by SS-Oberfuehrer Dirlewanger, a perverted sadist who had once been sent to a concentration camp for molesting a female child. (The sexual acts he is said to have committed upon the dead bodies of some of his victims will not be recounted here.) Like their commander, his men included the scum of the earth, some of the worst thugs in the Third Reich. The brigade included four thousand men in two regiments, as well as three artillery batteries. Hoefle was also given Colonel Martin Bieber's 271st Volksgrenadier Division (7,200 men), the 708th Volksgrenadier Division (six thousand men), and SS Major General August Wilhelm Trabandt's 18th SS Panzer Grenadier Division "Horst Wessel" (eight thousand men), and three more battalions from the 14th SS (four thousand men) organized as Kampfgruppe Wittenmeyer. In exchange, OKH directed Hoefle to return Panzer Division Tatra and KG Schill; Hoefle, however, did not believe he could defeat the rebels without these forces (his best), so he ignored the order. By October 18, Hoefle had forty-eight thousand combat troops, as opposed to thirty-six thousand for the rebels. Many of the Slovak forces, however, were considered unreliable.

Map 7.1
The Slovak Military Mutiny

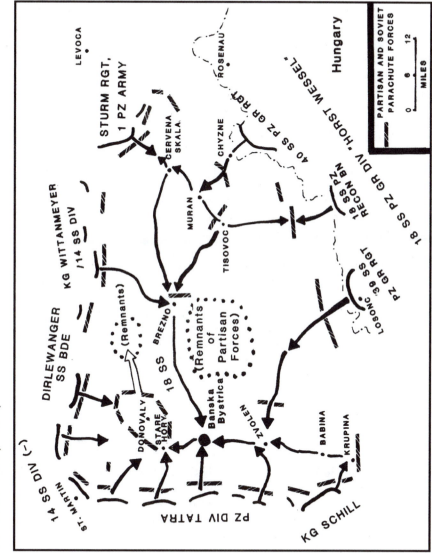

Hoefle took advantage of the lull to tighten the encirclement of the pocket. Meanwhile, Stalin hurled his divisions against Heinrici's 1st Panzer Army, in a desperate attempt to push through the Carpathians and rescue the encircled rebels. General Heinrici, however, was a past master of defensive tactics; he took full advantage of the terrain and gave ground very slowly. The Red Army lost twenty thousand men killed and sixty thousand wounded in August, September, and October; it did not get near the Dukla Pass, the gateway to Slovakia, until the first week in October. By then Hoefle had tightened the noose around the pocket and was nearly ready to crush it.[13]

The major German push to obliterate the pocket began on October 18, with the 14th SS Grenadier Division attacking from the northeast, the 18th SS Panzer Grenadier Division advancing from the southeast, SS Regiment Schill striking from the south, Panzer Division Tatra pushing on Banska Bystrica from the west, and the Dirlewanger Brigade attacking from the northwest. Enemy resistance was stiff until October 21, when the partisan brigade facing the 18th SS Division suddenly collapsed. Even so, Banska Bystrica did not fall until the morning of October 27, when it was captured by SS Regiment Schill. Over the next three days, all surviving mutineer units either surrendered or "took to the hills." In all, the rebels lost five thousand killed and fifteen thousand captured. The prisoners were generally treated humanely by the Germans, as were the civilians, unless they were unfortunate enough to fall into the hands of the Dirlewangers. Partisan activity continued until the Red Army overran the sector (Banska Bystrica fell on March 26, 1945, and the Soviets occupied Bratislava on April 4), but it never again constituted a serious threat to the German Army at the front. SS KG Schill had fought so well that it was used as the nucleus to form the 32nd SS Volunteer Grenadier Division "30 Januar."[14]

THE RETREAT CONTINUES

By the middle of September, Friessner had completed his retreat to the Muresul. His southern flank (in the area called the Szekler Strip) was still overextended and exposed, but Hitler refused to allow him to pull it back, due to the political effect that might have on the Hungarians, even though General of Infantry Hans von Greiffenberg, the OKW representative to the Hungarian High Command, assured the Fuehrer that the Hungarians were reconciled to the loss of Szekler. Friessner's northern flank was also threatened by the Slovak Military Mutiny. Seeing an opportunity to crack the German defenses, the Soviets launched an offensive on September 8, but the Germans were too quick for them. They disarmed the Slovak divisions (as we have seen), and Heinrici's 1st Panzer Army absorbed the main blow of the Soviet 1st Guards Army. Heinrici was nevertheless slowly pushed back by sheer weight of numbers, and on October 6 he was finally forced to abandon the Dukla Pass to the 1st Ukrainian Front.

On September 23, the Red Army penetrated into eastern Hungary and captured the towns of Temesvar and Arad. Hitler was shocked and deeply upset by the news; it was critical that Germany retain Hungary, which was the Reich's principal source of oil, bauxite, and grain.[15] He decided to reinforce Friessner at once.

Friessner's command was redesignated Army Group South on September 23, and Harpe's Army Group North Ukraine was renamed Army Group A on September 24. By the end of the month, Friessner was reinforced with SS Major General Fritz Schmedes's 4th SS Panzer Grenadier Division "Police," a fairly good formation from Army Group F, and with General of Panzer Troops Friedrich Kirchner's Headquarters, LVII Panzer Corps; in addition, the 23rd and 24th Panzer Divisions were on their way to Hungary, traveling as rapidly as the damaged German railroads would allow. By the end of September, Woehler's 8th Army had a strength of three German and three Hungarian divisions, while Fretter-Pico had four German and six Hungarian divisions. Friessner nevertheless faced the threat of a double envelopment, but Hitler again refused to allow him to retreat.

Friessner was given a relatively long respite in September, while Stalin's legions conquered Bulgaria and pushed into Yugoslavia. The lull ended on October 6, when the Soviets launched a massive offensive against Army Group South. They planned a giant envelopment, aimed at encircling and destroying Army Group South and Armeegruppe Heinrici (1st Panzer and 1st Hungarian Armies). The attacking forces included Malinovsky's 2nd Ukrainian Front and Petrov's 4th Ukrainian Front, which were coordinated by Marshal Timoshenko. Malinovsky alone had six Soviet rifle armies, a tank army, and two Rumanian armies: forty-two Russian rifle divisions, twenty-two Rumanian divisions, 750 tanks, and 1,100 airplanes.[16] Table 7.1 shows the forces Timoshenko was trying to encircle.

The Russians' plan was far too ambitious. They had the forces to carry it out but not the logistics. Because of the differences in gauges, the Rumanian railroads were of little use to the Soviets, and everything had to be brought up by truck from east of the Dnestr. The overextended Soviet supply lines were simply not able to adequately supply an offensive of this scale.

On the first day of the offensive, the 4th Ukrainian Front, on the Soviet right, routed the 1st Hungarian Army. After that, however, Petrov had to deal with the Germans. Performing with his usual brilliance, Colonel General Gotthard Heinrici, the commander of the 1st Panzer Army, again took maximum advantage of the excellent defensive possibilities in the Carpathians and quickly checked the 4th Ukrainian Front in the mountains. Friessner, however, had less suitable defensive terrain and less reliable troops; he was soon in serious trouble. On his left, the Soviet 53rd Army

Table 7.1
Order of Battle, German Forces in Hungary and Eastern Slovakia (South to North), September 28, 1944

Army Group South:

3rd Hungarian Army:
LVII Panzer Corps:
    4th SS Panzer Grenadier Division
    1st Hungarian Panzer Division
    22nd SS Cavalry Division[1]
II Hungarian Corps:
    23rd Hungarian Reserve Infantry Division
    8th Hungarian Reserve Infantry Division
    20th Hungarian Infantry Division
    6th Hungarian Reserve Infantry Division

Armeegruppe Fretter-Pico:
6th Army:
    III Panzer Corps
        23rd Panzer Division
        27th Hungarian Light Division
    VII Hungarian Corps
        4th Hungarian Reserve Division
        12th Hungarian Reserve Division
2nd Hungarian Army
    2nd Hungarian Panzer Division
    25th Hungarian Infantry Division
    9th Hungarian Reserve Division
    Group von Kessel
    1st Hungarian Reserve Brigade
    2nd Hungarian Mountain Reserve Brigade
    7th Hungarian Reserve Division

8th Army:
XXIX Corps:
    8th SS Cavalry Division "Florian Geyer"
    Group General Winkler
    4th Mountain Division
    Group General Schopper
XVII Corps:
    3rd Mountain Division
    Group Rath
    8th Jaeger Division
    9th Hungarian Guards Jaeger Brigade
    46th Infantry Division
    2nd Hungarian Reserve Infantry Division
Army Group Reserve:
    LXXII Corps z.b. V.
    Group Siebenbuergen
    76th Infantry Division[2]

Table 7.1 (*continued*)

OKH Reserve:
13th Panzer Division[2]
10th Panzer Grenadier Division[2]
Feldherrnhalle Panzer Grenadier Division[2]
3rd Panzer Division
337th Volksgrenadier Division[2]

Armeegruppe Heinrici
1st Hungarian Army:
    VI Hungarian Corps:
          10th Hungarian Infantry Division
          24th Hungarian Infantry Division
          1st Hungarian Mountain Brigade
    V Hungarian Corps:
          13th Hungarian Infantry Division
    III Hungarian Corps:
          2nd Hungarian Mountain Brigade
          6th Hungarian Infantry Division
1st Panzer Army:
    XXXXIX Mountain Corps:
          101st Jaeger Division
          100th Jaeger Division
    XI Corps:
          168th Infantry Division
          254th Infantry Division
          96th Infantry Division
          97th Jaeger Division
    XXIV Panzer Corps
          68th Infantry Division
          75th Infantry Division
          24th Panzer Division
          1st Ski Jaeger Division
          357th Infantry Division
Armeegruppe Reserve:
    153rd Field Training Division
    154th Reserve Division
    1st Panzer Division

Notes:
[1]Minus major elements
[2]In transit

Source: Mehner, ed., *Geheimen Tagesberichte*, vol. 12, p. 342.

and the Pliev Mechanized Cavalry Group broke through the 3rd Hungarian Army and gained fifty miles in three days. Fortunately for him, Major General Josef von Radowitz's 23rd Panzer Division put up a magnificent defense at Oradea, on the northern shoulder of the 3rd Hungarian Army, and stopped the entire 6th Guards Tank Army cold, forcing the Pliev Group to come back to assist it.[17] Even so, Friessner realized that his front could not hold indefinitely, and on October 8 warned Guderian that it would take Woehler's 8th Army six days to withdraw behind the Theiss River. Hitler, however, would not allow a timely retreat. When Radowitz finally lost Oradea on October 12, most of the 76th Infantry Division was cut off and destroyed. In the meantime, Friessner decided that he could wait no longer and on October 12 ordered a retreat on his own responsibility. Cluj was abandoned, and much of the army group fell back toward the Theiss (see Map 7.2).

Malinovsky was slowed by his supply problems, but on October 17 he launched an attack aimed at cutting off the retreat of the German 8th and Hungarian 1st and 2nd Armies east of the Theiss. The Germans made their stand at Debrecen, the third-largest city in Hungary; it did not fall until October 20. Then the Pliev Mechanized Cavalry Group, which included the 1st Tank and 2nd Guards Cavalry Corps, knifed into the rear of the 8th Army and captured Nyiregyhaza on October 22, cutting Woehler's main line of retreat. This time, however, Friessner was ready for them. Acting on a plan originated by Major General Helmuth von Grolman, the army group's chief of staff,[18] General of Panzer Troops Hermann Breith's III Panzer Corps of the 6th Army, spearheaded by the ever-reliable 23rd Panzer Division and backed by the veteran 1st and 13th Panzer Divisions, struck from the west on October 23, while Woehler attacked from the east with Lieutenant General Kurt Roepke's XXIX Corps and part of General of Mountain Troops Hans Kreysing's XVII Corps. The 4th Ukrainian Front tried to break up the impending encirclement by launching heavy attacks against Woehler's front, but without success. Woehler's recaptured Nyiregyhaza on October 29 and linked up with Radovitz's 23rd Panzer, cutting off the Pliev Group. Some of the Russians managed to escape in small groups, but by the time the Debrecen Pocket was cleared, the Russians had lost twenty-five thousand men (including 6,662 dead) and 632 tanks.[19] The entire operation resembled the blitzkrieg campaigns of old.

Although tiny by Soviet standards, German losses were severe, when the depleted state of their armored regiments is taken into account. The 23rd Panzer Division alone lost thirty-seven tanks and AFVs during the battle. The total armored strength of 6th Army had been reduced to fourteen Panthers, twelve PzKw IIIs, and forty-one assault guns.[20]

When they recaptured Nyiregyhaza and the surrounding villages, the Germans had ample opportunity to see how the Soviets were going to behave in occupied Axis territory. Hungarian women of all ages had been raped; after-

Map 7.2
Army Group South, October 5–29, 1944

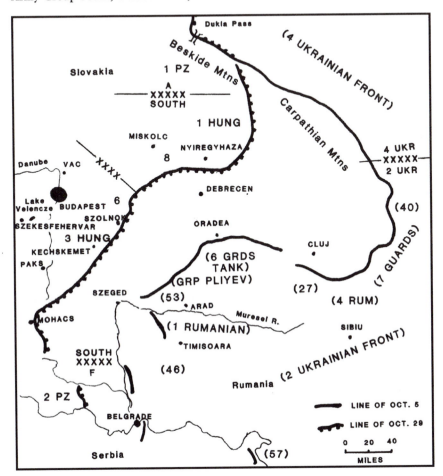

wards, many had been murdered. Mothers and fathers had been nailed to doorposts and forced to watch as their children were raped, mutilated, and murdered.[21] These sights nauseated the German soldiers and greatly reinforced their determination to hold off the Russians and prevent them from reaching German territory, and thus greatly increased the resistance of the Wehrmacht.

Meanwhile, Admiral Nicholas Horthy pursued his efforts to try to take Hungary out of the Axis. In late September, his representatives arrived in Moscow to negotiate an armistice with the Soviet Union. Stalin's diplomats somehow persuaded Horthy, his thirty-odd-year-old playboy son, also named Nicholas, and their representatives that the Soviets would allow the dynasty to survive within the Russian orbit. The treaty was concluded on October 11, but without a fixed date to take effect.

Hitler, however, was much better prepared to meet an attempted defection in Budapest than he had been in Bucharest six weeks earlier. He had already sent the brutal General of SS Erich von dem Bach-Zelewski to Hungary, as well as SS Major Otto Skorzeny, his most famous and skillful commando. Skorzeny entered the country secretly—on a tourist visa, using the alias "Dr. Wolf"—and was soon at work planning a secret coup against Horthy. Bach-Zelewski had considerable experience in putting down uprisings, most recently at Warsaw. Skorzeny, one of Hitler's favorites, was most famous for his daring rescue of Mussolini in 1943. Horthy, on the other hand, had ruled Hungary for a generation but had lost most of his support and faced a pro-German cabinet and parliament. The army was split, and many of the generals wanted to keep on fighting.

Unlike the case in Rumania, or in Italy the year before, Nazi agents had many well-placed informants in Budapest and in the Hungarian High Command. They learned that the German embassy on Castle Hill (the seat of the government in Budapest) was being discreetly surrounded by Hungarian forces. They also learned that General Miklos, the commander of the 1st Hungarian Army, had secretly met with Red Army officers in the Carpathians; they were planning to spring the armistice at just the right moment, so that most of Army Group South and hundreds of thousands of German soldiers would find themselves cut off behind enemy lines—just as had happened in Rumania.

The crisis began on October 15, when Skorzeny captured Nicholas Horthy, the admiral's son, designated successor, and a man who had played a major role in the secret armistice negotiations, but only after a shoot-out with Nicholas's bodyguards. During this firefight, SS Captain Otto Klages, the chief of the SD (Security Service) in Budapest, was mortally wounded when a bullet ripped through his stomach. Meanwhile, young Horthy was knocked out, rolled up in a Persian rug, tied with a curtain rope, rushed to the airport, and flown to Germany as a prisoner. Moscow, perhaps learning what had happened, demanded that Hungary accept the armistice terms by the next day, October 16. By early afternoon on the 15th, all approaches to the German Embassy had been barricaded, and Radio Budapest broadcast Admiral Horthy's armistice declaration, which ended with the statement. "It is clear today that Germany has lost the war.... Hungary has accordingly concluded a preliminary armistice with Russia, and will cease all hostilities against her."[22] But by this time Horthy had been effectively isolated politically. The Lakatos cabinet promptly resigned on the grounds that it did not approve the armistice. More importantly, the typical Hungarian soldier at the front did not lay down his arms. A declaration by the regent, after all, did not amount to an order.

In Budapest, the situation was extremely tense. There were three Hungarian divisions in the area against the equivalent of less than one German division; in addition, Horthy had a two-thousand-man bodyguard unit in and around the Royal Palace. There were, however, no indications that the Hungarian Army would stand with Horthy in a confrontation with the Germans. In addition, German reinforcements were converging on Budapest, including the army's 503rd Heavy Panzer Battalion (with forty superheavy King Tiger tanks), the elite 600th SS Parachute Battalion, Jaeger Battalion "Center," and several SS and police units that had fought in Warsaw. The brutal and murderous Bach-Zelewski had brought with him a huge twenty-five-inch mortar, which had been used very successfully by Field Marshal von Manstein when he reduced the Soviet naval fortress of Sevastopol in 1942. Bach-Zelewski himself had used it in the Warsaw Uprising, although with less success. Now he wanted to smash the Royal Castle to rubble. Skorzeny, however, stood firmly against this course of action. Hitler wanted Hungary back in the Axis; the attack Bach-Zelewski wanted to launch would surely throw it into Stalin's camp, Skorzeny declared. The other Germans—civilians, police, Gestapo, and military—sided with Skorzeny, so Bach reluctantly backed down.

Skorzeny seized the Royal Palace the following morning. He commandeered four Panthers that were on their way to the front and, with every German soldier and SS man that he could lay his hands on, simply marched up Castle Hill. Skorzeny was at the head of the column, gambling that the Hungarians would not fire on him. Boldly the column advanced down the mile-long road that led from the German Embassy to the Castle Square, the War Ministry, and Horthy's palace. Here some scattered shooting took place, in which seven men were killed and twenty-six wounded. Skorzeny did not report the nationalities of the casualties separately; the next day they were buried in a joint military funeral, as befit allies. The Austrian SS commando, in fact, did a masterful job in smoothing over the entire coup. To reward himself, Skorzeny promptly moved into the regent's wing of the Royal Palace, tapped the royal wine cellar, and lived a life of luxury for several days. General Bereckzy, a pro-German, was soon named the new war minister, and Hungary was back in the Axis. It would remain so until it was completely overrun by the Soviets.

Apparently to avoid capture by Skorzeny, Horthy appeared at the home of General of Police and Waffen-SS Karl von Pfeffer-Wildenbruch, a relative of the last kaiser, and turned himself in. Pfeffer-Wildenbruch, who was also the Waffen-SS Commander, Hungary, forced him to "request" asylum in Germany. Three days later, Skorzeny arrived at Pfeffer-Wildenbruch's home and was formally presented to Admiral Horthy. The regent was informed that he would be housed in Hirschberg, a castle in Bavaria, to which Skorzeny would personally have the honor of escorting him, using Horthy's own train. There was little conversation on the trip.[23] The deposed regent remained at Hirschberg until the end of the war.[24] His son ended up in a concentration camp. As his last official act, the old admiral was forced to appoint Ferenc Szalasi, the leader of the Arrow-Cross Party (the Hungarian version of the Nazi Party), as his successor.

Szalasi, who was of Hungarian, Slovakian, and Armenian ancestry, was the son of an authoritarian Austro-Hungarian army officer. Born in 1897, he had nevertheless served on the General Staff in World War I and by 1932 seemed to be on the threshold of a highly successful military career. Then he left the service and entered politics, because he honestly believed that God had preordained him to create a great Magyar state, under which Hungary would dominate the Balkans.

According to Earl Ziemke, Szalasi's chief claim to distinction to date had been "his incoherence both in speech and in writing." He promptly named himself *Nador* (Fuehrer), with all of the powers of the prince regent.[25] His first act was to renounce the armistice with the Soviets. An extremist and violent anti-Semite, he fully participated in the Holocaust. As early as the night of October 15–16, Arrow Cross members (mostly teenagers) were running wild in the streets, murdering Jews at their whim, shooting many and throwing them off the famous Margarethe Bridge. The Hungarian police did nothing to stop the killing; in fact, they were soon assisting Eichmann et al. in "cleansing" Hungary of Jews (i.e., sending them to the extermination camps). They were still rounding up Jews in Budapest even after the Hungarian capital was surrounded. (This practice reportedly ended in Budapest only when Major General Gerhard Schmidhuber, the commander of the 13th Panzer Division, took matters into his own hands and ordered it stopped—and that was after the city was surrounded.)[26]

Under Szalasi's puppet government, the Wehrmacht's rear in Hungary was secure.[27] The same, however, could not be said of its front. Like most of the front, the terrain around the Theiss (Tisza) was flat and well suited for mobile operations, and the Soviet forces in Hungary—equipped largely with American vehicles—were much more powerful and mobile than Army Group South. Malinvosky's 2nd Ukrainian Front alone had 635,000 men, 750 tanks, and 1,100 airplanes. Friessner had 330,000 Germans and 150,000 Hungarians (not all of whom were reliable)[28] but was even more heavily outnumbered in armored fighting vehicles (AFVs). The 6th Army, for example, had four panzer and two panzer grenadier divisions (the 1st, 13th, 23rd, and 24th Panzers and the 4th SS and Feldherrnhalle Panzer Grenadiers), but all told, these formations could now muster only sixty-seven tanks and fifty-eight assault guns. In short, Friessner's armies now held a continuous front, but it was weak and thinly manned; it could not hold long against a determined attack. Friessner also did not have firm contact with Weichs's Army Group F to the south and west, since elements of the 2nd Ukrainian Front had already crossed the lower Theiss and occupied much of the Hungarian Plain between the Theiss and the Danube.

Hitler nevertheless commanded Friessner to fight for every foot of soil and to allow no voluntary withdrawals.

The fall of Horthy and the advent of Szalasi also had a negative effect on Hungarian morale, which was already low. Hungarian soldiers began to desert in large numbers; in some places entire units went over to the Russians, including much of the 2nd Hungarian Armored Division. General Janos Voeroes, the Hungarian chief of staff, defected (crossing the lines in a Mercedes that Heinz Guderian had given him a few weeks before), as did General Bela Miklos, the commander of the 1st Hungarian Army—only an hour or so before a German general arrived to arrest him. Colonel General Verres, the leader of the Hungarian 2nd Army, was arrested on Friessner's orders.[29]

On the other side of the lines, Marshal Malinovsky planned a massive offensive that had as its objective the capture of Budapest. It was to be spearheaded by General I. T. Schlemin's 46th Army, which was to attack to the northwest, take Kecskemet, and then move rapidly on to the Hungarian capital. General M. S. Schumilov's 7th Guards Army to Schlemin's north was to attack across the Tisza, while still farther north the 40th, 27th, and 53rd Armies were to attack toward Miskolc, to tie up the German forces in that sector. To add speed and weight to these attacks, 46th Army was reinforced with the 2nd and 4th Mechanized Corps; the 7th Guards Army was reinforced with General Pliev's Mechanized Cavalry Group (4th and 6th Guards Cavalry Corps and the 23rd Tank Corps); and the 27th Army was given the 5th Guards and 7th Mechanized Corps. Malinvosky wanted a couple of weeks to rest his troops, perform much-needed maintenance, and replenish his supplies, but Stalin insisted that the offensive be launched at once.

Friessner's respite on the Theiss was very brief. On the afternoon of October 29, Malinovsky struck. Once again, he focused on the Colonel General Zoltan Heszlenyi's 3rd Hungarian Army. The German elements of this army, under the command of Kirchner's LVII Panzer Corps, held their positions, but most of the Hungarians scattered almost immediately. The Russians captured Kecskemet on the 31st and by November 1 had advanced fifteen to thirty miles all along the front. The 2nd and 4th Mechanized Corps poured into the rear of the German 6th Army and headed for Budapest.

To the north, the Germans were also in trouble. Within three days, the 7th Guards Army had pushed across the Tisza and had established a bridgehead six miles deep and twenty miles wide. General Fretter-Pico, the commander of the 6th Army, decided that the Soviet drive on Budapest represented the greatest threat. He decided to let his forces to the north fend for themselves, and sent the 23rd and 24th Panzer Divisions into a counterattack against the Soviet mechanized spearheads. They were joined by the 4th SS Panzer Grenadier Division "Police" from Kirchner's corps.

Mindful not to expose themselves to another disaster like Debrecen, the Soviets did not send huge numbers of tanks surging forward without regard for their flanks or rear; rather, they disposed them in small concentrations along the entire front, each backed by infantry, artillery, and anti-tank units. Major General Gustav-Adolf von Nostitz-Wallwitz's 24th Panzer Division in particular did a brilliant job in delaying the Soviets but could not stop them.[30] On November 4, the 7th Guards Army broke through the 20th Hungarian Infantry Division and reached Cegled, within ten miles of Budapest.

By now, Friessner had concentrated the III Panzer and LVII Panzer Corps, including the 1st, 23rd, 24th, and Feldherrnhalle Panzer Divisions, in this sector.[31] Together they halted the Soviets within a few miles of the suburbs of Budapest. Here the panzer troops managed to cut off a Red spearhead, which lost twenty of its thirty-five tanks before it could escape. A Russian infantry battalion was also destroyed. One Russian vanguard actually broke into the suburbs of eastern Budapest, much to the shock of the residents of the Magyar capital. The invaders, however, were quickly annihilated by ad hoc German battle groups, using *Panzerfausts* and PzKw IVs. Meanwhile, German defenders were reinforced by the 8th and 22nd SS Cavalry Divisions, while elements of the 8th SS Cavalry and the Feldherrnhalle Panzer Grenadier Division counterattacked and recaptured the town of Vecses, just southeast of the city. (The 60th Panzer Grenadier Division "Feldherrnhalle" had been redesignated Panzer Division "Feldherrnhalle" on October 1, after it absorbed the 109th Panzer Brigade.)[32]

In the meantime, the 23rd and 24th Panzer Divisions launched repeated attacks on the Soviet flanks, tying down the 23rd Rifle Corps (of the 46th Army). The Soviet spearhead was smashed by these determined counterattacks. Mindful of the disaster they had recently suffered at Debrecen, Stalin's forces withdrew to the southeast on November 5.[33] By this time, the Soviet 2nd and 4th Mechanized Corps were down to about a hundred tanks, combined.

Meanwhile, twenty thousand workers in Miskolc (mostly armaments workers) revolted, went on strike, and—no doubt expecting the Red Army to arrive at any time—adopted a hostile and belligerent attitude toward the Germans. The Soviet retreat allowed Friessner to send in a sizable *kampfgruppe* and put down the embryonic rebellion.

Between Miskolc and Budapest, however, the 7th Guards Army continued to expand its bridgehead across the Tisza (see Map 7.3). Because Fretter-Pico had sent his panzers south, to deal with the threat to Budapest, a Soviet breakthrough was all but inevitable. The German 6th Army had no choice but to abandon the entire Tisza River line and retreat to the west. This, however, also worked to its advantage: the Tisza line was very

Map 7.3
Army Group South, October 29–December 30, 1944

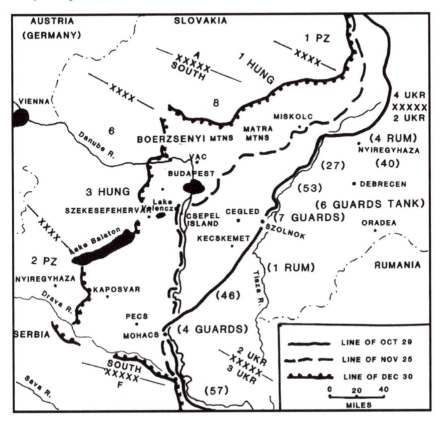

irregular, and any retreat would shorten (and thus strengthen) this front. The veteran German infantry completed this move during the first week of November and desperately began to dig in before the next onslaught. They were aided in their preparations by stragglers from the Hungarian Army rounded up by field police units, grouped into sapper formations, and put to work digging foxholes, trenches, and field fortifications. Fretter-Pico initially concentrated south of Budapest, where he expected the main enemy attack to come.

During the first week of November, Timoshenko also regrouped his forces and prepared for an offensive on a much broader front. On his left, Tolbukhin's 3rd Ukrainian Front, which had captured the Yugoslav capital on October 19, entered Hungary from the south with the 57th and 4th Guards Armies and the 18th Tank Corps in early November and was given control of the 46th Army, which was now just south of Budapest. East and northeast of the Hungarian capital lay Malinovsky's 2nd Ukrainian Front, with the 7th Guards, 53rd, 27th, and 40th Armies, plus the 1st and 4th Rumanian Armies.

The German forces available to meet this massive threat included the 2nd Panzer Army (of OB Southeast) and Army Group South, which deployed the remnants of the 2nd Hungarian Army, Armeegruppe Fretter-Pico (German 6th Army plus a few Hungarian units), and Armeegruppe Woehler (German 8th and 1st Hungarian Armies).

On the German southern flank lay de Angelis's 2nd Panzer Army, which was primarily responsible for defending the Hungarian oilfields in the Nagykanizsa area. Despite its impressive title, it had not controlled tank units since 1943. It was a motley collection of mediocre German Army units, mediocre to poor SS units (composed mainly of foreign volunteers), and three Croatian divisions. The only good division in the entire army was the battered 1st Mountain (see chapter 6).

Fretter-Pico's 6th Army held the line between Lake Balaton and Hatvan, about twenty-five miles north of Budapest. From south to north, it included Breith's III Panzer Corps, General of Infantry August Schmidt's LXXII Corps, SS Lieutenant General Karl Sauberzweig's IX SS Mountain Corps (inside the capital), and Kirchner's LVII Panzer Corps on the extreme left. Covering the German northern flank was Armeegruppe Woehler, which deployed Ulrich Kleemann's IV Panzer Corps, Roepke's XXIX Corps, and Kreysing's XVII Corps, which in turn was interlaced with the 1st Hungarian Army on Army Group South's extreme left flank. In all, Friessner had the equivalent of fifteen German divisions, including three panzer, two panzer grenadier, and two SS cavalry divisions.

The Soviet offensive finally started on November 7, when the 3rd Ukrainian Front attempted to cross to the west bank of the Danube near Mohacs, Batina, and Apatin. Most of this area was flooded and easily defended, so 2nd Panzer Army managed to put up an effective resistance until November 22, when Tolbukhin finally began to break out of his bridgeheads. Aided by a miners' revolt, the Soviet 57th Army (64th and 75th Rifle Corps and 6th Guards Rifle Corps) took Pecs (about fifty-five miles south of Lake Balaton) on November 29, in spite of fierce resistance from SS Major General Gustav Lombard's 31st SS Volunteer Grenadier Division "Bohemia-Moravia," which was fighting much better than anyone had expected. This mixed and partially equipped German/Volksdeutsch unit (which had been in the process of forming in southern Hungary when Tolbukhin's offensive struck) managed to evacuate eighty thousand ethnic Germans from southern Hungary and fell back to Lake Balaton to reform.

To the east and northeast of Budapest, Malinovsky's 2nd Ukrainian Front launched another major offensive on November 11. It expected to gain ground rapidly, but German infantry and some Hungarian units put up a dogged resistance, and the Reds had to fight for every inch of ground.

The German *feldgrau* were aided by repeated counterattacks from the 1st, 13th, 23rd, and 24th Panzer Divisions, as well as the 503rd and 509th Heavy Panzer Battalions, both of which were equipped with the newest King Tiger tanks. The Reds gained ground only slowly, but after a week of attacks, they were threatening Miskolc.

Meanwhile, to the south, the Soviets were now almost out of the low hills between the Drava and the Danube, beyond which the terrain was much more suitable for armored operations. Field Marshal Baron Maximilian von Weichs, the OB Southeast, believed that Tolbukhin intended to continue the offensive to the west, in order to cut off his (Weichs's) retreat from the Balkans; Friessner, on the other hand, was convinced that he intended to make a two-pronged drive to the northwest. His left prong, Friessner predicted, would be aimed at the southern tip of Lake Balaton and the oil fields and refineries near Nagykanizsa; his right would continue north of the lake to envelop Budapest from the south and west, while Malinovsky enveloped the city from the north. Tolbukhin's intentions were not clear until December 1, when the 57th Army began a quick advance to the northwest from Pecs, and the 4th Guards Army drove rapidly north along the Danube.

Now that it was clear that Friessner was correct, Hitler gave him control of 2nd Panzer Army. On December 2, Friessner ordered de Angelis to break contact with Army Group F and concentrate on holding a front between the southern tip of Lake Balaton and the Drava southwest of Nagykanizsa (the "Margarethe position"). To keep this line from collapsing and to close the gap between Lake Balaton and the Danube, Friessner had to rush several of his armored and motorized units to the south to reinforce it, significantly weakening his northern flank. Meanwhile, the 2nd Ukrainian Front attacked with thirty-five rifle divisions and pushed into the Matra Hills (sometimes called the Matra Mountains), northeast of Budapest, where it was halted by the 8th Army. It continued its probing attacks, however, and managed to capture Miskolc on December 4. Malinovsky resumed his offensive on a major scale on December 5, when the 6th Guards Tank Army (5th Guards Tank Corps and 9th Guards Mechanized Corps), supported by the Pliev Group (4th and 6th Guards Cavalry Corps and the 4th Guards Mechanized Corps) and the 7th Guards Army attacked in the Hatvan sector, at the junction of the 6th and 8th Armies. This zone was defended by the 357th Infantry, 18th SS Panzer Grenadier, and 13th Panzer Divisions—all understrength. They were hit by more than five hundred tanks and assault guns the first day. The Soviets penetrated the German lines in several places and poured their armor through the gaps.[34] By December 8, the Russians had captured the city of Vac on the Danube bend north of Budapest, about ten miles due north of the capital, and were also on the outskirts of Estergom, about twenty-five miles northwest of Budapest.

South of the Magyar capital, the 37th Rifle Corps of the Soviet 46th Army hurled itself at Colonel Bieber's 271st Volksgrenadier Division, which put up unexpectedly fierce resistance.[35] It delayed the Soviets long enough for Fretter-Pico to bring up the 8th Panzer Division, the 1st Hungarian Tank Division, and an SS police regiment, which counterattacked and brought the 2nd Ukrainian Front's southern offensive to an abrupt stop northwest of Erd. "No one thought of giving up," Sergeant Major Walter Boehm of the 8th Panzer Reconnaissance Battalion said later. "We attacked again and again, destroying several Soviet infantry units and stopping others dead in their tracks."[36]

Like waves against the shore, the Russians kept on coming. The 4th Guards Army of Tolbukhin's 3rd Ukrainian Front pushed toward the Lake Balaton–Lake Velencze line, southwest of the city, only to be stopped by the 1st and 23rd Panzer Divisions.

It was now clear that a Soviet encirclement of Budapest was in the offing. With Hitler's permission, OKH reinforced Friessner with two panzer divisions and three Tiger battalions for a counterattack. Guderian believed that the main Soviet effort was in the north; Friessner felt that the greater danger lay to the south, between the two lakes. Hitler finally decided to deploy the reinforcements along the general lines Friessner advocated, largely because he was worried about losing the bauxite mines near Szekesfehervar, between the lakes.

Once again, Friessner was right, although both north and south of Budapest the German fronts were in critical condition. On December 11, Malinovsky sent the 6th Guards Tank Army (5th Guards Tank and 9th Guards Mechanized Corps) into the attack, with the objective of reaching the Hron River valley, north of the city. Major General Josef Rintelen's 357th Infantry Division and the 2nd Hungarian Tank Division slowed it down but were unable to stop it, and it reached the valley on December 13. The next day, the Russians captured the town of Ipolysag north of Budapest, and began working their way through the small Boerzsenyi Mountains north of the city. Friessner had no choice but to defend Sahy with the Dirlewanger Brigade, which had recently come down from Slovakia. The army group commander visited it on the 14th, and what he saw amazed him. Dirlewanger, who was responsible for many of the terrible atrocities committed in putting down the Warsaw uprising a few months before, was sitting calmly at his desk, with a monkey on his shoulder. Neither he nor his staff knew anything about the situation in their sector of the front, but Dirlewanger nevertheless wanted to withdraw. Friessner ordered him to stay put. Then Friessner visited the 24th Panzer Division and passed through the Sahy sector again that evening, where he narrowly avoided being captured by the Russians. Dirlewanger had ignored his orders and pulled out anyway; no one knew where his brigade had gone.[37]

Friessner and Fretter-Pico countered this latest threat by rushing most of the 3rd and 6th Panzer Divisions to the Boerzsenyi Mountains sector and then splitting them into several battle groups, where they plugged holes in the battered German line. They were able to further slow—but not to halt—the 6th Guards Tank Army, which continued to slowly push through the Boerzsenyis, despite the cold, wet weather (which hampered their air support) and the bitter German resistance.

By December 18, the situation in the northern sector had deteriorated to the point that Friessner was forced to commit all of Froelich's 8th Panzer Division to the northern wing, to defend against the Russian 6th Tank Army. Hitler, in the meantime, ordered Army Group South to launch a major armored offensive southwest of Budapest against the 4th Guards Tank Army, between Lakes Balaton and Veleneze.

At the same time, Friessner and Guderian were having another series of arguments, because Friessner did not use his limited panzer reserve to counterattack right away. The weather was bad for the use of armor—with rain and above freezing temperatures—and the entire area around Budapest was a giant field of mud. On December 14, Friessner categorically refused to assume responsibility for the attack until the ground had frozen, but still Guderian persisted in ordering him to strike. Their arguments became so heated that Friessner personally flew to Zossen on December 18 for a showdown. Nothing of the sort happened, however. It turned out that Guderian had merely been repeating the orders of the Fuehrer; both he and Major General Bodislaw von Bonin, his operations officer, appeared to be in full agreement with Friessner's ideas. Friessner went on to advocate that Budapest be evacuated. Hitler had declared the city a "fortress" and had ordered it be defended house by house, but it was in no way prepared for a siege. Life, in fact, was going on as if there were no war. The shops were open, Christmas decorations were out, and many of the Hungarian officers were even spending their days at the front and their nights at home. They were literally commuting to and from the front—which, for most of them, involved little more than a streetcar ride. Guderian said that he would relay Friessner's views to the Fuehrer, but he would promise nothing else vis-à-vis Budapest.[38]

The next day, the 8th Panzer Division's counterattack failed, and the Dirlewanger Brigade mutinied. Several companies went over to the Reds while other units shot their officers and deserted. Most of its men had disappeared by the next day.

With this latest reversal, Hitler and Guderian took over the tactical conduct of the battle from Fuehrer Headquarters, hundreds of miles away from the battlefield. Hitler again ordered that a major armored thrust be made between Lakes Balaton and Velencze. As originally planned, it was to be directed by Breith's III Panzer Corps and would include the 3rd, 6th, and 8th Panzer Divisions, as well as two battalions of Panthers. Because the marshy terrain over which it had to attack was still not frozen, Hitler commanded that the 3rd and 6th Panzers leave all of their tanks, personnel carriers, assault guns, and self-propelled artillery behind; the dismounted infantry of the panzer grenadier regiments were to conduct the attack on foot, while the mobile units (without their infantry) remained committed to the north, against the Soviet 6th Tank Army. This ridiculous order was relayed to Friessner through the mouth of Heinz Guderian, the "father" of the blitzkrieg and the world's first master of armored operations. The attack naturally came to nothing, and when III Panzer Corps was counterattacked a few days later it was unable to hold, because it had no infantry.[39]

Meanwhile, the Soviets closed in on Budapest. The withdrawal of the 8th Panzer Division and much of the 3rd and 6th Panzers had significantly weakened the defense north of the city. On December 20, the 6th Guards Tank Army of the 2nd Ukrainian Front overran the 357th Infantry Division and advanced to the south, out of the Boerzsenyi Mountains on both sides of Sahy, while Tolbukhin advanced to the north, on both sides of Lake Velencze. By December 22, Val had fallen to the 2nd Guards Mechanized Corps (of the 46th Army), while the 3rd Panzer Division was pinned down in heavy fighting in the important communications center of Szekesfeherevar. Budapest was in danger of encirclement.

Once again, on December 23, Friessner called for the abandonment of the city. Both he and Fretter-Pico were sacked that night.[40] The quiet, cigar-smoking Woehler was given command of Army Group South, General of Panzer Troops Hermann Balck (the commander of Army Group G) was transferred from the Western Front to assume command of the 6th Army (an obvious demotion), and General Kreysing succeeded Woehler as commander of the 8th Army.[41] Guderian signaled the new commanders that they should have but one battle cry: "Attack!"—whether by patrols, locally, or on a large scale.[42]

Woehler responded by calling the chief of OKH and arguing that, historically, Budapest had always been defended from the west bank. Listening to his arguments, Guderian changed his tune completely and even agreed to speak to Hitler about abandoning Budapest. Three hours later, he relayed the Fuehrer's decision to General Woehler: the city, including the bridgehead on the eastern side of the Danube, was to be defended; OKH would launch a rescue attack, using the IV SS Panzer Corps (3rd SS and 5th SS Panzer Divisions) from Army Group Center; and Woehler had permission to withdraw two divisions from the city.

It was already too late for that, however; the 18th Tank Corps of the 46th Army and the vanguards of the 6th Guards Tank Army linked up at Estergom on Christmas Eve Day, December 24. Budapest was surrounded.

THE SIEGE OF BUDAPEST

What was happening in the Budapest sector itself?

Since November 5, the city of Budapest had been defended tenaciously by the 8th SS and 22nd SS Cavalry Divisions (both dismounted), the 13th Panzer Division, the 60th Panzer Division "Feldherrnhalle" (the FHH), the equivalent of a flak brigade (including Colonel Ernst Jansa's 12th Flak Regiment), a battalion-sized *kampfgruppe* from the 271st Volksgrenadier Division,[43] the 1st SS Police Regiment (of the 4th SS Panzer Grenadier Division "Police"), and the Hungarian I Corps (Hungarian 1st Armored and 10th and 12th Infantry Divisions, a regiment from the 1st Hungarian Cavalry Division, the Budapest Guard Battalion, and a few battalions of Hungarian police and Arrow Cross Party militia). The Hungarian forces were well commanded by Colonel General Ivan Hindy. All forces in and around Budapest, as of November 5, were under the control of Breith's III Panzer Corps. In all, Budapest was defended by thirty-three thousand Germans and thirty-seven thousand Hungarians. The quality of the Magyar units was highly varied, from good to poor, but overall was fair to mediocre. They were of higher quality than the average Hungarian army unit in late 1944. The quality of the German divisions was at least good, and the 8th SS Cavalry, 13th Panzer, and FHH were excellent, although all were plagued by equipment shortages of every description even before the siege began. The strongest army division in the garrison was the Feldherrnhalle Panzer Division, which had eight thousand men, twenty-five PzKw IV and V tanks, and a battalion of the superb Hummel 150 mm self-propelled howitzers. The 13th Panzer Division, which had penetrated into the Caucasus only two years before, was down to three thousand men, about twenty PzKw IVs and Vs, and a reduced panzer artillery regiment. The 8th SS Cavalry Division "Florian Geyer" contributed eight thousand men, about half of whom were ethnic Germans (Volksdeutsche). Most of its men were veterans of the Eastern Front. The 8th SS also had ten assault guns, three battalions of artillery, and a battalion of towed 88 mm anti-aircraft guns. The Luftwaffe contributed the excellent 12th Flak Regiment (of the 15th Flak Division), which included sixty 88 mm guns. Table 7.2 shows the Axis Order of Battle during the Siege of Budapest.

On November 10, a strong Russian armored column took the key town of Vecses from SS Major Walter Drexler's 8th SS Panzer Reconnaissance (Recon) Battalion. SS Colonel Joachim Rumohr, the commander of the 8th SS Cavalry Division, launched an immediate counterattack with the 15th SS Cavalry Regiment, the 3rd (Assault Gun) Company of the 8th SS Recon, and an assault-gun detachment from the Feldherrnhalle, supported by the 8th SS Artillery Regiment and the 8th SS Division's heavy flak battalion. Elements of the 12th Hungarian Infantry Division also joined the battle, which was fierce. The SS men retook the town in bitter, house-to-house fighting. They

Table 7.2
The Defenders of Budapest, November 1944–February 1945

III Panzer Corps: General of Panzer Troops Hermann Breith (replaced by the SS General
Karl von Pfeffer-Wildenbruch's IX SS Mountain Corps on December 4)[1]
    (60th) Panzer Division "Feldherrnhalle":[2] Colonel Guenther Pape[3]
    13th Panzer Division: Major General Gerhard Schmidhuber
    8th SS Cavalry Division "Florian Geyer": SS Colonel Joachim Rumohr
    22nd SS Cavalry Division "Maria Theresia": SS Colonel August Zehender
    1st SS Police Regiment:[4] SS Oberfuehrer Helmut Doerner
    Kampfgruppe, 271st Volksgrenadier Division: Lieutenant Colonel Herbert
      Kuendiger

I Hungarian Corps: Colonel General Ivan Hindy
    10th Hungarian Infantry Division
    12th Hungarian Reserve Division
    Elements, 1st Hungarian Armored Division
    One regiment, 1st Hungarian Cavalry Division
    Arrow Cross Party Militia
    Several police and auxiliary units

Notes:
[1] SS Obergruppenfuehrer von Pfeffer-Wildenbruch was named Wehrmacht Commander, Budapest, on December 25, 1944.
[2] Parts of the FHH Division, including the 13th Tank Destroyer Battalion, were outside the city when it was surrounded.
[3] Colonel Pape was promoted to major general on December 1, 1944. He was commanding an ad hoc battle group outside the fortress and was not with the part of the FHH Division that was inside Budapest.
[4] Part of the 4th SS Panzer Grenadier Division "Police."

found that most of the citizens of the town had been murdered; the women
had been raped, and most of them murdered. Over and over again, women
cried to the SS cavalrymen: "My God, my God, why did you leave us?" Several SS cavalrymen who had been captured were also found, but their bodies
were so badly mutilated that they were difficult to identify.[44] For the Waffen-
SS, Vescus set the tone for the battle. Quarter was seldom given, and the SS
men never gave up a position voluntarily. The Soviets were not able to recapture Vecsus, for example, until the end of December.

The 8th SS and 22nd SS Cavalry Divisions, now fighting as infantry,[45]
barred the direct route to Budapest and were subjected to repeated attacks,
all of which they repulsed, except for one. On November 17, the Soviets
broke through the German trenches and barreled into the western sector
of Vecses, but they were quickly surrounded by an SS counterattack. The
cavalrymen sealed off the breakthrough and wiped out the attacking force.

On December 4, 5, and 6, the Soviets penetrated the Hungarian lines in
several places. Most of these penetrations were liquidated by counterattacks

by Major General Gerhard Schmidhuber's 13th Panzer Division or by Colonel Guenther Pape's FHH Panzer Division. Between Alag and Kisalag, the Russians broke through the 10th and 12th Hungarian Infantry Divisions in several places, and the *panzertruppen* lacked the strength to seal off all of the penetrations, so they had to fall back into the "Budapest bridgehead" positions, on the very outskirts of the city. On December 9, the Soviets established a bridgehead on Csepel Island, in the middle of the Danube, due south of the city. By December 11, Budapest was tightly ringed in from the north, east, and south, and the Russians had brought up ten thousand heavy artillery pieces and were hammering the city from three directions. The Hungarian civilians, however, tried to go on with their everyday lives as if nothing was happening. The shops remained open, the streetcars still operated, and Christmas was celebrated in the usual manner—insofar as that was possible.

Meanwhile, on December 11, SS Colonel August Zehender's 22nd SS Cavalry Division "Maria Theresa" assumed operational control of the 1st Hungarian Armored Division and was placed in charge of the German defenses on Csepel Island. Two days later, the IX SS Mountain Corps replaced the III Panzer Corps and took charge of the defense of the Hungarian capital. This corps, which was initially commanded by SS Lieutenant General Karl G. Sauberzweig, had been formed in the summer of 1944 to control the training and operations of the 13th and 23rd SS Volunteer Mountain Divisions "Handschar" and "Kama." It was thus basically a training command. Its divisions, however, proved to be the worst in the Wehrmacht. They had been made up largely of Croatian Moslems who were not particularly interested in serving the Greater German Reich and only fought with enthusiasm when they had the opportunity to attack defenseless Christian villages. The 23rd SS had been dissolved due to its lack of discipline and the lack of time to train it, and the 13th had been scaled back to regimental size, to increase its efficiency. This had left the IX SS Mountain free for employment at the front.

In early December, General Sauberzweig was replaced by SS-Obergruppenfuehrer Karl von Pfeffer-Wildenbruch, who was also a general of police.[46] This veteran officer had been born on June 12, 1888, in Kalkberge-Ruedersdorf near Berlin, the son of a physician. His Protestant family was from Salzburg, Austria, but had moved to East Prussia two centuries before. Pfeffer-Wildenbruch joined the Imperial Army in 1907 as an officer cadet with the 22nd Artillery Regiment in Muenster, Westphalia. Commissioned in 1908, he served three years as battery officer. In 1911 he was sent to the Military Technical Academy in Berlin, where he remained until World War I broke out. He rejoined his old regiment in the field, served as adjutant of the 237th Field Artillery Regiment in 1915, and was then assigned to the staff of Field Marshal Baron von der Golz in Baghdad,

Iraq, as part of the special military mission to Persia. In 1917, he was chief of staff to General Liman von Sander, the head of the German military mission to the Ottoman Empire. The following year, he served as a general staff officer with the 11th Infantry Division, the LV Corps z.b.V. ("for special purposes"), and the XXIV Reserve Corps. He was decorated with both grades of the Iron Cross. After the war, Pfeffer-Wildenbruch was not selected for retention in General von Seeckt's four thousand-officer Reichsheer, so he joined the Order Police, serving in the Rhineland-Westphalia district. Later he was an advisor to the Interior Ministry and commander of police detachments in Osnabrueck and Magdeburg. From 1928 to 1930, he was an instructor with the Mobile State Police in Santiago, Chile. He then returned to Germany, where he commanded police units in Berlin and Kassel before taking charge of the state police regiment at Frankfurt-am-Main. Three years later he was appointed inspector of Police Schools in the Interior Ministry. He was promoted to major general of police in 1937 and to lieutenant general of police in November 1939. Meanwhile, on October 10, 1939, he become the first commander of the SS Motorized Division "Polizei," which he led on the Western Front in 1940. He was named SS-Gruppenfuehrer (lieutenant general of SS) on April 20, 1940.

From 1941 to 1943, Pfeffer-Wildenbruch was chief of the Colonial Police Bureau of the Interior Ministry, which oversaw police operations in the occupied territories. On September 27, 1943, he was named commander of the VI (Latvian) Volunteer SS Corps, which he led on the northern sector of the Eastern Front, until he was named commander of Waffen-SS forces in Hungary. As commander of the IX SS Mountain Corps, he led the German forces in Budapest throughout the rest of the siege. A tough veteran, he had already lost both of his sons. The oldest was killed in action as a *Fahnenjanker* (officer cadet) in North Africa in 1941, and the youngest, an army second lieutenant, was killed in France in 1944. Despite his SS status (as opposed to Waffen-SS status), Pfeffer-Wildenbruch was considered a reasonably competent commander by most of the army generals in Hungary, and most of them had a certain amount of respect for him. General Balck, however, did not. The new 6th Army commander was an extremely capable and sometimes brilliant leader. He was one of the best armored commanders the Wehrmacht produced in World War II—and he knew it. "People" skills, however, were not his strong point. He was arrogant, irascible, insensitive, and intractable when dealing with anyone whom he did not consider to be on his professional level, and that was almost everyone who was not a member of the General Staff and/or a veteran panzer officer. He even occasionally clashed with some of them, including Field Marshal Gerd von Rundstedt, the OB West, who Balck felt was not up to date professionally. (There was a considerable amount of justification in Balck's position concerning Rundstedt.) Balck had also clashed with Himmler, because of the general's open disdain for all SS divisions. Balck was, in fact, highly prejudiced against the Waffen-SS and all of its officers, and he did nothing to hide his contempt for them. The fact that his close personal friend and chief of staff, Major General Heinz Gaedcke, shared his views did nothing to improve Army-SS cooperation.[47]

The Russian infantry continued to launch frontal attacks against the IX SS Mountain Corps, while the 2nd and 3rd Ukrainian Fronts tried to cut the city off from the west and complete the encirclement. Casualties were high on both sides. On December 14, part of the 8th SS Cavalry Division was transferred from the southern to northern sector, to supplement the low infantry strength of the 13th Panzer and FHH. The next day, the army's 751st Engineer Battalion arrived in the city and was also sent into the trenches and bunkers.

Budapest, a city of almost a million people, still tried to ignore the siege. The 8th SS Cavalry Medical Battalion, for example, set up its main dressing station in the wine cellar of the elegant Hotel Britannia. Affluent Hungarians, however, continued to patronize the dining room, in spite of the fact that mud-covered and filthy wounded SS men were often carried past them, dripping blood as they went.

There was relatively little fighting in the trenches around Budapest during the week of December 17–23, and an ominous silence descended on the German positions. The troops tried not to think about the deteriorating strategic situation and concentrated on celebrating Christmas instead. The festivities were dampened considerably on December 24, when the news reached the soldiers: Budapest was completely encircled. Pfeffer-Wildenbruch wanted to launch an immediate breakout and sent the "Floian Geyer" SS Cavalry Division to Buda, on the western side of the pocket, to lead the way. Then came the order from Fuehrer Headquarters: "Budapest must be held under all circumstances!"[48] Instead of attacking, the 22nd SS Cavalry dug in to defend the western approaches to the "fortress." Unfortunately for the defenders, their supply depots were located too far west of the city and the staff of the IX SS Mountain Corps did not start moving them into the perimeter until it was too late. Most of their 450 tons of ammunition and three hundred thousand rations were lost to the Russians on Christmas Eve. Once again, the Waffen-SS demonstrated its major weakness as a combat force: poor staff officers and faulty staff work.

On December 25—Christmas Day—the fighting escalated again as the Soviets tried to batter their way into Budapest. There were few lulls during the rest of the siege. "In sheer horror," Ziemke wrote later, "nothing since Stalingrad compared with the Budapest siege. Almost the entire population, normally over a million, was trapped in the city without the barest provisions for subsistence or health, driven to the cellars by air and artillery bombardments. In most quarters, the electricity, gas, and water services failed in the first days."[49] Thousands died due to the cold and illness. On Christmas Day, FHH held Budaors in fierce fighting. The next day the Russians suffered heavy losses at Budakesci, which was held by the 8th SS Recon Battalion. Along the Danube, the Soviets managed to capture the main heights on Csepel Island. The Russians had committed around twenty rifle divisions and several armored and mechanized units to this battle, and they were attacking everywhere. Disaster was frequently averted only by counterattacks by the last battalions. All Pfeffer-Wildenbruch had left in reserve was a *kampfgruppe* from Oberfuehrer Helmut Doerner's 1st SS Police Regiment.[50] He signaled Fuehrer Headquarters that he wanted to evacuate the east (Pest) sector of the pocket, so he could concentrate his forces on the western side of the Danube. Needless to say, permission to retreat was not forthcoming from Fuehrer HQ.

The situation continued to worsen on December 27, when Drexler's 8th SS Panzer Reconnaissance Battalion was finally pushed out of Vecses, this time for good. The Soviets continued to gain ground on December 28 and broke through the eastern bridgehead. By now, the defenders were outnumbered about five to one in men and much more than that in guns, tanks, and virtually every other material category. There were no operational airfields within the pocket, so Russian domination of the air was total. Supplies were also running low; the IX SS Mountain predicted that it would be out of ammunition by January 3 and out of food by January 12. Even so, Gerhard Schmidhuber's 13th Panzer Division launched a vicious counterattack and wiped out the Russian penetration of the day before.

The IX SS could now only be resupplied by air and then usually only at night. The corps determined that the city's racetrack was the best landing site left in Budapest; twenty-seven He-111s and Ju-52s landed during the night of December 29–30, depositing seventy-five tons of ammunition and ten tons of fuel. Another forty-five tons were air-dropped, and another twenty-nine supply planes landed on December 30, during daylight hours, although several were shot down by Soviet fighters. Resupply was almost impossible that night, due to low temperatures, snowfall, and poor visibility.

Meanwhile, the Soviet attacks continued without respite. Near Csomor, the Soviets penetrated the lines of the 10th Hungarian Division, and the 13th Panzer was not able to close the gap completely. The two divisions had to retreat to a shorter defensive line to the west.

Malinovski and Tolbukhin had been sure that they would capture Budapest within three or four days after completing the encirclement, but the battle was developing contrary to their expectations. The Budapest garrison was tying up more than a quarter of a million Soviet troops, including nineteen Soviet and Rumanian divisions, three mechanized or tank brigades, and several specialized artillery and assault units. The Russian generals therefore tried diplomacy: and issued an ultimatum. On December 29, a team of four "parliamentarians" crossed the line under a flag of truce. They were first taken to the command post of SS Colonel Zehender, the commander of the 22nd SS Cavalry Division. Zehender, however, was full of contempt for the very idea of surrender and refused to even look at the terms. Colonel Rumohr, the commander of the 8th SS Cavalry, heatedly told the emissaries that Budapest would never surrender and sent them packing. What happened next is the subject of dispute. What is known is that as the Soviet representatives crossed German lines under a flag of truce their jeep exploded, killing all four occupants.

One SS man who witnessed the incident stated that the jeep was fired on by a Hungarian anti-tank gun, hidden nearby, where the Budaorcsi Road crossed the Hamszabegi railroad line. The Hungarians denied the charge and stated that the vehicle must have struck a mine. Other Hungarians put the blame on a battery of Hummels from the FHH. Two Feldherrnhalle veterans later testified that the men were killed in a Russian mortar attack. The Soviets claimed that the Waffen-SS had murdered the men and had committed a serious war crime. They swore revenge via loudspeakers and radio broadcasts, and the Germans and Hungarians knew that if the city ever fell, they could be counted upon to take it. Resistance became all the fiercer, and the Siege of Budapest became one of the bitterest battles of the Second World War.

By December 30, all of the German flak guns were concentrated in the zone of the 13th Panzer Division around Csomor, where the racetrack/airfield was located. To the west, in the hilly suburbs of Buda, the 8th SS Cavalry (supported by elements of the 271st Volksgrenadier Division) was also hard pressed by repeated attacks from the 23rd, 37th and 10th Guards Corps. SS Sergeant Friedrich Buck, then twenty-two years of age and commanding a four-hundred-man battle group in the 8th SS, later recalled that the street fighting in Buda "was the most savage I had ever seen. We fought man to man with bayonets, entrenching tools and grenades. The Soviets hit us night and day without let up."[51]

Everywhere the story was the same: the Germans fought for every block. "The closer the Soviet troops drew into Budapest, the more desperate the enemy's resistance became." Red Army Colonel M. M. Malakhov recalled, "The advancing troops had to overcome a maze of trenches, wire entanglements, anti-tank ditches and concentrated fire. . . . [T]hey had to take each building by storm."[52]

Soviet casualties were enormous, but the Russians outnumbered the Germans between fifteen and twenty to one in most categories. Slowly the pocket shrank. Inside Axis lines, food became scarce, and wool, coal, and heating oil were virtually exhausted. Old people, children, and the wounded died in the cold. Since every soldier was needed at the front, the dead were abandoned in the rubble or were left to rot in the streets. By

December 31, the 15th Cavalry Regiment of the 8th SS had been pushed to within half a mile of the Margarethe Island bridge on the Danube.

During the night of December 31–January 1, the entire front around Budapest came alive with the sound of thousands of guns, followed by massive Soviet attacks all along the line. The Reds broke through the 13th Panzer near Csomer and forced it back to the west. All along the eastern half of the bridgehead the Germans were forced to commit their last reserves, and the fighting was hand to hand in several places. "My wounds are not so bad," a soldier from the 18th SS Cavalry Regiment wrote to his parents in Duesseldorf:

On the 29th I received a splinter in my left foot, had it bound up and went back on duty. On the 30th I got a shell fragment from a Russian anti-tank gun in my left thigh which was worse. . . . There were five floors in the Hotel Imperial, all full of wounded. . . . The situation in the city is crazy. The Hungarians have really lost their heads. We must fight in the streets. . . . [T]he Russians are shooting with their artillery from all sides. . . .

The last days forward at the front were terrible, we never stopped fighting. Three times the Russians broke through a little bit with tanks and each time we had to counterattack with units made out of thin air! My platoon has gone from 42 men to 14. We don't get much food—only a loaf of bread for each 18 men. Our planes come early each evening taking the wounded out and bringing supplies in, but yesterday they could not land as the Russians had the airfield covered with their anti-tank guns. . . .

The Russians are coming ever closer. . . . [T]he streets are fully blocked up. Dead men, horses, animals and ruined cars are all over.[53]

The man who wrote this letter was more fortunate than most: the next day, he was flown out of the pocket to Papa, Hungary, by a Ju-52. Inside the pocket, however, his comrades continued to fight and die. Of the thirty-three thousand German soldiers trapped in Budapest, approximately two thousand had been killed, and more than seven thousand had been wounded. The Hungarians had also suffered heavy casualties, and about one-third of the Hungarian troops deserted to the Soviets by the time the battle was over. The Reds helped speed up this process by promising Hungarian deserters that they could go home if they lived behind Russian lines.

During the night of January 1–2, fifty-six He-111s dropped 73.5 tons of ammunition and supplies into the garrison, as well as a small quantity of fuel. In spite of the great bravery shown by the Luftwaffe pilots in the face of Soviet flak and hundreds of Red Air Force fighters, this was not enough.

Meanwhile, the rescue operation began.

To save the garrison at Budapest, Hitler gave Army Group South (and 6th Army) SS General Herbert Gille's IV SS Panzer Corps, which included the 3rd SS Panzer Division "Totenkopf" and the 5th SS Panzer Division

"Viking."[54] Both were considered elite divisions. The Totenkopf had originally consisted of paramilitary concentration camp guards, but, after three years on the Eastern Front, most of these men were dead. Just in the period June 22, 1941, to December 31, 1944, the Death's Head Division had suffered an absolutely astounding total of 53,794 casualties,[55] especially when one considers that its total strength probably never exceeded twenty-one thousand. During World War II, there were Allied armies that did not suffer fifty-three thousand casualties. The 3rd SS had been annihilated, rebuilt, annihilated, rebuilt, annihilated, and rebuilt again. After the war, Soviet Marshal Zhukov paid it a high left-handed compliment when he complained: "Everywhere I went I ran into the Totenkopf Division." Viking was also considered an elite unit. Unlike Totenkopf, it consisted not just of Germans but also of volunteers from Denmark, Norway, the Netherlands, Belgium, Sweden, and Finland—idealistic men who joined the SS to fight against Communism. Together, the two SS divisions constituted a formidable strike force, even in the sixth year of the war.

There were two possible routes for the relief attack. From southeast of Komarno to Budapest, the most direct route, the IV SS Panzer would have to travel about thirty miles, but half of the distance was through the heavily wooded Vertes Mountains. From northeast of Szekesfehervar to the capital the distance was about forty miles; the terrain was much better for tanks, but it would require Gille about five extra days to assemble here, and considerably more gasoline would be needed. Despite strong doubts, Army Group South opted for the direct route. The operation was codenamed Konrad I (Map 7.4).

Early on the morning of New Year's Day, 1945, Colonel Hermann Harrendorf's 96th Infantry Division crossed the frozen Danube five miles west of Estergom in the predawn darkness.[56] When day broke, the men of the Soviet 31st Guards Rifle Corps found that the Germans were already in their rear. As they battled the 96th, the IV SS Panzer Corps detrained and assembled for the attack. It struck at 10:30 P.M. with the 3rd SS Panzer and 5th SS Panzer Divisions—about 250 tanks in all, some of them Tigers. (The tank strength of the IV SS, however, would decline rapidly in this offensive, due to combat losses and mechanical breakdowns. By this stage of the war, many of the panzers were simply worn out, and the German spare-parts industry—which had been a problem since 1941—was now in complete disarray because of Allied bombing.) The SS panzers were supported by elements of Lieutenant General Joseph Reichert's 711th Infantry Division, although part of this two-regiment unit was still en route from Holland when the battle began. South of the IV SS, Group Pape (6th and 8th Panzer Divisions) attacked the 34th Guards Rifle Division, overwhelmed it, and achieved a breakthrough there as well.

To the south, the III Panzer and I Cavalry Corps launched a diversionary attack just west of Szekesfehervar, in the zone of the 135th Rifle Corps.

Map 7.4
Operation Konrad I: January 1–6, 1945

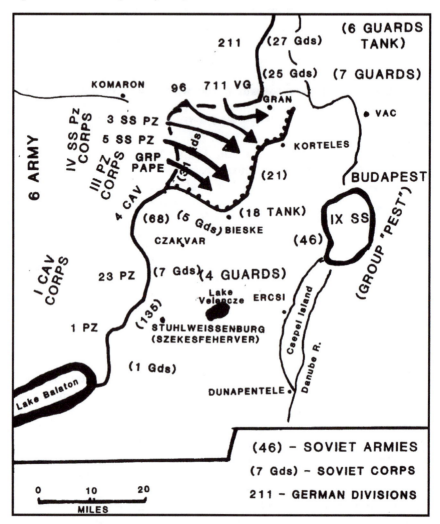

Marshal Malinovsky had incorrectly guessed that the main German relief attack would come here, so he had positioned his mobile reserves nearby. He committed the 1st and 7th Guard Mechanized here, while simultaneously sending the 18th Tank Corps to reinforce the 31st Guards.

The III Panzer and I Cavalry Corps were quickly checked, but the IV SS and Group Pape inflicted heavy casualties on the 31st Guards Rifle and 18th Tank Corps. The Russians (many of whom were still drunk or hung over from New Year's parties) were pushed back toward Budapest, along the Komarno-Budapest road, but the combination of the unfavorable terrain, lack of air support, mined roads, and enemy resistance was enough to deny the Germans a decisive breakthrough. Soviet fighter-bombers were particularly effective in slowing the advance of the panzers.

It was not until January 3, 1945, that Marshal Malinovsky—alarmed over the progress made by the Vikings and the Death's Head Division—concluded that this was the main attack. He ordered the 7th Guards Mechanized, 1st Guards Mechanized, 5th Guards Cavalry, and 21st Rifle Corps north, to deal with the threat.

As late as this move came, it was not too late. On January 4, the 5th SS could only advance three miles. It ran into the 41st Guards Rifle Division at the vital road junction of Bicske (Bieske) and was stopped cold. That night, SS Lieutenant Colonel Fritz Darges, the commander of the 5th SS Panzer Regiment, probed the Soviet line for weak spots and found one. He led a predominantly panzer grenadier battle group through it and, about dawn, ambushed and destroyed a Soviet task force, knocking out four 122 mm guns, four 76 mm antitank guns, a dozen trucks, and a number of supply wagons. Pushing forward, he attacked Regis Castle (Hegykastely), which was located on a commanding hill about a mile from Bicske. The Russian garrison scattered, but Malinovsky's reinforcements were already descending on the endangered sector. Soon the shoe was on the other foot, and Darges found himself surrounded. The SS colonel quickly hedgehogged (formed an isolated, all-around defensive perimeter) and repulsed attack after attack. Three days later, during the night of January 7–8, a Viking battle group crashed through Russian lines and rescued him. KG Darges (which included SS Lieutenant Colonel Fritz Vogt's Norge Battalion, a unit of Norwegian volunteers) left behind thirty burned-out Soviet tanks, ringed around the castle. But it was clear that there was going to be no breakthrough in this sector.[57]

On January 6, other elements of the IV SS were stopped near Perbal, about fifteen miles from the Budapest perimeter, and the 6th Guards Tank and 7th Guards Armies launched a powerful counterattack to the north, threatening the rear of the SS panzer corps. The next day, General Balck (acting on General Woehler's orders) struck the Russian lines to the south with his I Cavalry Corps (3rd and 23rd Panzer Divisions and the 4th Cavalry Brigade) and gained several miles, but the Russians again reacted quickly by sending in the 4th Guards Army. By January 7, both attacks were stalled. That day, January 7, Balck (after another verbal clash with Gille) signaled that the order for the breakout must be given within twenty-four hours. Hitler, however, refused to allow it. Woehler therefore had no choice but to continue hammering at the Russian lines, hoping to punch a hole deep enough to allow a relief force to reach the garrison.

To reinforce Konrad I, Woehler had taken what he knew was a serious risk: he had transferred Colonel Wilhelm Soeth's 3rd Panzer Division from the north side of the Danube to the Zamoly sector.[58] This move had achieved some success, but it had also severely weakened the defenses on the north side of the river. All that now defended the vital northern flank was the severely depleted 8th Panzer Division, the unreliable Hungarian St. Laszlo Division, the 211th Volksgrenadier Division, and the static 711th Volksgrenadier Division, which had just arrived from the Netherlands and was equipped with Dutch bicycles. Described by author Perry Pierik as a "rather shabby bunch," the 711th had been routed in France in the autumn of 1944. Many of its soldiers had just been transferred from the navy and still wore blue uniforms. They were, however, very well led by Lieutenant General Josef Reichert.[59] Despite its condition, Woehler ordered that the 711th launch a diversionary attack on the communications center of Gran (Estergom), a city of twenty thousand on January 6. To everyone's amazement, Reichert barreled through a gap in the Russian lines and took the city, almost without loss.

That same day, just north of the 711th Volksgrenadier, the Soviet 7th Guards and 6th Armies launched an offensive clearly aimed at Komaron. This city was important for three reasons: it was a communications center, it was the site of the only permanent bridge link to Slovakia, and it was the home of one of the few sizable oil refineries still in German hands. The 8th Panzer, 211th Volksgrenadier, and St. Laszlo Divisions were soon in rapid retreat. Woehler quickly ordered a bridgehead formed around Komaron; he and Balck reinforced it with the 13th Tank Destroyer Battalion, the 286th Army Flak Battalion, the twelve tanks of the independent 208th Panzer Battalion, and several ad hoc emergency (Alarm) battalions. Woehler placed General Herhudt von Roden in overall command of the bridgehead and Balck, who held Major General Gottfried Froelich responsible for the poor performance of his 8th Panzer Division, relieved him of his command.

Meanwhile, local German counterattacks, notably by Lieutenant Colonel Waldemar von Knoop's 98th Panzer Grenadier Regiment of the 8th Panzer, slowed the Russian advance.[60] Still the situation was desperate, and Woehler was even considering redeploying the III Panzer Corps when Hitler and OKH intervened in a positive manner, for a change. Fortunately for Woehler and Balck, the 8th Army had posted Major General Hermann von Oppeln-Bronikowski's 20th Panzer Division on its far southern flank, not far north of Komarom. Hitler transferred it to 6th Army, and it arrived just in time to turn back the Soviet attack.

In the meantime, General Woehler decided that Konrad I had been checked, so he quickly pulled the 5th SS Panzer Division out of the line and ordered it to reassemble just south of Gran about eighteen miles north of Bieske, on the right flank of the 711th Volksgrenadier and on the left flank of the 96th Infantry Division, from which it could launch a second relief attempt, Konrad II (Map 7.5). The Vikings went forward at 10:30

Map 7.5
Operation Konrad II: January 6–11, 1945

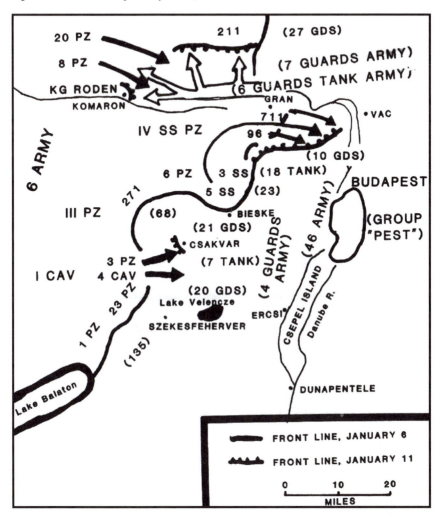

P.M. on January 10, once again catching the Soviets flat-footed. The 86th Guards Rifle Division was soon overrun. The Red Army again reacted quickly, however, and counterattacked with the 2nd Guards Mechanized Corps, but this time the Vikings would not be stopped. Prior to 1943, the Waffen-SS had been a fairly small and unusually close-knit organization—almost a brotherhood. Almost everybody in the Viking Division had close friends in Budapest, and they were very eager to save them. Morale was sky high, and it was even difficult to get the wounded to go to the rear, so anxious were they to rescue their comrades.

The drive continued to make relatively rapid headway on January 11, and on January 12 it captured Pilisszentkereszt. The next day it was within fourteen miles of the capital, and from one hill near the health resort of Dobogokoe the SS men could see the steeples of the city through their field glasses. One more day, they were convinced, would give them the city. Hospitals were ordered to prepare to move to Budapest on short notice, and soup was prepared for the wounded. Then, at 10 P.M. on January 13, to their shock and disbelief, they were ordered to halt and pull back. SS General Gille protested immediately to Generals Balck and Woehler, only to be informed that the halt order had come from the Fuehrer himself. From his headquarters four hundred miles away, Hitler had decided that the northern relief attack had gone as far as it would go. Nothing could be done to change his mind.

Hitler's order flew in the face of every concept of common sense and German military convention, which traditionally held that tactical and operational decisions should be made by the commanders on the spot. Herbert Gille, Karl Ullrich, and most of their officers would go to their graves convinced that they could have freed their comrades, had they been allowed to do so.

Hitler's fertile imagination had, in fact, produced another grandiose plan, one that went far beyond just a relief operation: he had decided to destroy the bulk of the 46th and 4th Guards Armies by launching a double envelopment west of Budapest. The IV SS Panzer and III Panzer Corps would form the southern pincer, while the 6th Panzer Division and 3rd Cavalry Brigade enveloped the Soviets from the north. Simultaneously, IV SS Panzer would relieve Budapest. Although few German officers believed this operation had a chance, there was nothing left for them to do but try it. The offensive was dubbed Operation Konrad III.

On January 12, Hitler ordered Army Group South to shift the IV SS Panzer Corps southward seventy miles, to the northern tip of Lake Balaton, for Konrad III (Map 7.6). It would take days to complete this move. Meanwhile, inside the pocket, the Russians continued to pound at the Budapest perimeter with all of the subtlety of a sledgehammer. "Frontlines as such no longer existed," Landwehr wrote later.

Machine gun nests and foxholes in the ruins provided the key points of resistance, and wherever they were located, there was the "front." The defending artillery pieces and heavy weapons now had very constricted fields of fire and in any event there was not enough ammunition to go around for all of the big guns, so their use was growing increasingly sporadic. House-to-house fighting, with hand grenades, revolvers, machine-pistols, bayonets and spades, was the order of the day. The streets were so shell-cratered and plowed up that tanks and vehicles could no longer move through most of them. Behind the "front," the Russians and their Hungarian

Map 7.6
Operation Konrad III: January 12–25, 1945

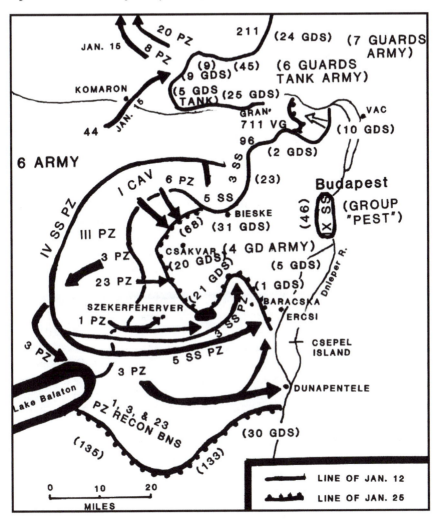

communist counterparts went on a rampage of murder, rape and plunder. No civilian was safe from their reign of terror.[61]

By January 7, food was in critically short supply, and the garrison's main source of water was melted snow. On January 12, a Russian force broke into the eastern parts of the city of Pest; it was wiped out in bitter street fighting.

The next day, another breakthrough took place to the south at Kispest, but again it was eliminated by a prompt counterattack. On the 15th, the Reds launched an all-out attack with every available unit, but it only managed to gain a few blocks in eastern Budapest. It was, however, becoming increasingly evident that the days of the German defenders east of the Danube were numbered. Most of the bridges across the river had already been destroyed by the Red Air Force, and the divisions east of the river were out of fuel, had lost most of their heavy weapons, and were almost out of food and ammunition. Pfeffer-Wildenbruch practically begged Army Group South and Fuehrer Headquarters for permission to pull back across the Danube.

Hitler finally relented at 7:25 P.M. on January 16. The evacuation began early at 10 P.M. on January 17 and continued until after daylight on January 18. During the crossings, the bridges were continually strafed by the Red Air Force, despite the fact that they were jammed with Hungarian men, women, and children. While this was going on, the remnants of the FHH, 22nd SS Cavalry, and 13th Panzer Divisions crossed the river. The historic Franz-Joseph Bridge was destroyed by Russian bombers on January 17, and the Elisabethen Bridge and the last pontoon bridges were blown up by German engineers at 7 A.M. on January 18. The eastern side of the Danube was now clear of Axis forces.

Meanwhile, the IV SS Panzer Corps marched back to Komarno (about sixty miles northwest of Budapest), reboarded trains, and moved off to the west, to redeploy for Konrad III. Its two SS panzer divisions now had about thirty operational tanks apiece, so when it arrived north of Lake Balaton, Army Group South reinforced it with the 1st and 3rd Panzer Divisions, the 509th Heavy Panzer Battalion (which was equipped with about thirty King Tigers), the 303rd Assault Gun Brigade, the 17th Volks Mortar Brigade, the 1335th Assault Gun Battalion, and the 219th Assault Panzer Battalion.[62]

The disappearance of the Viking and Totenkopf divisions obviously lulled the Soviet generals into a false sense of security, for when the IV SS and III Panzer Corps attacked the Russian 135th Rifle Corps near the northern tip of Lake Balaton on the night of January 17–18, they achieved complete surprise and smashed it. "It was like 1940 all over again," a member of the 3rd Panzer Division would recall later.[63] The army and SS *panzeriruppen* then advanced rapidly to the east, reaching the Danube at Dunapentele on January 19, cutting off most of the 3rd Ukrainian Front from its supply bases. Fighting was very heavy. The Soviet 18th Tank Corps was virtually wiped out, and the Red Army lost 193 tanks, 229 guns, and 257 antitank guns between January 18 and 21 alone. With the Soviet armor crushed, Gille then turned northwest and advanced to the western bank of the Danube, to a point only a dozen miles south of the Budapest perimeter, while General Breith covered his southern flank. The Viking Division, supported by Major Kokott's 303rd Assault Gun Brigade, reached the point where the Vali Canal flowed into the Danube and fired into terrified Russians as they tried to escape across the river. The situation became so desperate that Marshal Tolbukhin signaled Moscow and asked for permission to abandon the western side of the Danube. Stalin, however, refused to allow it. Pfeffer-Wildenbruch would have broken out had he been allowed to, but Hitler's orders were also firm. For him, the recapture of the Magyar capital was the only solution to the problem. So, as was the case with Stalingrad, the garrison of Budapest was forced to pass up its last real chance to break out and escape.

Suddenly, a dozen miles from the Budapest perimeter, the steam ran out of the offensive. The IV SS now had fewer than thirty operational panzers. The Viking Division proved unable to cross the Vali and lost one of its best men in the fighting: SS Lieutenant Colonel Hans Dorr, the commander of the legendary SS Panzer Grenadier Regiment "Germania," who was famous throughout the Reich. An incredibly brave officer, he had been wounded fifteen times before. Now, during the drive to the Vali and the Danube, he was hit from shrapnel from a Russian grenade. Evacuated back to Vienna, he died in a military hospital. His loss had a depressing effect on the entire Viking Division, which had come to regard him as nearly immortal. Even more depressing was the fact that Tolbukhin committed his last reserves to the fighting on the Vali, including several units that had been taking part in the siege. He could afford to do this, since he no longer had to contend with seventy thousand defenders. The number of Axis troops still fighting was less than twenty-five thousand and they were extremely short on food and ammunition. Medical supplies for the ten thousand wounded were exhausted.

By January 19, the Budapest pocket extended about a mile along the Danube and was between six-tenths of a mile and one mile in depth. The men were eating horse meat or cats—when they were available. By now, there were no more airfields in the garrison's hands, and resupply attempts were sporadic and haphazard. Supply canisters, dropped by parachute, frequently landed behind Russian lines or in no-man's land, and quite a few provoked savage little battles.

The southern fork of the relief attempt, meanwhile, became a series of wild running battles. Major General Eberhard Thunert's 1st Panzer Division fought a fierce three-day battle at Szekesfehervar before it finally threw a Guards rifle division out of the town. The loss of this critical road junction compelled the Reds to abandon all of their positions south and west of Lake Velencze, thus freeing the 1st Panzer Division for employment elsewhere. Gille sent it to join the 3rd SS Panzer Division "Totenkopf" in an attack against Kapolnasnjek, a key town on the eastern side of Lake Velencse. The two divisions took the place almost immediately, jeopardizing the entire Soviet position south and west of Budapest.

Meanwhile, to the northeast, the 6th Panzer Division and 3rd Cavalry

Brigade broke through the Russian lines east of Bieske and smashed two Soviet infantry divisions in the process. Only fifteen miles now separated the northern and southern pincers, and it looked for a moment as if Hitler might successfully pull off his improbable double envelopment after all. The weather, however, mitigated against the Wehrmacht, as did the numbers. Malinovsky committed the 68th Rifle and 5th Guards Cavalry Corps at Baracska and pulled another corps out of the Siege of Budapest to reinforce his sagging line. He also used about four other divisions to reinforce other endangered points. Heavy snow fell on January 24 and 25, limiting the mobility of the panzers.

The Battle of Baracska was fought in near-blizzard conditions. Temperatures dropped to minus five degrees Centigrade. Russian soldiers inflicted heavy casualties on the advancing Germans, who quickly returned the favor. The King Tigers of Major Hans-Juergen Burmester's 509th Heavy Panzer Battalion, for example, destroyed fifteen Red tanks and fifty antitank guns in one twenty-minute attack. Finally, on January 25, the 1st Panzer and 3rd SS Panzer overpowered the 223rd Rifle Division and advanced to the southwest bank of the Vali Canal—the last barrier between them and Budapest. Unlike the exhausted Vikings to the east, it was able to cross it the next day, January 26. Then they pushed on to the outskirts of Val—twelve miles from Budapest and six or seven miles from the spearheads of the I Cavalry Corps—but it could go no farther, since Malinovsky had reinforced this sector with the fresh 23rd Tank and 104th Rifle Corps. Gille's corps, on the other hand, was down to a strength of five PzKw IIIs and IVs, twenty-seven Panthers, eleven Tigers, and seven assault guns—only fifty AFVs in all. The I Cavalry had also shot its bolt and had gone over to the defensive the day before.

On January 27, the Soviets launched a desperate series of counterattacks against IV SS Panzer Corps salient, using the 26th and 4th Guards Armies, as well as the 23rd Tank, 1st Guards Mechanized, and 5th Guards Cavalry Corps.[64] Soon Gille was forced to retreat, but still Hitler would not authorize a breakout attempt, even though it was clear that there would be no further relief attempts. Since Konrad I began, the Totenkopf Division had lost 4,350 men, and Viking had lost 3,079. The 96th Infantry Division had suffered 2,107 casualties, the 711th Volksgrenadier had lost 1,174 men, the 211th Volksgrenadier's losses exceeded 1,500, and both cavalry brigades had lost more than a thousand men each. All told, Army Group South had suffered approximately thirty-five thousand casualties. Material losses were also devastating. The 3rd SS Panzer Division had only fourteen operational tanks left, the 5th SS had nine, and the 1st Panzer Division had only six.[65] Even if two or three fresh panzer divisions had been available for another attempt, Army Group South no longer had the fuel or ammunition to supply them.

That same day, January 27, the last members of the IX SS Mountain

Corps staff were thrown into the battle as infantrymen, fighting to seal off the numerous Russian penetrations. Losses were high on both sides. Two days later, IX SS reported that the number of its wounded would soon exceed the number of effective combatants. The Feldherrnhalle Division had already dissolved one of its panzer grenadier regiments (the 93rd) and transferred its survivors to its other P.G. regiment (the 66th). Daily rations were reduced to five grams of lard, a slice of bread, and one piece of horse meat per man per day. These rations were supplemented by large quantities of Schnapps and wine, of which Budapest had an abundant supply. No one in the pocket was safe; everyone was in the infantry. On January 29, SS Major Leander Hauck, the commander of the 22nd SS Divisional Supply Unit, was killed at the front. He had previously been chief musical inspector of the Waffen-SS and had founded the SS Music School at Brunswick, before he volunteered for duty in the combat zone. Not one member of his unit would escape the siege.

On January 30, the twelfth (and last) anniversary of Hitler's assumption of power, IX SS Corps signaled: "Famine and disease are spreading. The people have lost all faith and hope. . . . [T]he situation is very critical. The last battle has begun."[66]

Despite the fact that the garrison was nearing the end of its endurance, house-to-house fighting continued with unrelenting savagery. On February 3, for example, the starving defenders destroyed eight Soviet tanks, two anti-tank guns, an antiaircraft gun, and an armored car. So it went day after day, as the Russians cleared one block at a time. On February 5, they captured the tactically important Alder Hill and further compressed the pocket; the garrison lacked the strength to take it back. By February 6, there were eleven thousand wounded in the cauldron. Several squadrons of the 8th SS Cavalry Division were surrounded in the area of the main rail-road station on February 7, and the men of the 8th SS Flak Battalion (which had shot down seventy-five enemy airplanes during the siege and had received a special commendation from General Guderian) abandoned their empty guns on the grounds of the university at Castle Hill and went into the battle as infantry.[67]

On February 9, the Russians tried to drive a wedge between Castle Hill (the former seat of the Hungarian government) and the Budapest citadel. It failed in fierce fighting, but the end was obviously not far off. Pfeffer-Wildenbruch again signaled Fuehrer HQ for permission to break out, even though few of his men now believed the effort could succeed. On February 11, he signaled OKH that the attempt would take place that night.

As the men prepared for the breakout, their mood became strangely relaxed, almost carefree. One SS cavalry squadron ate its first hot meal in days—meatballs (made from horsemeat) and gravy. The men knew it was probably their last meal, but they did not let that disturb the festivities. For them, life was over, so there was nothing to worry about—or at least that was the attitude most of them took. Not long before the breakout began, a dispatch runner from the 8th SS Cavalry entered the command post of SS General Rumohr. There were several high-ranking officers seated around the conference table (the runner recognized General Schmidhuber, the commander of the 13th Panzer, among others), but no serious discussions were going on. The mood was relaxed—very relaxed—and the table was piled high with Schnapps bottles. All thought of rank was forgotten. "Come and drink up my boy!" General Rumohr greeted the runner. "Once we leave here we'll be dodging the shit soon enough!"[68] There was no fear, but there were no illusions left, either; all of those present realized that most of them would soon be dead. But at least they would be through with the Siege of Budapest.

The breakout attempt began at 8 P.M. on February 11. After leaving their ten thousand seriously wounded to the care of the Papal Nuncio and destroying their heavy equipment, as well as everything else they could not carry, approximately sixteen thousand soldiers (six thousand of whom were walking wounded) moved out into the attack. Someone must have informed the Russians as to the exact time of the attack, because as soon as it got under way the Soviets hit it with every gun in their arsenal, including the dreaded Stalin organs. Within minutes, the first wave—the infantry assault elements of the 13th Panzer and 8th SS Cavalry Divisions—was slaughtered.

Without surprise, the breakout had virtually no chance of succeeding, but there was nothing left to do but keep trying. General Schmidhuber led the second wave of his 13th Panzer Division across the open terrain northwest of Vienna-Strasse, into a hail of bullets and artillery fire. Schmidhuber was killed instantly, and his troops dispersed, only to be rounded up later by the Reds.

Lieutenant Colonel of Reserves Wilhelm Schoening, the commander of the FHH's 66th Panzer Grenadier Regiment, followed by Lieutenant Colonel Joachim-Helmut Wolff of the same division, chose another route, with better luck. With about six hundred men they overran a Russian blocking position at Budakesci and made their way to a forest, which was full of ravines and gullies. Following these, they managed to weave their way past the Russians and out of the city. By February 14, almost half of this *kampfgruppe* had reached the main lines of Army Group South, although Schoening was wounded on the way. It was the largest single force to escape the fall of Budapest.

Despite heavy resistance, Pfeffer-Wildenbruch's second breakout attempt succeeded in clearing the built-up area of Budapest, which was now a field of ruins. Making surprising progress, it advanced about twelve miles, reaching the area of Perbal, near where the IV SS Panzer had been halted a month before, before it was scattered by Soviet armor on February 12. The survivors tried to make their way back to German lines, but very few succeeded. Lieutenant Colonel Arthur von Ekespare, the chief of operations of the 13th Panzer Division, was among those killed in the attempt.[69]

Most of the ten thousand wounded left behind in Budapest were murdered by the Russians, many in the most brutal manner. Many were doused with gasoline and set on fire. Others were doused with water and left to freeze to death. Others were simply sealed off in their underground hospitals and left to starve. A large number, such as Lieutenant Colonel Fritz Kucklick, the badly wounded commander of the 13th Panzer Regiment, committed suicide rather than fall into the hands of the Soviets.[70] They knew better than to expect mercy from Stalin's legions.

With the battle over, the Red Army vented its fury upon Budapest. German bodies were mutilated, pulverized, and ground into the mud and snow by Russian tanks, while Hungarian homes and businesses were plundered. Hungarian civilians were indiscriminately shot—sometimes just for fun—while many women (some as young as twelve) were raped repeatedly. The drunken orgy of rape and violence continued for days. Then the violence became more systematic. Arrow Cross men and women were hunted down and murdered. Using the telephone book, the Soviets arrested and deported everyone with a German surname. About thirty thousand people were deported to the East in this manner.[71] Most of them ended up in Siberia. Many of them were never seen again.

Budapest has been called "the Stalingrad of the Waffen-SS." Only about seven hundred soldiers of the armed SS ever made their ways back to German lines. Most of the rest were murdered by the Soviets after they surrendered or died subsequently in "death marches" or in slave labor camps. About twenty-five thousand German soldiers and Waffen-SS men were put to death after the fall of Budapest—perhaps more.

SS General Pfeffer-Wildenbruch was severely wounded and captured on February 12, when his corps was scattered; like many Soviet prisoners, he was not returned to Germany until 1955. (Hitler had awarded him the Oak Leaves to his Knight's Cross on February 1.) He died in Germany on January 29, 1971. Most of his men, however, never reached old age. Joachim Rumohr, the commander of the Florian Geyer Division, and August Zehender, the commander of the 22nd SS Cavalry Division, were both killed in the breakout attempt, although there were unverified reports that Rumohr shot himself to keep from falling into Russian hands. Both officers had been promoted to SS-Brigadefuehrer und Generalmajor der Waffen-SS (SS major general) in the last days of the siege, and both had been decorated with the Oak Leaves to their Knight's Crosses.

None of the three of the commanders of the cavalry regiments of the 8th SS Cavalry Division escaped. SS Lieutenant Colonel Oswald Krauss and SS Major Hans von Schack, the commanders of the 15th and 16th SS Cavalry Regiments, respectively, were reported as missing in action and apparently have not been heard from since. SS Major Hans-Georg von Charpentier, the commander of the 18th SS Cavalry Regiment, was killed in action on February 11, according to his comrades. On the other hand, both of the commanders of horse regiments of the 22nd SS Cavalry Division—SS Colonel Karl-Heinz Keitel of the 52nd SS Cavalry and SS Reserve Lieutenant Colonel Anton Ameiser of the 54th—escaped the disaster. Both had been wounded and flown out of the pocket near the end of the siege. Both were given regimental commands in the new 37th SS Cavalry Division "Luetzow," which was formed using the horses given up by the now-defunct 8th and 22nd SS Cavalry. SS-Oberfuehrer Helmut Doerner, the commander of the 1st SS Police Regiment, a bona fide war hero and a holder of the Knight's Cross with Oak Leaves and Swords, was killed near the Boinay Academy (west of Budapest) on February 11.

SS Major von Mitzlaff, the Ia of the 8th SS Cavalry Division, was the highest-ranking SS officer to escape the pocket, although he was wounded in the process. The Waffen-SS, however, lost some of its best men in the siege of Budapest. The Knight's Cross holders alone included SS Major Walter Drexler, the defender of Nescus and commander of the 8th SS Reconnaissance Battalion, who went missing in action during the breakout; SS Captain Albert Klett, commander of the 6th Squadron, 15th Cavalry Regiment, captured on February 14 and shot by the Russians in June 1946; SS 1st Lieutenant Werner Dallmann, adjutant of the 53rd SS Cavalry Regiment, who died of his wounds in February; SS Lieutenant Dr. Siegfried Korth, commander of the 3rd Squadron/18th SS Cavalry Regiment, captured; SS Lieutenant Colonel and Reserve Lieutenant Colonel of Police Reiner Gottstein commander of the Security Police and SD in Budapest, killed in action northwest of the city on February 13; SS Reserve Lieutenant Franz Liebisch, squadron commander in the 8th SS Cavalry Division, wounded in the foot on February 9 and subsequently declared missing in action; and SS 1st Lieutenant Erhard Moesslacher, commander of the 6th Squadron, 16th Cavalry Regiment, killed in action during the breakout. SS Captain Artur Kessler, the commander of the 8th SS Anti-Tank Battalion, was also killed in action.[72]

Two men were very lucky. SS Captain Harry Phoenix, the commander of the II Battalion, 8th SS Artillery Regiment, destroyed his guns and led a battle group out of the city. He was fortunate enough to miss the major Soviet concentrations and reached German lines "without any particular difficulty." Also escaping was SS Sergeant Hermann Maringgele, a platoon leader in the 15th SS Cavalry Regiment, who had led forty-seven successful assault operations during the Siege of Budapest without suffering so much as a flesh wound. The Fuehrer summoned both men to Berlin and decorated them with the Knight's Cross on February 20; in addition, Maringgele received a battlefield commission as second lieutenant of Waffen-SS. No amount of posturing, "spin," or celebration of individual heroism on the part of Hitler, however, could obscure the fact that he had needlessly sacrificed the IX SS Mountain Corps on the altar of his own inflexibility. On the other hand, the courageous sacrifice of the defenders of Budapest had given tens of thousands of people the opportunity to escape the Red flood that was now about to engulf Central Europe. "Finally, on February 12, 1945, the guns ceased firing in Budapest," SS Captain Peter Neumann wrote,

An oppressive silence suddenly hung over the city like a curtain of lead, a silence even more tragic than the deafening roar of bombs and street fighting.

Budapest had not surrendered.

But there were no men left alive to stop the screaming hordes who now poured into the city. . . . Drunk with fury and vodka they murdered, raped, pillaged and set fire to what remained of the ruined buildings.[73]

With the fall of Budapest, Hitler's empire in the East had, for all intents and purposes, ceased to exist. The war was now in its sixth year, and the Third Reich had finally been thrown back to roughly where it had been when it started its march of conquest in 1939. The next battles against the Red Army would be in the Reich itself. Nazi Germany was entering its death throes.

NOTES

1. The 15th Flak Division suffered heavy losses in Rumania and was in remnants by the time it reached Hungary. Its commander, Colonel Ernst Simon, had been captured on August 29. He was temporarily replaced by Colonel Arnost Jansa, the commander of the 12th Flak Regiment. The 15th Flak Division had, however, temporarily absorbed the 5th Flak Division at the end of August.

Colonel Jansa was replaced as divisional commander by Major General Theodor Herbert on September 12, 1944. Major General Hans-Wilhelm Doering-Manteuffel, the last divisional commander, assumed command on January 26, 1945. In 1944, the 15th Flak Division was motorized; it controlled the 4th, 12th, 104th, and 133rd Flak Regiments. Peter Schmitz, Klaus-Juergen Thies, Guenter Wegmann, and Christian Zweng, *Die deutschen Divisionen, 1939–1945* (Osnabrueck: 1993–1997), Band 1, *Divisionen 1–5,* p. 379; Horst-Adalbert Koch, *Flak: Die Geschichte der deutschen Flakartillerie, 1935–1945* (Bad Nauheim: 1954), p. 189.

Colonel Hans Simon (1896–1970) was promoted to major general effective October 1, 1944—three days after he was captured. (His promotion was confirmed before its effective date.) He remained in Soviet captivity until late 1949. Simon had previously commanded the 131st Flak Regiment (1939–40), the 9th Flak Regiment at Nuremberg (1940), the 14th Flak Regiment at Cologne (1940), the 2nd Searchlight Regiment in the West (1940–42), the Field Flak School (1942–44), and the 17th Flak Division (1944). Hildebrand, vol. 3, pp. 309–10.

2. Nicholas Horthy was born in Kenderes in 1868. His was an old family of

landed gentry. Nicholas joined the Austro-Hungarian navy, was educated at the naval academy at Fiume, became an aide to Emperior Franz Joseph, and at the end of World War I was commander in chief of the Austro-Hungarian navy. Settling in Hungary, he helped organize the anti-Bolshevik counterrevolution of 1919 and became C-in-C of the Hungarian armed forces. He became regent on March 1, 1920. It was an anomalous position, since Hungary had no monarchy.

3. Pierik, pp. 83–85.

4. SS-Obergruppenfuehrer and General of Police Dr. Otto Windelmann was born in 1894 and fought in World War I, where he was wounded and earned both grades of the Iron Cross.

5. Pierik, pp. 83–85. Endre was executed in 1946. Eichmann, who was born in the Rhineland in 1906, was executed in Israel in 1962. He was chief of the IV-B-4 (Jewish) Office in the Reich Main Security Office (RHSA).

6. Ibid.

7. Daniel P. Bolger, "Undercover," *World War II* 5, no. 3 (March 1990), p. 62.

8. Landwehr, *Freedom*, p. 141.

9. Richard Landwehr, "The Waffen-SS and the Crushing of the Slovak Military Mutiny," *Siegrunen* 5, no. 6, p. 23.

10. Gottlob Berger was born in Gerstetten, Wuerttemberg in 1896 and joined the army as a volunteer in the infantry in 1914. He was wounded four times, earned a battlefield commission, and was discharged as a first lieutenant in 1919. Berger joined the Nazi Party in 1922 and, as a stormtrooper, took part in Hitler's unsuccessful Beer Hall Putsch of 1923. A high-ranking brownshirt, he joined the SS in 1936. Berger was chief of the powerful SS Central Office from April 1, 1940, until the end of the war, and he played a major role in the growth and development of the Waffen-SS. After the war, he was tried by the U.S. Military Tribunal and was sentenced to twenty-five years' imprisonment. His sentence was commuted, and he was released in 1951. Gottlob Berger died at Gerstettin on January 5, 1975.

11. Landwehr, "Slovak," p. 26.

12. Ibid., pp. 27–28.

13. Hermann Hoefle was born in Augsburg, Swabia, on September 12, 1898. He joined the army during World War I, serving in the infantry and then in a Bavarian aviation unit. He retired from the Reichswehr as a major in 1934. He joined the NSKK (the National Socialist Motor Corps) shortly thereafter and rose to the rank of NSKK brigadefuehrer (major general). This position was more important than it might sound to many Americans, as the vast majority of Germans in the 1930s did not know how to drive, and the rapidly expanding military had neither the personnel nor the resources to teach them. The NSKK, therefore, essentially provided basic training for Germany's mobile forces of all branches. Hoefle transferred to the SS on July 1, 1943, as a lieutenant general of Waffen-SS and police. He was Higher SS and Police Leader "Center" (headquartered at Brunswick) until he was named to succeed Berger. SS General Hoefle was Higher SS and Police Leader in Slovakia until the end of the war. He was hanged in Bratislava in 1947.

14. Landwehr, "Slovak," pp. 28–30.

15. Lucas, *Last Year*, p. 192.

16. Seaton, *Russo-German War*, p. 494.

17. Josef von Radowitz was born in Frankfurt-am-Main in 1899 and joined the

army as a *Fahnenjunker* in the dragoons in 1917. Discharged at the end of the war, he returned to active duty in 1924 and was a major and adjutant of III Corps when the war broke out. He served on the staff of 2nd Panzer Army (1942–43) and commanded the 28th Panzer Grenadier Regiment (1943–44) before assuming command of the 23rd Panzer Division in June 1944. He was promoted to major general on September 1, 1944, and to lieutenant general on March 1, 1945. He was a major general in the Bundeswehr at the time of his death in 1956 (Keilig, p. 266).

18. Helmuth von Grolman was promoted to lieutenant general in November 1944. At the end of the war, he was commander of the 4th Cavalry Division.

19. Friessner, pp. 151–53.

20. Pierik, p. 57.

21. Friessner, pp. 151–53; Seaton, *Russo-German War*, p. 494.

22. Charles Foley, *Commando Extraordinary* (New York: 1955), p. 92.

23. Ibid., p. 100. Skorzeny later commanded the 150th Panzer Brigade in the Battle of the Bulge and led a brigade on the Oder in 1945. He escaped to Spain after the war and died in Madrid on July 5, 1975. He had been born in Vienna on June 12, 1908.

24. Admiral Horthy was a witness at Nuremberg after the war. He chose not to return to Hungary, since the Communists were in control, and moved to Estoril, Portugal, where he died in 1957. His body was returned to Hungary in 1993, and he was reburied in the town of his birth.

25. Ziemke, p. 363.

26. Gerhard Schmidhuber was a Saxon. He joined the army as a volunteer in 1914 (at age seventeen) and received a reserve commission in the infantry in 1915. Discharged in 1920, he reentered the service as a territorial officer in 1933. In 1935 he earned regular-officer status and was a major commanding a battalion in the 103rd Infantry Regiment when the war broke out. He was promoted to lieutenant colonel in 1941, to colonel in mid-1942, attended the Panzer Troops School, and was given command of the 304th Panzer Grenadier Regiment in November. He was named deputy commander of the 7th Panzer Division in May 1944, and acting commander of the 13th Panzer Division on September 9, 1944. This post was made permanent on October 1, 1944, the day he was promoted to major general (Keilig, p. 303).

27. Szalasi was hanged in Budapest on March 12, 1946.

28. McTaggart, p. 345.

29. Friessner, p. 146. General Voeroes (Voroes) died in 1968. General Dezso Laszlo succeeded Miklos as commander of the 1st Hungarian Army and led it until the end of the war. General Jeno Major succeeded Verres and led the 2nd Hungarian Army until December 1, 1944, when it was disbanded. General Zoltan Heszlenyi, who assumed command of the 3rd Hungarian Army on September 19, 1944, led it until the end.

30. A Silesian, Gustav-Adolf von Nostitz-Wallwitz was born in 1898 and joined the army as a *Fahnenjunker* in 1917. He had spent the entire war commanding artillery and panzer artillery battalions and regiments before assuming command of the 24th Panzer Division on August 1, 1944. He was promoted to major general on November 11, 1944, and was mortally wounded on the Eastern Front on March 28, 1945.

31. All of these units were placed under the command of Group Breith (under General of Panzer Troops Hermann Breith, the commander of the III Panzer Corps).

32. Rolf O. G. Stoves, *Die Gepanzerten und Motorisierten deutschen Grossverbaende (Divisionen und selfstaendige Brigaden) 1935–1945* (Friedberg: 1986), p. 246.

33. McTaggart, pp. 346–47.

34. Ibid., p. 348.

35. Martin Bieber (born 1900) was promoted to major general on January 1, 1945. He surrendered the 271st Volksgrenadier to the Soviets at the end of the war and spent the next ten years in captivity. He died in Duesseldorf in 1974.

36. McTaggart, p. 348.

37. Ironically, the remnant of the Dirlewanger Brigade was upgraded into the 36th SS Grenadier Division (36. Waffen-Grenadier-Division der SS) on February 20, 1945, absorbing several army units (including the 681st Heavy Tank Destroyer Battalion, 687th Army Engineer Brigade, and the 1244th Grenadier Regiment) in the process. It was sent to the Oder sector of the Eastern Front, where it was smashed. The survivors of the unit surrendered to the Russians. Dirlewanger himself escaped the debacle and made his way to Wuerttemberg, where he surrendered to the French. Here another prisoner recognized him, and he was apparently beaten to death by French soldiers on June 7, 1945. His body was exhumed and identified in 1960. Tessin, vol. 14, p. 62; Kraetschmer, p. 785.

38. Friessner, pp. 194–95.

39. Ibid., pp. 198–201; Maximilian Fretter-Pico, *Missbrauchte Infantrie* (Frankfurt-am-Main: 1957), pp. 141–43.

40. General Friessner was never reemployed. Fretter-Pico was named commander of Wehrkreis IX (a definite demotion) in March 1945.

41. Otto Woeher joined the army as a *Fahnenjunker* in the infantry in 1914. He was a colonel and chief of operations of the 14th Army during the invasion of Poland. He advanced rapidly, becoming chief of staff of XVII Corps (late 1939), chief of staff of 11th Army (1940), chief of staff of Army Group Center (1942), commander of I Corps (1943), commander of 8th Army (1943) and commander in chief of Army Group South (1944). Hitler relieved him of his command on March 3, 1945, and he was never reemployed.

42. Ziemke, p. 385.

43. The KG from the 271st Volksgrenadier Division was led by Major Herbert Kuendiger, who was normally commander of 1st Battalion, 978th Grenadier Regiment. Promoted to lieutenant colonel around the end of the year, he was awarded the Knight's Cross and then the Oak Leaves during the siege (on December 9, 1944, and January 21, 1945, respectively) (Seemen, pp. 53, 211).

44. Landwehr, "Budapest," p. 6.

45. They had left their horses behind, outside the city.

46. SS General Otto Winkelmann, the Higher SS and Police Fuehrer, Hungary, was initially named commandant of Fortress Budapest, but he lacked senior military experience, and his appointment lasted only five days. He held his post as Higher SS and Police Leader until February 11, 1945. Winkelmann died in Bordesholm in 1977.

47. Heinz Gaedcke was born in Guben in 1895 and joined the army as an infantry *Fahnenjunker* in 1925. He was commissioned in 1927 and rather quickly

became a member of the General Staff. A major on the staff of OKH when the war began, he was Ia of the 25th Infantry Division from 1940 until 1943. After briefly serving on the staff of the War Academy (1943), Gaedcke was acting chief of staff of the XXIV Panzer Corps (1943), chief of staff of the IX Corps (1943–44), acting chief of staff of 4th Army (1944), and chief of staff of the 6th Army (August 15, 1944–end). He was promoted to major general on November 1, 1944. A prisoner of war until 1947, he joined the newly formed Bundeswehr as a brigadier general and commander of the 1st Army Officers' School. In 1957, he became commander of the Leadership Academy of the Bundeswehr in Hamburg, and he was commander of the III Corps in Koblenz from 1961 to 1965. He retired as a lieutenant general in 1965 and died in Waldesch on December 21, 1992.

48. Landwehr, "Budapest," pp. 19–20.

49. Ziemke, p. 433.

50. The son of a businessman, Helmut Doerner was born in Munich-Gladbach in 1909 and joined the SS as an officer-cadet in 1927. He did not attend the officers' training course, however, until 1936. Instead, he completed his education (he was trilingual by 1931) and became an NCO in the Landespolizei in Bonn and then Munich. Commissioned second lieutenant in the SS in 1937, he was promoted to first lieutenant in 1938 and to captain in 1939. He joined the newly formed SS Police Division in November 1939. Doerner served as adjutant and then company commander in the division's anti-tank battalion (1939–40); he was commander of the antitank company of the 1st Police Rifle Regiment of the same division (1940–42) until he was wounded by a hand grenade on the Eastern Front in January 1942. Upon recovery, Doerner was promoted to SS major and was given command of the 2nd Battalion, 2nd SS Police Infantry Regiment (1942–43), and then the regiment itself (1943–44). Promoted to SS lieutenant colonel (1943) and colonel (1944), he briefly succeeded to the command of the 4th SS Panzer Grenadier Division "Police" when Karl Schumes was killed in action on August 18, 1944. He was given command of an SS battle group under the IX SS Mountain Corps in January 1945. Doerner was promoted to SS Oberfuehrer on January 15, 1945. One of the bravest men in the German armed forces, he was awarded the Knight's Cross with Oak Leaves and Swords on February 4, but it is not known if he ever received news of the award.

51. McTaggart, p. 353.

52. Ibid.

53. Landwehr, "Budapest," pp. 19–20.

54. A holder of the Knight's Cross with Oak Leaves, Swords, and Diamonds, Herbert Otto Gille was, along with Sepp Dietrich, the most decorated soldier in the history of the Waffen-SS. Born in Gandersheim-am-Harz in 1897, the son of a factory manager, he was educated in various cadet schools and attended the War Academy at Berlin-Lichterfelde, Germany's equivalent of West Point. He left the academy in 1914 when World War I broke out but was nevertheless commissioned second lieutenant in early 1915. He served in the artillery in World War I and was discharged in 1919. He spent the next ten years managing private agricultural estates. When he joined the SS in 1931, he was running his own business. He was commissioned SS second lieutenant in 1933.

Herbert Gille transferred from the Allgemeine-SS (General SS) to the SS-Verfuegungstruppe (the forerunner of the Waffen-SS) in 1935. He served as a company commander in the SS Germania Regiment (1935–37), as a battalion commander in the Germania (1937–39), and as a battalion commander in the first SS artillery regiment (1939–40). Promoted to SS lieutenant colonel in 1939, he was commander of the 5th SS Artillery Regiment of the "Viking" Division (1940–43) and commander of the 5th SS Panzer Division "Viking" from May 1, 1943, to July 20, 1944. Gille distinguished himself as a divisional commander on the Eastern Front. In one three-month period, for example, his division destroyed more than four hundred Russian tanks. He assumed command of the IV SS Panzer Corps on July 20 and held it for the rest of the war. Gille was promoted to SS-Obergruppenfuehrer and General of Waffen-SS on November 9, 1944.

Although he was undoubtedly highly intelligent, historical assessments of Gille's abilities as a corps commander vary. Mark Yeager, one of the most distinguished historians of the Waffen-SS, refers to him as an "exceptionally gifted strategist and leader," noted for his calm and humor in difficult situations, who was "undoubtedly among the very best" divisional or corps commanders in the Waffen-SS. Other historians have criticized him as a corps commander, however, because his units suffered very high casualties. Whether or not these losses were avoidable is still a disputed topic.

Gille surrendered to the Americans at the end of the war and was released from prison in 1948. He then operated a small bookstore in Stemmen and founded the SS veteran magazine *Wiking Ruf* (now *Der Freiwillige*). Married with a daughter, he died of a heart attack on December 26, 1966.

The 3rd SS Panzer Division was still commanded by SS Major General Hellmut Becker. The 5th SS Panzer Division was led by SS Colonel Karl Ullrich, who had served as acting commander of the Totenkopf Division in June, 1944. SS Colonel Hannes Muehlenkamp had, in the meantime, been named inspector of panzer troops for the Waffen-SS. Schmitz et al., vol. I, p. 247. A former Brownshirt, Ullrich volunteered for the SS in 1934. He commanded the SS-VT Engineer Battalion (1939–40), the 3rd SS Engineer Battalion (1940–42), and the 6th SS Panzer Grenadier Regiment "Theodor Eicke" (1943–44). Ullrich also served as chief engineer officer of the SS Panzer Corps (1942–early 1943). Ullrich celebrated his thirty-fourth birthday on December 1, 1944. Promoted to SS-Oberfuehrer on April 20, 1945, he surrendered the 5th SS to the Americans at the end of the war. He was released from the POW camps in 1948 and was still alive at last report.

55. Pierik, p. 149.

56. Mehner, vol. 11, p. 364. Hermann Harrendorf was promoted to major general on January 30, 1945.

57. McTaggart, pp. 358–59. Fritz Darges was born in Duelsberg, Altmark, in 1913. He joined the SS in the late 1920s or early 1930s and attended the first officers' training class to graduate from the famous SS Junkerschule, at Bad Toelz. He served in the Germania SS Regiment until 1939, when he was transferred to the Deutschland Regiment. Then he became a company commander in Der Fuehrer SS Panzer Grenadier Regiment. He fought in Poland, France, and on the Eastern Front. In 1942, he assumed command of a panzer company in the Viking Division. After commanding a tank battalion in the same division (1943–44), he was given command of the 5th SS Panzer Regiment.

Fritz Vogt was an officer famous for his recklessness.

58. Wilhelm Soeth assumed command of the 3rd Panzer Division on January 1, 1945. He would be promoted to major general on January 30.

59. Joseph Reichert was born in Burgfeld, Bavaria, on December 13, 1891, the son of a customs official. He joined the Bavarian army as a *Fahnenjunker* in the infantry in 1910. During World War I, he rose to the command of a battalion but was captured by the French in October 1918. Released in 1920, he was retained in the Reichsheer and in 1938 was a colonel commanding the 6th Infantry Regiment. He fought in Poland, the Netherlands, Belgium, France, and Russia (1939–41) before returning to Germany as commander of the 177th Replacement Division. He briefly commanded the 714th Infantry Division (1943) before assuming command of the 711th on March 15, 1943. His division was crushed in the Normandy fighting; Reichert rebuilt it in the Netherlands and led it on the Eastern Front until April 14, 1945, when he was seriously injured in an automobile accident. Captured by the Americans the following month, Reichert was released from prison in July 1945. He settled in Gauting and died there on March 15, 1970. He was promoted to major general in 1941 and to lieutenant general in 1943. Georg Meyer, "Josef Reichert," Amy Hackett, trans., in David G. Chandler and James Lawton Collins, eds., *The D-Day Encyclopedia* (New York: 1994), p. 454; Keilig, p. 270.

60. As a major, Waldemar von Knoop had commanded the 8th Motorcycle Battalion of the 8th Panzer Division (1943).

61. Landwehr, "Budapest," p. 21.

62. Pierik, p. 177.

63. Ibid., p. 178.

64. Seaton, *Russo-German War*, p. 501.

65. Pierik, p. 184.

66. Landwehr, "Budapest," p. 26.

67. Ibid., p. 27.

68. Ibid., p. 20.

69. Arthur von Ekespare had previously commanded II/25th Motorized Regiment. He received the Knight's Cross on January 15, 1945. Pabst was the former commander of the 34th Reconnaissance Battalion. Seemen, p. 119; Pierik, p. 144; Scheibert, p. 89.

70. Kucklick formerly commanded I/13th Panzer Artillery Regiment.

71. Pierik, p. 145.

72. Kraetschmer, pp. 402, 630. Zehender was born on April 28, 1903, in Aalen, Wuerttemberg. After twelve years' service as an enlisted man in the Reichsheer, he joined the SS in 1935. Rumohr was born in Hamburg on August 6, 1910.

73. Peter Neumann, *The Black March* (New York: 1960), p. 266.

Table of Equivalent Ranks

U.S. Army	German Army
General of the Army	Field Marshal (*Generalfeldmarschall*)
General	Colonel General (*Generaloberst*)
Lieutenant General	General of (Infantry, Panzer Troops, etc.)
Major General	Lieutenant General (*Generalleutnant*)
Brigadier General*	Major General (*Generalmajor*)
Colonel	Colonel (*Oberst*)
Lieutenant Colonel	Lieutenant Colonel (*Oberstleutnant*)
Major	Major (*Major*)
Captain	Captain (*Hauptmann*)
First Lieutenant	First Lieutenant (*Oberleutnant*)
Second Lieutenant	Second Lieutenant (*Leutnant*)
none	Senior Officer Cadet or Ensign (*Faehnrich*)
Officer Candidate	*Fahnenjunker* (Officer Cadet)

*Brigadier in British Army

German Army	Waffen-SS
Commander in Chief of the Army	*Reichsfuehrer-SS* (Himmler)
Field Marshal (*Generalfeldmarschall*)	none
Colonel General (*Generaloberst*)	*Oberstgruppenfuehrer* (SS Colonel General)
General of (Infantry, Panzer Troops, etc.)	*Obergruppenfuehrer* (SS General)

Lieutenant General (*Generalleutnant*)	*Gruppenfuehrer* (SS Lieutenant General)
Major General (*Generalmajor*)	*Brigadefuehrer* (SS Major General)
none	*Oberfuehrer*
Colonel (*Oberst*)	*Standartenfuehrer* (SS Colonel)
Lieutenant Colonel (*Oberstleutnant*)	*Obersturmbannfuehrer* (SS Lt. Colonel)
Major (*Major*)	*Sturmbannfuehrer* (SS Major)
Captain (*Hauptmann*)	*Hauptsturmfuehrer* (SS Captain)
First Lieutenant (*Oberleutnant*)	*Obersturmfuehrer* (SS 1st Lieutenant)
Second Lieutenant (*Leutnant*)	*Untersturmfuehrer* (SS 2nd Lieutenant)

German Units, Ranks, and Strengths

Unit	Rank of Commander	Strength[1]
Army Group	Field Marshal/Col. Gen.	2 or more armies
Army	Colonel General/Gen.	2 or more corps
Armeegruppe	General of . . . [2]	German army plus 1 allied army
Army Detachment	General of . . .	2 or more corps; intermediate temporary headquarters between corps and army levels
Corps	General of . . . /Lt. Gen.	2 or more divisions
Corps Detachment	Lt. Gen./Maj. Gen.	3 division groups (decimated divisions)
Division	Lt. Gen./Maj. Gen./Colonel	10,000 to 18,000 men[3]; 150 to 200 tanks if panzer[3, 4]
Brigade[5]	Colonel	2 or more battalions
Regiment	Colonel/Lt. Colonel	Normally 2 or 3 battalions
Kampfgruppe	Lt. Gen./Maj. Gen./Colonel	A burnt-out division of approximately regimental combat value
Battalion[6]	Lt. Col/Maj./Captain	2 or more companies (approximately 300 to 600 per infantry battalion; usually 17 to 60 tanks per panzer battalion)
Company[7]	Captain/Lieutenant	3 or 4 platoons; approx. 80 to 100 men; Panzer: 8 to 15 tanks

Platoon	Lieutenant/Sergeant Major	20 to 30 men; Panzer: 3 to 5 tanks
Section	Warrant Officer/Sergeant	2 squads (more or less)
Squad	Sergeant/Corporal/	Infantry: 7 to 10 men; Panzer: 1 tank

NOTES

1. Authorized or theoretical strength; the actual strength of German units in 1944 was usually considerably less.

2 General of infantry, panzer troops, artillery, engineers, signal troops, flak artillery, cavalry, paratroopers, fliers, etc.

3. SS divisions normally had more men and tanks than army divisions; Volksgrenadier divisions typically had six to eight thousand men; most infantry and panzer grenadier divisions had eight to twelve thousand men.

4. Few army panzer divisions had a hundred tanks in 1944.

5. Rarely found in the German Army in 1944. Assault gun brigades actually had the strength of a reinforced battalion.

6. Called "squadrons" in the cavalry branch.

7. Called a "battery" in the artillery branch (including assault gun units, which were part of the artillery branch).

APPENDIX **III**

Characteristics of Opposing Tanks

Model	Weight (in tons)	Speed (mph)	Range (miles)	Main Armament	Crew
AMERICAN (in Soviet Service)					
M4A3 Sherman	37.1	30	120	176 mm	5
RUSSIAN					
T34/Model 76	29.7	32	250	176 mm	4
T34/Model 85	34.4	32	250	185 mm	5
KV 1	52	25	208	176.2 mm	5
JSII Joseph Stalin	45.5	23	150	1 122 mm	5
GERMAN					
PzKw II	9.3	25	118	120 mm	3
PzKw III	24.5	25	160	150 mm	5
PzKw IV	19.7	26	125	175 mm	5
PzKw V Panther	49.3	25	125	175 mm	5
PzKw VI Tiger	62.0	23	73	188 mm	5

German Staff Abbreviations

Chief of Staff (Not present below the corps level)

Ia—Chief of Operations

Ib—Quartermaster (Chief Supply Officer)

Ic—Staff Officer, Intelligence (subordinate to Ia)

IIa—Chief Personnel Officer (Adjutant)

IIb—Second Personnel Officer (subordinate to IIa)

III—Chief Judge Advocate (subordinate to IIa)

IVa—Chief Administrative Officer (subordinate to Ib)

IVb—Chief Medical Officer (subordinate to Ib)

IVc—Chief Veterinary Officer (subordinate to Ib)

IVd—Chaplain (subordinate to IIa)

V—Motor Transport Officer (subordinate to Ib)

National Socialist Guidance Officer (added 1944)

Special Staff Officers (Chief of Artillery, Chief of Projectors [Rocket Launchers], etc.)

Bibliography

Absolom, Rudolf, comp. *Rangliste der Generale der deutschen Luftwaffe nach dem Stand vom 20, April 1945.* Friedberg: 1984.

Adair, Paul. *Hitler's Greatest Defeat: The Collapse of Army Group Center.* London: 1994.

Ailsby, Christopher. *SS: Hell on the Eastern Front.* Osceola, Wis.: 1998.

Barnett, Correlli, ed. *Hitler's Generals.* London: 1989.

Bender, Roger James, and Hugh Page Taylor. *Uniforms, Organization and History of the Waffen-SS.* Palo Alto, Calif.: 1971–1985. 5 volumes.

Bethell, Nichols, and the editors of Time Life Books. *Russia Besieged.* Alexandria, Va.: 1980.

Black, Peter R. *Ernst Kaltenbrunner.* Princeton, N.J.: 1984.

Bolger, Daniel P. "Undercover." *World War II,* 5, no. 3 (March 1990), pp. 10, 62–66.

Bradley, Dermot, Karl-Friedrich Hildebrand, and Markus Roevekamp. *Die Generale des Heeres, 1921–1945.* Osnabrueck: 1993–1999. 5 volumes to date.

Brandt, Allen. *The Last Knight of Flanders.* Atglen, Penn.: 1998.

Brett-Smith, Richard. *Hitler's Generals.* San Rafael, Calif.: 1977.

Brown, Anthony C. *Bodyguard of Lies.* New York: 1975.

Brownlow, Donald G. *Panzer Baron: The Military Exploits of General Hasso von Manteuffel.* North Quincy, Mass.: 1975.

Buchner, Alex. *Ostfront, 1944.* Translated by David Johnston. West Chester, Penn.: 1991.

Carell, Paul. *Hitler Moves East.* Boston: 1965. Reprint ed., New York: 1966.

———. *Scorched Earth: The Russian-German War, 1943–1944.* Boston: 1966. Reprint ed., New York: 1971. "Paul Carell" was the pseudonym used by Hans Karl Schmidt.

Chandler, David G., and James Lawton Collins, eds. *The D-Day Encyclopedia.* New York: 1994.

Chant, Christopher, ed. *The Marshall Cavendish Illustrated Encyclopedia of World War II.* New York: 1972.

Conze, Werner. *Die Geschichte der 291. Infanterie-Division, 1940–1945.* Bad Nauheim: 1953.

Dallin, Alexander. *The Kaminsky Brigade: 1941–1944: A Case Study of German Military Exploitation of Soviet Disaffection.* Technical Research Report No. 7. Maxwell Air Force Base, Ala.: 1952.

Deac, Wilfred P. "City Streets Contested." *World War II 9*, no. 3 (September 1994), pp. 39–44, 66.

D'Este, Carlo. "Model." In Correlli Barnett, ed. *Hitler's Generals.* London: 1989.

Dunn, Walter S., Jr. *Second Front Now—1943.* Tuscaloosa, Ala.: 1980.

Eisenhower, John D. S. *The Bitter Woods.* New York: 1969.

Foley, Charles. *Commando Extraordinary.* New York: 1955.

Fretter-Pico, Maximilian. *Missbrauchte Infantrie.* Frankfurt-am-Main: 1957.

Friessner, Johannes. *Verratene Schlachten.* Hamburg: 1956.

Gackenholz, Hermann. "The Collapse of Army Group Center." In H. A. Jacobsen and J. Rohwer, eds., *Decisive Battles of World War II: The German View.* New York: 1965.

Goerlitz, Walter. *Walter Model: Strategie der Defensive.* 2nd ed. Weisbaden: 1975.

Graber, Gerry S. *Stauffenberg.* New York: 1973.

Greenberg, Lawrence M. "Army with No Way Out." *World War II 6*, no. 1 (May 1991).

Guderian, Heinz. *Panzer Leader.* Translated by Constantine Fitzgibbon. New York: 1957. Reprint ed., New York: 1967.

Hart, B. H. Liddell. *The Other Side of the Hill.* London: 1978.

Haupt, Werner. *Army Group Center: The Wehrmacht in Russia, 1941–1945.* Translated by Joseph G. Welsh. Atglen, Penn.: 1997.

———. *Heeresgruppe Nord, 1941–1945.* Bad Nauheim: 1966.

———. *Army Group South: The Wehrmacht in Russia, 1941–1945.* Translated by Joseph G. Welsh, Atglen, Penn.: 1998.

Hildebrand, Hans H., and Ernst Henriot. *Deutschlands Admirale, 1849–1945.* Osnabrueck: 1988–1996. 3 volumes.

Hildebrand, Karl F. *Die Generale der deutschen Luftwaffe, 1935–1945.* Osnabrueck: 1990–92. 3 volumes.

Irving, David. *Hitler's War.* New York: 1977.

Jacobsen, H. A., and Rohwer, J. eds. *Decisive Battles of World War II: The German View.* New York: 1965.

Keilig, Wolf. *Die Generale des Heeres.* Friedberg: 1983.

Kennedy, Robert M. *The German Campaign in Poland (1939).* U.S. Department of the Army Pamphlet 20–255. Washington, D.C.: 1956.

Kissel, Hans. *Die Panzerschlachten in der Pussta im October, 1944.* Neckargemuend: 1960.

Koch, Horst-Adalbert. *Flak: Die Geschichte der deutschen Flakartillerie, 1935–1945.* Bad Nauheim: 1954.

Kraetschmer, Ernst-Guenther. *Die Ritterkreuztraeger der Waffen-SS.* 3rd ed. Preussisch Oldendorf: 1982.

Kramarz, Joachim. *Stauffenberg.* London: 1967.

Kriegstagebuch des Oberkommando des Wehrmacht (Wehrmachtfuehrungstab). Frankfurt-am-Main, 1961. 4 volumes.

Landwehr, Richard. "Budapest: The Stalingrad of the Waffen-SS." *Siegrunen*, no. 37 (1985), pp. 1–35.

———. *Fighting for Freedom: The Ukrainian Volunteer Division of the Waffen-SS*. Silver Spring, Md.: 1985.

———. "The Waffen-SS and the Crushing of the Slovak Military Mutiny." *Siegrunen* 5, no. 6, pp. 23–30.

Landwehr, Richard, Jean-Louis Roba, and Ray Merriam. "The 'Walloon': The History of the 5th SS-Sturmbrigade and 28th SS Volunteer Panzergrenadier Division." *Weapons and Warfare/Siegrunen Series No. 1*. Bennington, Vt.: 1984.

Logusz, Michael O. *Galicia Division: The Waffen-SS 14th Grenadier Division 1943–1945*. Atglen, Penn.: 1997.

Lucas, James. *Hitler's Enforcers*. London: 1996.

———. *The Last Year of the German Army: May, 1944–May, 1945*. London: 1994.

Mansfield, Stephen. *Never Give In: The Extraordinary Character of Winston Churchill*. Elkton, Md.: 1995. Reprint ed., Nashville, Tenn.: 1996.

Manstein, Erich von. *Lost Victories*. Novato, Calif.: 1982.

McTaggart, Pat. "Budapest '45." In editors of *Command, Hitler's War: The Evolution and Structure of the German Armed Forces*. Conshohocken, Penn.: 1995, pp. 343–74.

Mehner, Kurt, ed. *Die Geheimen Tagesberichte der deutschen Wehrmachtfuehrung im Zweiten Weltkrieg, 1939–1945*. Osnabrueck: 1984–1995. 12 volumes.

Mellenthin, Friedrich Wilhem von. *German Generals of World War Two*. Norman, Okla.: 1977.

———. *Panzer Battles*. Norman, Okla.: 1956; reprint ed., New York: 1984.

Melzer, Walter. *Geschichte der 252. Infanterie-Division*. Bad Nauheim: 1960.

Meyer, Georg. "Josef Reichert." Translated by Amy Hackett. In David G. Chandler and James Lawton Collins, eds., *The D-Day Encyclopedia* (New York: 1994), p. 454.

Mitcham, Samuel W., Jr. *Hitler's Legions*. New York: 1985. Reprint ed., London: 1985.

Mitcham, Samuel W., and Gene Mueller. *Hitler's Commanders*. Latham, Md.: 1992.

Moll, Otto E. *Die deutschen Generalfeldmarschaelle, 1939–1945*. Rastatt/Baden: 1961.

Munoz, Antonio J. *The Kaminski Brigade: A History, 1941–1945*. Bayside, N.Y.: 1996.

Neumann, Peter. *The Black March*. New York: 1960.

Niepold, Gerd. *Battle for White Russia: The Destruction of Army Group Center, June, 1944*. Translated by Richard Simpkin. London: 1987.

Otte, Alfred. *The HG Panzer Division*. West Chester, Penn.: 1989.

Padfield, Peter. *Doenitz: The Last Fuehrer*. New York: 1984.

Pierik, Perry. *Hungary, 1944–1945*. Nieuwegein, The Netherlands: 1996.

Plocher, Hermann. "The German Air Force Versus Russia, 1943." U.S. Air Force Historical Studies Number 155. Maxwell Air Force Base, Ala.: Air University Archives. Unpublished manuscript written about 1965.

Bibliography

Scheibert, Horst. *Die Traeger des deutschen Kreuzes in Gold: Das Heer.* Friedburg: n.d.

Schlabendorff, Fabian von. *Revolt against Hitler.* Edited by Gero von S. Gaevernitz. London: 1948.

Schmitz, Peter, Klaus-Juergen Thies, Guenter Wegmann, and Christian Zweng. *Die deutschen Divisionen, 1939–1945.* Osnabrueck: 1993–1997. 3 volumes.

Seaton, Albert. *The German Army, 1933–1945.* New York: 1982. Reprint ed., New York: 1982.

———. *The Russo-German War, 1941–1945.* New York: 1970.

Seemen, Gerhard von. *Die Ritterkreuztraeger.* Friedburg: 1976.

Snyder, Louis L. *Encyclopedia of the Third Reich.* New York: 1976.

Stahlberg, Alexander. *Bounden Duty.* Translated by Patricia Crampton. London: 1990.

Stoves, Rolf O. G. *Die Gepanzerten und Motorisierten deutschen Grossverbaende (Divisionen und selfstaendige Brigaden), 1935–1945.* Friedberg: 1986.

Strassner, Peter. *European Volunteers.* Translated by David Johnston. Winnepeg: 1988.

Taylor, Telford. *Sword and Swastika: Generals and Nazis in the Third Reich.* New York: 1952. Reprint ed., Chicago: 1969.

Tessin, Georg. *Verbaende und Truppen der deutschen Wehrmacht und Waffen-SS im Zweiten Weltkrieg, 1939–1945.* Osnabrueck: 1973–1982. 16 volumes.

Tiemann, Reinhard. *Geschichte der 83, Infanterie-Division, 1939–1945.* Friedburg: 1986.

Warlimont, Walter. "From the Invasion to the Siegfried Line." *ETHINT 1* (European Theater Historical Interrogation 1), U.S. Army Historical Division, 1945. U.S. Army Institute of Military History, Carlisle Barracks, Penn.

———. *Inside Hitler's Headquarters.* New York: 1964; reprint ed., 1991.

Williamson, Gordon. *Infantry Aces of the Reich.* London: 1989.

Wilmot, Chester. *The Struggle for Europe.* New York: 1981.

Wistrich, Robert. *Who's Who in Nazi Germany.* New York: 1982.

Yeager, Mark C. *Waffen-SS Commanders.* Atglen, Penn.: 1997.

Zaloga, Steven. *Bagration, 1944: The Destruction of Army Group Center.* London: 1996. Reprint ed., Danbury, Conn.: 1997.

Ziemke, Earl F. *Stalingrad to Berlin: The German Defeat in the East.* Washington, D.C.: 1966.

General Index

Index of German Military Units

(Estonian Nr. 1), 119, 130, 149, 157
21st Infantry, 118, 121, 130, 146, 149, 150
21st Luftwaffe Field, 118, 126
22nd Air Landing, 198, 200
23rd Infantry, 5, 118, 125, 133, 138, 142, 153, 160
24th Infantry, 118, 120, 121, 123, 130, 142, 154
26th Infantry, 65, 66
28th Jaeger (Light), 31, 50, 54, 56
29th SS Waffen Grenadier Division (Russian Nr. 1). *See* Brigades: Kaminsky Brigade
30th Infantry, 118, 125, 130, 133, 146, 150, 158
31st Infantry, 11, 27, 29, 32, 34, 49, 52, 134, 146, 149, 150
31st SS Volunteer Grenadier Division "Bohemia Moravia," 228
32nd Infantry, 118, 126, 130
32nd SS Volunteer Grenadier Division "30 Jaegeranuar," 216
35th Infantry, 12, 23, 25, 31
36th Infantry, 12, 23, 32, 47, 49
36th SS Waffen Grenadier. *See* Brigades: Dirlewanger Brigade
41st Fortress, 200
45th Infantry, 12, 32, 34, 47, 49
46th Infantry, 165, 218
50th Infantry, 31, 55
52nd Security, 31, 57, 141
56th Infantry. *See* Division Groups: 56
57th Infantry, 11, 13, 22, 32, 34, 52
58th Infantry, 119, 126, 130, 142, 147, 151
61st Infantry, 119, 125, 130
62nd Infantry, 164, 182
68th Infantry, 219
69th Infantry, 32, 58, 118, 124
70th Infantry, 122
72nd Infantry, 66, 88
73rd Infantry, 96, 100, 111, 114, 115, 201
75th Infantry, 66, 219

76th Infantry, 165, 173, 176, 188, 218, 220
78th Assault, 11, 22, 30, 32, 34, 37, 39, 52
79th Infantry, 164, 176, 179, 186, 187–88, 192
81st Infantry, 118, 121–22, 123, 126, 130, 131, 133, 136
83rd Infantry, 118, 120, 126, 130
86th Infantry, 213
87th Infantry, 8, 36, 118, 122, 123, 130, 134, 142, 156
88th Infantry, 66
93rd Infantry, 58, 124, 125, 126, 130
95th Infantry, 20, 24, 32, 34
96th Infantry, 66, 219, 244, 250
97th Jaeger, 165, 166, 190, 219
98th Infantry, 200
100th Jaeger, 66, 219
101st Jaeger, 67, 219
102nd Infantry, 12, 31
104th Jaeger, 200
106th Infantry, 181, 182
110th Infantry, 11, 32, 34
117th Jaeger, 200
118th Jaeger, 200
121st Infantry, 118, 120, 125, 130, 143
122nd Infantry, 119, 132, 140
126th Infantry, 118, 125, 130
129th Infantry, 12, 31
131st Infantry, 32, 65
132nd, 50, 118, 122, 126, 130, 136
133rd Fortress, 200
134th Infantry, 12, 25, 26, 32, 34, 47
137th Infantry, 31
140th Special Purposes, 145
153rd Field Training, 165, 177, 178, 182, 188, 189, 192, 219
154th Reserve, 219
161st Infantry, 164, 182, 189
163rd Infantry, 145
168th Infantry, 219
169th Infantry, 145
170th Infantry, 31, 50, 58, 118, 122
178th Infantry, 212, 214

183rd Infantry. *See* Division Groups: 183
196th Infantry, 32
197th Infantry, 11, 20, 32, 34
199th Infantry, 145
201st Security, 13, 32
203rd Security, 12, 31
205th Infantry, 117, 118, 120, 121, 124, 130, 150, 154
206th Infantry, 11, 23, 24, 33, 34
207th Security, 118
208th Infantry, 66
210st Infantry, 145
211th Infantry (later Volksgrenadier), 12, 66, 244, 250
212th Infantry, 23, 32, 55, 118
214th Infantry, 66
215th Infantry, 123, 130, 132, 147, 148, 150
217th Infantry. *See* Division Groups: 217
218th Infantry, 118, 126, 130, 150, 154
221st Security, 13, 31, 50
225th Infantry, 118, 124, 127, 125, 130, 136, 142
227th Infantry, 118, 130, 146, 152
239th Infantry, 164
246th Infantry, 11, 23, 33, 34
250th Infantry, 159
251st Infantry, 31
252nd Infantry, 11, 20, 32, 55, 119, 120, 154
253rd Infantry, 65
254th Infantry, 66, 219
256th Infantry, 11, 20, 24, 32, 34
257th Infantry, 164, 182, 192, 195, 196
258th Infantry, 164, 182
260th Infantry, 11, 32, 34, 52
263rd Infantry, 118, 124, 125, 130
264th Infantry, 200
267th Infantry, 11, 13, 27, 29, 30, 32, 34, 39, 40, 49, 52
269th Infantry, 145
270th Infantry, 145
271st Volksgrenadier, 214, 230, 233, 234, 239, 258,

274th Infantry, 145
280th Infantry, 145
281st Security, 6, 118, 125, 130, 147
282nd Infantry, 164, 182, 185
285th Security, 118, 119
286th Security, 13, 33, 52
290th Infantry, 6, 23, 118, 120, 121, 122, 126, 130, 132, 136, 147, 148
291st Infantry, 66, 94, 167
292nd Infantry, 12, 31
294th Infantry, 164, 182, 183, 184
295th Infantry, 145
296th Infantry, 12, 25, 32
299th Infantry, 11, 20, 24, 32, 34
300th Special Purposes, 118
302nd Infantry, 164, 182, 183, 184
304th Infantry, 164, 166
306th Infantry, 164, 175, 177, 178, 179, 182
320th Infantry, 164
329th Infantry, 118, 125, 130, 143
335th Infantry, 164, 182
337th Infantry (later Volksgrenadier), 11, 22, 32, 33, 34, 50, 219
339th Infantry. *See* Division Groups: 339
340th Infantry, 66, 166, 193
342nd Infantry, 65, 66, 68
349th Infantry, 66, 68, 75, 76, 78, 79, 81, 84, 166
357th Infantry, 68, 76, 219, 229, 230, 232
359th Infantry, 66
361st Infantry, 66, 75, 76, 78, 82, 84
367th Infantry, 31, 55
369th Infantry, 200
370th Infantry, 181, 186, 187, 192
371st Infantry, 66, 168
373rd Infantry, 200
376th Infantry, 164, 179, 182, 186, 192
383rd Infantry, 12, 32, 34, 47
384th Infantry, 164, 182, 184
389th Infantry, 118, 130, 142
390th Field Training, 13, 33, 55, 88

Index of German Military Units

391st Security, 13, 100
392nd Croatian Infantry, 200
454th Security, 66, 75, 76, 78, 82, 84
539th Special Administrative Division Staff, 212
540th Special Administrative Division Staff, 212
541st Volksgrenadier, 100, 101
542nd Volksgrenadier, 100, 101, 114
543rd Volksgrenadier, 100
544th Volksgrenadier, 100, 101, 167
545th Volksgrenadier, 100, 101, 167
546th Volksgrenadier, 100
547th Volksgrenadier, 100, 101
548th Volksgrenadier, 100, 101
549th Volksgrenadier, 100, 101
550th Volksgrenadier, 100
551st Volksgrenadier, 100, 101, 151
552nd Volksgrenadier, 100, 101
553rd Volksgrenadier, 100
558th Volksgrenadier, 100, 101
559th Volksgrenadier, 100
560th Volksgrenadier, 100, 145
561st Volksgrenadier, 100, 101
562nd Volksgrenadier, 100, 101
563rd Volksgrenadier, 100, 101
702nd Infantry, 145
707th Infantry, 13, 22, 23, 25, 33, 34, 47
708th Infantry, 214
710th Infantry, 145
711th Infantry, 241, 244, 250, 261
Field Training Division North (formerly 388th Field Training), 123, 156
Divisions, Mountain:
1st, 198, 201, 202, 205, 208, 228
2nd, 145
3rd, 165, 178, 184, 190, 218
4th, 218
6th, 145
6th SS, 145
7th, 145
7th SS, 200
13th SS Volunteer Mountain Division "Handschar," 200, 205, 235
23rd SS Volunteer Mountain Division "Kama," 235
Divisions, Panzer:
1st, 66, 76, 78, 81, 85, 161, 205, 219, 220, 224, 226, 229, 230, 248, 249, 250
3rd, 166, 219, 231, 232, 243, 248, 261
3rd SS "Totenkopf," 31, 55, 100, 101, 102, 110, 112, 114, 232, 240, 241, 243, 249, 250, 260
4th, 31, 54, 56, 101, 141
5th, 23, 27, 29, 30, 31, 47, 58, 63, 64, 89, 138, 141
5th SS "Viking," 32, 65, 100, 101, 102, 110, 112, 232, 240, 241, 243, 244, 245, 249, 250, 260
6th, 32, 55, 58, 231, 232, 241, 246
7th, 32, 50, 58, 141, 150, 152, 158
8th, 66, 68, 76, 78, 80, 82, 95, 94, 167, 230, 231, 232, 241, 244
12th, 31, 38, 48, 49, 55, 56, 63, 121, 141
13th, 170, 175, 176, 177–78, 179, 182, 184–85, 188, 192, 219, 220, 224, 229, 233, 234, 235, 237, 238, 239, 240, 248, 252, 253, 257
14th, 141, 151, 166
16th, 66, 85
17th, 66, 85
19th, 100, 101, 112
20th, 22–23, 25, 26, 37, 47, 48, 49, 55, 56, 63, 165, 188, 244
23rd, 166, 167, 217, 218, 220, 224, 225, 226, 229, 230, 243, 257
24th, 217, 219, 224, 225, 226, 229, 230, 257
Hermann Goering (Parachute) Panzer, 101, 110, 112
"Tatra," 214, 216
Divisions, Panzer Grenadier:
4th SS "Police," 169, 200, 217, 218, 224, 226, 233, 234, 259
10th, 165, 173, 176, 182, 188, 219
11th SS Volunteer "Nordland," 130, 150, 157
14th, 34

292

Index of German Military Units

About the Author

SAMUEL W. MITCHAM, JR. is an internationally recognized authority on Nazi Germany and the Second World War and is the author of more than 15 books on the subject, including this title's companion volume, *Retreat to the Reich* (Praeger, 2000), *Why Hitler?* (Praeger, 1996), and *The Desert Fox in Normandy* (Praeger, 1997), as well as several dozen articles. A former army helicopter pilot and company commander, he is a graduate of the U.S. Army's Command and General Staff College. He lives in rural Louisiana.